Information
and Democratic
Processes

Information
and Democratic
Processes

Edited by
John A. Ferejohn
and
James H. Kuklinski

University of Illinois Press
Urbana and Chicago

Library of Congress Cataloging-in-Publication Data

Information and democratic processes/edited by John A. Ferejohn
  and James H. Kuklinski.
      p.   cm.
    Bibliography: p.
    Includes index.
    ISBN 0–252–01679–3 (cloth : alk. paper).—ISBN 0–252–06113–6 (paper :
alk. paper)
    1. Democracy. 2. Political participation. 3. Political
socialization. 4. Public opinion. 5. Elections. I. Ferejohn,
John A. II. Kuklinski, James H.
JC423.I49   1990
321.8—dc20   89–35123
                                                                      CIP

Contents

Preface

The chapters in this book began as working papers that the authors presented at the Conference on Information and Democratic Processes, held at the University of Illinois, March 9–11, 1986. Our principal debt, of course, is to the authors who participated in the two-day meeting. The Department of Political Science and the College of Liberal Arts and Sciences at the University of Illinois provided generous financial support. Two individuals, Roger Kanet, then head of the department, and William Prokasy, then dean of the college, were especially instrumental in securing the monetary resources necessary to make this project a reality. Lawrence Malley at the University of Illinois Press provided incalculable guidance and encouragement. Given his intimate knowledge of political science, Larry functioned as much as disciplinary adviser as editor. Finally, we thank Grace Ashenfelter and Mary Giles for their editorial assistance. Inviting them to be co-editors of this volume might well have been the most appropriate way to acknowledge the magnitude of their contributions. The same applies to Michael Frank, whose thorough and careful readings of the manuscript eliminated many errors.

INTRODUCTION

Information and the Electoral Process

John A. Ferejohn

Nothing strikes the student of public opinion and democracy more forcefully than the paucity of information most people possess about politics. Decades of behavioral research have shown that most people know little about their elected officeholders, less about their opponents, and virtually nothing about the public issues that occupy officials from Washington to city hall. Those attitudes they express to interviewers are usually ephemeral and transient. In what sense, then, can the policies of any government be said to reflect the will of the governed when that will cannot even be said to exist?

Indeed, even if mass opinions existed and were strongly held on the full range of public issues, how could they be transmitted to elected officials? The language that citizens can use to transmit their desires to public officials is, after all, extremely limited. People may cast votes in elections, petition their officeholders, and participate in campaigns in various ways. But such methods are often costly and difficult to use, ambiguous to interpret, and are only occasionally employed by most citizens. Thus officeholders are likely to receive an incomplete message at best, and one that is hard to decipher.

Moreover, even if public preferences were well articulated on important issues, and even if the electoral mechanism were able to allow the transmission of the full range of possible public sentiments, officials might, nevertheless, choose to pay less heed to the expressed wishes of their electors than to their own desires. Officeholders are not mere ciphers who simply gauge public sentiment and enact it directly into public legislation. They may be men and women of unusual talent and public spirit, but they are not much more virtuous than the rest of us. They have the same passions and vices and are subject to the same petty temptations and are likely to hear what they wish from the public and to employ such information for their own purposes. Can we expect them neutrally to translate public desires into legislation?

Concerns of this sort have often led thinkers to a profound skepticism about possibilities of popular rule. Antidemocratic theorists, from Plato and Aristotle to Mosca and Pareto, have asserted the impossibility of democracy in the strong sense in which public policy is simply a reflection of public opinion. They thought that public sentiment is relatively unenlightened and at best a poor guide to good legislation. Most such theorists have instead advanced recommendations to assure that the best people enter public life and that public officials are motivated to act in a public-spirited fashion.

Democratic theorists, following Rousseau, have sought ways to allow the direct reflection of the public will in the laws. Such theorists have attempted to find ways to increase the level of information in the electorate and reduce whatever biases to which the election process might be susceptible. Thus Rousseau's famous recommendations in favor of a small political unit, the prevention of political parties and interest groups, and the restriction of public questions to general issues of public policy, were advocated as means to encourage the development and expression of informed public opinion and to limit the temptations to which citizens and their officials would otherwise be exposed.

There is a hoary quality to these arguments. They have been repeated for thousands of years without being fundamentally influenced by increasing scientific understanding of political processes. While antidemocrats argue that behavioral research supports their skepticism about public opinion, democratic theorists respond that these conclusions are drawn from poorly constructed polities that would be expected to produce biased and ill-informed public sentiments. Others respond that public opinion is, in fact, clearly defined on the fundamental issues connected to everyday life, if not on the complex policy issues that occupy the editorial pages of the *New York Times* and the *Washington Post*. Thus, insofar as political institutions permit the transmission of these mundane public sentiments to public officials who formulate policy, and insofar as these leaders may be motivated to translate these expressions into good legislation, democratic rule is achievable by modern society.

Perhaps we are condemned, after all, to regard these as eternal issues to be debated and discussed with no more sophistication two thousand years from now as they have been since Alexander's time. The contributors to this volume believe otherwise. While each of them is concerned with addressing a scientific question about information flow and information acquisition in democratic electoral systems, their answers have broad implications for the normative assessment of democratic institutions. And, for the most part, these implications permit a more sanguine assessment of the possibility of democratic government than might have been expected.

While information levels are indeed low and information about public issues unevenly distributed, citizens are generally found to employ sensible decision rules, or heuristics, in acquiring and storing information about politics. These decision rules do, in fact, entail remaining ignorant on most issues most of the time, making inferences about the likely behavior of officeholders from very little information, and basing one's vote or other political actions on a relatively sparse set of signals about governmental activity. Even if individuals, taken alone, are remarkable for their ignorance and even if most individuals make poor inferences a lot of the time, as Condorcet noted long ago, electorates like juries can exhibit a high level of aggregate sophistication. And, insofar as politicians are motivated to compete for public office, they have strong incentives to make appropriate inferences about these aggregated public wishes and base their actions on them. If they don't, they risk losing their offices to opponents who will. The result is that even in situations of incomplete information, there are powerful equilibrating forces pushing public policy in the direction of the representation of public sentiment.

In view of these findings, it seems worthwhile to begin this collection by assessing what we now know or can conjecture about information and democratic processes. These speculations are tentative and controversial, and the authors in this volume ought not to be expected to endorse them. I will focus on three problems that I believe are central to an evaluation of the significance of informational issues for democratic rule: the controllability of representatives by constituents; the informational content of public opinion; and the capacity of democratic institutions to permit the transmission of information between citizens and politicians. I will argue that the limitations on the free flow of information may in fact be a good thing for the operation of democratic institutions. Frictions on information flow may act to restrain officials from the temptations they would otherwise face in democratic systems.

REPRESENTATION, DELEGATION, AND THE PROBLEM OF CONTROL[1]

Political institutions are an expression of the division of labor: they permit small numbers of officials to regulate and direct social processes without having to consult regularly with the rest of us. In this sense, political institutions economize on the distribution and processing of information. We elect officials to learn about things that might affect us and then to act on our behalf as we would if we had the same information.

In choosing representatives, in delegating to them the authority to act on our behalf, we surrender to an enormous informational disadvantage. We will never be able to know enough about the choices faced by our leaders to be sure that they are always acting in our interests. As a result, we face the eternal problem of political control: how may we ensure that our chosen representatives act in our interest as well as in our names? Who shall guard the guardians?

We cannot hope to circumvent the officials' informational advantages without forgoing the advantages of the division of labor itself and requiring, in that sense, irrational behavior of citizens. As Madison recognized two centuries ago, the best hope for establishing control lies in the architecture of political institutions themselves. We must arrange institutions in such a way that officials will be motivated to pursue our interests rather than (or, as well as) their own, and to reveal to us the information we must have to make intelligent electoral choices.

It is useful to examine the problem of political control from the standpoint of the theory of institutions pioneered by economists. In the last decade economists have devised methods to study what is often called the problem of agency. How can you ensure that an agent employed to represent your interests will act as you would if you had his or her information and were acting on your own behalf? Although perfect control is not generally possible, the theory of agency shows that if you—the principal—are able to commit to a schedule of rewards and punishments that depends on the outcomes of the agent's actions, a very high degree of control is achievable. Indeed, in the special case in which the principal can observe the agent's actions perfectly, the agent can be induced to act exactly as the principal would wish. Only the opportunities for deception offered by the fact that the agent has an informational advantage permit the agent any discretionary leeway at all, and that leeway is quite limited by the structure of the relationship.

Indeed, in one respect, simple agency models with one principal and one agent may actually understate the degree to which the agent may be controlled by the principal. If the principal could employ any of several agents, competition among agents permits the principal even better control than in the situation of simple agency. This is good news for individuals who are seeking the services of a doctor or an automobile mechanic; even if information asymmetries are enormous, if you are sufficiently careful to take advantage of competition in the market for such services, you should not be taken advantage of too badly.

But the economics of agency differs in a fundamental way from the problem of the political control of officials. In agency models, the principal can know exactly what he or she wants the agent to do in each conceivable situation. In political life the principal cannot know exactly what he or she wants the agent to do in each conceivable situation. In political life the principal is not a single individual at all: rather it is a collectivity, an electorate, and it is not likely to have well-defined preferences in all circumstances. Rather, the normal case is one in which there is substantial disagreement within the electorate. In this circumstance it is not clear how one might even define the notion of control.

At the deepest level, this problem has nothing at all to do with imperfect information, although it is exacerbated by it. We may, therefore, illustrate this problem in a simple model of perfect information. Suppose there is an office whose task it is to divide a dollar among a three-person constituency governed by majority rule, and whose occupant is permitted to keep whatever is not given to constituents. Assume that the incumbent seeks to retain office by promising to deliver payments to voters and that a citizen votes for the incumbent if he or she offers a sufficiently high payment. What payment will citizens require of the incumbent in order to vote for his or her re-election? It is easy to see that the required payment cannot be greater than zero: if some individuals demand a positive amount, the incumbent will simply deliver payments to the least costly majority, which of course must be of minimum size (containing two voters in this case). The citizen with the highest required payment will anticipate receiving nothing in this situation and will therefore be motivated to lower his or her required payment enough to enter the least costly majority. In this model, competition among voters allows the official to exploit the electorate completely.

The problem of political control arises because the collective principal—the electorate—finds it difficult to precommit itself to a reward schedule for the incumbent that depends on performance in office. If electors could somehow bind themselves not to listen to the blandishments of officials seeking to play one group off against another—if, to use Elster's (1984) metaphor, they could lash themselves to the mast—officials would be unable to exploit divisions among them. Thus, to the extent that methods of arranging such commitments can be devised, the problem of control may be mitigated.

It seems worth working out a few implications of the notion of electoral control. Where there is little electoral control, public office is relatively valuable because officeholders will be able to extract the rents of public office. And, if the public sector is sufficiently large, competition for office will be intense. Indeed, rational office-seekers will be willing to spend substantial resources to gain control of public office. In this way the value of office will be dissipated in electoral competition, with substantial sums and efforts diverted into campaigning or even, if institutions are arranged in such a way that votes may be exchanged, the bribing of the electorate.

There are a number of institutional "solutions" to this problem that the citizens might attempt. For example, political parties might be seen as a way for citizens to coordinate their voting strategies—precommiting if you will—in order to prevent politicians from exploiting divisions in the electorate. If electors all "agree" to hold all members of the party in control of the presidency responsible for aggregate economic performance, for example, elected officials will have little incentive to differentiate themselves from their party or to exploit latent divisions in the electorate. They will face, instead, a unified principal who has well-defined preferences and be forced into a situation of simple agency. Analytically, this is the wisdom of the responsible parties doctrine.

Where the control of officials is weak, one would not expect citizens to allow officials to command many resources. Thus, if strong, well-disciplined parties exert stronger control over politicians than do weak, fragmented parties, citizens in strong-party systems should be willing to have a relatively large public sector. Because their officeholders are relatively free to seek their own interests, weak party systems would be more likely to experience periodic "taxpayer" revolts aimed at restricting the proportion of the economy that is governed by elected officials.

Constitutional provisions of various sorts may also achieve the same effect—Rousseau's constitutional stricture that public issues must not involve any issue of private distribution is one such example. Each of these devices involves the following simple notion: find a way to get the electorate to commit itself to act as though it is a simple principal with a one-dimensional set of rewards. In this way, incumbents will be prevented from taking advantage of the conflicting interests in the electorate.

The whole idea is to employ institutions to allow the electorate to commit itself to a special sort of compensation scheme—one that does not allow officials to appeal to subgroups of the citizenry. Commitment is hard to achieve because politicians have an incentive to subvert it: to try to entice subsets of the population to break their "commitment" and accept a better deal.

Students of political history know, however, that institutional solutions to the problem of political control are fragile at best. Parties sometimes decay or become mere creatures of officeholders; constitutional provisions are corrupted or distorted. In the long run, the problem of control recurs; in this sense it is endemic to political institutions.

INCOMPLETE INFORMATION, DECEPTION, AND CONTROL

In an election system, politicians have information about their own activities and abilities that is not freely available to voters. This asymmetry of information gives political actors opportunities to mislead or lie to others for their own benefit. They can send deceptive signals or try to establish reputations for having abilities or proclivities they may or may not have. What does this imply for the problem of control?

Consider a new member of Congress, elected to represent some district remote from Washington, and who, as it happens, detests the idea of doing constituency work back in the district. The legislator realizes, however, that being reelected means being thought to be accessible to constituents and at least appearing to be willing to help them with their problems.

Now suppose that constituents believe that there are two types of members of Congress: those who don't mind doing constituency work and those who loathe it. Assume that citizens value constituency service and would not knowingly vote to reelect someone of the second sort. In these conditions it is clear that if the office is sufficiently valuable, our legislator will find it worthwhile to pretend to enjoy constituency work, at least until retirement.

This example illustrates the importance of reputational phenomena in politics. Calvert (1985, 1986) has illustrated that the establishment and maintenance of reputations underlie important aspects of political leadership in a variety of settings ranging from the establishment of international hegemonic stability to the maintenance of power in Congress. Leaders retain their hold on their positions by convincing others, citizens and potential challengers, that they are willing to undertake retaliatory actions that appear to be costly. In effect, they successfully convince others that such actions may not really be costly to them. And the striking thing about the logic of reputations is that leaders do not actually have to convince us that these actions are not costly, only that they *may not* be. As long as followers are not sure that acts of leadership are costly, they won't find it worthwhile to challenge the politician's authority.

Reputational phenomena are inherent in settings of asymmetric information, and so we should expect them to be ubiquitous in the political world as well. What do they imply for the problem of political control over representatives? In one sense the congressional member's constituency in the example is poorly represented: they reelect someone of the sort they dislike. In a more important sense, they are well represented in that their legislator behaves as they wish (until the last term). It is also clear that electoral control is possible in this case only if the value of office is sufficiently high to make reputation formation useful.

Where elections are relatively frequent and candidates seek reelection, the fact that officials have much more information than voters does not eliminate the possibilities of electoral control. Madison's prescription in *Federalist,* Number 51, that the Constitution employ the ambitions of officeholders to discipline them, works in this setting as well as in the ones he envisioned.

THE ACQUISITION OF POLITICAL INFORMATION

Let us set aside for now the basic problem of political control and ask about other informational aspects of representation in democratic polities. Democratic representation seems to require that public wishes, where those are defined, are made known to representatives and are the principal object of legislation. This requirement seems to demand that representatives concern themselves with the effects of public acts on their constituents. And, in turn, this seems to require that citizens learn enough about legislative alternatives to codify and convey this information to their delegates. What do citizens learn about the complex world of politics, and how do they organize this information?

Although research in this area is still in its youth, current understanding of this question suggests that individuals resort to a number of cognitive strategies or heuristics to help them deal with complicated informational environments. Exactly what these psychic mechanisms are and how they work is not yet clear, but this much is widely agreed upon (Kahneman, Slovic, and Tversky, 1982). Individuals employ psychic economizing devices to search for, store, and retrieve information. These produce biased patterns of cognition that appear to be, nevertheless, fairly efficient in allowing humans to deal with complex environments.

For most of us, political information is both difficult to acquire and of dubious value. Thus, as in other arenas of life, we resort to heuristics to economize in organizing the acquisition and storage of information about public life. As a result, political learning is characterized by such mechanisms as selective attention, framing, the accessibility heuristic, and various other cognitive biases. Citizens make use of simple informational shortcuts long familiar to political scientists under other names: party images, ideologies, and the like. These images change slowly in response to new information, and they appear to organize the collection and retention of new information. The changeability of political images depends negatively on the size of the information base on which they are founded.

Research reported in this book suggests that information is retained in rough proportion to the existing stock of information on the topic. Those who know most about a topic acquire the most new information and are able to retain more of it than those who know less. The organization of political information depends on how it is presented, or "framed." Individuals do not remember or retrieve information about politics in an unbiased fashion. Rather, they recall information that is relatively accessible, ignoring or forgetting the rest.

Although research in this area is new, it seems clear that cognitive processes can have important implications for the operation of a democratic polity and particularly for what we have called the problem of control. The use of cognitive strategies such as the accessibility heuristic may allow elites to manipulate public beliefs and perceptions. Conversely, the relative stability of belief systems and the peripherality of politics to most people may limit the ability of officials to sway ordinary citizens very much.

Without implying that the contributors to this volume would concur, I speculate that, on balance, the fact that citizens use heuristics to economize on the acquisition and handling of information may very well increase their ability to discipline or control officials. Precisely because citizens care so little about politics, political evaluations and attachments are relatively stable and slow to shift. Thus, competitors for office are induced to regard them as external "facts" about their environment and not really subject to intentional manipulation. In a sense, citizens are able to act "as if" they have precommitted to a reward scheme. Thus, the fact that citizens do not pay much attention to new information, and that politicians know this, implies that politicians are limited in their ability to take advantage of the heterogeneity of their constituency to build new coalitions. Rather, they are well advised to regard their constituents as having committed themselves to a collective strategy of delivering rewards and punishments conditional on how public officials are behaving. And, in the language of agency theory, if citizens are able to commit to simple compensation schemes such as negative voting based solely on (say) aggregate economic performance rather than on the benefits they personally receive from public policy, they may effectively control the behavior of incumbents.

THE DISTRIBUTION OF POLITICAL INFORMATION

Because information acquisition is costly, individuals will generally not choose to be completely informed about anything. They will acquire information on an issue only as long as the value to them of the information exceeds the costs of its acquisition. This observation applies equally to citizens and their representatives.

How may citizens place a value on information? If one person casts an "incorrect" vote in an election—a vote he or she would have cast otherwise if more were known—what does it matter? There is little chance that a switch in vote would affect the outcome of the election. To a first approximation, then, the electoral value of a piece of political information must be near zero. Moreover, even if a piece of information has a positive electoral value, why should any particular voter acquire it? Why not just let someone else acquire and interpret the information? That person will then presumably wish to communicate it cheaply to those with whom he or she agrees to get them to vote the same way. Thus, not only is information nearly valueless in elections, it shares some of the attributes of what economists call a public good: individuals have an incentive to try to "free ride" on those who agree with them.

On this view, no one would rationally and purposefully acquire information about office seekers or public issues, and the distribution of information should be quite even: no one should know anything. In this volume, Fiorina remarks that what is most puzzling about democratic polities is that the level of public knowledge is as *high* as it is, not that ignorance is widespread. As Dahl (1961:279) put the matter, writing almost thirty years ago, "Instead of seeking to explain why citizens are not interested, concerned, and active, the task is to explain why a few citizens are."

In his commentary, Fiorina attempts to explain this puzzle by arguing (among other things) that although information acquisition is generally costly, a lot of information is essentially free; it comes with the ordinary performance of social and economic roles. From this perspective the distribution of political information may be seen as a side effect or consequence of broader social processes.

The crucial observation is that *what* information is free varies widely over the electorate. What a stockbroker on Wall Street picks up from a client or from observing the movement of stock prices is vastly different from the information freely available to a truck driver (traversing inadequately maintained highways) or a hash-slinger in a coffee shop (observing competition from newly arrived immigrants). Electorally relevant information may actually be directly valuable to all of these people in their everyday work, but it is different sorts and amounts of information. Thus, if account is taken of the differentiation of occupations in the economy and of the variability of social settings, one would expect to find an uneven distribution of politically relevant information that reflects, in some respects, variable costs of acquisition.

Indeed, insofar as information acquisition opportunities vary among social, political, and economic settings, information distributions will differ by issue area. Citizens will, in effect, specialize in information about some things rather than others. And, as Iyengar and Ottati and Wyer show, the tendency toward specialization may be reinforced and amplified by the operation of cognitive mechanisms such as selective attention and the accessibility bias.

Communication of information among citizens depends on the social and economic context. MacKuen's chapter illustrates this dependence. He shows that if individuals prefer to avoid disagreeable discussions, the expression of political information will be extremely sensitive to the distribution of opinion in "local" areas. Where a sentiment is held by a majority—even a relatively small majority—it will be expressed and transmitted to the exclusion of opposing views. From this perspective, social communication of political ideas may easily produce the misleading impression of consensus where, in reality, diverse viewpoints exist. Although MacKuen does not speculate on this possibility, to the extent that this process affects the acquisition of opinions as well as their expression, real consensus can follow false ones.

While MacKuen examines the effects of the relative density of political opinions on their social transmission, Huckfeldt and Sprague ask about the effects of complex social differentiation on political expression. They find that the "structural effects" of the social environments of citizens are mediated by the somewhat freer choice of social context. In a highly differentiated society, individuals are able to exercise some degree of choice in choosing to whom to listen and what to read. These choices, in turn, haunt the subsequent flows of political information in the electorate.

What do these considerations imply about the content of public opinion on political issues? First, of course, it is clear that one cannot expect many citizens to know very much about politics; most political information is too costly and of too little use for most of us to bother to try to acquire it. Second, the distribution of information will be uneven, with some people knowing much more about politics than others. Third, the distribution of political information is differentiated by subject matter and reflects aspects of social communication and economic structure. The overall picture is one of substantial amounts of information distributed unevenly in an electorate that pays sporadic attention to political events.

Of course, even if each of us knows relatively little about politics, it is likely that constituencies, taken as aggregates, might contain quite a lot of dispersed information. Each of us is only an occasional and unreliable observer of political life, but, together, we have a lot of information about politics. Moreover, as Converse, Stimson, and McKelvey and Ordeshook illustrate, electoral processes aggregate information in ways that "cancel out" random components and magnify the "signal to noise ratio." From an aggregate point of view, public perceptions of political life are remarkably accurate—the law of large numbers is a potent force in large electorates. However, MacKuen and Huckfeldt and Sprague suggest that social communication of public opinion may produce systematic biases, and that we must ask how the communication of public sentiment through the electoral mechanism affects its content.

INFORMATION TRANSMISSION IN ELECTORAL PROCESSES

Students of democratic life are often deeply troubled by the uneven distribution and biased communication of information in the electorate. As Sniderman and his collaborators illustrate, well-informed citizens vote and act differently than those with less information. They are able to base their political activities on much more differentiated information about political life and, presumably, exert more discipline on their representatives. And the well informed are not merely well informed. They are relatively well educated and tend to be employed in higher-status occupations. In view of these correlations, it is natural to suspect that such people are somehow able to take advantage of their knowledge for their own benefit.

But in a world of incomplete information, does more information really translate into better control of officeholders? Are those who know the most about politics really advantaged in this regard, or have they foolishly overinvested in useless information that they cannot use without divulging its content to their less-informed peers? Are those who find political information useful in their economic activities able to use that information to their advantage in political contexts?

Using information entails communicating it to others. Thus, if stockbrokers trade on political knowledge, stock prices will reflect that information and come to summarize the political information available to the traders. But experienced traders will realize this and know that they can "free ride" on other traders by merely watching stock prices. In this sense, the value of political information to stockbrokers will tend to be small, putting the stockbroker in the same situation as the rest of us.

The research reported by Rahn and her coauthors seems consistent with this perspective. They emphasize that a lot of the political information relevant to evaluating presidential candidates is provided for free in "entertaining" settings and that it is highly redundant. Citizens must, in any case, reduce whatever information into a simple "yes-no" judgment in the voting booth. Rahn, Aldrich, Borgida, and Sullivan suggest that the simplicity of the voting decision induces all voters to rely heavily on judgments of candidate competence and other personal qualities. In fact, Rahn and her collaborators find little difference in evaluative strategies between informed and uninformed voters.

Although economists have long known that economic signals convey information in markets, McKelvey and Ordeshook (and Carmines and Kuklinski) argue that political action sends informative signals as well. If some members of the electorate are informed about the likely behavior of elected officials, this information may be inferred from their voting behavior and from their responses to opinion polls, and the information will spread throughout the electorate. In this sense, once again, the electorate, like the market, will aggregate and pool information.

In an electoral setting, information pooling and aggregation allow competitors for office to make inferences about the likely rewards of differing campaign strategies. McKelvey and Ordeshook provide analyses of a number of electoral settings in which informational flows are quite sparse and in which, nevertheless, candidates make remarkably precise judgments about the collective preferences of the electorate. Their results suggest that electoral institutions may economize on informational costs in the sense that relatively little information need be held by participants for electoral competition to produce the same outcome as would be observed in a world of perfect information. Most significantly, they demonstrate that information transmission in electoral processes is self-correcting: politicians end up having correct beliefs about majority sentiment and are motivated to respond to it.

These results appear to imply that what I called the problem of control is somehow overcome in the McKelvey-Ordeshook model of elections. In one sense it is. These authors are working in a setting in which politicians are unable to distribute benefits in a discretionary fashion to groups of voters. In a sense, they have imposed a unidimensional structure on the set of actions of the politicians, and this is sufficient to allow for their complete control by the electorate.

But where the assumption of unidimensionality fails—where politics is concerned with the distribution of resources among a number of competing groups—the acquisition of information by these groups may actually reduce the degree to which political leaders may be subject to popular control. To the extent that subgroups in the electorate are aware of their gains and losses from political life, they can base their voting strategies on this information. In turn this will produce the sort of competition among "principals" that allows officeholders complete autonomy. In this sense, once again, too much information in the electorate may be a bad thing.

From this point of view, the costliness of information and the difficulties of its transmission may actually be valuable to democratic processes. Many of the contributors to this volume have emphasized just this point. Iyengar, Rahn, Aldrich, Borgida, and Sullivan, and Ottati and Wyer suggest that citizens resort to simple and efficient cognitive strategies for learning about public affairs. Converse argues that even if relatively little information is held by each citizen, the aggregate electoral responses are still likely to be quite informative. Fiorina and Shepsle, and Chappell and Keech, emphasize that citizens

john

quiring very little information to motivate poli-
l" public policy. On these views, there is much
cerned about the sparseness of political infor-
distribution than previous theorists have been.

l life may be characterized by a "booming, buzz-
amount of information acquisition and trans-
effective representation may actually be quite
icy to respond to public opinion, maybe all that
know is that their constituents are displeased
iblic activity. This information by itself may be
fficials to search for new alternatives. Perhaps
the electoral process is that it economizes on
l permits the formulation of good legislation
ation flowing from one place to another and
.... lons.

An investigation into information and elections requires that one
address questions of institutional evaluation. Do our electoral institutions, single-member geographic constituencies with plurality rule
elections, somehow distort the representation of public opinion? Do
they force policymakers to choose inefficient or otherwise inferior
courses of action for "political" reasons? Are some citizens better represented than others? Are there other institutions, electoral or otherwise, that are to be preferred to the ones we have in place?

One is tempted in such discussions simply to borrow normative
conceptions from other disciplines. The obvious candidates are the
efficiency criterion employed ubiquitously in economics, or one or
another of the equality criteria put forward by philosophers. But although the application of such criteria to the evaluation of political
institutions might be illuminating, it is important to identify in advance
what notion of goodness is most appropriate. For some purposes the
efficiency criterion seems useful; it would be disturbing if fiscal choices
by democratic governments were inefficient. Indeed, Chappell and
Keech's argument—contrary to the standard political business-cycle
story—that democratic politics is not necessarily inefficient in the
realm of macroeconomic policymaking is important and consoling.[2]
Inefficiency is a real demerit of an institution.

But politics is concerned largely with matters of disagreement
and conflict, and so the efficiency test is likely to be rather weak. Just
because an outcome is efficient does not mean that citizens will find

it satisfactory from a normative point of view. Put more abstractly, the set of efficient alternatives is too large to serve as more than a necessary condition for the approval of an institution.

If the efficiency criterion is too weak to serve as a standard for institutional evaluation, the equality criterion seems far too strong. Virtually no process that is remotely democratic can achieve egalitarian outcomes, no matter how those might be defined (but see Baron and Ferejohn, 1987). The use of such a standard virtually entails the rejection of democracy. Are there alternative standards that are more appropriate to the evaluation of political institutions?

One such standard, implicitly put forward in several of the chapters, has its roots in the theory of collective choice (Arrow, 1951): responsiveness. Representation seems to require that policy be responsive to public opinion in the sense that if this opinion shifts in some significant way, policy shifts as well. This criterion is problematic even in the informationally simple situation in models of collective choice. Classical results in that area demonstrate the impossibility of finding a general coherent and democratic relationship between the distribution of opinion and policy choices. In most interesting cases, there is no policy choice that can be said to be the right or appropriate choice for a given electorate (cf. Riker, 1982). Thus, a responsiveness criterion is only useful in empirically rare cases in which the appropriate policy choice is clear. Some such examples are found in the McKelvey-Ordeshook chapter.

Another standard is suggested by the work in informational economics. It is surely a virtue of democratic electoral processes that they serve to pool dispersed information in the electorate and transmit it to officeholders, and that, conversely, they are also sufficiently effective in conveying information from officials to citizens to allow citizens a modicum of control. These institutions appear to be compatible with human capacities and incentives, as well as with the functioning of a large-scale society with an extensive division of labor. This suggests that one sort of useful comparative standard might be "informational efficiency": one institution is to be preferred to another on this basis if it requires the transmission of less information.

Still another possible standard is implied by the notion of control. Governmental institutions that require less wealth transfer to officials or competitors for office should be preferred to those that require a large transfer. On this ground we should prefer institutions that permit greater control over politicians to those that permit less. This is simply the efficiency criterion applied to everyone outside the political profession and views the transfer of wealth to specialized politicians as a cost of running governmental institutions.

While each of these criteria seems attractive to me, there is much too little research on alternative institutional structures to apply them to real comparisons. We cannot say, as yet, whether single-member district electoral systems are or are not to be preferred to multimember systems, nor whether either type of system is definitively better than some nondemocratic alternative. Nor are we ready to address the presumably simpler issues of the evaluation of reforms of existing institutions. One can hope, however, that considerations of the sort examined in this volume will permit such issues to be posed and addressed in the future.

NOTES

1. This idea is developed more fully in Ferejohn (1986).

2. There are, of course, many other authors who argue that democratic mechanisms are inherently inefficient. This literature is too large to be discussed here, but the interested reader should consider Shepsle and Weingast (1984a).

I

SOCIAL INTERACTION AND THE TRANSMISSION OF POLITICAL INFORMATION

2

Social Order and Political Chaos: The Structural Setting of Political Information

Robert Huckfeldt
John Sprague

Political information is obtained at particular times in particular places. Time and place, in turn, are intimately related to content and effect, and thus the transmission of information is neither simple nor direct. Dan Rather's nightly television reports, presidential news conferences, and wire service reports have different consequences in Amarillo than they have in Scarsdale, and their import varies as a function of temporal salience. In terms of the dynamic logic inherent in an election campaign, information transmitted during the early primaries has a different significance than information transmitted during the week before the election.

This chapter conceives of political information as being simultaneously social, environmental, and dynamic. It is social because it is frequently conveyed through the medium of human interaction. It is environmental because human interaction is environmentally structured, and because political information is judged and evaluated relative to a particular political setting. Finally, it is dynamic because attentiveness is dynamic, and thus social influence is dynamic as well. The success of information transmission depends fundamentally upon the motivation of the receiver, and motivation responds to the systematic dynamics of politics and social structure.

We undertake several tasks in this chapter: (1) to articulate the structural basis of voting and identify several elements of social structure; (2) to consider the dynamic consequences of social influence and posit a learning model of social influence; (3) to evaluate evidence regarding structural effects in the 1972 and 1976 presidential elections; and (4) to address the political consequences of structural effects more generally both in terms of the relationship between class and politics and in terms of information, rationality, and democratic politics.

THE STRUCTURAL BASIS OF POLITICS

Casting a vote in the isolation of a voting booth is an act of individual choice, but for many voters it is also the end product of a systematic social and political process (Hoare and Smith, 1971; Eulau, 1986). Even though the voting act is individualistic in nature, the voting decision is part of a social experience that is structurally based. Voters employ a variety of information sources during the course of a political campaign: newspapers, radio, television. Here, we are primarily concerned with an alternative, informal source of information and influence—the information that voters receive from one another. Every information source is potentially influential because each includes its own particular bias. Thus, the vote decision depends upon the particular configuration of a voter's informational environment and the receptivity of the voter to the various information sources (McPhee and Smith, 1962; McPhee, Ferguson, and Smith, 1963; Fiorina, 1981; Calvert, 1985; MacKuen and Brown, 1987).

The extent to which voters control the content of the information they receive is problematic. They may or may not turn off an offensive television news broadcast, but the damage is already done when the offense is taken. Voters may or may not avoid political discussions with politically disagreeable neighbors, but they cannot avoid seeing the yard signs and bumper stickers on neighborhood cars and lawns. They may or may not avoid eating lunch with a co-worker who vocalizes divergent political viewpoints, but they cannot so easily shield themselves from the co-worker who shares the same work area. In short, voters react in systematically different ways to the same stimulus, but some reaction is inevitable. Thus, the social structure of the vote is crucial, because it shapes the social experiences and political information that are brought by the voter to the voting booth.

ELEMENTS OF SOCIAL STRUCTURE: ENVIRONMENTS AND CONTEXTS

For purposes of this research, social structure is defined in terms of environments and contexts. These terms are often used interchangeably in discussions of social and political behavior, but Eulau (1980:216) argues that context and environment are concepts that should not be mistaken for each other: "*Context* is a compositional phenomenon that *emerges*, and there is nothing deterministic about it as there is likely to be about the environment." We adopt Eulau's distinction and define the social context according to the social or political composition of an environment. That is, an environment is a structured setting that shares one or more common characteristics: spatial boundaries, political functions, institutions of governance, political organization, and so forth. In contrast, a context is defined in terms of an environment's social composition and the resulting consequences of social composition for social interaction and the social transmission of information and influence. In adopting this definition for context, we are anchoring the analysis in a tradition whose modern origin traces to Blau's work (1957) on structural effects and the work of Davis, Spaeth, and Huson (1961) on compositional effects.

Contextual theories of politics are organized by a variety of social influence arguments that emphasize the consequences of population composition for the political behavior of individuals within the population. These explanations are supported by a number of empirically documented relationships: (1) Blue-collar workers are more likely to vote for left-leaning parties if they live among other blue-collar workers (Tingsten, [1937], 1963; Langton and Rapoport, 1975). (2) Low-status people are more likely to participate in politics if they live among other low-status people, and high-status people are more likely to participate if they live among other high-status people (Giles and Dantico, 1982; Huckfeldt, 1986). (3) Democratic autoworkers employed in a workplace environment dominated by other Democrats are indiscriminate regarding the political party leanings of associates, but Republican autoworkers in the same environment prefer to associate with other Republicans (Finifter, 1974).

These contextual relationships are very different in their substantive and theoretical implications, but they share several important similarities. First, they emphasize that the behavior of individuals is affected by various forms of social influence, but the nature and content of that social influence varies systematically across both individuals and contexts. Second, contextual explanations point toward a time-ordered process of social influence: an individual is embedded within a particular context, the context structures social interaction patterns, political information is conveyed through social interaction, and the individual forms a political response based upon this information. The process is, of course, a cyclical one, with the most recent political response but an occasion for the further response of others.

In contrast, the environment is defined to include population composition and many other factors as well. Our concern is with the county as a political environment, and although our measure of the environment is the county proportion voting Democratic, we treat it as a surrogate measure for a variety of environmental features. Everything else being equal, people who live in Democratic counties are more likely to interact with Democrats. But they are also more likely to see local politicians who are Democrats on television, to be contacted by Democratic campaign workers, to read a newspaper with a Democratic bias, and so on. In contrast, our concern with the neighborhood is in terms of social composition, social interaction, and socially based political influence. Thus our primary conceptual distinction is between a generalized political environment and a more specific and localized social context.

THE INTERDEPENDENCE BETWEEN CONTEXTS AND ENVIRONMENTS

The importance of the political environment for the voting behavior of individuals is well demonstrated by the work of Warren Miller. In a classic analysis, Miller (1956) examines the impact of one-party politics at the county level upon the voting choices made by individual voters. He shows that voters with the same partisan motivations—defined in terms of party identification, issue positions, and candidate evaluations—were less likely to vote in correspondence with their partisan leanings if they lived in counties where these predispositions placed them in a political minority. As Miller puts it (1956:715): "the minority fails to receive its 'fair share' of votes if the relative incidence of supporting motivations is used as the criterion of fairness." Furthermore, individuals who were members of a partisan minority—defined in terms of 1952 presidential vote choice—were less homogeneous with respect to issue opinions and candidate evaluations than members of the majority.

What are the sources of these effects? In a rich analysis, Putnam (1966) shows that the relationship between the respondent's vote and the county political environment was strongest among respondents involved in secondary organizations. He also shows that the political composition of respondents' primary groups reflected the county's political environment, and that this relationship between the partisan composition of the county and the partisan composition of primary groups was strongest among the members of secondary organizations. Putnam's logic is straightforward: people integrated within the community are also those most highly exposed to community sentiment through repeated social interactions.

Segal and Meyer (1974) seemingly contradict Putnam's work by showing that residents of several northeastern cities who belonged to secondary organizations were *less* influenced by the neighborhood social context than those who did not belong. But Segal and Meyer measure highly localized environments (precincts), a point picked up by Cox (1974:161–162). Cox resolves the anomaly when he observes that most organizations better represent the county environment than the neighborhood context. (These interactions between contexts and group membership relationships have been intensively investigated by Brown, 1981). Thus, Cox's observation points toward the complex interdependence of the larger environment and the more immediate surroundings of the individual voter.

The classic statement of the interaction between the larger political environment and the voter's immediate social surroundings is contained in the early voting studies of the Columbia sociologists. In their identification of a breakage effect, Lazarsfeld, Berelson, and Gaudet (1944) show that the potential for environmental influence is heightened when the voter's immediate circumstances push in opposite directions. That is, if a voter's intimate surroundings are dissonance-producing, then the likelihood is increased that he or she will vote in line with the larger environment. Conversely, Segal and Meyer (1974) show that voters who reside in political environments without a clear partisan leaning are *more* affected by stimuli from the local social context. Thus, effects from both levels are interactive: localized contextual effects depend upon the larger political environment, and the effects of the larger political environment depend upon the more immediate context of the voter.

DYNAMIC CONSEQUENCES OF SOCIAL STRUCTURE

The authors of *Voting* show that the social structure produces a predictable, systematic dynamic during an election campaign: those who discuss politics with people holding compatible views remain stable in their vote intentions; people who cannot recall any political conversations are generally unstable and often lapse into neutrality or nonvoting; and people who come into contact with opposition preferences demonstrate more volatility in their vote choices (Berelson, Lazarsfeld, and McPhee, 1954:120). The authors catalog a number of sources of social influence responsible for producing volatility: opposite political preferences within the family, opposite preferences among friends, and opposite preferences among co-workers. In general, voters were more likely to change their vote intentions during the course of the campaign if they occupied social locations that conflicted with their original vote intentions: volatility was higher among Protestants and white-collar workers who initially favored Truman and among Catholics and blue-collar workers who initially favored Dewey. In the words of Berelson and his associates: "The stability of a preference, then, varies with the chances of social support for it. And the chances of social support for given political choices, in turn, vary with the distribution of such preferences in the particular segment of the community" (1954:126).

Short-run political volatility among individuals during the campaign is, however, responsible for political stability in the longer run at the level of groups (Berelson, Lazarsfeld, and McPhee, 1954; Huckfeldt, 1983). As one political campaign ends, and politics recedes from its place of prominence in people's minds, the level of informal social control exercised by a group over its members with respect to political matters recedes as well. Political preferences become more idiosyncratic, and political cohesiveness within groups reaches a low ebb. As the next campaign heats up, politics becomes more salient, and the social control exercised by groups is increased. Thus, the political campaign has the potential to increase homogeneity within, and polarization between, politically significant social groups. Individual volatility is the price of political stability within groups across time.

In summary, Berelson and his associates describe a social influence process that occurs during election campaigns in which "political preferences are 'contagious' over the range of personal contacts" (1954:122). What happens during behavioral contagion? Voters share their preferences with other voters during social exchanges, and preferences change as the result of these exchanges in at least partially predictable ways. Thus, behavioral contagion is a learning process where individuals learn appropriate political preferences and opinions from one another.

A LEARNING MODEL OF CONTEXTUAL INFLUENCE

A learning model of contextual influence can be articulated in the tradition of the Columbia sociologists and especially in the tradition of William McPhee (1963). In his work on a voting simulator, McPhee supplies logical structure for a process of serially occurring, politically significant events: (1) an individual receives a stimulus from the political environment in the form of an event, a media report, a campaign speech; (2) based upon individual preconceptions, the individual forms a response to the stimulus; (3) the response is evaluated through social interaction that provides either negative or positive reinforcement; (4) negative reinforcement leads to information search in an informationally biased context; and (5) the initial response is modified or confirmed on the basis of both the search and social experience. And the process is recurring, so that an endless feedback loop of political stimulus, response, reinforcement, search, and changed or confirmed choice is formed.

Sprague (1982) identifies the dynamic features of a contextually based learning process, and several of these features are directly related to the changes that occur in preferences, opinions, and attitudes during the course of a political campaign. First, the efficiency of learning is increased as delay in reinforcement is decreased, and frequency of reinforcement is increased. Thus, the face-to-face encounters that occur through routine patterns of social interaction have an especially high potential for political influence. Furthermore, regular associates, even if they are not close or trusted friends, may be more influential than the best friends whom we seldom see because regular associates occupy a more strategic position for imposing frequent and immediate reinforcement.

Second, continuous reinforcement of short duration produces short-term effects of large magnitude that decay rapidly at the end of reinforcement. This characteristic is especially germane to opinions and preferences connected with political campaigns. Before the campaign begins, many opinions regarding campaign issues and candidates are generally matters of private concern (or of no concern), and hence they are idiosyncratic (McPhee, Anderson, and Milholland, 1962). Thus, such opinions are susceptible to the effects of social learning because they are not anchored in any prior history of discussion and reinforcement. As politics comes to dominate the content of discussions previously devoted to other subjects, we should expect to see important contextually based changes in opinions and preferences that were previously idiosyncratic. In turn, as the campaign is displaced by other subjects of concern, continuous reinforcement comes to an abrupt end, and the effect of context dissipates rapidly.

Viewed in a different light, reinforcement regarding basic political orientations accumulates in an irregular and intermittent manner, but it occurs over long time periods. Opinions regarding candidates and issues are subject to reinforcement that is more continuous for shorter time periods. Thus, party identification is learned slowly and intermittently over the long haul, thereby becoming resistant to decay. In contrast, attitudes toward Carter's handling of the Iranian hostage issue obey the rule, "out of sight, out of mind."

Finally, the individual's motivational state is of central importance in determining learning efficiency: learning occurs more efficiently when motivation is high. In terms of the political campaign, motivation is high when politics is salient, and politics becomes more salient as the campaign progresses. Furthermore, the process is self-accelerating: salience increases motivation, motivation increases attention, attention increases expressive response to political stimuli, and expressive response increases the frequency of politically significant social interaction. As Converse (1962) observes, however, incoming information must compete with previously stored information. Thus, it is not clear that the highly motivated will show the greatest contextual effect, because they are also likely to possess large amounts of stored information (Orbell, 1970).

EXPECTATIONS REGARDING STRUCTURAL EFFECTS

These ideas lead to a number of observational expectations:

1. The influence of social contexts should interact with the influence of political environments; the effect of each level should depend upon the effect of the other level.

2. Campaign-related behaviors affected by both contexts and environments should be highly volatile and rapidly altered due to the nature of the social learning process and to the episodic quality of political campaigns.

3. The effects of contextual learning should vary as a function of individual motivation; politically attentive and inattentive individuals should demonstrate different patterns of effects.

ENVIRONMENTS AND CONTEXTS IN 1972 AND 1976

These expectations are examined relative to people's preelection expected votes and postelection reported votes. Our research strategy is to examine the patterns of relationships among the context, the environment, and vote preference during the general election campaign and after the election is over. The data base for the analysis builds upon the pre- and postelection waves of the American National Election Studies for 1972 and 1976 conducted by the Center for Political Studies of the University of Michigan. So that the data base serves our purposes, we have altered it in two major ways. First, the analysis is limited to white respondents in a conservative effort to avoid any exaggeration of contextual effects. Our concern is with social contexts, social status, and social influence. Thus, including nonwhites would exaggerate contextual relationships: a large majority of non-whites live in lower status contexts and Democratic counties.

Electoral histories for respondents' counties and census data for respondents' tracts are merged with the survey, and this leads to a second alteration in the data base. Roughly one-third of the respondents live in untracted areas and cannot be included in the analysis. What remains of the original sample? All major urban areas in the United States are tracted, and the resulting data base should approximate a (random) sample of whites living in major urban areas. Although we make no formal claims to randomness for the resulting sample, there is no reason to expect that any extraordinary bias has been introduced that might compromise the results. We do not make use of the case weight for the 1976 data. Using unweighted data compromises the representativeness of the sample, but the logistic procedure used herein does not accommodate a weighting procedure. Thus, the only way to incorporate the weight would be to resample randomly from the portion of the sample that is to be weighted greater than one. The disadvantage of this procedure is that it makes replicability of our results impossible without access to the same weighted data set.

The logistic model is employed in this analysis because all dependent variables are dichotomous in nature (Hanushek and Jackson, 1977). This model is well suited to our task of estimating the contingent probability of a political preference. In order to determine the magnitude of an effect due to an explanatory variable, predicted probabilities are calculated across the range of a particular explanatory variable with all other explanatory variables held constant. Our practice in this chapter is to display figures in the text illustrating the magnitudes of effects, but to defer discussions of the underlying logit model to the Appendix.

The incorporation of social structure within the model builds on our earlier discussion. The political environment is defined at the level of the county, and the social context at the level of the neighborhood, defined as a census tract. These are, of course, crude instruments of aggregation: counties vary in population from the hundreds to the millions, and census tracts are blunt surrogates for the emergent compositional phenomenon identified by Eulau (1980). These operational devices possess several distinct advantages, however. Perhaps most important, they are widely used, and thus our results can be directly interpreted relative to what has gone before. Further, the levels of measurement are biased in conservative directions, and the empirical issue is whether or not these crude but readily available proxies provide sufficient predictive power to overcome the noise inherent in such aggregates of convenience. As it turns out, the measures we use appear capable of bearing the burden asked of them.

The county political environment and the neighborhood social context are measured separately in the model, and their interaction is measured as a simple multiplicative product. A number of individual-level controls are also included to guard against the contextual fallacy of inferring a contextual effect that is actually an artifact of excluded individual-level variables (Hauser, 1974). Five individual-level variables are included either because they are standardly accepted as predictors for the partisan direction of voting, or because they are individual-level surrogates for living within a given social status milieu: age, education, income, working-class occupational status, and partisan self-identification. These five are entered into the model both for 1972 and also for 1976. A final individual-level control is unique to the 1972 analysis: respondents' attitudes regarding withdrawal of American forces from Vietnam—a powerful predictor of the vote and perhaps the most important issue of the election.

The direction and magnitude of environmental and contextual effects in the 1972 election are displayed in Figure 1. For both the expected and reported votes, age, income, and education are held constant at the sample means, partisan self-identification at Independent, and occupational class at middle class. Each line represents a different value for the proportion of high school graduates in the neighborhood. We use the county proportion voting Democratic as a general measure of the political environment rather than as a time-specific measure of a particular election. The county Democratic vote in 1972 is highly correlated to the county Democratic vote in 1968 and the county Democratic vote in 1976. We use the 1976 measure in Figure 2 and the 1972 measure in Figure 1 because they provide the most up-to-date measures of the counties' general political environments in the particular election campaigns.

At first consideration it might seem obvious that the lines should slope positively: the variable on the y axis is in one sense a microsample version of the variable on the x axis, taken before the event in part A and after the event in part B. Recall, however, that party identification is controlled in these models. In these instances it is not a tautology to report that people are more likely to vote Democratic if they live in counties where more people vote Democratic. Figure 1 shows that political Independents are more likely to expect to vote Democratic, and to report voting Democratic, if they live in counties where other people are more likely to vote Democratic. The same

Figure 1. Probability of McGovern Vote Preference in 1972 Among Political Independents, with Individual-Level Controls

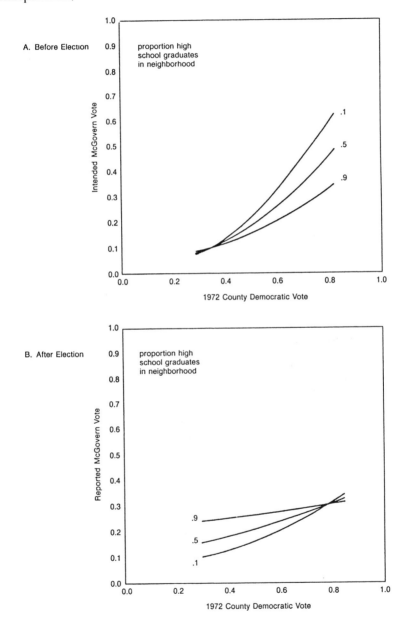

Source: Table 1 logit model

general pattern of effects holds true for Democrats and for Republicans as well. The central interpretive fact is this: citizens are more likely to vote Democratic in Democratic counties regardless of their own partisan inclinations.

Several features of the political environment's effect stand out. First, for Independents at least, the effect decreases from the expected vote to the reported vote. Second, in both instances, the effect of the political environment is mediated by the social context: the county's partisan complexion has a greater effect among people living in lower-status neighborhoods.

The effect of the social context is more complex. For the expected vote, higher-status contexts generally produce a lower Democratic vote probability. Further, the effect of context becomes more pronounced in more Democratic environments. The social context's effect is completely transformed for the reported vote: higher-status contexts encourage a Democratic vote. This effect becomes smaller as a function of more Democratic environments until, in strongly Democratic counties, the effect is extinguished. Thus, the *strength* of the contextual effect varies across political environments, and the *direction* of the contextual effect varies across the campaign. (These somewhat puzzling effects may be products of the statistically marginal logit coefficients that generated Figure 1. See Table 1 in the Appendix.)

Figure 2 shows the magnitudes of structural effects for the same basic model applied to the 1976 presidential election. As before, age, education, and income are held constant at the sample means, partisan identification at Independent, and social class at middle class.

In terms of intended votes before the election, Figure 2A shows that Independents are more likely to plan on voting Democratic if they live in Democratic counties, and plots could also be generated to show that Democrats and Republicans are more likely to plan on voting Democratic in Democratic counties. Thus, a moderate environmental effect appears to be present in Figure 2A: living in a Democratic or Republican county has a modest effect upon vote intention. In contrast, part A of the figure shows a contextual, as opposed to environmental, effect that is, as a practical matter, nonexistent.

The same procedure is employed in Figure 2B for respondents' reported votes, but the pattern of relationships is dramatically altered. Among individuals living in the lowest-status contexts, the effect of the political environment is strong and positive. But among respondents living in the highest-status contexts, the political environment has an effect that is actually reversed in direction. Figure 2B also shows

Figure 2. Probabilty of Carter Vote Preference in 1976 Among Political Independents, with Individual-Level Controls

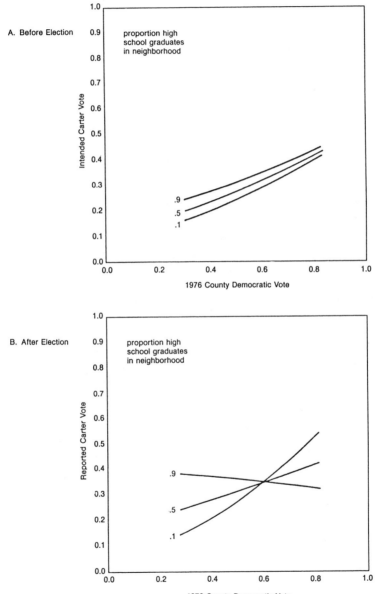

Source: Table 2 logit model.

that the effect of context depends upon the political environment. In moderately Democratic environments the effect of context is non-existent. In strongly Democratic environments the contextual effect is strong and lies in the expected direction: higher-status contexts discourage a Carter vote. But in strongly Republican environments the effect lies in a reversed direction: higher-status contexts are related to higher levels of Carter support.

Figure 3 replicates the procedure of Figure 2B, but partisan identification is controlled at strong Democrat in part A of the figure and at strong Republican in part B of the figure. Clearly, the magnitudes of contextual and environmental effects depend upon where an individual lies on the probability distribution. Especially in the case of Republicans, the strength of the partisan cue tends to overwhelm environmental influence. That is, the political significance of being a strong Republican far outweighs the political significance of being a strong Democrat, and it also overwhelms a pronounced structural effect. To paraphrase F. Scott Fitzgerald in the words of Robert H. Salisbury: Republicans really *are* different from you and me.

The model of Figure 2 is replicated once again in Figures 4 and 5; Figure 4 includes only respondents who report being very interested in the campaign at the first interview, and Figure 5 only those who report being marginally interested or disinterested. Figure 4 shows that the preferences of politically attentive citizens are socially structured both before and after the election. The major difference between the pre- and postpatterns of effects is that environmental effects tend to diminish while contextual effects generally tend to intensify. In particular, the reversal of effect for social contexts in Republican environments shows up very strongly in the postelection interview for these respondents.

In contrast, the pattern of structural effects is much different for less attentive citizens. The structural effects shown in Figure 5A present a perverse pattern suggestive of white noise, and thus it would appear that the preferences of the less attentive are likely to be *unstructured* early in the campaign (see Table 4). The postelection structural effects of part B take on a more familiar pattern: (1) an environmental effect that lies in the expected direction for respondents in lower-status contexts and is diminished (and reversed) in higher-status contexts, and (2) a contextual effect that lies in the expected direction in Democratic environments but in a reversed direction in Republican environments. Although the reported votes of the less attentive are structured less than the more attentive, their preferences also show the most *movement* during the course of the

Figure 3. Probability of Reported Carter Vote After the 1976 Election, with Individual-Level Controls, for Strong Democrats and Republicans

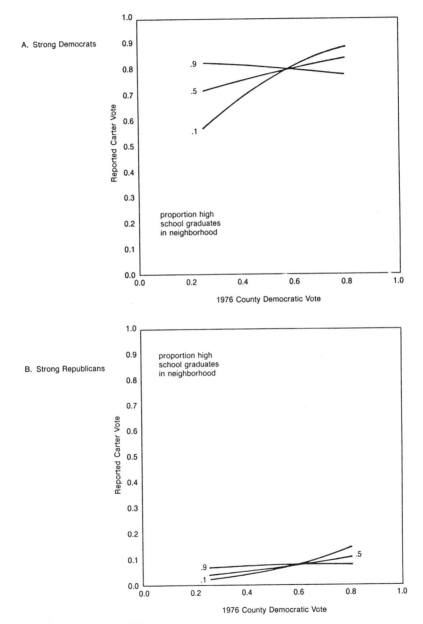

Source: Table 2 logit model

Figure 4. Probability of Carter Vote Preference in 1976 Among Political Independents, with Individual-Level Controls, for Respondents Very Interested in the Campaign

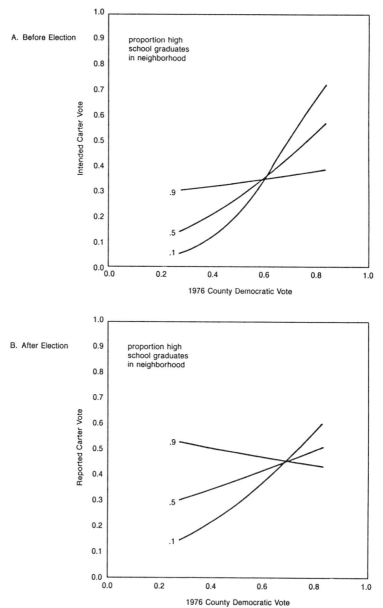

Source: Table 3 logit model

Figure 5. Probability of Carter Vote Preference in 1976 Among Political Independents, with Individual-Level Controls, for Respondents Less Interested in the Campaign

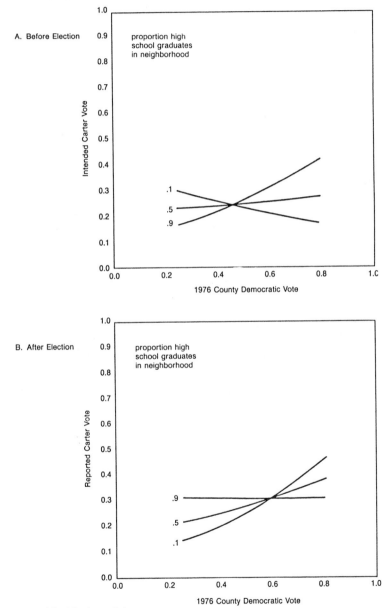

Source: Table 4 logit model

campaign, and this movement systematically brings them into correspondence with the social structure. In short, their preferences appear to be transformed from being individually idiosyncratic and socially unstructured to being at least moderately structured in terms of environments and contexts.

The results displayed for 1976 are consistent with our expectations. First, there is a marked interaction between the social context and the political environment: effects at both levels depend upon conditions at the other level. Second, great volatility appears in the social structure of political choice: the political stimulus of an election campaign sets in motion a process of social influence, and this process produces systematic changes in the structure of the candidate preference distribution. Third, the impact of social structure varies as a function of individual motivation, conceived both in terms of partisan inclination and in terms of attentiveness to the campaign. Thus these results are supportive of a social learning interpretation of politically significant social interaction in election campaigns. Finally, and perhaps most important, these results also produce a number of questions, and it is to these questions that we now turn.

WHAT DO THESE RESULTS MEAN?

First, why is the effect of social structure upon the reported vote so much more apparent in 1976 than in 1972?

The presidential elections of 1972 and 1976 differ in a number of important ways, but no difference is more fundamental than the alteration of electoral coalitions that occurred between the elections. Both partisanship and class voting were at low ebb in the 1972 election. Indeed, class voting in 1972 was at its lowest level in post-New Deal American political history: support for the Democratic party was virtually identical among the working class and middle class. In contrast, the 1976 election demonstrated at least a temporary resurgence of traditional party coalitions, and the level of class voting in 1976 was equal to the post-Truman high points of 1952 and 1964 (Lipset, 1981). Thus, the political and social boundaries separating Democratic and Republican voters were altered between the elections; the ideological politics of 1972 gave way to class and party in 1976.

Elections without structure by party and class are typically unstructured by context and environment as well. Ideological politics stimulates a high level of individual idiosyncrasy unless ideology is successfully institutionalized within a party organization, or unless it becomes strongly identified with a major social group. Such was not the case in 1972. When the traditional bases of party support are disrupted as they were in 1972, the social structure is not so readily invoked in support of a party or candidate. And this is a direct result of the fact that political preferences were heterogeneous within the structural boundaries of class and party.

Second, why does the campaign produce different dynamic consequences in 1972 and 1976? In 1972, a fairly modest set of structural effects is weakened during the course of the campaign. In 1976, an even weaker set of structural effects is invigorated and accentuated by the campaign.

In both campaigns the Democratic candidate lost ground during the course of the campaign, but the structural logic underlying these losses differed dramatically. McGovern's campaign resulted in the deterioration of the traditional Democratic party coalition. Carter's campaign began with an inflated lead that slowly but surely deteriorated as the campaign developed into a fairly classic partisan contest between a predominantly working-class Democratic party and a predominantly middle-class Republican party.

Political campaigns possess a logic that is not only related to issues and media events, but to social structure as well. Some campaigns successfully mobilize voters within social and political categories while others do not. Some campaigns begin with an electorate that is already mobilized according to class and party while others do not. A successful mobilization effort does not enlist supporters in single-file fashion. Rather, the successful mobilization of a party or a group exploits the social structure: the campaign serves as a stimulus or a catalyst that puts a social process into action across a broad front operating simultaneously on many individuals who very well may reinforce each other's behavior. And thus, at the culmination of the 1976 campaign, the individual probability of voting for Carter varied significantly and interactively across political environments and social contexts.

Third, how do the effects of the localized social context compare with the effects of the larger political environment? In 1976, the post-campaign reported vote shows a higher level of contextual influence. The effect of the social context becomes more evident during the course of the campaign because the slow-but-steady persuasion of this locally defined setting continues to increase in importance as channels of informal communication are increasingly dominated by politics. At the culmination of the campaign, its effect appears to overshadow the effect of the political environment defined more broadly. In short, the campaign serves as a stimulus that pushes people toward a social equilibrium defined on the basis of their immediate surroundings—

on the basis of the people who are *most* strategically positioned to affect their vote preferences.

These results also point to the importance of the social context as an interceptor of environmental influence. Environmental effects in 1976 cannot be understood except in reference to the more immediate social context. Lower-status contexts accelerate environmental influence, while higher-status contexts greatly diminish the environmental effect. People living in lower-status neighborhoods are more susceptible to environmental influence and, as a result, lower-status contexts encourage conformity to the political environment. Higher-status contexts provide an alternative source of political information that competes very effectively with information from the larger political environment. Lower-status contexts do not.

Fourth, why are there reversals in direction both for the effects of political environments and social contexts? Figure 2B shows that, in high-status contexts, people are more likely to vote Democratic if they live in *Republican* counties. In Republican political environments, people are more likely to vote Democratic if they live in *higher* status contexts.

Further statistical analyses, detailed in the Appendix, make the sign reversal disappear for the effect of county political environments, but the sign reversal persists for neighborhood social contexts. Higher-status contexts encourage Republican voting in Democratic counties, but higher-status contexts are related to higher levels of Democratic voting in Republican counties. It is very difficult to explain these contextual social status effects with traditionally and simply stated class arguments. A straightforward expectation regarding the effect of contextual social status is that higher-status contexts should produce a greater likelihood of Republican voting, but this is not uniformly the case. Why?

Any discussion of this sign reversal for context must be undertaken from the standpoint that partisan loyalties are controlled, and thus any demonstrated structural effect is purely informational in content. That is, we are ignoring the role of structural factors in affecting basic political orientations, and the figures displayed here must always be evaluated for a particular partisan category. In addition, class and status are controlled as well, and thus the analysis isolates the purely informational effects of social structure.

The strong interdependence between the county political environment and the neighborhood social context produces the inversion of the commonly expected relationship between contextual social status and partisan choice. This reversed direction of the expected relationship between context and vote must be judged relative to the more general influence of higher-status contexts toward political nonconformity. At the same time, lower-status contexts accelerate environmental influence, thereby leading to a situation in which these contexts encourage Democratic voting in Republican environments and Republican voting in Democratic environments. One way to think about this nonconformity effect is that higher-status contexts compete effectively with political environments as an alternative source of political information. Lower-status contexts do *not* compete effectively as sources of information, and thus people living in lower-status contexts demonstrate very strong environmental effects and high levels of environmental conformity.

An interesting contrast can be made between these results and the results that Segal and Meyer (1974) report. Our findings show that the influence of context is seemingly diminished in competitive environments, but Segal and Meyer show that the effect of context is generally greatest in competitive environments. These differences in results can probably be accounted for in terms of the criterion variables employed in the respective analyses: we examine vote choice, whereas Segal and Meyer examine party identification. Thus, their analysis relates to a fundamental decision regarding partisan orientation that is affected by the social context to a greater degree when the political environment gives no clear-cut cue. Our analysis relates to a more ephemeral decision regarding vote choice, which is subject to competing short-term cues from the environment and from the context. Ironically, when environments are more competitive, the effect of context appears weakest. However, even in these situations, the social context plays an important mediating role between the political environment and the individual. Any examination of contextual influence that is undertaken in a single political environment is destined to ignore this intervening function.

Finally, how can the variation in structural effects across individuals be explained?

This analysis has focused upon two different types of individual effects. First, a powerful partisan cue is able to overcome and extinguish disagreeable information emanating from the social structure. As a result, strong Republicans were effectively immunized against structural infections. This is not to suggest that they are necessarily shielded from structural influences, although this might certainly be a possibility (Finifter, 1974). Rather, it is to indicate that powerfully held beliefs are in some instances capable of overpowering dissonance-producing information.

A second type of individual characteristic, the level of political attentiveness, appears to determine levels of exposure to structural influence. The learning model anticipates that the interested would be more structured than the disinterested, but not that the campaign effect would be so powerful in the disinterested. The disinterested are, of course, embedded in social contexts and political environments before the campaign begins, but at this early stage the embedding is, apparently, politically irrelevant. What emerges from the comparison is the extraordinary power of the campaign, of the manipulation of political information and events by elites to activate politically relevant social interaction and hence induce the consequent socially learned political responses. What the campaign achieves, then, is to insure the power of social coercion. Free democratic politics coerces men and women to pay attention to politics, and this has the inevitable outcome of inflicting the correlation between social distributions and political preference distributions on individual choices. The mass political world is social and interactive.

POLITICAL CONSEQUENCES

What then can be said regarding social structure and the vote in 1972 and 1976? First and foremost, the structural basis of the vote depends upon the nature of the campaign. Some candidates and some campaigns exploit the social structure as a vehicle for political mobilization. Others do not. For elections in which the social structure is exploited, such as the 1976 election, we see social order being imposed upon political chaos. At the beginning of such a campaign, preferences tend to be idiosyncratic and heterogeneous across environments and contexts. By the end of such a campaign, however, individual preferences are brought into line with their surroundings, thereby creating political integrity and homogeneity within social structural boundaries.

Second, these results suggest that, as sources of political information, social contexts and political environments generate a joint effect that reduces the level of class politics. This is primarily due to the competitive disadvantage of lower-status contexts as sources of political information. Although higher-status contexts produce an effect that shields individuals from environmental influence, lower-status contexts expose individuals to environmental cues. Thus, the relationship between contextual social status and the vote is reversed across political environments, necessarily leading to an aggregate decline in the influence of social status on voting.

These observations produce an irony: (1) if politics is not structurally based, then lower-status groups and parties are unlikely to obtain the internal homogeneity necessary for furthering their interests, but (2) if politics is structurally based, then the natural social order produces lower-status contexts exposed to environmentally structured information and cues. Stated in different terms, lower-status groups are at a disadvantage because the breakage effect is inherently asymmetric. Lower-status groups tend to be exposed to environmental influence, but higher-status groups do not.

In summary, the contextual and environmental bases of these structural effects put lower-status groups at a distinct disadvantage in terms of their political interests. In particular, it exposes them to environmental influence that limits their potential for political cohesiveness. Thus we are led to a realization that has been brought forward by many writers at many times and in many settings: lower-status groups are especially dependent upon organizations that structure and mobilize their votes. The demise of political parties and labor unions as agents of political mobilization is felt most acutely among these people, and we are reminded once again that politics without parties and organized groups is inherently biased against lower-status groups.

THE SOCIALLY RATIONAL BASIS OF DEMOCRATIC POLITICS

Rational citizens act politically in concert and competition with other rational citizens. We have argued, and also have attempted to demonstrate empirically, that these behaviors are anchored in social contexts and political environments in complex ways. It is now time to sketch some consequences for democratic politics arising from this view of mass political behavior.

The nub of the issue lies in the conceptualization of interdependence. This was recognized long ago by McPhee, who treated this issue as the theoretical puzzle of social determinism. How can it be that (statistical) nonindependence is so pervasive in groups, the more pervasive as the groups tend toward the end point of family? Our reasoning has been profoundly influenced by McPhee, who resolved this puzzle—and puzzle it is because you do not choose your family—by placing a rational, self-interested, calculating person in the center of a dynamic process of social interaction, which itself was structured and informationally biased in probabilistic ways.

Indeed, when a rational actor buys a house in a neighborhood, he or she chooses a complicated probability distribution of social interaction opportunities across the lives of the household. College chances and marriages are conditioned by these choices, choices of enormous consequence in the lives of those held dear, but uncertain, distant, and not easily calculated. But calculate we do, not because we are independent rational beings, but because we are rational and socially interdependent beings, and we comprehend that harsh (or wonderful) fact and act upon it. We choose a neighborhood because we are rationally aware that day-to-day living entails contingent social interactions that can only be controlled, if at all, by buying into one set of probabilities as compared with others. We care where we live because the world is social and hence ineluctably interdependent.

This common behavior, residential choice, can serve to bring us back to McPhee's formulation of the social influence process in politics. The heart of his formulation lies in the mechanisms governing the consequences of disagreement. When you discover that someone you talk with disagrees with you, what does rational behavior dictate? If it is a friend whom you love and respect, good sense as well as rationality require that you reassess your own position. McPhee's insight was to see that the information-gathering behavior consequent on opinion disagreement among close associates is undoubtedly conducted in an informationally biased (socially structured) context (compare Calvert, 1985).

Hence Downs's rational citizen might, among other information-gathering behaviors, seek a second opinion from "someone he knows who has selection principles like his own" (Downs, 1957:229). In short, he asks another friend. But this friend is similarly situated and, probabilistically, either is more likely to support the first friend or the questioner. The argument is symmetric. As long as the informational context is systematically biased, which must be the case with a probability of unity, then one will be reinforced more than once and the other will be punished more than once. If rational humans choose on the basis of the weight of the evidence in hand, they very well may thus choose to modify their policy preferences, or, alternatively, to be confirmed in their evidently correct original opinion. Rough homogeneity of preferences within groups is the outcome of these dynamic processes, and they are wholly the outcome of rational people making rational decisions under the naturally occurring conditions of social interdependence.

Interdependence and *information* are the key words. Much political information is acquired through social interaction. Social interactions are informationally biased by a (biased) nonrandom structuring of social relations—social structure. The joint consequence is that ra-

tional citizens in democratic politics tend, as distinct groups, to advance the interests of others similarly situated. This fact is known and
acted on by political leaders, especially when political organization is
in process. The coercive power of the group over the opinions of its
members is no less coercive because it arises from rational behavior.
Democratic politics both exploits and arises from this group basis, for
it produces aggregates, occasionally well organized, with sufficiently
common and well-articulated opinions that public debate is possible.

In democratic politics, leaders of coalitions must manage leaders
of groups. And the groups, unlike the coalitions, have an underlying
organizational logic rooted in social interdependence. Information in
democratic politics is aggregated by rational social processes initially.
This aggregation produces coherence in public issues sufficient for
debate and discussion. Socially structured information and opinion
formation processes thus constitute an important enabling condition
for democratic politics.

Appendix

This appendix addresses three tasks: a description of analytic
procedures, a discussion of the logit models that undergird the prior
analyses in Figures 1 through 5, and an analysis of the direction reversals in structural effects shown in Figure 2B.

PROCEDURE

The logit model for micro data provides a useful technique for
estimating the effects of various factors upon the probability of an
event. Here, the "event" is the report of a vote preference by a survey
respondent. The technique resembles ordinary least squares regression in that each respondent is treated as an observation, and a coefficient is estimated for each independent variable. The coefficient
predicts change in a dependent variable as a function of change in
some particular independent variable for a fixed set of coefficients,
and values, for all other independent predictors in the equation.

The logistic functions for the probability of an event's occurrence
(P) and nonoccurrence ($1 - P$) are expressed as:

$$P = 1/(1 + e^{-XB})$$
$$1 - P = 1/(1 + e^{XB})$$

where X = matrix of independent variables including the constant,
and B = vector of coefficients to be estimated. Clearly, the coefficients

do not provide a linear estimate of the probability. They do provide a linear estimate of the logit, or the natural log of the odds ratio:

$$XB = L = ln(P/(1 - P))$$

The logit has several features worth noting. A unit change in the logit is related to a larger change in the probability when the probability is closer to .5, corresponding to the normal manner in which probabilities vary as a function of exogenous influences. Moreover, as the logit varies from negative infinity to positive infinity, the corresponding probability varies from zero to one, thereby eliminating the problem of predicting probabilities that lie outside the meaningful unit interval.

The logit model employs a maximum likelihood technique to estimate the coefficients. Locating the actual maximum of the likelihood function requires that a system of nonlinear equations be solved for the coefficient values. Absent a closed form solution for these equations, an iterative procedure is used to arrive at a numeric solution for the coefficients.

The logit model is inherently nonlinear, and thus the magnitudes of coefficients cannot be interpreted directly. Rather, judgments regarding the magnitude of an explanatory variable's effect can be based upon variations in the predicted probabilities that result from changes in one explanatory variable while other explanatory variables are held constant. This method is used in the construction and interpretation of Figures 1 through 5, and it is necessary because the model explicitly assumes that the effect of any single explanatory variable depends upon values of other explanatory variables and their coefficients jointly (Hanushek and Jackson, 1977; Fiorina, 1981; Huckfeldt, 1986).

In order to make the figures in this chapter directly comparable, common baseline values for the control variables are required. Thus, most controlled variables are held constant at the same values for all the figures. Social class is held constant at middle class: the dummy variable for household working-class status is set equal to zero. The 1972 Vietnam withdrawal scale is held constant at "3": a moderate position leaning slightly toward the "immediate withdrawal" end of the spectrum. Values for age, education, and household income are held constant at mean values. These mean values are calculated for that part of the unweighted 1976 white sample that has valid (nonmissing) values for the variables included in the analysis of Table 2B. Coding conventions for 1972 and 1976 data have been brought into correspondence by the authors. The mean values are as follows: mean age of respondent = 44, mean years of school for respondent = 13, mean household income for respondent = 11.

For reasons that are discussed below, two different status measures are employed for census tracts. The value for median education in the tract is held constant as a linear function of the proportion of adult tract residents who are high school educated. This linear function is estimated using ordinary least squares for 1976 white respondents with valid (non-missing) values on the variables included in the analysis of Table 2B. The equation is as follows:

$$Y = b_1 + b_2X$$

where

Y = median education in tract
X = proportion high school graduates in tract
b_1 = 8.4
b_2 = 6.1
R^2 = .83

In all the figures, the two structural properties are varied across their observed range for the 1976 respondents. The Democratic proportion of the presidential vote varies from .28 to .83, and the tract high school educated proportion varies from approximately .1 to approximately .9.

THE LOGIT MODELS

Table 1 shows two estimated logit models: one for the respondents' expected votes in 1972 and another for their reported votes in the same year. The county political environment is entered as a single variable measured by the proportion of the vote that is Democratic in 1972, and it is also included in an interaction term. The interaction variable measures the interdependent effect of the neighborhood social context, measured as a status density variable, and the county political environment. The neighborhood social context is also entered as a single variable measured by median school years completed. Thus, the context is measured as the median education of the census tract in its single variable form, and as the percentage of high school graduates in its interactive form. This practice helps to relieve problems caused by multicollinearity in the models. Both education measures stand as proxies for the relative social status of the tracts as social contexts.

Table 1. Logit Model of 1972 Vote Choice among Likely Voters as a Function of Individual, Contextual, and Environmental Factors (t-Values in Parentheses).

McGovern vote $= 1/(1 + e^{-f})$; $\quad f = a_0 + a_1X_1 + \ldots + a_9X_9$

	Preelection Expected Vote	Postelection Reported Vote
a_0 (constant)	-1.53	-2.35
	(.60)	(.96)
a_1 (age)	$-.010$	$-.012$
	(1.52)	(1.79)
a_2 (party identification: 7 pt. scale, 0–6)	$-.72$	$-.62$
	(10.1)	(10.12)
a_3 (working-class household, dummy coded)	$-.15$	.063
	(.68)	(.30)
a_4 (household income)	$-.081$	$-.05$
	(2.93)	(1.94)
a_5 (respondent education)	$+.074$	.058
	(1.46)	(1.20)
a_6 (Vietnam withdrawal opin- ion)	$-.46$	$-.49$
	(7.64)	(8.39)
a_7 (median education in census tract)	.17	.34
	(.84)	(1.74)
a_8 (Democratic proportion of county presidential vote)	5.76	2.96
	(2.82)	(1.49)
a_9 (product of county Demo- cratic vote and proportion high school educated in tract)	-3.05	-2.69
	(.93)	(.86)
$N =$	888	839

Absent a commonly accepted overall measure of fit for the logistic model, we emphasize two technical features of results in interpretation. First, the t-ratios, and in particular their change from the expected to reported votes, are taken as pointers to the structuring of the vote. Second, the plots in the figures display the arrayed equivalent of a simple coefficient in a linear model. An entire figure with the relevant range of variation thus displays the behavior compared to the partial derivative in the linear model case. After all, it is the behavior through the range, rather than the instantaneous change at a point of the range, that is of interest. It is merely a happy accident of algebra that both types of information are conveyed by only the derivative in a linear model without interaction terms. The graphic displays are given for those relationships most germane to our overall concern with context and environment interaction. The numerical details are set forth in the tables, however, and given a knowledge of mean variable values (set out above), any probability trace of particular interest to a reader may be generated.

The Table 1 t-values present a mixed picture regarding changes that occur in the structural effects upon the vote. The t-value for tract status increases substantially from expected to reported vote, whereas the t-value for county partisanship decreases. The variable measuring the interaction between these two has a t-value that is anemic both before and after the election.

Table 2 presents a nearly identical model, estimated for the 1976 vote, with the exception that the statistical control for Vietnam withdrawal attitudes is eliminated. The Table 2 t-values show that the model does a better job in explaining the reported vote than it does in explaining the expected vote. In particular, the coefficients for the political environment, the social context, and the interaction terms acquire crisp t-ratios in the postelection survey. Thus, the reported vote is socially structured in a way that the expected vote is not.

Table 3 replicates the postelection logit model shown in the second column of Table 2 for respondents with high levels of interest in the campaign, and Table 4 replicates the model for respondents with moderate and low levels of interest. As Table 3 shows, the directions of coefficients for social structure variables do not change before and after the election for respondents who report being very interested. However, the magnitudes of t-values do tend to decline, especially for the county environment variable and for the context-environment interaction variable.

The pattern of change is more dramatic in Table 4 for respondents who report being somewhat or "not much" interested in the campaign. The directions of coefficients for the social structure variables take on a perverse pattern before the election that is exactly opposite that seen elsewhere in this discussion. After the election, these coefficients take on the expected pattern. The t-values are not especially impressive either before or after the election.

There is, of course, a more appropriate way to evaluate the consequence of the campaign if our argument is that the campaign produces substantial differences in structural effects. The postelection coefficients should not be evaluated on the basis of a null hypothesis of zero, but more appropriately we should evaluate changes in the

Table 2. Logit Model of 1976 Vote Choice among Likely Voters as a
Function of Individual, Contextual, and Environmental Factors (t-Values
in Parentheses).

Carter vote $= 1/(1 + e^{-f})$; $f = a_0 + a_1X_1 + \ldots + a_8X_8$

	Preelection Expected Vote	Postelection Reported Vote
a_0 (constant)	-1.41	-5.92
	(.61)	(2.42)
a_1 (age)	$-.0032$	.0077
	(.54)	(1.26)
a_2 (party identification: 7 pt. scale, 0–6)	$-.73$	$-.72$
	(13.03)	(12.70)
a_3 (working-class household, dummy coded)	.17	.04
	(.85)	(.19)
a_4 (household income)	$-.028$	$-.022$
	(1.08)	(.79)
a_5 (respondent education)	.025	0.34
	(.63)	(.81)
a_6 (median education in census tract)	.15	.52
	(.84)	(2.74)
a_7 (Democratic proportion of county presidential vote)	2.38	4.17
	(1.41)	(2.34)
a_8 (product of county Democratic vote and proportion high school educated in tract)	$-.91$	-5.29
	(.38)	(2.11)
$N =$	822	732

coefficients directly. When this is done, the following t-values appear
for the postelection structural changes: t-value for a_6 (neighborhood)
= 2.97, t-value for a_7 (county) = 2.32, t-value for a_8 (interaction) =
2.73. Clearly, these pass most testing criteria.

DIRECTION REVERSALS FOR STRUCTURAL EFFECTS

Figure 2B shows a reversal in direction for both environmental
and contextual effects. The effect of higher-status contexts goes from
anti-Carter to pro-Carter as county environments become more Republican, and the effect of more Democratic environments goes from

Table 3. Postelection Logit Model of Table 2, Estimated for Respondents "Very" Interested in Campaigns (t-Values in Parentheses).

Carter vote $= 1/(1 + e^{-f})$; $f = a_0 + a_1X_1 + \ldots + a_8X_8$

	Preelection Expected Vote	Postelection Reported Vote
a_0 (constant)	−8.50	−6.03
	(2.22)	(1.59)
a_1 (age)	.0028	.0083
	(.28)	(.85)
a_2 (party identification: 7 pt. scale, 0–6)	−.84	−.78
	(9.58)	(9.39)
a_3 (working-class household, dummy coded)	.035	−.24
	(.10)	(.66)
a_4 (household income)	−.050	−.078
	(1.14)	(1.81)
a_5 (respondent education)	−.0093	−.017
	(.15)	(.27)
a_6 (median education in census tract)	.76	.68
	(2.49)	(2.23)
a_7 (Democratic proportion of county presidential vote)	7.83	4.66
	(2.73)	(1.67)
a_8 (product of county Democratic vote and proportion high school educated in tract)	−7.86	−6.10
	(1.83)	(1.41)
$N =$	354	320

pro-Carter to anti-Carter as neighborhood contexts become higher status. Are these reversals the result of a statistical artifact?

The structural effect upon the "logit" can be extracted from the argument of the model and expressed as:

$$S = a_6M + a_7C + a_8CN$$

where

S = the structural effect
M = median school years in tract
C = county Democratic vote proportion
N = proportion high school graduates in neighborhood

Table 4. Postelection Logit Model of Table 2, Estimated for Respondents "Somewhat" or "Not Much" Interested in Campaigns (t-Values in Parentheses).

Carter vote $= 1/(1 + e^{-f})$; $f = a_0 + a_1X_1 + \ldots + a_8X_8$

	Preelection Expected Vote	Postelection Reported Vote
a_0 (constant)	4.98	−5.07
	(1.52)	(1.51)
a_1 (age)	−.010	.0018
	(1.32)	(.22)
a_2 (party identification: 7 pt. scale, 0–6)	−.67	−.70
	(8.73)	(8.64)
a_3 (working-class household, dummy coded)	.21	.23
	(.85)	(.88)
a_4 (household income)	−.021	.017
	(.62)	(.48)
a_5 (respondent education)	.035	.038
	(.64)	(.62)
a_6 (median education in census tract)	−.36	.40
	(1.42)	(1.55)
a_7 (Democratic proportion of county presidential vote)	−1.75	3.62
	(.78)	(1.51)
a_8 (product of county Democratic vote and proportion high school educated in tract)	4.54	−4.03
	(1.47)	(1.26)
$N =$	467	411

Recall that the previously estimated relationship between M and N is expressed as:

$$M = b_0 + b_1N$$

Then the structural effect can be rewritten as:

$$S = a_6b_0 + a_6b_1N + a_7C + a_8CN$$

The rate of change in the structural effect with respect to the neighborhood social context becomes:

$$\partial S/\partial N = a_6b_1 + a_8C$$

And the rate of change in the structural effect with respect to the county political environment becomes:

$$\partial S/\partial C = a_7 + a_8 N$$

The effect of the neighborhood context is extinguished when:

$$a_6 b_1 + a_8 C = 0, \text{ or}$$
$$C = -a_6 b_1/a_8$$

We place special emphasis upon this value of C, denoted as C^*, the environmental point at which contextual influence is extinguished, or the environmental point at which contextual influence changes direction.

Likewise, the effect of the environment is extinguished when:

$$a_7 + a_8 N = 0, \text{ or}$$
$$N = -a_7/a_8$$

Once again, we place special emphasis upon this value of N, denoted as N^*, the contextual point at which environmental influence is extinguished, or at which contextual influence changes direction.

So long as the signs on the structural effects maintain the pattern observed in the second column of Table 2, it will be the case that:

1. Values of N greater than N^* produce a direction reversal in the county environmental effect.

2. Values of C less than C^* produce a direction reversal in the neighborhood contextual effect.

The second column results of Table 2 generate the following values for N^* and C^*:

$$N^* = .79$$
$$C^* = .60$$

As Figure 2B shows, these values lie well within the bounds set by the ranges of the observed data, but it is possible that the values might change across context and environment. The interaction effect may be strongest at intermediate ranges of context and environment, and thus the direction reversals at the extremes may be statistical artifacts.

In order to explore this possibility, the postelection logit model of Table 2 is estimated four more times: above and below the median for the 1976 county Democratic proportion, and above and below the median for the neighborhood social context (see Tables 5 and 6). The important issues are as follows:

1. When the sample is stratified by county environment (C), how

Table 5. Postelection Logit Model of Table 2, Estimated Above and Below Median of County Democratic Proportion in the 1976 Election (t-Values in Parentheses).

Reported Carter vote $= 1/(1 + e^{-f})$; $f = a_0 + a_1X_1 + \ldots + a_8X_8$

	County Democratic Proportion Less than .49	County Democratic Proportion More than .49
a_0 (constant)	−6.79	−6.82
	(1.71)	(1.92)
a_1 (age)	.0078	.0084
	(.87)	(.99)
a_2 (party identification: 7 pt. scale, 0–6)	−.68	−.75
	(8.69)	(9.04)
a_3 (working-class household, dummy coded)	.58	−.47
	(1.90)	(1.60)
a_4 (household income)	−.047	−.014
	(1.10)	(.39)
a_5 (respondent education)	.037	.030
	(.59)	(.51)
a_6 (median education in census tract)	.69	.60
	(2.26)	(2.20)
a_7 (Democratic proportion of county presidential vote)	3.64	4.80
	(1.04)	(1.66)
a_8 (product of county Democratic vote and proportion high school educated in tract)	−9.30	−5.81
	(1.88)	(1.76)
$N =$	371	361
C^*(county point at which contextual effect is zero)	.45	.63

large is the observed range of values less than C^*—the values that produce a direction reversal in the effect of the neighborhood context? Table 5 shows that the direction reversal is maintained across much of the observed ranges, especially in the first column, as we would expect.

2. When the sample is stratified by the neighborhood social context, how large is the observed range of values greater than N^*—the values that produce a direction reversal in the effect of the county environment? As Table 6 shows, the observed range that produces

Table 6. Postelection Logit Model of Table 2, Estimated Above and Below Median of Proportion High School Graduates in Census Tract (t-Values in Parentheses).

Reported Carter vote $= 1/(1 + e^{-f})$; $f = a_0 + a_1X_1 + \ldots + a_8X_8$

	Proportion High School Educated in Census Tract: Less than .618	Proportion High School Educated in Census Tract: More than .618
a_0 (constant)	−11.85 (2.70)	−5.71 (1.37)
a_1 (age)	.016 (1.96)	−.00022 (.02)
a_2 (party identification: 7 pt. scale, 0–6)	−.67 (8.33)	−.77 (9.55)
a_3 (working-class household, dummy coded)	.15 (.55)	−.084 (.24)
a_4 (household income)	−.023 (.62)	−.024 (.54)
a_5 (respondent education)	.087 (1.52)	−.0028 (.04)
a_6 (median education in census tract)	1.03 (2.73)	.51 (1.63)
a_7 (Democratic proportion of county presidential vote)	6.49 (1.98)	7.85 (1.88)
a_8 (product of county Democratic vote and proportion high school educated in tract)	−14.44 (2.14)	−7.53 (1.46)
$N =$	366	366
N^*(contextual point at which county effect is zero)	.45	1.04

the direction reversal is much less significant. Indeed, the direction reversal *only* occurs in the first column of Table 6, where the observed range of N extends to .62 and N^* is .45. Even in this case, however, most of the observed range lies below .45.

In summary, this analysis shows that N^* varies significantly across neighborhood contexts (N), while C^* does not vary significantly across county political environments (C). In other words, this effort sustains the direction reversal in contextual effects, but largely fails to sustain the direction reversal in environmental effects. It would thus appear that the informational effect of the county environment lies uniformly in the direction of its partisan cue even though the effect is extinguished in higher-status contexts and exaggerated in lower-status contexts. In contrast, the effect of the local context is considerably more complex: the direction of contextually based information effects depends upon environmental factors.

NOTE

The survey data utilized in this chapter were collected by the Center for Political Studies at the University of Michigan, and they were made available by the Inter-university Consortium for Political and Social Research. The contextual and environmental data were collected by John Sprague and Louis P. Westefield under National Science Foundation grants SOC-7719938 to Washington University and SOC-7720363 to Southern Illinois University in Edwardsville. With the exception of Sprague, the original collectors and disseminators of the data are freed from any blame for the analyses and interpretations put forward here. Analyses were supported under National Science Foundation grants SES-8319188 to Washington University and SES-8415572 to Indiana University.

3

Speaking of Politics:
Individual Conversational Choice,
Public Opinion, and the Prospects
for Deliberative Democracy

Michael MacKuen

John Wockenfuss stumbles into work one drizzly October morning during an election campaign. He runs into an acquaintance on the elevator and, to pass the moment, initiates a conversation. Well, the weather is a reasonable subject. However, it's election season, and he wants to say something humorous or terribly insightful about current political events. Dare Wockenfuss open his mouth? The last time he made an innocent comment, his elevator partner turned on him, told him how foolish his ideas were, and smugly wandered down the hall. On the other hand, this time may be different. After all, this is a sensible fellow, one who might agree with real wisdom. To talk or not to talk?

When citizens cast their ballots in the secrecy of the polling booth, they are engaged in a democratic act: their choices reverberate through the entire policymaking apparatus. Yet, a political system encompasses much more than the institutions that translate private preferences into public policy. Although much work needs to be done on how institutions may determine outcomes, additional efforts need to be aimed at assessing how political preferences are formulated and articulated as the raw material of politics. Of particular interest here are the factors that shape the ways in which the participants interact with one another. Those interactions set the political and intellectual contexts for democratic decisions.

The quality of political life is affected by political intercourse. Ideas discussed with others carry with them the force of interpersonal encounter, they are subject to clarification and argument, and they take place in the context of each individual's personal scene (Wiebe, 1973). Views picked up from the mass media will be affected by the individual's immediate political environment.[1] Finally, the act of public expression itself transforms subconscious sentiment into conscious cognition and provides the basis for an active rather than a passive political involvement.

Broadly speaking, these political interactions may take one of two forms. On the one hand, they may occur between those who hold similar views. Each participant will gain a richer sense of his or her original understanding, translate vague notions into concrete ideas, and be encouraged to carry on. These discussions serve as reinforcement. When any individual engages only in reinforcing interactions, then he or she will face social consensus. On the other hand, interactions may occur between individuals of differing views. Only in this case will the discussion process allow genuine debate and an exchange of ideas. Each participant will have the opportunity to choose from a broader menu, and the composite social process may serve as a marketplace of ideas. Call this mixing of ideas in conversation a public dialogue.

This distinction between types of conversational settings is important. Should citizens experience only social consensus, then the collective result is akin to the dynamics of mob rule. Citizens may become more and more passionately committed to a single course of action. A public dialogue, on the other hand, more closely resembles the social deliberation on alternatives that underlies the classical argument for democratic rule (Speier, 1950; Lazarsfeld, 1957). With citizens being exposed to different appeals, social awareness should grow, with the result that pure self-interest may be tempered with sensitivity to the welfare of others. For the citizen, the difference between social consensus and public dialogue is that between the homogeneity of a socially imposed propriety and the richness of varied choice. Social consensus restricts political freedom in the sense that it smothers the spark to political imagination with the uniformity of accepted reality. Without the ability to choose from alternative political visions, the individual becomes a product, rather than a producer, of political action. From the individual's perspective, public dialogue forms the foundation of political liberty. For the community, deliberative democracy is at stake.

This chapter is about political interaction and the prospects for deliberative democracy. The central idea is that individuals are not passively subjected to political discussion, but instead actively choose when and where to engage in political discourse, and that such choices have implications for the collective political milieu. By abstracting a few central features of political interaction, the following discussion develops an analysis of how the context of individual choices may produce different collective outcomes for the polity. It suggests the conditions under which political interaction will generate social consensus, on the one hand, or public dialogue, on the other. The results depend on the distribution of individual political views, on the distribution of individual feelings about political discussion, and on the strategies individuals develop for political interactions. The more general result, however, is that the quality of political life produced by *individual* choices made in a *collective* context differs fundamentally from one that might be expected from a simple aggregation of individual preferences. This phenomenon implies an indirect, subtle, and often misleading association between citizens' privately held political views and those that are expressed in public.

The analytics below develop three ways in which individuals may exercise conversational choice. The first section (TALK/CLAM) describes a simple choice between talking politics with one's peers or avoiding the subject altogether. The collective outcomes of such choices lead to dramatically unexpected social dynamics. The second section introduces an intermediate passive strategy (REACT) and shows how the collective results may change in character. The third part (SIGNALING) applies the notion of signaling to individuals seeking ways to create agreeable conversational environments. Finally, the last section lays out some speculations about how the theoretical ideas might be useful for substantive or normative political analysis.

TALK/CLAM

For each citizen, as for John Wockenfuss in the preceding example, the choice is about strategies.[2] Should one engage in public discourse, seeking the reward of self-expression and mutual interaction, or ought one clam up and thus avoid embarrassing conflict? The answer depends not only on how much one enjoys discussion or hates controversy, but also on the likelihood of running into sympathetic and contrary viewpoints.

Consider a simple game involving a player and a partner. Each participant may choose one of two strategies. The first is to TALK. That is, when running into a conversational partner, the player *initiates* political discourse. The second strategy is to CLAM. The player never initiates political discussion, picking instead weather, film, family, or sport. Should the opposite number TALK (politics), the first player changes the subject.[3]

What happens when like-minded people run into each other?

Table 1a. Payoff Matrix for Player Encountering Friend

		Friend's Strategy	
		TALK	CLAM
Player's	TALK	Reinforcement	Bluster
strategy	CLAM	Music	Pass

Table 1b. Payoff Matrix for Player Encountering Opponent

		Opponent's Strategy	
		TALK	CLAM
Player's	TALK	Disagreement	Embarrassment
strategy	CLAM	Grate	Pass

The outcomes might look something like Table 1a. The only real conversation takes place if both individuals choose TALK. Call this Reinforcement, because the player finds a sympathetic soul who rewards self-expression. When the player TALKs but the partner CLAMs, the payoff may be mildly positive—the player gets to hear himself speak (Bluster). However, the partner will switch topics, and the benefit will be short-lived. Similarly, should the player CLAM and the partner TALK, the player might find the commentary mildly satisfactory (Music), but, not being prepared to carry on an extended conversation, he or she lets the moment pass.[4] Both individuals CLAMming results in a nonpolitical conversation—a Pass.

Two potential adversaries produce the outcomes in Table 1b. Should the player TALK and run into a similarly expressive foe, then a Disagreement results. If the partner chooses CLAM, a slight Embarrassment might follow. CLAMming in the face of a TALKing foe produces a slight Grating noise before the topic can be shifted to the weather. Of course, a pair of CLAMs produces a political Pass.

Assume the player's preferences for outcomes rank order something like this:

Reinforcement >> Bluster > Music > Pass >
Grate > Embarrass >> Disagreement

with the relative ordering of Reinforcement, Pass, and Disagreement being the most important elements. The fundamental idea is that people like to talk with friends and do not care for disagreements.[5]

For convenience, norm the payoffs relative to the opportunity cost of talking about something else. That is, score Pass as zero. Further, in order to simplify the formalization, ignore the payoffs for Bluster, Music, Grate, and Embarrass. Because those conversations will be brief, their values should be similar to that of Pass (or zero).[6]

If the player knows the views of each conversational partner, then the strategy choice is easy. If the partner is Friend, then TALK; if an Opponent, then CLAM. A more interesting circumstance arises when the player does not know how the potential conversational partner will react. Instead, all that can be done is to place some a priori probability on the situation. Let P_f and P_o be the player's subjective prior about the probability that the conversational partner will have Friendly and Opposing views. (This simplification of making opinion distributions dichotomous may seem unsatisfactory, but it need not limit the generalizability of the model to continuous distributions.[7]) Likewise, allow each player to choose a mixed strategy—with some assigned probability of playing TALK and of playing CLAM.[8] Call these T_i and C_i for the player and T_f and C_f for a Friend and T_o and C_o for an Opponent. The player's *expected* payoff for choosing TALK is

$$\text{Payoff (TALK)} = P_f[T_f(\text{Reinforcement}) + C_f(\text{Bluster})] + P_o[T_o(\text{Disagreement}) + C_o(\text{Embarrass})],$$

or, more simply,

$$\text{Payoff (TALK)} = P_f[T_f(\text{Reinforcement})] + P_o[T_o(\text{Disagreement})]. \tag{1}$$

The value depends on the probability of encountering a Friend or an Opponent and on the other's strategy choice. Likewise, the expected value for choosing CLAM is

$$\text{Payoff(CLAM)} = P_f[T_f(\text{Music}) + C_f(\text{Pass})] + P_o[T_o(\text{Grate}) + C_o(\text{Pass})],$$

or

$$\text{Payoff(CLAM)} = 0. \tag{2}$$

The player's problem is to choose a probability of TALKing that maximizes his or her expected value—T_i times the first quantity, and $(1 - T_i)$ times the second.

Putting equations (1) and (2) together and taking derivatives with respect to T_i produces the following condition:[9] TALK if

$$\frac{|\text{Reinforcement}|}{|\text{Disagreement}|} > \frac{P_o T_o}{P_f T_f} \tag{3}$$

where the terms on the left are absolute values. Call this ratio of pleasure (from rewarding conversation) to pain (of disagreements) *Expressivity*. It reflects the individual's positive incentives to engage in conversation and his or her tolerance of opposing viewpoints.[10] The entries on the righthand side of the inequality are simply the subjective probabilities of encountering Friends and Opponents who choose to TALK.

If the ratio of Talking Opponents to Talking Friends exceeds the Expressivity criterion level, then the individual avoids political conversation; if not, then the individual will TALK. Low levels of Expressivity require Friendly environments to make conversation worthwhile. High levels of Expressivity make political discussion attractive even in the face of opposing majorities. To be sure, it is difficult to say how the values of Expressivity translate into real experience. Disagreements will be brief, yet even a hint of conflict will be unpleasant for many citizens. It is also hard to think of how much joy comes from political talk. A helpful benchmark is the Expressivity value of unity. If "pleasure" is greater than "pain," the case for Expressivity greater than one, then the individual will TALK when his or her subjective probability of encountering Friends is not less than that of running into Opponents. That is to say that such an individual will TALK when he or she is not in a minority, or alternatively, when in complete ignorance of the partner's views (when the subjective probabilities are equal). An Expressivity of two will encourage conversations so long as the ratio of Opponents to Friends does not exceed 2:1, and so on. The point is that an individual will engage in political interaction when he or she expects that conversations will be *sufficiently* Friendly to be rewarding. More Expressive types are perfectly willing to encounter substantial contrary sentiment. They need not limit their interactions to purely Friendly environments; in fact, they may seek out interactions in adverse contexts provided that the prospects are *sufficiently* Friendly.

Expressivity will vary in the population. Some individuals may relish harmonious discussion, whereas others may loathe disagreements. Politics being a marginal topic for most citizens, we should certainly expect considerable variation in individual Expressivity. Because other potential conversational partners will like conversation more or less than any individual actor, the collective result will depend on how Expressivity is spread in the society.

A stylized example illustrates the social dynamics. Consider the situation, adapted from Schelling (1971, 1978), represented in Figure 1.1. The picture presents the number of individuals (on the vertical axis) arranged by their Expressivity (on the horizontal axis). Look first at the slashed line showing the uniform[11] distribution of one hundred Friends whose Expressivity ranges from 2.0 to 0.0. At the extreme left, a few individuals choose to TALK when the opposition ratio is 2:1 (their pleasure is twice their pain); at the other end, some individuals will never TALK (they see no pleasure in politics). The rest range in between. The cumulative density (the solid line) shows the number of individuals whose criteria are sufficiently Expressive to allow them to enter conversations given the ratio of Opponents to Friends shown on the horizontal axis. One-half (fifty of the hundred) enter conversations if they are not in the minority, three-quarters will enter so long as they are in a substantial majority (an Opposition:Friend ratio of no more than 1:2).

Two factors allow a calculation of the number of Opponents any number of Friends will tolerate and remain in dialogue. First, note that the individuals may be ordered by their Expressivity. If the seventy-fifth (most Expressive) individual will TALK, then the preceding seventy-four will TALK as well. Second, with T_o and T_f, the number of TALKing Opponents and Friends, note that the individual chooses TALK when

$$T_o/T_f < \text{(Expressivity)}$$

from equation (3), or when

$$T_o < T_f(\text{Expressivity}) \tag{4}$$

In this example, the seventy-fifth most Expressive individual has an Expressivity of one-half: if he or she finds it worthwhile to TALK, so will at least seventy-four other Friends (giving a total $T_f = 75$). Thus seventy-five Friends will tolerate up to 37.5 [$= 75(1/2)$] TALKing Opponents. The fiftieth individual's Expressivity is one, so fifty Friends will TALK in the presence of 50 [$= 50(1)$] TALKing Opponents. And so on.

The relationship between Expressivity and the configuration of Friends and Opponents generates an elementary dynamic. The general curve for equation (4) is drawn in Figure 1.2: it is the convex curve relating the number of Friends (on the horizontal axis) to the number of Opponents that they will tolerate (on the vertical axis). It is worth a moment to study the dynamics here. To see what happens, posit an initial condition composed of (1) a number of Friends (on the horizontal axis) and (2) a number of TALKing Opponents (on the vertical axis). When the starting combination of Friends and Oppo-

Figure 1. Cumulative Density Function and Dynamic Equilibria for Uniform
Distributions of Expressivity (Mean of 1.0)

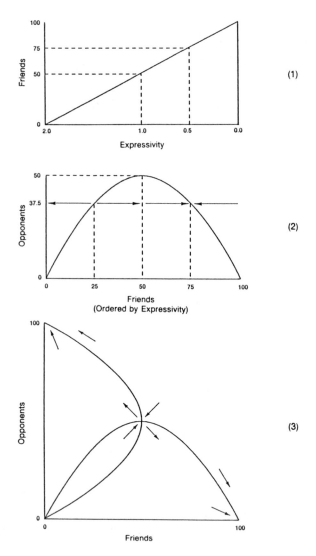

Note: The broken line in Figure 1.1 illustrates a uniform density function of Expressivity ranging from 4.0 to 0.0 (with a mean of 2.0). The solid line represents the
cumulative density function. Figure 1.2 illustrates the dynamics of 100 Friends encountering 37.5 TALKing Opponents. Figure 1.3 depicts the full dynamics and equilibria of 100 Friends and 100 Opponents taken from the uniform Expressivity
distribution (mean of 1.0) in Figure 1.1

nents lies *beneath* the convex criterion curve, then conditions will be so Friendly that additional Friends will wish to speak. The number of TALKing Friends will grow (the point will move horizontally to the right) until the criterion curve is met. For example, start with 25 Friends and 37.5 Opponents in the field. The twenty-sixth (most Expressive) Friend will also choose to TALK, as will the twenty-seventh, the twenty-eighth, and so on up to the seventy-fifth. Only when the seventy-sixth comes to decide does CLAM prove the better strategy. Likewise, when the starting point lies *above* the criterion curve, the dynamics move the point horizontally to the left. The number of fellow Friends cannot support TALK for the least tolerant individual, so he or she will choose CLAM, and this process will unravel until the criterion curve is met or no one remains. In the example of Figure 1.2, if a hundred Friends run into 37.5 Opponents, the number TALKing will unravel to seventy-five; if twenty-four Friends meet 37.5 Opponents, the social situation will spiral into the safety of Noelle-Neumann's (1974) silence.

Of course, the Opponents simultaneously make the same calculations. Say that in our population there also exist a hundred Opponents who must choose TALK or CLAM. Their criterion curve may be turned on its side and superimposed on that for the Friends to produce Figure 1.3. The dynamics of the composite numbers of each group TALKing are shown by the arrows. In the area to the upper right of both curves, both groups unravel downward. (The relative speed of the movement will determine the relative slope of the arrows.) In the region "below" the two curves, both groups' TALKing will increase until one or the other criterion curve is reached. In the region under one curve but above the other, the dynamics show that the first group grows while the second diminishes (here to zero).

In this example, three equilibria exist.[12] There are three combinations of Friends and Opponents for which there is no incentive for some CLAMS to TALK or some TALKers to CLAM. The two straightforward ones lie in the *pure* combinations where one group has all members TALKing, while the other remains entirely silent. The third equilibrium lies at the intersection of the two curves. Here both groups are happy, and the next most tolerant CLAM of each group has no incentive to TALK. However, this is an *unstable* equilibrium; should someone make a "mistake," then the point will jump off in one direction or the other and eventually result in one of the two pure equilibria. Given these criterion curves, the clear expectation is that one group or the other will completely dominate conversations, and the other will remain (politically) mute.

This is important because half of each group is perfectly willing to TALK even if in a minority. In fact, any combination of Friends and Opponents that lies under both curves can merrily converse. However, further entrants from one group or the other will show up and eventually drive out the other group's previously content TALKers. Because the decision of each individual depends on decisions made by all the others and the others' criteria vary, the results unravel to extreme solutions. Thus, while half of the members find political interaction worthwhile even if they expect to encounter more contrary than sympathetic views, the social dynamic generates the uniformity of social consensus rather than the deliberation of public dialogue.

Two factors might generate a stable equilibrium of dialogue, that is, one that supports conversations between the two sides. The simplest is an increase in the overall Expressivity level. Figure 2.1 illustrates the criterion curves for two groups whose pleasure/pain ratios now are uniformly distributed from 4:1 to zero (a mean Expressivity of 2.0; three-quarters of the individuals are willing to be in a minority). Now three stable equilibria appear. The most interesting has a mixture of 75 percent of each group talking with members of the other. The stability derives from the observation that any relatively small "mistake" will be self-correcting. In this example, this public dialogue equilibrium (distinguished from the social consensus solutions) is an attractor over a large part of the space of possible starting conditions. This is important, because the initial conditions represent individuals' prior expectations about the nature of the environment, expectations that get "corrected" through experience but that are also subject to mistaken perceptions.[13]

Note, however, that this public dialogue equilibrium is subject to discontinuities as the relative size of the two groups varies. Assume that there exist only eighty-two Opponents (instead of a hundred), making the Opponents a minority of 45 percent and Friends a majority of 55 percent. The resulting criterion curves in Figure 2.2 show that the public dialogue equilibrium completely disappears. The dominant attractor is an equilibrium composed entirely of Friends.

The fragility of public dialogue in the face of even modestly imbalanced populations is made evident in Table 2. The first column represents varying mean Expressivity levels, and the second column presents the maximum majority that can still support a public dialogue for that level of Expressivity. The example illustrated in Figure 2 is found in the third row. A mean Expressivity of 2.0 can sustain public dialogue when one side commands 53.5 percent of the population and no more. Should the majority grow only slightly (say to 55 per-

Figure 2. Dynamics and Equilibria for a Uniform Distribution of Expressivity (Mean of 2.0) for Evenly Balanced and Slightly Unbalanced Mixtures of Friends and Opponents

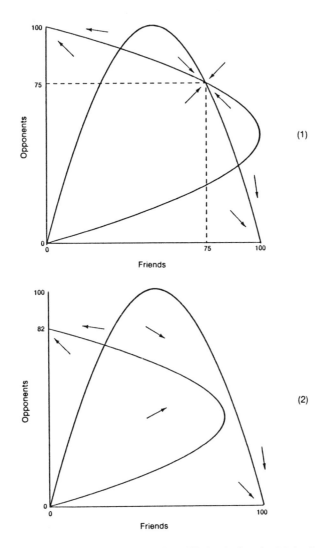

Note: Figure 2.1 illustrates the dynamics and equilibria of a hundred Friends and a hundred Opponents drawn from a uniform Expressivity distribution (with mean of 2.0). Figure 2.2 demonstrates the fragility of the "public dialogue" equilibrium. It disappears when the balance of Friends and Opponents becomes slightly uneven (here a hundred Friends and eighty-two Opponents).

Table 2. Maximum Majorities and Conversation Levels for Mean Levels of Expressivity

Mean Level of Expressivity	Maximum Majority	Number of Majority	Conversants Minority	Proportion of Conversants from Majority
1.55	50.2	36.0	31.4	.53
1.75	51.5	41.5	28.0	.60
2.0	53.5	46.0	25.7	.64
2.5	57.7	52.6	22.9	.70
3.0	61.4	57.8	20.4	.74
3.5	64.6	61.9	18.4	.77
4.0	67.4	65.1	17.2	.79
4.5	69.8	68.0	15.6	.81
5.0	71.9	70.3	14.8	.83
5.5	73.7	72.4	13.7	.84
6.0	75.3	74.2	12.6	.86
6.5	76.7	75.7	12.4	.86
7.0	78.0	77.1	11.6	.87
7.5	79.1	78.3	11.0	.88

Note: These results apply to uniform distributions of Expressivity (the criterion level at which the derivative for TALKing politics changes from negative to positive). The mean levels represent uniform distributions ranging from twice the mean to zero.

The numbers are numerical approximations for a population of one hundred. Thus, a mean Expressivity of 2.0 (the distribution for which ranges from 4.0 to 0.0) can sustain a maximum majority of (about) 53.5 majority members. The mixed conversation equilibrium at that maximum includes 46.0 and 25.7 members of the majority and minority, respectively. Sixty-four percent of those 71.7 individuals choosing to TALK are from the majority faction.

cent), then open debate gives way to conversational uniformity. The nature of the problem is illustrated in column five. The conversational mixture is always more one-sided than the mix in the population as a whole. Even the more Expressive of the minority begin to CLAM as more and more of the majority are lured into conversations by increasingly majoritarian mixtures.

Two points are of interest. First, note that imbalances of 60/40 or 75/25 require mean Expressivity levels of about 3.0 and 6.0 in order to produce stable cross-factional interaction. This means that such imbalances need populations of whom 84 percent and 93 percent are willing to TALK when in a minority. Thus, for all but the most modest of imbalances, a remarkable degree of overall Expressivity is required to sustain public dialogue. Second, the underlying logic suggests real limits on the power of social influence. The disappearance of dialogue equilibria implies that the members of one group (usually the minority) CLAM or disengage themselves from public politics. They remain beyond the reach of the majority's influence, and they are unable to enjoy the social reinforcement of conversations with co-believers. Interpersonal politics is limited to members of the majority.[14]

This is not to say, however, that a homogeneous equilibrium will always be comprised of majority members. Look at Figure 2.2 again. If, for some historical reason, conversations had been dominated by Opponents, then no growth in the number of Friends (however large) could get Friends into the conversational field. For Friends, this is a classic collective action problem. All friends would be better off if they all TALKed because they command a sufficient majority to dominate conversation completely. Yet each individual Friend, acting alone, cannot get started TALKing because he or she faces a uniformly Disagreeable field. In this way, a majority may be "silenced" by the elements of conversational choice.

The second factor that might give rise to a dialogue equilibrium involves the shape of the underlying Expressivity distributions. The problem in much of the space is that at any given point the conversants may be content with the mixture, but as even more members join in the fray, they eventually drive out the previously content of one of the groups. Stable dialogue equilibria result when no more members of the groups wish to enter. Consider the Expressivity distribution in Figure 3.1. Here the maximum Expressivity is the same as in Figure 1.1, but the lower ranges are even less inclined to get into conversation (yielding a slightly less expressive composite). The gap in the middle serves as a "firebreak" to prevent the spread of interaction. The resulting criterion curves (in Figure 3.2) generate a stable public dialogue because in the region of the equilibrium the decrease in tolerance is sufficiently great to dissuade further entry by members of one group or the other. Thus, the stability derives not from greater overall Expressivity (more pleasure or less pain), but from lower Expressivity in the relevant range.

These equilibrium-inducing factors may be more than mere curiosities. Consider how the Expressivity ratio for individuals might vary over time. Assume that the reward for interaction depends on the number of (favorable) political facts the individual carries into the encounter: the information fuels Reinforcing conversations to new levels and insulates the individual against the awkwardness of Disagreement. In one case, political news for each side may be considerable and favorable. Friends, talking with one another, will have more

Figure 3. Cumulative Density Function and Dynamic Equilibria for a "Fire-break" Distribution of Expressivity (Mean < 1.0)

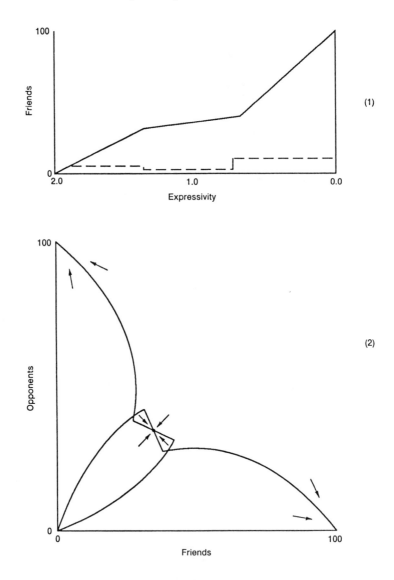

Note: Figure 3.1 presents an example of a "firebreak" cumulative density comparable to the uniform distribution in Figure 1. Figure 3.2 shows the resulting dynamics and equilibria. The stable "public dialogue" equilibrium is an attractor over only a small region of the space.

to share, and the conversation will be more rewarding. Conversations among persons of different persuasions will be less threatening and hence more tolerable. Thus, Expressivity may increase for an entire community. Such a situation might be produced by an evenly matched and intensely fought election or referendum campaign. This is, of course, what produced the stable public dialogue in Figure 2.1, and one might expect that stimulating and evenly balanced public campaigns will generate generous levels of cross-group discussion. Of course, if the political news is one-sided, the result may be different. Disproportionately good news for the minority's viewpoint will produce a stable mixed equilibrium (of considerable proportions) where only the majority had talked before. Even more dramatic, stimuli that encourage a "silenced" majority to TALK may produce discontinuous swings in the tenor of social discussion—changing it instantly from one completely dominated by the minority to one completely dominated by the previously silent majority.[15] Of course, when external forces advantage a dominating majority, they will continue to frighten away any potential minority conversationalists.

A similar result might be produced by differential acquisition of the political facts. Imagine a situation in which the favorable political arguments are made available only to those most inclined to TALK in the first place. (Say that the public campaigns are presented at an abstract level accessible to only a small, activist portion of the public.) The remaining members of each group will have less to talk about and will find themselves with lower Expressivity. Such a change would transform the distribution in Figure 1.1 and its resulting social consensus into the distribution of Figure 3.1 and the modest political interaction of Figure 3.2. Of course, if the acquisition of political information is positively associated with normal Expressivity, then such situations may arise naturally. On the other hand, if such a natural dialogue of the politically involved exists, it might be eliminated by a public information campaign that excites the heretofore uninvolved. Counterintuitively, a stimulus to conversation might destroy ongoing debate. One side or the other would dominate the field (as in Figure 1).

REACTORS

The distinction between TALK and CLAM can stand for all sorts of political involvement, and for this reason it is useful to consider that simple dichotomy. However, when examining the specifics of political conversations, it is clear that individuals may choose strategies

Table 3a. Payoff Matrix for Player Encountering Friend

		Friend's Strategy		
		TALK	REACT	CLAM
Player's strategy	TALK	Reinforcement	Reinforcement	Bluster
	REACT	Reinforcement	Pass	Pass
	CLAM	Music	Pass	Pass

Table 3b. Payoff Matrix for Player Encountering Opponent

		Opponent's Strategy		
		TALK	REACT	CLAM
Player's strategy	TALK	Disagreement	Embarrass	Embarrass
	REACT	Grate	Pass	Pass
	CLAM	Grate	Pass	Pass

other than a mixture of TALK and CLAM. One possibility is to REACT to others, cheerfully responding to Friendly TALKers and remaining silent before Opposing viewpoints. The REACTor never initiates a (political) conversation, but instead waits for the partner to unmask. The resulting payoffs for an individual encountering Friends and Opponents are displayed in Table 3. Note that this strategy is parasitic in the sense that the individual pays no price of Disagreement and yet enjoys the rewards of Friendly conversations initiated by Friendly TALKers (who must bear the burden of encountering Opposing views).

The introduction of this strategy changes the conversational equilibria. REACT clearly dominates CLAM because the payoffs are the same on encountering an Opponent, and there are benefits to be had should any Friends choose TALK. Even the most reticent individuals will do at least as well in choosing REACT as they do in choosing CLAM. Thus, the real choice for individuals is between TALK and REACT. The question is, Will anyone choose TALK?

Certainly if all other Friends TALK, then any individual will be better off switching to REACT simply because this strategy avoids Disagreements. However, if all Friends REACT, then the REACTor will be handsomely rewarded for TALKing. *Any* encounter with a Friend will produce harmonious conversation, there being no CLAMs to shun initiatives. The prospective TALKer will, of course, have to pay the price of running into Opponents, so the choice will depend on his or her

Expressivity. Now, as the number of TALKing Friends increases, the attractiveness of REACT will also increase because the individual may take advantage of others bearing the burden of initiative. Thus, the choice between TALK and REACT will depend on the individual's Expressivity, on the probability of running into a TALKing Opponent, and on the number of Friends who choose to TALK.

The payoff for any level of T_i (where $1 - T_i$ is now REACT) is:

$$\text{Payoff}(T_i) = P_f\{T_i[\text{Reinforcement}] + (1 - T_i)T_f[\text{Reinforcement}]\} + P_o\{T_iT_o[\text{Disagreement}]\}.$$

Taking derivatives indicates the individual will TALK if:

$$\frac{|\text{Reinforcement}|}{|\text{Disagreement}|} \cdot \frac{(1 - T_f)}{T_f} > \frac{P_oT_o}{P_fT_f}$$

or,

$$\text{Expressivity} \cdot \frac{(1 - T_f)}{T_f} > \frac{P_oT_o}{P_fT_f}.$$

Note how this alternative changes the effect of Expressivity. If T_f is 0.5, then all remains as before. However, if T_f is less than 0.5 (less than one-half of the individual's co-believers choose to TALK), then those individuals who had previously barely opted for CLAM will now join the conversational mix. On the other hand, when T_f is greater than 0.5, the marginal individual who had before just chosen TALK will now opt for REACT (avoiding Disagreement and freeloading on those Friends already choosing TALK).

The introduction of the REACT option has an interesting effect on the probability of obtaining public dialogue equilibria. In the earlier model, the disappearance of such equilibria stemmed from majority members gleefully joining a previously content mixture and forcing out even the most Expressive minority conversants. Now, as the proportion of TALKing majority members begins to increase, the relative payoff (compared to freeloading REACT) diminishes so that the less Expressive majority members may be less inclined to TALK and thus silence the contented members of the minority.

This impact is dramatic. Consider the criterion curves and the resulting equilibrium in Figure 4. Here the Expressivity ratios come from a uniform distribution with a mean of 1.0 and a maximum of 2.0 (comparable to that of Figure 1). There exists only one equilibrium. However, it is a stable public dialogue equilibrium, and it serves as an attractor over the entire space. Any initial mix of conversing

Figure 4. Dynamics and Equilibria for a Uniform Distribution of Expressivity
(Mean 1.0) Strategy Choice TALK/REACT

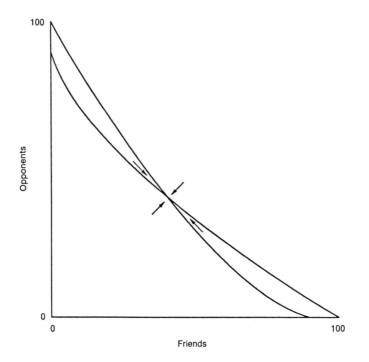

Note: The dynamics produce a single equilibrium. However, it is stable, it is an attractor over the entire space, and it is a "public dialogue" equilibrium.

Friends and Opponents will produce this result, so the solution is
robust against errors. More importantly, any combination of Friends
and Opponents will generate a stable public dialogue as long as the
number in the majority does not exceed the product of the number
in the minority times the maximum Expressivity level in the minority.[16] (Of course, as this limit is approached, the conversational imbalance can become pronounced.)

The passive nature of REACT permits cross-factional discussion
by supporting minority TALKers with their more timid allies while
reducing the need for less Expressive majoritarians to initiate discussion. Thus, TALK/REACT/CLAM generates public dialogue for a broader
range of conditions than the TALK/CLAM strategy set. Figure 5 compares the two "existence" regions over the space defined by imbalance
of opinion and by the population distribution of Expressivity. It is

Figure 5. Existence Region for Public Dialogue (TALK/CLAM and TALK/REACT/CLAM)

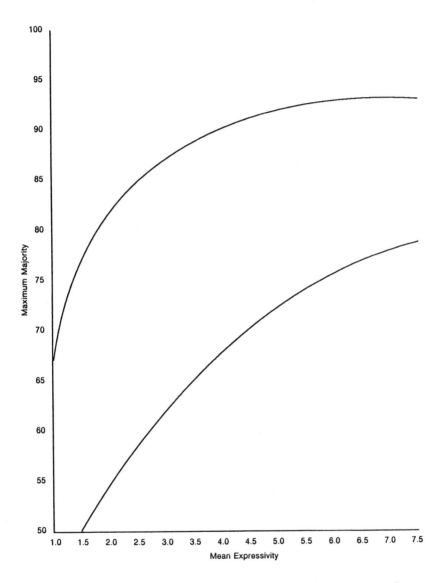

Note: The smaller region contains the space in which TALK/CLAM may produce a public dialogue. The larger and inclusive region sets the boundaries for TALK/REACT/CLAM.

clear that the TALK/REACT/CLAM region is considerably larger and that its advantage is most dramatic for lower levels of Expressivity. This is important because these are the ranges that seem intuitively most plausible in typical mass publics.

While the introduction of REACT certainly increases the likelihood of public dialogue, it does so at a cost. The crucial feature of REACT is the way it limits the attractiveness of the TALK option. At low levels of composite Expressivity, it encourages conversation among the more Expressive because they are sure to reap the rewards of all Friendly encounters. However, a rise in the conversational level leads to an increase in the attractiveness of freeloading and encourages many modestly Expressive citizens to take a passive stance. Thus, the scope of public dialogue is constrained. Further, because it is so easy for the less-inclined to engage in conversation with like-minded types, the proportion of conversations that take on an exclusively Reinforcement character is increased.

The impact of these phenomena may be illustrated by calculating the proportion of cross-factional and reinforcing conversations that one might expect in a particular situation. (Alternatively, one may think of the probability that any interaction, chosen at random from a population of a given imbalance-Expressivity character, will be a political conversation between people who do not already agree or between people who have similar opinions.) The results of such calculations for several typical combinations of opinion imbalance and Expressivity are depicted in Figure 6, which graphs the expected probabilities of both public dialogue (on the vertical axis) and of reinforcing conversations (on the horizontal axis). The slashed line at 45 degrees represents the path where reinforcement equals public dialogue. Graphed in the space are the expected probabilities for the TALK/CLAM model (connected by a solid line) and the TALK/REACT/CLAM model (connected by a dotted line) for rising levels of Expressivity (the three points represent mean levels of one, two, and four). For each model there are three paths representing the results for three levels of imbalance with majorities of .50 (evenly balanced), .60, and .75. First note that when a public dialogue equilibrium does not exist, all outcomes lie along the bottom of the horizontal axis (for TALK/ CLAM this includes the first two outcomes with a majority of .60 and all three outcomes with a majority of .75). Also note that, as one should expect, the paths move upward (more dialogue) and to the right (more reinforcement) as Expressivity rises.

Two substantive points are of direct interest here. First, whenever it can sustain a public dialogue equilibrium, TALK/CLAM generates

Figure 6. Probability of Dialogue and Reinforcement (TALK/CLAM and TALK/REACT/CLAM)

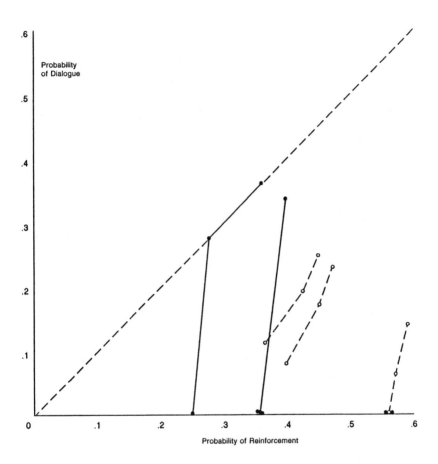

Note: Conversations are typified by the probabilities of Dialogue and Reinforcement (at equilibrium). Plotted here are the results for the two models TALK/CLAM (connected by the solid lines) and TALK/REACT/CLAM (connected by the dotted lines) under typical conditions of opinion imbalance and mean population Expressivity. The connected paths for each model represent increases in political conversation levels as Expressivity increases. The three paths for each model represent opinion majorities of .50 (evenly balanced), .60, and .75 from left to right (the entire path for TALK/CLAM with a majority of .75 is completely exhausted at the single point at the lower right).

considerably more cross-factional discussion than does TALK/REACT/ CLAM. Thus the effects of the self-containment implicit in the passive stance are manifest. Second, note that the overall levels of public dialogue (on the vertical axis) remain modest—especially so at the lower levels of Expressivity. Particularly noticeable here is the realization that the REACT model (for all nine conditions of imbalance and Expressivity) produces considerably more reinforcement than dialogue (the points lie well below the 45-degree line).

Thus, the fact that TALK/REACT/CLAM is more likely to produce public dialogue does not indicate that the ensuing amount of cross-factional discussion will be substantial. By any standard the absolute levels of dialogue are fairly modest. The mere existence of such conversations may be important because they do provide citizens the opportunity to hear opposing viewpoints. However, even these modest levels of dialogue are marked by increases in the levels of reinforcing conversations with the result that the pattern may be typified as virtual (if not absolute) consensus. While TALK/REACT/CLAM can more readily generate political interaction, the overall picture is one of very limited public debate.

SIGNALING

The preceding results depend on individuals possessing imperfect information when they choose strategies. Should one know with certainty that the partner be Friend or Opponent, then a conditional strategy is obvious: TALK to Friends, CLAM in front of Opponents. In the absence of certainty, the elements of choice generate interaction when individuals can expect a *sufficiently* sympathetic response to their views. Thus, it makes sense for the individual to use all available information about the prospects of any particular conversation before making a strategy choice. The only information assumed so far is that the individual knows the distribution of opinion in the general environment (this is assumed to be learned).[17] However, one may send signals to others in order to increase the probability of encountering Friends and avoiding Opponents (for comparison, see Spence, 1974). Two types of signals may be sent: intentional and inadvertent.

Individuals may choose to signal potential partners in advance about their own political views. If the signal is sufficiently clear, then potential Opponents will shy away from conversation with the signaler, and whatever conversations that the signaler has will be Friendly in tone. For example, a Republican worker in an automobile plant would normally find himself or herself in a distinct minority, one that inhibits political conversations on his or her part. However, the worker may choose to wear a Republican campaign button.[18] Only other Republicans will choose that individual as a conversation partner because Democrats would know in advance that any conversation would produce an argument. Thus, the Republican autoworker can create a Friendly environment by engaging the strategic choices of others.

Similarly, individuals may establish reputations. The Republican autoworker may let others know that he or she will always support the Republican line. Of course, this tactic sends a more subtle signal than the campaign button simply because reputations depend on the information levels of others. In fact, the sensitivity to signals may vary. Minority members might be cautious, investing much time and effort in ascertaining the prospects for a Friendly conversation. Majority members may safely ignore signals. A Democratic autoworker is so unlikely to run into a TALKing Republican that he or she may find it unnecessary to decode signals or learn reputations. Thus, one would expect minority members to be more selective about the conversations that they initiate, and that their mix of partners should be more Friendly than one might expect on average (for evidence, see Finifter, 1974). Majority members will be more likely to run into Opponents. Nevertheless, when individuals signal potential partners, Friendly conversational activity can flower in normally inexpressive groups. However, the effectiveness of signaling reduces the prospects for cross-factional interaction. The attractiveness of signaling for individual choice produces a community of isolated groups and eliminates meaningful public dialogue.

Of course, not all individuals will choose to signal their views explicitly. Signaling's benefits depend on the individual's Expressivity (the pleasure of rewarding conversation and the pain of disagreement), on the distribution of political views in the social environment, and on the ability or desire of others to interpret signals of varying ambiguity. However, signals also impose direct costs on the signaler. Imagine wearing an NAACP button to a Ku Klux Klan rally or a three-piece suit to a union strike meeting. When the signal is clear, when the individual is most sensitive to social approbation, and when the distribution of views is most one-sided, the incentives to signal are at their greatest, but so are the direct costs.

Further, signaling has interesting consequences when one considers complex issue domains. An individual may have views that do not perfectly coincide with easily projected signals. A traditional conservative might, for example, support hand-gun control or increased Social Security payments. If the individual chooses a signaling strategy (say, by cultivating a reputation of conservatism), then he or she will encounter only conservative views on all issue domains. On any specific incongruent issue, the general reputation will prevent Friendly discussions and instead will produce Disagreements. Certainly, this indirect cost of signaling will be less important to the extent that each individual's views are consistent with commonly used signals. Those who take positions marked by ideology or consistent with broad-band symbols will escape these indirect costs. Those holding more complicated views may shun public labels.

In fact, signaling may encourage "consistent" thinking. Because signaling orchestrates harmonious discussion groups, discordant ideas will find no support in the social setting. Should our conservative have a liberal thought, it will die of loneliness. Signaling not only prevents a consideration of alternative views, but it also generates a consistency of opinions around the symbols embodied in the signal itself. Popular ideologies or mass belief systems may be built out of the strategies for political interaction. Thus, the substance and availability of signals may do much to define the patterns of social interaction and the organization of political beliefs themselves.

In addition, individuals may inadvertently send off signals about their views. Say a society is comprised of Blue- and White-collar workers and that the overwhelming majority of Blues and Whites are liberal and conservative, respectively. Any individual can make a judgment about the prospects of a potential partner merely by observing the color of his or her collar. Liberal Blues and conservative Whites can cheerfully choose a conditional TALK/CLAM strategy depending on the partner's plumage. The preponderance of the society can then enjoy political discourse (although, of course, no cross-factional dialogue takes place), even with very low overall Expressivity.

A conservative Blue-Collar type, however, is in an unhappy situation. She would like to select a strategy of TALK(White)/CLAM(Blue). However, the conservative Whites she seeks out will simply CLAM up once they see her as Blue-Collar. The only people who will TALK to her are other Blue-Collar types, and, of course, their views are disagreeable. Given any mild discomfort at being shunned, the optimal strategy is an unconditional CLAM. The same choice is forced on liberal White-Collar types. The situation is self-reinforcing in the sense that those choosing TALK express views consistent with the stereotype; individuals testing the preconception will discover that Blue-Collars talk the liberal line and that White-Collars talk the conservative line. In fact, the preponderance of views in a subgroup need not be large (note Table 2) to generate a self-reinforcing stereotype. Substantial minorities within each group may be silenced.

The importance of signaling is that although it encourages political interaction, it eliminates public dialogue. The impact of political discourse will be to reinforce already existing divisions, not to encourage consideration of alternatives. To the extent that such signals carry information, we should expect an increase in political activity but also more strongly divided polities. Political involvement may grow at the expense of deliberative democracy.

STRATEGY SETS AND PUBLIC DIALOGUE

Each of these options, TALK, CLAM, REACT, and SIGNAL, captures a bit of reality, but each represents an abstraction from a more complicated picture. Because the theoretical chances for public dialogue depend on the strategies abstracted for individuals, it is important to choose which strategy set or model applies to a problem. That choice is not easy.

For practical reasons, the model development has assumed a randomly interacting population of strangers. Of course, most real-life political discussions take place among friends, neighbors, relatives, and work-mates who know each other and develop relationships over time. The abstract models need to be, and can be, translated into such settings. Think of each partner as someone marked with a given probability of being Friend or Opponent on any given topic and whose Expressivity at the moment comes from a distribution with a known expected value. Then, at any moment, the choice about engaging an acquaintance in conversation looks like the choice about engaging a stranger who comes from a known population. Dynamics similar to those governing the collectivity will govern pairwise conversations, and they will produce the same characteristic results.

It is in the context of daily life that the distinct strategy sets may be considered. To begin, the fuller menu of TALK/REACT/CLAM appears most attractive. The passive REACT strategy allows the timid to enjoy Friendly conversation without risking Disagreement. Personal experience suggests that such passive behavior exists. Decisions about conversations may be made on the spur of the moment in a way that reflects the give and take of typical conversation. Further, TALK/CLAM seems too sterile because it forces individuals to CLAM in front of Friendly initiatives. This does not make intuitive sense.

On the other hand, such a harsh dichotomous choice may apply when individuals develop long-standing expectations of their own and others' behaviors. A simple rule of thumb about politics being either a suitable or an unsuitable topic for conversation may typify individual approaches to political conversation better than the active monitoring needed in TALK/REACT/CLAM. Finally, SIGNAL captures the sense that individuals do acquire reputations among their friends with the result that genuine arguments among acquaintances are rare. However, often such signals will be imprecise when it comes to the shifting topics in everyday political discussion. When imprecise, signals represent nothing more than the a priori expectations about friendliness incorporated in the TALK/CLAM and TALK/REACT/CLAM models.

While the three models outlined here are categorically distinct, they may be placed along a (loosely defined) continuum. In TALK/CLAM, the individual has only indirect information about the views of any particular partner; in TALK/REACT/CLAM, the partner must reveal his or her preferences before many individuals will engage in conversation; and when SIGNALing is widely used, all individuals will know with certainty their potential partner's political stance. For the TALK/CLAM model, the results suggest that conversation levels will be low and that public dialogue will be unlikely, but that when it does arise, it will be robust. When individuals may REACT to others' initiatives, then we should expect that more political conversations will take place and that public dialogue will be possible in more circumstances. However, the ensuing levels of public dialogue will be constrained, and the bulk of political conversations will be reinforcing. Finally, when SIGNALing dominates, no cross-factional dialogue will occur, and reinforcing conversations will universally dominate. Political interaction may flower where it otherwise might die off, but the collective result generates islands of uniformity, each isolated from the rest. Thus, while the precise expectations may vary across the models, the overall picture is a bleak one with regard to the possibilities for any substantial dimensions of public dialogue.

SOME IMPLICATIONS FOR POLITICAL ANALYSIS

The social product of individual decisions depends on how much individuals value political interaction (Expressivity), on the distribution of those preferences, and on the social balance of alternate viewpoints (the ratio of Friends and Opponents). *Public dialogue,* where individuals engage in political discussions with others who hold different viewpoints, is more likely to arise when overall Expressivity is high and when political views are evenly distributed. When the political balance is (sometimes only slightly) skewed, the social dynamics will easily produce communities of *social consensus*. When political symbols, slogans, and ideologies fall to hand, then citizens are likely to turn to signaling as a way to ensure agreeable interactions. The overall implication is that public, if not private, conformity is likely to occur even when many individuals are perfectly willing to encounter contrary views.

This discussion is meant to present a tool for thinking about politics. To be sure, the theory's merit will depend on its accord with the empirical world (Appendix A). Nevertheless, it may be helpful to suspend disbelief and speculate a bit. Consider three propositions: (1) the prospects for public dialogue vary predictably across communities and over time; (2) the expected dominance of social consensus facilitates the operation of democratic institutions while, at the same time, undermining their character; and (3) the probability that social structure may shape the context of political discussions requires a social, rather than an individual, foundation for democratic theory.

First, the overall level of Expressivity, and thus the chances for public dialogue, will depend both on political culture and on historical circumstance. Two stories illustrate the point.

> Immediately after the Iranians took Americans hostage in 1979, President Jimmy Carter invoked national honor. In the first week, Senator Edward Kennedy tentatively questioned the President's wisdom in the matter only to discover himself shouted down as traitorous. As patriotism burst forth, public dialogue vanished.

> Mansbridge (1980) closely examined two cases of community democracy, one in a Vermont town and the second in a Boston social services center. In both cases, she found that the participants' willingness to engage in political debate varied with how the issues were defined. When matters involved the integrity of individual members of the community, when distinctly personal interests were at stake, the communities bent over backward to avoid debate. Yet, when matters involved smaller, not to say trivial, affairs, public deliberation became the norm.

The rewards and penalties associated with public discussion, and thus the chance for individuals to entertain contradictory views, vary with the social and historical context and with the ways the issues are framed. Cross-culturally, a tradition of moderation encourages discussion by minimizing the pain of Disagreement. Similarly, conversation is easier when opposing sides disagree about how to achieve consensual goals rather than disagree about the goals themselves: Opponents are Fools, not Villains. When a political culture stigmatizes political conflict and when politics elicits the passions of righteousness, citizens face social consensus.

Of course, the level of public dialogue may vary with circumstance. To the extent that the tone and volume of mass-mediated political information affect Expressivity, then lively and competitive public discussions will encourage public dialogue. Conversely, when elite debate is mute, social consensus rules. Again, when political conflicts are cast as moral rather than practical questions, then public spirits may rise and blood may boil, but public dialogue will suffer.

More subtly, the prospects for debate may depend on exclusion. As a community's distribution of Expressivity becomes bifurcated, as the distinction between willing and unwilling TALKers becomes marked, it may be possible to sustain public dialogues among political activists. As in our "firebreak" example, the uninterested majority will refrain from entering the conversational mix, and the minority activists will not be silenced. Thus, for example, in societies where political interest is found only in the highly educated strata, one might expect political life to sustain modest levels of public debate. Yet, should political interest be democratized, the fragile public dialogue will shatter, leaving the field to the driving passions of social consensus.

Further, signaling alters the prospects for public dialogue: when individuals signal, interfactional debate disappears. This phenomenon may vary across cultures and through historical periods. The match between political views and socially visible characteristics such as social class or readily recognizable symbols, slogans, or ideologies will enhance the effectiveness and the meaningful range of signals and lead to active, although isolated, political groups. One might expect socially divided and politically polarized societies to yield highly charged but also highly insulated political talk. More pluralistic polities, ones that encompass any array of views resistant to facile symbolization, should generate lower levels of political involvement but also permit the cross-fertilization of public dialogue.

A second matter is the status of public opinion and its effect on democratic politics. Consider the following examples.

St. Louis is a Catholic town. It is also pro-life. All three members of Congress and both Senators are pro-life. Members of the state legislature have continuously voted measures intended to circumvent *Roe v. Wade*. When an enormous sign advertising that "God is Pro-Life" was argued to be larger than allowed by city ordinance, the city council ruled it was not advertising but instead a work of art. That St. Louis is pro-life is a simple social fact. Yet, public opinion surveys of the area show that residents of St. Louis are much like Americans in general, marginally favoring the *pro-choice* position.

In the late 1960s, Fields and Schuman (1976) wanted to see if residents of Detroit perceived how others in Detroit felt about civil rights and interracial relations. Asking whites a battery of questions about integration sentiment (concerning if and where one would allow one's child to play with a black child) and also asking about the feelings of Detroit residents in general, the team ascertained both the "private" opinions of a sample of Detroiters and also their perceptions of others' opinions. While the general perception was that Detroit was a segregationist town, in fact the survey showed that Detroiters were modestly integrationist.

This "pluralistic ignorance" appears common (O'Gorman and Garry, 1976; D. Taylor, 1982), and the phenomenon has been used to argue that public opinion doesn't exist—it is only an analyst's creation. To be sure, individuals might not be expected to know the views of an entire city. Thus, Fields and Schuman asked about the views of the individual's neighbors as well as the city in general. The same result obtained. The correlation between any individual's perception of neighborhood opinion and expressed neighborhood opinion hardly registered. Yet, Fields and Schuman went beyond the ordinary line of inquiry and looked at the congruence of neighbors' perceptions. The correlation between any individual's perception of neighborhood opinion and the neighbors' perceptions of neighborhood opinion was substantial. That is, neighbors may not have known what each other thought, but they agreed on the climate of expressed opinion.

In both these cases, public opinion exists. It is a social fact. Yet, it bears no relation to individuals' privately expressed opinions. This disjunction between genuine public opinion and private opinions might be accounted for by the conversational choice mechanism and the social dynamics predicted by our models. First, we might expect that Expressivity on the topics of abortion and race relations will be fairly low. Individuals hold strong and fixed opinions, and the subjects are laced with emotional overtones: disagreement may be particularly unpleasant, not to say threatening. Next, for historical reasons, one or the other opinion might dominate a neighborhood's discussions about abortion or race matters, even when actual opinion is equally (or otherwise) distributed. Thus public dialogue of any proportions will hardly exist; a "silenced majority" might never reveal itself. Given the histories of Detroit and St. Louis, it would not be surprising that the composition of neighborhood conversations remained Conservative while a growing number of individuals took on differing views in private. More generally, one might expect that perceptions of others' expressed views should lag behind genuine, although privately held, attitude change. Such is the pattern that typifies results in this field. Public opinion and private opinions are not merely alternate measures of the same thing. They are distinct social phenomena.

This is important because the democratic character of political institutions will depend on how they take into account the distinction between preferences held in private and views expressed in public. There exists no direct link between the two. Given the right historical circumstances, majorities may be silenced by the social mechanisms of conversational choice. More often, majorities are likely to dominate public opinion, leaving little room for minority opinions to show themselves. In either case, opposition is crushed. When political institutions reflect socially expressed public opinion rather than aggregations of private views, then the social dynamic makes the democratic process easier. Decisions take on the appearance of consensus and generate little conflict.

Yet, easier is not better. When portions of the public are silenced, then politics may ignore their preferences and plainly violate elementary democratic norms. Being unable to open discussion, current losers cannot even hope to persuade fellow citizens for the future. Public decisions will not reflect a consideration of all sides of an issue. Instead they will merely ratify the public opinion outcome. Thus the quality of decisions will not benefit from serious deliberation in the classic sense. Further, because majority discussants face no active opposition, they need not develop tolerance for alternative views. Absent contradiction, the winning position may take on a moral flavor and further exacerbate the majoritarian bias. This self-reinforcing dominance of public opinion sheds the original legitimacy of democratic government and takes on the mantle of mob rule.

Finally, the strong pressure toward homogeneity generated by these social dynamics disappoints classic democratic hopes. Yet the consequences for democratic rule are not unambiguously deleterious. While the classical model implicitly assumes that citizens actively consider the nature of policy alternatives, decades of empirical research indicate that most citizens pay only casual attention to public affairs. Only rarely do they engage their full capabilities when considering political argument. When faced with the kaleidoscope of politics, such casual observers may fail to develop the conceptual framework necessary to distinguish form and meaning. Having no perspective, such citizens might be susceptible to transitory demagogic appeal.

Homogeneous environments can provide structure to political tastes. The reinforcement (and belief immunization) that the social dynamic produces may crystallize views for otherwise confused citizens. Of course, to the extent that interaction patterns are consistent with individuals' genuine political interests, then this social structuring of political beliefs may yield a potential for meaningful democratic rule where none existed before. However, there remains an ineluctable tension between a potentially healthful social definition of belief and the classic desire for citizens to be open to new perspectives. Individual citizens entertaining novel ideas will find themselves in social isolation while those considering dominant views will be encouraged by mutual reinforcement. The meaningful interaction of various views must occur in the setting of formal political institutions rather than in the formulation of the raw material of political preferences.[19] An entire community's belief structure, derived from historical social and ideological divisions, may lock it into a pattern of politics that cannot easily respond to exogenous change. The result may be political stagnation punctuated by revolutionary shifts in the configuration of political preferences. These outcomes may be more desirable than democratic government founded on confusion, but they do not represent the spontaneously deliberative system classical theorists had in mind.

All these speculations sound a little overly dramatic, the result of a theorist's taking license to paint a picture more starkly than necessary. They are. Yet the rule of public opinion, in the sense of closing off debate about accepted truths, carries with it a cloak of invisibility. Its power lies not in what is produced but in what is precluded.

GENERALIZATION

The analytic results for this model suggest an exceedingly strong pressure toward a false social consensus even when many individuals can tolerate a substantial amount of disagreement. The pattern surely makes sense for mass publics whose incentives to engage in political interaction are marginal at best. Yet, the results may be applicable to more highly politicized institutional settings. The crucial theoretical building block is individual Expressivity, the ratio of the incentives and disincentives associated with political interaction. One might imagine that the incentive structures might be different in a legislative assembly, a policymaking committee, or a scientific panel. Surely they are. The participants interact not merely to pass the time but for instrumental reasons: they seek political information and the opportunities for gaining political power. Further, institutional arrangements often produce rewards for public activity that dwarf the soft incentives outlined so far. One must expect Expressivity to be higher than in mass publics and that the proportion of Evangelicals and Chameleons (Appendix B) will be greater. Nevertheless, to the extent that participants prefer interactions with sympathetic rather than contrary partners, then the same analytic results will apply. There exists a substantial expectation that social consensus (perhaps broken down into isolated groupings) rather than public dialogue will arise in many political circumstances. Again, the prospects for genuine deliberation suffer.

Appendix A: Empirical Evidence

First, it must be noted that we might expect only a rough correspondence between the theoretical abstraction and the real world. The analytics are essentially those of comparative statics. At any given moment, we might expect to find portions of the population in disequilibrium. That is, individuals may be reacting to changes in their environment (or in their own expressivity) and not yet settled on optimal strategies. Analyses of individual behavior during politically interesting periods (say, during election campaigns or immediately subsequent to dramatic events) will require a comparative dynamic component to supplement the steady state expectations posited here. However, an examination of individuals in disequilibrium states may help confirm the rough outlines presented here. For example, one might expect that the effects of social influence ought to be greatest for new members of a community simply because they may have not yet adjusted their conversational patterns to fit the new environment. Minority newcomers may misjudge the social situation and engage in conversations that (in the long run) prove unrewarding, or they may not signal effectively. Cox's (1974) analysis of newcomers to Columbus, Ohio, presents a confirmation of the expected contrast between citizens in equilibrium and those still adjusting.

More importantly, citizens may not live in a unitary social environment. Many individuals interact with different sorts of people at work, in family groups, in the neighborhood, in voluntary associations, and in personal friendship circles. The effects of the social dynamics outlined above may be confounded for the individual who experiences a multilayered social mix. The empirical expectation, then, is that the homogeneity-induced reinforcement associated with this model ought to be most evident for those citizens who develop interlocking social networks (where one's friends all know each other) rather than radial networks (that include friends from many different social environments). Laumann (1973) reports that individuals experiencing a more closed community of friends are significantly more likely to have strong partisan orientations than are those who have friends from a variety of environments.[20]

The isomorphism between the simple theoretical construct and the observable world is far from complete. Nevertheless, some tendencies in the more complex reality are consistent with the broadband predictions emanating from the abstract model. Of course, citizens are more willing to TALK in compatible rather than contentious political environments (Glynn and McLeod, 1984; for a sensitive and rich examination of how citizens handle political communication, see Graber, 1984). In more detail, the model suggests that cross-factional interaction ought to be more prevalent in relatively evenly balanced political environments. Thus, the expectation would be that the social influence on individual views ought to be greatest when the political division is fairly even and ought to be minimal when the environment is most one-sided. These are exactly the results reported by Segal and Meyer (1974) in their examination of comparative social influence in small New England towns. In addition, Putnam's (1966) classic analysis of community influence suggests that the political environment is most influential on those who are exposed to a variety of views, those choosing to join community organizations.

Huckfeldt and Sprague's (1986) South Bend survey, in which both members of a conversational dyad are interviewed, provides some crucial evidence on our theoretical propositions. In a thoughtful analysis, they report only a modest relationship between an individual's voting preference in 1986 and the voting preference of the discussant. Thus, individuals do in fact talk with disagreeing partners. Huckfeldt and Sprague convincingly argue that most individuals choose friends for reasons that have nothing to do with politics and that, once having chosen friends, those individuals go ahead and discuss politics.

This apparent disconfirmation, however, merely highlights the subtlety of the social dynamics operation. Huckfeldt and Sprague not only measure each partner's voting choice, but also his or her perception of the other's voting choice. These measures allow one to examine the accuracy of perception, or equivalently, the extent to which any individual's political preference is revealed to the partner.

Our models suggest that two factors ought to impede perceptual accuracy. First, when the partner disagrees, then the individual will dissemble or, more likely, avoid meaningful political discussion. In addition, when the social environment is unfriendly, then the individual will similarly avoid articulating his or her true feelings. Both predictions are sustained in Huckfeldt and Sprague's analysis. The data show that individuals are reticent to make their feelings known when they face social consequences.

Overall, bits and pieces of empirical evidence lie in accord with the general outlines predicted by the abstract models. These are not only occasional fragments: their patterns sustain both the broadest of theoretical predictions and also subtleties around the edges that otherwise might seem odd. However, unless one is willing to interpret previous work very closely, the data do not very well distinguish among the alternative formulations. The lay of the data does not conclusively confirm the models presented here, but instead it suggests that the theoretical results lie in the domain of plausibility.

Appendix B: Some Odd Members of the Menagerie: Evangelicals, Jays, and Chameleons

Extreme forms of Expressivity may alter the prospects for public dialogue. At one end of the continuum lie the highly involved Evangelicals and Jays; at the other repose the indifferent Chameleons.

One might expect some portion of each side to positively value talking with members of the other persuasion. They may entertain the hope of converting the heathen to their cause. Call these *Evangelicals*. Alternatively, they may see political talk as a social "blood sport," a way of asserting dominance. Call these *Jays*. The critical factor is that, for different reasons, these types enjoy political discourse with anyone. They prefer arguing with opponents to nonpolitical activity. When these individuals are placed in the conversational mix, they alter the equilibria. Trivially, they generate "almost pure" equilibria comprised of almost all members of one side talking with the chatterboxes of the other. Under unusual circumstances (when overall Expressivity is low or the proportion of Evangelicals and Jays is high), they also may generate a public dialogue equilibrium of Evangelicals and Jays talking only with (or at) each other. In general, however, their existence does not alter the conditions that are likely to generate a substantially mixed equilibria of public dialogue. Nevertheless, the appearance of such incongruent yet insistent TALKers in an otherwise homogeneous environment may be sufficient to break the social pressure of conformity. Asch's (1951) experimental data suggest that the effects of social environment (on willingness to express contrary views) fall off dramatically once absolute uniformity is lost.

On the other hand, some individuals may be so indifferent about politics that they have no views about any particular issues.[21] They simply take on the coloration of any potential partner who initiates discourse. These are *Chameleons*. Any widespread introduction of these types will lure *both* sides of the spectrum into political interaction. Because they appear Friendly to everyone, they may make the environment sufficiently sympathetic to encourage relatively large minorities into discussions despite the fact that they also will encounter opposing viewpoints. Such neutral lures can substantially increase the probabilities of public dialogue.

NOTES

This chapter has benefited from the close reading and comments of my friends and colleagues. I'd like to thank Randall Calvert, Paul Johnson, William R. Keech, Carol Kohfeld, Eugene S. Meehan, John Sprague, Herbert Weisberg, and of course James H. Kuklinski and John Ferejohn. Needless to say, as terrorists claim credit for their thoughtless destruction, I claim credit for the logical errors and faulty inferences that persist.

1. Messages that are directly transmitted to the citizen by newspapers, television, campaign advertisements, and so forth depend on the citizen's interpretation of their substantive meaning. Although intrapsychic mechanisms (such as selective perception) are surely paramount, it is also clear that the citizen's social environment amplifies (or dampens) the effectiveness of a message depending on the (in)congruence of message and environment. See, for example, Klapper (1960).

2. The *language* used here is that of game theory. The analytic, however, might just as easily be understood as "jointly learned behavior." For purposes of exposition, the results are generated by assuming that individuals actively decide, from moment to moment, what behavioral pattern (what "strategy") produces the best outcome. Think of this as a state of nature argument, one free of assumptions about cultural experience or personal habits. In the abstract, individuals develop a strategy choice for the supergame by repeating the dyadic game, time and time again, in conjunction with other individuals. Of course this is isomorphic with the descriptive notion of (myopic) learned behavior, and this identity makes the model conceptually powerful. See the discussion that follows. Although game-theoretic language connotes active volition, the analytic results do not depend on individuals making a cleverly calculated choice at every instance. A similar application of game-theoretic

analytics for less self-reflective actors can be found in Maynard Smith's (1982) analysis of genetic evolution.

Finally, this is not an adversarial game between competing players. It does have some competitive aspects, but it also contains a heavy cooperative flavor. The goal of each player is not to interact more than anyone else, but engage in political interaction. The true competitors are not the individual players, but instead the *strategies*. The interesting analytic outcomes are the winning mixes of strategies, not winning and losing players.

3. CLAM does not mean that the individual remains forever mute. He or she merely keeps the conversation on other topics. Instead of TALK and CLAM, one might read TALK POLITICS and TALK WEATHER. When considering a more narrow topic than politics, say a specific subject such as abortion, the individual may CLAM by shifting the topic to *another* political matter.

This model abstracts from many features of genuine political interaction. In any conversation the participants may steer the course toward areas of agreement. Compatible partners may find it easy to explore many aspects of the political world; contrary types may cut off argument after showing their colors. Although the dynamics of any particular interaction may generate subtly different results, the overall value that the participants place on the interaction will depend on the scope of their shared values.

4. This may be an unreasonable response. For the moment, keep things simple. For a consideration of another response, see the discussion of REACT ahead.

5. This is a weaker assumption than it might appear. The positive and negative values for Reinforcement and Disagreement are *relative* to Pass (which means TALK WEATHER or cutting off the conversation in favor of doing something else). Thus, Disagreement need not be absolutely "painful," but only less attractive than nonpolitical activity.

This notion demands little justification. A simple appeal to balance or dissonance theory will do. However, something more interesting may be afoot. Homans (1958) introduced the notion that individuals choose social relations with those who offer something in exchange, say social approval. Consider the possibility that individuals see themselves reflected in the reactions of their partners. For simplicity, say the individual sees himself or herself as one of the cultural "folk types" (Klapp, 1954): Hero, Villain, or Fool. Clearly, individuals want to see themselves as Heroes—which is to say that they want others to express admiring and sympathetic views. When the partner Disagrees, the reflection may indicate Villain (the speaker has evil motives) or Fool (the speaker is simply incompetent). One suspects that the threat of being seen as Villain is more serious than that of being seen as Fool. Now, the activation of one or the other of the negative images may depend on whether the subject matter elicits a sense of morality or merely a notion of expertise. Politics probably incorporates more of a sense of morality than many other topics of conversation (say, weather, film, or sport), and thus one would expect that individual choice to engage in *political* discussion should be particularly sensitive to the nature of the social environment. By way of extreme example, in times of crisis the moral component of politics is likely to be greatest, and one would expect to discover a single viewpoint dominating conversations. During the McCarthy period, the pressure to conform (on the subject of the communist threat) made it difficult for nonbelievers to raise their voices. Individuals opposing the dominant view were seen not as Fools, but as Villains.

   6. The essential point here is to focus on the attraction of Reinforcement and the pain of Disagreement. The marginal payoffs for the off-diagonal outcomes have less clear values, and their impact should not determine the results. We might expect these momentary encounters to be less important for individual choice. A more complete analysis indicates that the substantive conclusions do not depend on this simplification.

   7. Strictly speaking, P_f and P_o are the Player's subjective probabilities that any potential conversational partner will have something reinforcing or something disagreeable to say. For simplicity's sake, the rest of the discussion treats individuals as having a discretely Friendly or Opposing viewpoint. The results may be more generally applicable. Each individual may have a unique probability distribution of being either Friend *or* Opponent (or Neutral). For example, an individual may be primarily Friendly: his or her probability of Friend and Opponent might be (.75 and .25). For any individual's decisions, it does not matter whether the environment is made up of (on the one hand) seventy-five Friends and twenty-five Opponents, or (on the other) one individual who has a mixed political view that is distributed ($P_f = .75$; $P_o = .25$). The difficulty arises when anticipating others' decisions. An individual ($P_f = .51$; $P_o = .49$) will maximize Friendly encounters just as will the individual ($P_f = 1.00$; $P_o = 0.00$). The different mixtures of such preference distributions before utility maximization complicate the analytics considerably. However, consider the following abstraction. At any given moment an individual has a discrete viewpoint (with the probability of its being Friendly or Opposing being distributed continuously). A typically liberal academic might have a conservative notion pop into his or her head—and then have to decide about sharing it with his or her colleagues. The decision will depend on whether the colleagues are relatively more or less conservative. Given this abstraction, the results presented in the form of dichotomies in the text will be generalizable to a continuous distribution of opinion.

   Further, the analysis is presented as though there existed only one political continuum. Again, the results are more generally applicable. When an individual initiates political discourse that may range over a number of topics, he or she merely collapses the prospective partner's varying views into a composite. The question remains, Will the response contain a *sufficient* proportion of sympathetic rather than contrary reactions to make the interaction worthwhile? Of course, to the extent that individuals can limit the substantive range of the interaction, then it is easy to compartmentalize the issue domains into discrete continua.

   8. That is to say that an individual chooses a strategy in which he or

she will TALK with a probability of T_i and CLAM with a probability of C_i. The introduction of such mixed strategies allows the idea of TALK and CLAM to represent a rich variety of substantive meanings. T_i may represent not only the probability of TALKing, but also the personal commitment of time and effort dedicated to gathering political grist for the conversational mill. Further, consider the idea of waiting a portion of time (W_i) to see what the partner has to say where the payoff for each encounter is simply $(1 - W_i)$ times the substantive outcome. Such a strategy might allow the individual to avoid unpleasant situations, but it also reduces the benefits of rewarding conversations. This strategy may be represented in the T_i terms in the equations ahead, with the same results.

9. When this inequality holds, then the derivative for T_i is positive. The individual does best by choosing T_i on the boundary, here $T_i = 1$. When the reverse is true, the individual minimizes T_i to zero (that is, he or she chooses CLAM). Citizens, of course, do not use calculus when making their decisions. The theoretical meaningfulness of the formulation here relies on an implicit argument about learning. Citizens who choose sub-optimal strategies might learn through their own experience to TALK more or to TALK less. Alternatively, social norms that embody such past learning might develop as a matter of common culture. Because the payoff curves are monotonic, even gradual learning through casual experimentation will take individual citizens to their optima. Further, because the equilibria involve simple rules of thumb (pure strategies), one might expect individuals to latch onto them fairly quickly.

10. For modeling purposes, let this quantity Expressivity be fixed. Individuals then choose strategies that accord with the pleasure and pain they associate with agreeable and disagreeable conversations. Of course, Expressivity itself will vary over time for any individual as other circumstances heighten or dampen his or her interest in public affairs.

11. The qualitative character of these results (although not the precise numbers) depends little on the assumption of a uniform distribution. A broad range of curves (including normal and F distributions) will produce equilibria of the sort discussed here. The uniform density function is used here for simplicity. For a classic extension of this type of model to the normal distribution, see Granovetter (1978). For a substantive discussion of a more general class of distributions, look at Koppstein (1983, especially Chapter 3). See ahead for a discussion of what happens for some extreme departures from smooth distributions. (The density function in Figure 1.1 is not drawn to scale.)

12. In the simple uniform distribution problem, the criterion curves are given by: $TO = a \, TF \, (1 - TF/F)$ and $TF = c \, TO \, (1 - TO/O)$, where a and c are twice the mean Expressivity levels and F and O the total number of Friends and Opponents, respectively. The equilibria are found at the four roots of the pair of quadratic equations. The trivial $(0,0)$ point is ignored in the text. Unless they are at the intersections of the curves, the points on the curves are *not* equilibria.

13. The existence of attracting stable equilibria is important for trans-

lating the abstract model into the real world. The assumption here is that each individual learns to behave in ways consistent with his or her Expressivity level. In the long-run, all individuals might be expected to choose proper strategies. However, at any given time, some might choose sub-optimal strategies because their learning is imperfect, because they misperceive the social environment, or because random factors might compel them to TALK or to CLAM against their better judgment. Further, dissatisfied individuals (who may nevertheless be at their optima) might attempt new strategies as trial and error. Thus, the robustness of the equilibrium is important in "correcting" such deviant behavior.

Such robustness is a function of the levels of the composite Expressivity distributions and of the social balance of political views. The generation of public dialogue equilibria by skewed distributions (as in Figure 3) is typically not very robust in the sense that the distributions are attractors over only a small portion of space. Further, as the political imbalance approaches the limits in Table 2, robustness declines as well.

The notion of robustness enables the equilibria discussed here to attain the *stability* properties of a Collectively Stable Strategy (Axelrod, 1981 or 1984) or an Evolutionary Stable Strategy (Maynard Smith, 1982) in the sense that the equilibria may resist "invasion" by small groups of players choosing another strategy. Consider the equilibria in Figure 2.1. Should a small number of the previously silenced members (for some unexplained reason, say, they are new in the neighborhood) choose to TALK, they will soon find out that their efforts are unrewarded. On the other hand, the relatively unstable heterogeneous equilibrium of Figure 3.2 devolves into a homogeneous equilibrium when a modest portion of the population (perhaps inadvertently) chooses an "incorrect" strategy.

14. The way that individual conversational choice limits social influence depends on the model that one has in mind. The most elementary model (elegantly explored by Huckfeldt, 1983) approximates conversations by a series of randomized dyadic interactions. It yields the most straightforward restriction. Minority members simply exit the field after the social imbalance becomes too one-sided. Table 2 suggests that these limits are reached very quickly. A clever variant outlined by McPhee and Smith (1962) and McPhee, Ferguson, and Smith (1963), and elaborated by Sprague (1982), suggests that individuals put novel ideas to a social reality test among their conversational partners. When the new idea passes the test, it becomes crystallized. When it fails, the individual "goes fishing" back into the public information stream. The result is a reinforcement of those ideas consistent with the discussion network. In cases of conversational uniformity, those not engaged in political discourse lack the social reinforcement to develop firm political ideas and are susceptible to (say) mass-mediated political influence. Finally, individuals might be influenced by perceived political norms, even when they do not participate in political conversations. Noelle-Neumann (1974, 1977, 1984) convincingly suggests that a fear of social isolation motivates individuals to

take on political views consistent with the apparent consensus. Alternatively, the "silenced" citizens may simply disengage their egos from the political realm and thus remain largely impervious to social pressures.

15. The dynamics that might allow a "silenced majority" to take the field illustrate the advantage of analyzing the problem as a game rather than as simple learning. Consider the possibility that something dramatic occurs that might stimulate the previously silent majoritarians. Each individual, acting alone and knowing only the observable climate of opinion, sees no reason to think that a conversational initiative might be rewarded. However, if he or she believes that *other* majoritarians will also sense the stimulus and make similar calculations about his or her behavior, then the individual may anticipate a Friendly reception and begin to TALK. Now citizens surely do not actually make this sort of clever calculation. However, a "strategy" of TALK after a positive event will prove rewarding because that event will alter the "strategies" of other Friends and change the character of public discourse. Of course, myopic learning might produce this outcome if enough majoritarians "mistakenly" begin to talk without considering the nature of their likely conversational environment.

A straightforward possibility for this sort of phenomenon is the publication of a public opinion poll that reveals private preferences in the public domain. Bandwagon effects might be produced simply because individual expectations about the conversational environment might be substantially altered, and "silenced" majorities begin to feel their oats. Hollander (1979) reports an interesting case of a newspaper endorsement effecting a dramatic change in an electoral outcome, not directly (the impact lagged behind the endorsement) but by altering the climate of *expressible* opinion. In fact, these swings in the conversational environment may typically dwarf actual changes in private sentiments. For some excellent empirical work in this area see Noelle-Neumann (1984).

16. Alternatively, a public dialogue obtains if

$$\text{Maximum (Expressivity of Minority)} > \frac{\text{Minority}}{\text{Majority}}.$$

This may be seen as a conjecture for cases where at least one member of the minority has an Expressivity level of 1.0. A mirror-image region exists for lower Expressivity distributions although the resultant behavior there becomes bizarre.

17. The individual decision does not require a sense of the political balance in the population, only among those who converse.

18. At various times individuals may choose other meaningful symbols. During the 1960s, radicals wore their hair long and dressed in denim. Conservatives put flags in their lapels. Of course, fashions have since changed and so has the availability of signals. Alas, with modern campaign finance laws, even campaign buttons have become a memory.

19. Although the idea that elites are more tolerant of divisiveness and

thus more capable of integrating political differences has some merit, the sad histories of Northern Ireland and Lebanon are discouraging.

20. A direct empirical referent for the closed community abstracted in the model may be disappearing in socially mobile, industrial societies. For this reason, it may be useful to note the political behavior evinced in American small towns during the nineteenth century. These clearer examples of unitary communities exhibited the political uniformity in partisanship and voting choice that the model predicts. For a wealth of empirical data, see Kleppner (1970, 1979).

21. Thanks to Charles Hermann for suggesting this intriguing character.

4

The Structure of Interaction and the Transmission of Political Influence and Information

Michael A. Krassa

An individual forms political preferences and determines appropriate political actions through a dynamic, interactive, and continuing process. Contexts and environments shape actions and opinions, making them as much reflections of and reactions to elements within the social setting as political statements. Both the immediate and the broader milieus condition the preferences a person holds and his or her decisions about whether to act on them. This conditioning is an interactive process in which the context, the environment, and the individual all play an important role.

Eulau's (1980) important observation that the context is emergent and results from the interactions and exchanges of persons sharing either contact or living space serves as a launching pad for discussions of the interdependencies among structures, interactions, and the conveyance of political information. Contextual influences at once help mold individual behaviors and are themselves shaped by individual actions as well as by their particular relation to the larger environment. By patterning the interactions in which an individual participates, the context and environment jointly establish a person's social experience. But because the experience is social, usually involving multiple participants, the actions of one individual help shape not only his or her own future actions, but also those of others in the setting because they become a part of the context in which others must act and make decisions.

INDIVIDUAL INTERACTIONS, STRATEGIES, AND COLLECTIVE OUTCOMES

MacKuen deals explicitly with the interdependence of individual decisions within the same setting (chapter 3, this volume), showing how the choices and strategies of one person influence not only those among whom direct interaction is shared, but also help organize the entire social setting. His game-theoretic presentation of the decision whether to voice an opinion confirms Noelle-Neumann's (1974; 1984) recognition that the observed distributions of opinion assertion in some populations may bear little resemblance to the distribution of actual opinions across the same population. It also shows, using a different technology than Granovetter (1978) and Granovetter and Soong (1988), that social outcomes (e.g., equilibrium levels of public dialogue, levels of participation in riots, neighborhood integration) may be extremely sensitive to the exact population distribution of "thresholds" or proclivities to act (expressivity). Even where a majority would prefer some other outcome, the population distribution of expressivities or thresholds for some behavior may make that outcome less likely.

The simple threshold models of opinion assertion, in which an individual will speak his or her mind if and only if there exists an acceptable level of support (i.e., when the portion of the public voicing support is above that person's threshold), usually depict mass behavior as unstable and subject to wide swings in response to the actions of even one individual. Mixed equilibria such as the public dialogue equilibrium are usually found to be rather fragile, deteriorating rapidly to one of the pure (social-consensus type) equilibria in response to changes in individual behaviors or shifts in the population distribution of thresholds. Indeed, the fragility of its equilibria is one of the major criticisms of the threshold approach to modeling such binary choice phenomena as opinion assertion.

Such radical swings in aggregate behaviors, however, seem much more rare than the analytic results suggest they ought to be, and several attempts have been made to modify the logic to represent more realistically observed phenomena. Granovetter (1978) suggests that greater stability may result when such models are modified to incorporate the fact that not all individuals' decisions are of equal importance to the system-level (society's) behaviors. In these models each individual's behavior influences others' differently so that no one individual is highly likely to play the key role in determining system-level properties. Similarly, the system behaves more realistically when the model allows for the fact that individuals observe and interact with different population segments with varying probabilities (Krassa, 1988). Because not everyone is in contact with, or even knows of, every other person in a large population (such as that involved in the case of public opinion), and because people only see the behaviors of some population subset, the assumptions of random mixing are not met. It is convenient that, when the models are adjusted to account for these pieces of reality, the system behaviors it predicts also become more realistic.

To this same end, MacKuen's game-theoretic approach permits both a more realistic construction of the problem and the creation of more stable population behaviors. Adding the strategy of signaling, for example, allows greater levels of discussion to occur in a population by allowing people to avoid unpleasant conversations more easily, much as networks might bring people with common interests together more often than they mate opposites (Finifter, 1974). In either case, however, although higher levels of discussion result, the discussion is less likely to be cross-factional: the discussions are less likely to be socially productive in that they bring together persons of varying views. These discussions are most likely to be between partners who agree.

Signaling permits selectivity in picking conversation partners, which means that people with low thresholds for the social "pain" of engaging in conflictual discourse may avoid such conversations.[1] Networks provide another, although less individually effective, means of accomplishing the same end. Individuals form ties with others partially by choice and partially through circumstance. Ties made through choice (or mostly by choice) are most likely to be between individuals with similar views, and thus these strong ties are probably least likely to bring persons with conflicting views together. Weaker ties often form between persons brought together through circumstances of similar employment, group membership, and interests. When people with only a weak bond talk politics, there exists a somewhat greater possibility of disagreement,[2] and thus a greater probability that new information is transmitted among the individuals, which increases the chance that learning and social change may take place. Thus, although individuals may have a preference for biased information for reasons of comfort (as in MacKuen), protection (Finifter, 1974), or political preference (Calvert, 1985), the result may be socially sub-optimal, retarding any social change that may be made possible through cross-factional discussion.

INDIVIDUAL MEMORY AND SYSTEM BEHAVIOR

Another feature of the MacKuen model and other models that basically stem from threshold approaches is that there is no individual memory across encounters with the same other person. In small populations and in large populations over the long run, there are relatively high probabilities of encountering the same potential conversation partner more than once.[3] By remembering the payoffs from a prior encounter, an individual may "play" a different strategy and receive a higher payoff (if one exists) on future encounters. Thus, one may initially try a TALK strategy in every encounter, knowing that in some situations there will be disagreement but that reinforcement will occur in other meetings. Then, in future meetings with the same individuals, the better strategy becomes clear: TALK to friends and CLAM with opponents.[4]

In a game in which TALK and CLAM are the only actions (i.e., no SIGNALing and no REACTing), the best strategy for any individual is to TALK to everyone on first meeting, then TALK to friends and CLAM with opponents. Axelrod (1981) demonstrates that the same strategy (called Tit for Tat in his Prisoner's Dilemma game) is the most successful long-run strategy an individual may play and, furthermore, allows small groups of cooperators ("friends") to coexist and survive successfully (TALK to each other) in a relatively hostile environment. The problem is that the only discussion that will take place will be among friends. Although in this game the social-consensus equilibrium becomes less likely, so too does public dialogue (in the sense of cross-factional discussion). Although multiple points of view are represented in the big picture of public opinion, and the spiral of silence has been avoided, the discussion that occurs is always between friends (in the very long run).

The game MacKuen presents differs from the game Axelrod (1981) explores because individuals calculate a single strategy for all encounters based on their "expressivities" or willingness to bear the pain of rejection in order to enjoy the fruits of reinforcement (i.e., "thresholds" for opinion assertion). Thus, although in Axelrod's analysis individuals are affected (through total payoffs) by the mix of people in the environment, they are not allowed to react to the totality of the social environment, but only to individuals within the environment. By including a feature that allows individuals to calculate a strategy based on the environment, MacKuen moves a step closer to understanding how the world functions. However, it is probable that individuals base behaviors on both types of calculations: they react to the social environment, and they also react to their personal histories when encountering the same individual repeatedly.

INDIVIDUAL BEHAVIORS AND THE
INTERACTION OF MULTIPLE STRUCTURES

Huckfeldt and Sprague deal less with how individual interactions determine observable features of the social setting than with how contextual and environmental properties combine to influence individual behaviors. For the most part they do not distinguish among outward and underlying features of an environment—they do not distinguish the levels of opinion expressed from the underlying distribution of opinions, for example—although they do show how behaviors emerge and are structured over time by events such as campaigns and aspects of an individual's social niche such as the relationship among the individual, the context, and the environment. Thus, in a manner entirely different from MacKuen, they show an interdependence between contextual and individual properties.

In this model, individuals react to each other as individuals. The distribution of opinions across the environment governs the content of interactions, and individual attitude formation is influenced by the overall environment, although less directly than in MacKuen's model, where individuals react to the setting as a whole. For Huckfeldt and Sprague, by contrast, the totality of individual interactions shapes the social setting, which itself feeds back to influence the interaction probabilities among individuals, but the influence of the context is in a sense through the feedback rather than a direct response to the composition of the environment.

Implicit in Eulau's (1980) comment that the context is emergent is an explanation of contextual impacts as a time-ordered dynamic in which individuals continuously respond to and change the information content of their own social setting. It is a system of mutual feedback in which certain motivated individuals seek reinforcement for their opinions from others in the environment and base future actions and reevaluate opinions founded, in part, on the responses of those with whom they interact.[5]

Although this model, an extension of the McPhee (1963, chapter 2) model of information search, sounds superficially like the game examined by MacKuen and the threshold models considered in Granovetter (1978), Granovetter and Soong (1988), and Krassa (1988), it has one very different premise that, by definition, assumes that cross-factional dialogue occurs in a population. The assumption, present in both the McPhee model and Huckfeldt and Sprague's extension of it, is that when an individual does not find support (reinforcement of his or her position) in an encounter, other encounters are sought. Thus an information search takes place, with the result being that an initial bias is either confirmed or modified. What this implies is that conversations between opponents will occur frequently—until people change positions and a homogeneous context emerges.

If one were to formalize the logic in this model of information search and evaluation, one would find that under most initial conditions, it shows deliberation leading to social consensus in the very long run—but this is a social consensus not of opinion assertion but rather of real beliefs. The prospect for deliberative democracy seems very great in the short run, but the long-run prospects are very poor because over time a uniformity of opinions may occur. Unless the proponents of one view have a pedagogical or psychological advantage that makes it easier for them to win converts than their opponents, or unless the initial distribution of opinions is nearly perfectly balanced between two positions, the dynamics of the system are likely to lead, in the long run, to the extinction of one viewpoint (see Goldberg, 1958).

The episodic nature of elections and political campaigns, however, preserves the prospects for democracy. The learning model in McPhee (1963:73) implies that the process of encounters, discussion, and (re)evaluation is continuous and relatively stable over time. The contribution of Huckfeldt and Sprague is to note that the political campaign dramatically changes the rate at which the information search takes place. Without the stimuli of an election campaign, politics is often remote and of low saliency to most people. When people have political preferences in the absence of a universal stimulus such as a campaign, they are apt to be a low priority for discussion and validation,[6] and, by implication, therefore, unstructured.[7]

ELECTION AS CATALYST

Electoral campaigns are more than episodic. However, they also are more or less unique. In different years, different candidates—with different backgrounds, public images, and histories—compete for office, different issues emerge as salient, and the electorate is mobilized in different ways and along different cleavages. Thus, if elections are the catalysts to reactions of political information to social structures, they must act as slightly different catalytic agents each time and may therefore permit a somewhat different reaction to occur each time.

Elections act as catalysts by bringing political questions to greater salience for much of the general public. But they also contribute to the reaction, however, by advantaging different social structures in different elections and in different settings. Huckfeldt and Sprague document the differences between the class-based 1976 election and the more ideological 1972 contest and show that contextual or local-level influences were strengthened during the 1976 campaign, whereas structural effects were weakened during the 1972 competition. Because elections mobilize people differently at different times, they allow social structures to affect information flow (and hence the creation of social consensus) in a variety of ways over time.

Thus, over time, by providing periodic and slightly different stimuli to the structuring powers of contexts and environments, elections help make possible a kind of social evolution, even in stable (and homogeneous) social settings. The laws of logic and science dictate that the results should be the same each time that the same stimulus is applied to the same object (subject) in the same way. And in each election year, context, environment, and an information search come together to structure a public's behavior. But even when the context and the environment have changed only minimally,[8] the results have been shown to be very different over time. The variations in information searches and the competitive positions and interactions of environments and contexts *must* therefore have been elicited by differences in the two electoral contests. In other words, social change may be possible even in the absence of prior structural change because the relevant structures may be brought together in a variety of ways, and elections provide one of the mechanisms for fashioning the larger compound structure, the unique entity that emerges from the interaction of other structures.

Therefore, the distinctiveness of various elections plays a key role in creating the diversity of social and structural responses. As the only factor in the complex interaction that varies substantially over the short period between the two elections, the differences in the character of the elections must be responsible for the different outcomes. And indeed, the theory put forth by Huckfeldt and Sprague argues that elections shape the way that the three factors—individuals, contexts, and environments—interact to produce the very different results over the two years they examine. The argument, of course, is that when similar elections bring these same three factors together in more similar ways, the results are more similar; when the elections vary the way the factors interact, results can be very different, even if the three factors themselves have not changed.

PRIVATE PREFERENCES AND PUBLIC CONSEQUENCES

Using different methods and applications, Arrow (1951) and Olson (1965) each demonstrated that rational behaviors at the individual level may generate sub-optimal or even undesirable social outcomes. In a similar vein, MacKuen shows that when people choose a pattern of responding in their interpersonal interactions with others according to what is most comfortable for them as individuals, the social-level outcome may be imperfect and, indeed, may even be damaging to the long-run prospects for the society, as when debate is squelched.

The irony, of course, is that among the most stable equilibria are those in which there is no cross-factional discussion; a "tyranny of the minority" is as likely and as hard to eliminate as the tyranny of the majority. A majority preference may never be vocalized (and hence not acted upon) because a vocal minority inadvertently silences the majority by making the climate of opinion appear different than is actually the case, that is, by making majority views seem to have little social support. A social dialogue equilibrium is the only case in which asserted opinions may reflect the underlying distribution of attitudes. It may, however, be relatively uncommon because individuals calculate their strategies not in total isolation, but rather on the basis of observations of the apparent opinion climate.

Huckfeldt and Sprague illustrate a different public consequence of the interactions among individuals and their surroundings. They show that opinions change and become more coherently structured over time as a result of the way that the campaign helps organize discussion and interaction. Individuals, simultaneously reacting to each other and their social surroundings, evolve during the course of the campaign and in the process further influence each other and restructure their surroundings.

Opinions are patterned in different ways over the course of the two very different elections considered, 1972 and 1976. The differences found are logically consistent with a theory that attributes an active role not only to the various structures (contexts, environments, and individuals), but also to the peculiar processes and histories of each specific campaign. Two results in two campaigns, however, cannot confirm that the differences in attitudinal structures were due to the fact that one was an electoral contest in which ideology was important and the other one in which the class-basis of American partisan politics resurfaced. The evidence clearly conforms to such a hypothesis, but further research is necessary for confirmation.

The discussions by MacKuen and Huckfeldt and Sprague are also based on very different, even incompatible, understandings about the private preferences of individuals. MacKuen begins with an assumption that individuals desire "reinforcement" or "confirmation" of their attitudes but will avoid discussions with others when the environment appears hostile. Individuals view the environment as a whole, judging the level of social support for their views according to the relative sizes of vocal segments of the population, and determine the most appropriate behavior on the basis of their assessments of the environment and their tolerance for interaction with those who disagree. Individuals thus seek agreement and enjoy the accompanying reinforcement but prefer to avoid disagreement. Indeed, for all but the most assertive or expressive of individuals, the expectation (accurate or not) of many disagreeable interactions leads to a strategy that does not include political discussion.

On the other hand, in the model that underlies the chapter by Huckfeldt and Sprague, individuals seek information—a confirmation or refutation of their views—and have no preference for confirmatory/reinforcing discussions over disagreeable discussions with opponents. They sample their environment, interacting and conversing with others, and revise their attitudes on the basis of the character of their sample. Thus, under this model, the individual in a hostile environment will be highly interactive and engage others in conversation—and may eventually change views. Faced with this same prospect, MacKuen's assumptions lead to silence for the individual.

One key difference between the two theories, therefore, is in the understanding of human motivations and the calculations that individuals make about their interactions. Faced with an apparently hostile environment, will individuals continue to seek information even though it may be unpleasant, will they alter their opinions to become more like the others, or will they seek the relative comfort of a politically noninteractive life-style?

A single psychological perspective provides evidence on behalf of two different adaptive behaviors. When faced with a hostile environment, theories of cognition and cognitive dissonance argue, individuals will act to minimize the conflict in any of a number of ways. The famous experiments by Asch (1951) show that individuals will, over time, begin to agree with a socially dominant position, eventually viewing their original positions as incorrect. Further, this tendency is greater as the subject is a member of a smaller and smaller minority.

The Asch experiments, however, did not give the subject the option of failing to voice a preference. Thus, as Huckfeldt and Sprague show, repeated exposure to the unfriendly environment will change one's views.

However, in studies by Festinger (1957), individuals are allowed a wider range of behavioral responses to a hostile information environment. Among the reactions he finds is a behavior similar to the silencing (CLAM strategy) on which MacKuen's analysis is based. Individuals may simply become less interactive. Another dissonance minimization strategy that individuals choose involves increasing contacts with friendly individuals and decreasing them with opponents and adapting one's network of friends and acquaintances to increase the frequency of interaction with those who are politically similar. Thus, the networks may actively be used to control that to which one exposes oneself (Finifter, 1974) and indicate the general importance of recognizing that an individual has some control over his or her contacts, indeed, more individual-level control over interactions than the models underlying either MacKuen or Huckfeldt and Sprague suggest.

Two other strategies that Festinger observed involve attitude change. Like the individuals in Asch's studies, people may change their minds in response to an overwhelmingly hostile social environment. Alternatively, opinions may weaken in intensity but may not be completely reversed. When a person finds some support among friends and acquaintances for two sides of an argument, he or she may simply opt out of the disagreement by holding neither opinion, suggesting instead that the issue is unimportant. Note that this is not quite the same as a CLAM strategy because CLAM does not involve any change of preference. But neither is this a description of the information search that McPhee describes.

A second important difference highlights a substantial incompatibility among the theories. If some individuals remain conversationally inert or noninteractive on some topics because of their subjective assessment of the environment's character, then it becomes impossible for the information-seeker to sample the environment in an unbiased fashion. The sampling would be of assertive individuals and not of the environment as a whole. The correct measure of the informational bias encountered by this method of sampling the environment is not the distribution of attitudes across the whole environment, but rather the distribution of expressed attitudes across the relevant environment(s)—which MacKuen, as well as Noelle-Neumann, demonstrates may not be the same thing.

Thus, although both discussions present systems models in which individuals react to features of the larger environment *and* environments are simultaneously shaped by individual actions, they are distinguished by substantial differences in approaches, assumptions, and conclusions. Some of the distinctions may simply result from the fact that different aspects of human decision making are examined, whereas others may properly be classed as incompatibilities and contradictions and may derive more from the imperfect state of the discipline's understanding of human motivations and behaviors than the models and theories themselves.

Each model is based on sets of assumptions that seem to be relatively complete and sensible descriptions of behavior. Yet irreconcilable differences prevent the two models from addressing one another. The important contradictions, therefore, must stem not from techniques and methodologies, but rather from differences in premise and underlying theory.

CONCLUSION

The arguments of MacKuen and Huckfeldt and Sprague are most interesting when placed in juxtaposition. Each argument states that there is an interaction between individuals and the social setting. These two factors mutually influence each other to determine both system and individual behaviors. The arguments differ dramatically, however, in approach, underlying assumptions, and, consequently, results and implications.

The most important of the differences, as noted previously, is found among their assumptions about basic human behavior and reactions. For example, each attributes a different type of behavior to individuals who find themselves in a hostile social environment. MacKuen invokes a theory in which individuals may cease to be interactive in an excessively hostile environment; Huckfeldt and Sprague assume, by contrast, that individuals will continue interacting but may change their preferences over time in response to their interactions within the hostile social setting. Further, note that in MacKuen, an individual's behaviors may change over time—from assertive to silent or vice versa—but opinions remain fixed; Huckfeldt and Sprague, on the other hand, show behaviors as relatively fixed—always engaged in an information search—but opinions may change over time in response to the information obtained.

Moreover, both discussions show individuals shaping and being shaped by their environments, but the mechanisms presented differ greatly. In MacKuen's argument, individuals react to a perception of the social setting as a whole, whereas Huckfeldt and Sprague show individuals sampling the setting piece by piece in an effort to validate personal attitudes. MacKuen shows individuals as able to assess the totality of the environment at a single instant based on some overt and observable system properties, that is, the mix of opinions asserted in the public. Individuals then base their behaviors on these assessments. Huckfeldt and Sprague, on the other hand, show individuals responding strictly to other individuals without using a view of the environment in its totality as a basis for behavior. For them, individuals learn about the overall nature of the social setting through a series of interactions. A weighted average of opinions encountered in interactions is the available measure of the whole environment. However, because both models allow the character of the social setting to change over time, this change will affect individuals differently in each model.

In MacKuen's model, individuals will respond immediately to changes in the mix of opinions expressed in the population. Thus, in his model, feedback to the individual is fast. In Huckfeldt and Sprague's model, however, individuals will respond to change in the setting—without necessarily being cognizant of the change—because of the way it accumulates in their weighted averaging of interactions. If past interactions have some continuing importance (i.e., a non-zero weighting at all times), however, individual opinions will change relatively slowly (by comparison with MacKuen's model) in response to even a large environmental or contextual change.

Thus, the two models present results from very different understandings of human nature. Each in its own right presents a reasonable and believable depiction of human interactions and draws sensible conclusions based on the model. It is fascinating, and perhaps says more about the state of the discipline than about either chapter, that two such plausible models contain such dramatic differences and logical incompatibilities. If each addresses the same question, and if each sounds so plausible, why aren't they more similar?

NOTES

1. In the analysis MacKuen presents, the ability to avoid the social pain is relatively complete. In reality, this may not be entirely the case. As noted, wearing a campaign button is a signal, as was long hair in another era. These signals may prompt reactions from "evangelical" passers-by, producing the payoff "GRATE" at best, and perhaps producing a poorer payoff.

Also consider an example of supporters of two opposing candidates, both wearing campaign buttons, who meet in an elevator. Even without conversation there may be some recognition of an unpleasant circumstance. In the complete silence of the elevator each has communicated disapproval to the other, and the brief ride may, if nothing else, seem unnecessarily long.

Note, however, that if one considers the encounters in these two examples as "conversations," albeit silent ones, then there is greater hope for social dialogue equilibria. However, a possibility also exists that citizens will then make the same calculations about whether to signal as they made about whether to talk, and we merely move the logic back one step.

2. However, this probability is influenced strongly by the nature of the forces that forge the bond. Bonds arising through shared workplace experience may indeed bring rather similar individuals together if the workplace is homogeneous in its employment opportunities. Employees of a Tennessee auto assembly plant are likely to be more homogeneous than are the employees at the corporate headquarters, for example, because the headquarters will contain large white-, blue-, and pink-collar work forces, while the branch plant will be more heavily blue collar. These two forces help different sorts of networks emerge, with the result that one is more likely than the other to bring new information into conversations even though the ties between unlike individuals may be weak (see Granovetter, 1973).

Similarly, bonds arising through shared membership in groups will vary in the chance of bringing opponents together. A Southern Baptist church, for example, will be more homogeneous than will, say, a hobby-based club (unless, of course, a very expensive or class-biased hobby is involved). Different sorts of groups and associations, groups that form around different focuses, and groups that form for different reasons may all vary in both homogeneity and impact on individual behaviors. See Brown (1981) for a comprehensive discussion of the impact of group membership and its interaction with other contextual variables.

3. Similarly, when one considers networks as a measure of the proximity of individuals, the probability of any given encounter is a direct function of closeness (proximity) within the network. It is a noncontroversial social fact that we interact with some people on a much more regular basis than we do with others; those with whom we have the most regular contact are most central to us in the network in which we are embedded.

4. Although sounding similar on the surface to the REACT strategy that MacKuen discusses, this is in fact quite different. The difference is most clearly seen in the meeting of two REACTORs, in which conversation will never result, even if the two are friends.

5. Note how the dynamic underlying this argument is almost identical to the game described by MacKuen. The key differences are that in the description of the information search there may be change over time in opinions as a result of the information obtained. Also, as earlier noted, Huckfeldt and Sprague do not propose that individuals decide whether/how to carry out the information search (i.e., talk with others or not) in reaction to the external features of the context. They do, however, argue that networks within the

environment influence the selection of others with whom individuals will interact.

6. That is, such topics as baseball and the weather will be the bulk of most discussions.

7. "Unstructured," for Huckfeldt and Sprague, means socially or across the population. It is interesting to note, however, that in the absence of political stimuli and discussion, the many political opinions of an individual may themselves be unstructured and idiosyncratic—internally. Berelson, Lazarsfeld, and McPhee (1954), Campbell, Converse, Miller, and Stokes (1960), and Converse (1962) all support the notion that issue consistency will be lower in the absence of a reason for them to be ordered. Thus, with the exception of the relatively few *true* ideologues in the population, individuals will be less likely to have internally-structured sets of opinions in the absence of such stimuli as the campaign. The campaign, therefore, may serve as catalyst for the imposition of structure on opinions both within and across individuals.

8. This would be the case between 1972 and 1976. Note that not only are the amounts of change at the environmental (county) and neighborhood (tract) levels minimal across this period, but they are also so small that the 1970 census is able to provide contextual measures for both the 1972 and 1976 analyses by Huckfeldt and Sprague. Few neighborhoods demonstrated *great* change in important indicators (such as mean incomes, mean education levels, and racial composition), even over the entire decade between 1970 and 1980. Although everyone can make a lengthy list of neighborhoods that have undergone rapid change through gentrification, abandonment, decay, or urbanization, these neighborhoods are noteworthy precisely because they are comparatively rare in the national context of literally millions of relatively stable neighborhoods.

II

INFORMATION PROCESSING AND THE PSYCHOLOGY OF POLITICAL JUDGMENTS

5

Information and Electoral Choice

Paul M. Sniderman
James M. Glaser
Robert Griffin

That the average citizen tends not to know a lot about politics, lamentable though this is, has obscured the rather more crucial fact that some of them know markedly more than others. Some members of the public are knowledgeable about politics, follow it closely, and understand who stands for what politically; others are ignorant of politics, pay little attention to it, and have only a weak grip on who stands for what. In this chapter, we will explore the spectacularly obvious—yet curiously neglected—suggestion that voters who are quite well informed about politics and those who pay scarcely any attention to it may not make up their minds in quite the same way.

This seems a worthwhile undertaking for a number of reasons, two of which deserve particular mention. The first concerns the proper shape of a theory of voting. The established practice in electoral research is to aim at a model of voting, to develop a uniform explanation for the electorate as a whole. This is not an obviously winning strategy. Different people make up their minds in different ways. What is needed is a kind of explanation that takes account of this heterogeneity. Or, to put the point more exactly, it is necessary to consider whether or not certain pivotal factors not only condition the voting decision in their own right, but also condition the influence of other causal factors. There are not likely to be many such pivotal factors, but information is quite likely to be one of them.

There is a second, normative rather than causal reason to focus on information. It is a commonplace that information assists rational choice and, by implication, that the well-informed voter may be capable of it but the poorly informed one may not. This is by no means a foolish idea. Still, we will explore not merely the relatively straight-forward suggestion that voters who are well informed make up their minds in different ways than those who are poorly informed, but also the more challenging idea that, by making up their minds in a different way, voters who are *not* well informed about politics—as well as those who are—may make approximately rational electoral choices.

THE STRUCTURE OF ELECTORAL CHOICE

Electoral choices can be organized in two different ways: either as a referendum on the incumbent or as a choice between competing candidates.

Consider a presidential campaign with two candidates, typically an incumbent and a challenger. How can voters approach this choice? One approach is to focus on the incumbent and make a judgment about his past performance. If voters judge the incumbent's record to be satisfactory, they should support him. If the record looks poor, voters should consider the alternative. Voters may focus on many or few aspects of the incumbent's record, interpreting the notion of a record broadly or narrowly. It comes down, all the same, to voting the incumbent up or down. That is the choice being offered.

Alternatively, an electoral choice may take the form of an evaluation of the competing candidates. This evaluation may focus on many aspects of the candidates' claims or few, focus on what they have done or are likely to do. It comes down, all the same, to a comparison of alternatives.

The first kind of choice, then, focuses on the incumbent, the second on challenger as well as incumbent. The first involves evaluating the candidates serially beginning with the incumbent. The second involves evaluating them simultaneously. And because these choices differ in the form they take, they differ as well in the information they require and the way they are made.

Imagine two hypothetical voters. One is well informed about politics, a daily and devout reader of the *New York Times* who follows closely the major national and international issues. The second is a *Daily News* fan who devotes little time to public affairs and looks only at the sports page. Is it plausible to suppose that these two voters, asked to make a choice about who should be president of the United States, would make up their minds in the same way?

It is implausible, it seems to us. It is not reasonable to suppose that the voter who is well informed about politics and the one who is largely ignorant of public issues would enumerate potentially relevant considerations with the same exhaustiveness, or frame alternative considerations with the same precision, or foresee consequences of alternative choices with the same distinctness, or coordinate calculations, both about alternative means and alternative ends, with the same exactness. It is, in short, not plausible to suppose that the well-informed voter and the poorly informed one go about the business of making up their minds in the same way.

But what, more exactly, does it mean to say this? How does the nature of the choice before the voter vary with his or her informational level? Presidential elections typically pit an incumbent against a challenger. The incumbent has a prominence the challenger finds hard to match. He has been in the most visible public office for four years. The media have focused on the incumbent for his term and focus more on him during the campaign in his double role as both president and candidate, highlighting information about policies and performance. By contrast, the public knows less about the challenger; indeed, people may have known next to nothing about him before the primaries. So the challenger lags behind in public awareness.

But not uniformly. Some voters are politically knowledgeable. They have some overall sense of the political landscape. They know, broadly, who stands for what and who opposes whom. They are less likely to see the challenger as having come from nowhere and more likely to perceive him distinctly. They may know more about the incumbent, who has had, after all, the benefit not only of a term in office, but also his run for it. All the same, the well-informed voter is able to compare incumbent and challenger and vote his or her interests.

The poorly informed voter is not so fortunate. The president is perhaps a familiar enough figure, at least in broad outline, but not the challenger. Before his nomination, the latter was in all probability not well known to voters who habitually pay little attention to politics. Poorly informed voters, moreover, face an uphill battle in overcoming their lack of information about the challenger, partly for the very reasons that lead to their lack of information in the first place. And the consequence is that the incumbent tends to have a prominence that the challenger finds hard to match, especially among voters who are not politically informed.

This suggests that the way in which voters make up their minds may vary with information and attention levels. Well-informed voters can more readily hinge voting decisions on a comparison of the incumbents' and challengers' personal attributes and policy commitments. Precisely because they are well informed, they know something of the policy commitments of the two major parties. As a consequence, they are capable of gauging the policy preferences of the candidates and placing them in the context of the long-term differences in ideological orientation that have distinguished the two major parties over the last fifty years or so. Poorly informed voters, however, are less likely to make up their minds in quite this way. Certainly, it is unreasonable to suppose that they follow politics closely enough to track carefully the issue commitments of the parties or candidates. But poorly informed or not, they are in a position to form an opinion about whether the president is doing a satisfactory job. They know how the economy is faring and can judge how the president is performing.

A POINT OF DEPARTURE: THE SHANKS-MILLER MODEL

Voting is a field of study repeatedly, and profitably, plowed. It is thus sensible to recognize and take advantage of the labor of others. The model of voting developed by Shanks and Miller (1985), displayed in schematic form in Figure 1, seems to us especially suggestive.

The Shanks-Miller model features a single-strand causal chain. In this respect, the model exemplifies a consensual approach in the study of voting, specifying one sequence of variables, arranged in temporal order, *ex hypothesi* the same for all voters: variables farthest removed (in time) from the vote are farthest to the left; those closest to the vote are farthest to the right. The causal chain begins with fixed personal characteristics (gender, for example) and ends with the vote choice. In between are intervening factors (e.g., partisanship and candidate images), laid out in causal (or temporal) order.

The ordering of variables, as displayed in Figure 1, is far from decorative: it is rather a concise representation of the causal relations supposed to hold among variables in the model. Specifically, a variable may be a cause of a variable to its right, but only an effect of a variable to its left.

The Shanks-Miller model illustrates well some of the principal conventions of recursive, multistage accounts of voting. But it also has several features that recommend it particularly. First is its specific analytic objective: to compare the relative importance of two images of the voting decision. One way is to see the model as a calculus concerning policy. On this view, elections come down to a public judgment on the direction government policy should take or avoid taking. A second, quite different, image is a view of the vote decision as hinging on performance evaluation. On this view, what is decisive is

Figure 1. The Shanks-Miller Model

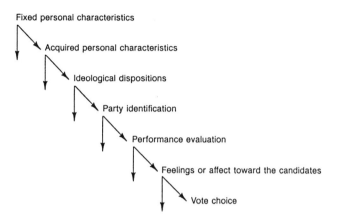

not the public's view of the policy direction government should follow, but rather its judgment of how good a job the incumbent has done. The distinction between these two images—policy direction and performance evaluation—is potentially of considerable importance.

The Shanks-Miller model has a second provocative feature, although this is a negative rather than a positive property. The model excludes a class of variables that voting models commonly include: the so-called issue proximities—a set of variables defining the (mean) discrepancies between the policies a voter prefers and those he or she perceives the candidates to support. This omission seems to us a helpful simplification. So much evidence has piled up on voters' low levels of political information and attention that it is hard to credit them with a steady grip on their own positions on many issues, let alone on the positions of candidates. Moreover, it is not obvious in what sense people's perceptions of where they stand on issues and of where the candidates stand are independent. Many voters derive their sense of what candidates think should be done partly from their own beliefs about what should be done. Indeed, it may be more plausible to conceive of the final arrangement of positions attributed to candidates that takes shape in the voter's mind as a result—rather than a cause—of the decision he or she has reached;[1] issue proximities, in the case of candidates, can give the appearance of a rational calculus without operating, in fact, as a causal mechanism. Shanks and Miller, in short, have reason to argue that "relatively few citizens actually compare 'issue distances' when they come to a vote decision" (p. 35).

The Shanks-Miller model, although it serves well as a point of departure, needs modification in two principal respects. The first, and more superficial, is that in Figure 1, ideological dispositions precede party identification. On this view, the former is cause, the latter effect. It is by no means obvious that this is the most plausible view to take. Many voters acquire a party identification early in life as a result of everyday socialization to politics. In addition, relatively few acquire ideological orientations, and they tend to do so later in their lives, typically not before attending college. So it seems more reasonable to suppose that party identification precedes, temporally and causally, ideological orientation, not the other way around.

The second, and more fundamental, difference is that the Shanks-Miller model assumes that acquired personal characteristics should be located near the beginning of the causal chain and—what makes this assumption crucial—presupposes as well that there is one set of variables, arranged in one sequence, that is the same for all respondents. But how much sense does it make to presume a uniformity of causal sequence? Why suppose that all voters make up their minds in the same way? We have argued that it makes more sense to suppose they take account of different considerations or make different use of the same considerations, depending on how politically well informed they are. If we are right, the assumption of a single, fixed causal sequence should be scuttled. It is instead necessary to allow for differing effects of various independent variables for voters of differing levels of information.

MEASURES

Some of the 1980 National Election Study measures we deploy are quite familiar—party identification, for instance, and ideological self-identification. Others are less so and deserve a word of description.

Two questions tapping retrospective voting concerns were asked. The first involves judgments about the past performance of the incumbent. Specifically, respondents were asked if they approved or disapproved of the way Carter was handling his job as president; then, if they approved (disapproved), whether or not they did so strongly. This question directly assesses performance evaluation. It yields a five-point measure with a range of 0 to 4 and a mean of 2.4, scored so that the higher the number the more negative the evaluation.

The second measure tapping retrospective voting concerns the past performance, not of the incumbent, but of the economy. A voter with even minimal political information can make a determination that too many people are out of work, or that gasoline is too expensive, or that the standard of living is lower than it should be. To get a grip on this kind of judgment, we take advantage of a question on national economic conditions. Specifically, respondents were asked whether, in their opinion, the economy has gotten much better, somewhat better, stayed about the same, become somewhat worse, or become much worse. This variable has a range of 0 to 4, with a mean of 3.2, and is scored so that a larger number indicates a more negative judgment.

Rather than focus on whether or not the incumbent has done a satisfactory job, the voter may try to determine which of the two candidates will, in his or her judgment, do the better job. One way to capture this kind of judgment is to measure the voter's comparative evaluations of the candidates. Accordingly, we have put together a six-item index of comparative competence. This index is based on a list of words or phrases that people use in evaluations of political figures. Six were read, with respondents asked whether each describes the candidates extremely well, quite well, not too well, or not well at all. The six were weak, knowledgeable, inspiring, solve our economic problems, provide strong leadership, and develop good relations with other countries. The comparative competence index was scored so that the larger the number, the stronger the tendency to judge Reagan more favorably than Carter. Conversely, the smaller the number, the stronger the tendency to judge Carter more favorably than Reagan. The competence index has a range of 0 to 12, with a mean of 7.0.

Voters, moreover, may be driven by public policy goals, particularly when candidates differ fundamentally in their policy objectives, as Reagan and Carter did. To tap this kind of consideration, a policy index was built. The policy index focuses on four issues: government spending for social services, government job guarantees, government aid to minorities, and defense spending. Opinions on these issues are correlated significantly and positively. The policy index is scored so that a larger number indicates a conservative orientation, a smaller number a liberal one. The index has a range of 0 to 24, with a mean of 13.9.

A final point. Conceptually, we speak of variations in information level. Operationally, we focus on variations in formal schooling. This may seem arbitrary. Education, clearly, is not the same thing as information level, but the two are highly correlated all the same. The person with considerable formal schooling, on average, is better able to pick up political information than the person with minimal schooling, is better able to remember it, and is better able to put it to use. Moreover, there is mounting evidence that education organizes policy reasoning in mass publics.[2] As a result, we expect education to organize the voting choice, too.

VOTING

To what extent do voters make up their minds in different ways depending on their level of education? Figure 2 lays out two causal models of vote choice. The first applies to the less educated, that is, those with eleven years of education or less (upper panel); the second applies to the well educated, that is, those with thirteen or more years of education (lower panel). The variables in each are the same and laid out in the same arrangement. Because vote choice is a dichotomous variate, direct effects on voting are estimated through logit; because the mediating variables—incumbent approval, comparative competence, and policy preference—are continuous variates, indirect effects are estimated through ordinary least squares, relying on (as is customary) unstandardized regression coefficients.

Obviously, impressions of the candidates constitute a prime consideration in deciding how to vote. But, as we have suggested, there is more than one way to form such impressions. One alternative is to focus on the incumbent, voting for (or against) him depending on approval (or disapproval) of his performance in office. Alternatively, a voter may compare both candidates in one or more respects, and on the basis of this comparison, choose between them. The incumbent approval measure captures the first sort of judgment, the relative competence measure, the second.

Look first at the less educated, and compare the impact of incumbent approval vis-à-vis relative competence on their voting decision. Both matter, but one predominates. Judgments about the incumbent are a more important consideration than a comparison of the two candidates.

This reliance on judgments of the incumbent's performance gives to the choice process of the less educated a flavor of retrospective voting, since the dominant consideration for them is whether the incumbent is doing a satisfactory job, not whether the challenger will do a better job. This impression of retrospective voting is strengthened on further examination of Figure 2. Look at the role of judgments of national economic conditions among the less educated. These, too, have a direct impact on the voting decision. Their impact is modest, not surprisingly, considering the limitations of a one-item measure. Nevertheless, a judgment about how well the economy is doing enters into the voting calculus of the less educated.

Figure 2. A Model of Vote Choice by Education (1980)

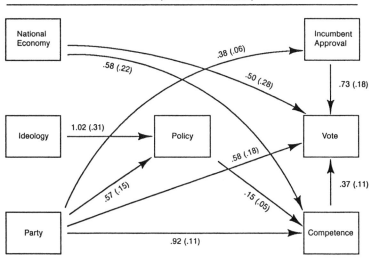

Less Educated (0-11 Years of Education)

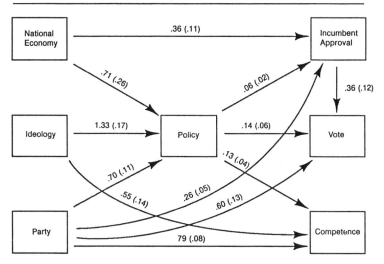

Well Educated (13+ Years of Education)

The results for the well educated are quite different. Look first at the role of candidate judgments. It is not impressions of incumbent performance that are the dominant consideration in voting; rather, it is a comparison of the two candidates' qualities. In this respect the kinds of considerations about candidates that drive the voting choice are different for the less educated and for the well educated: for the former, it is incumbent approval; for the latter, comparative competence.

There is a second point of difference between the poorly educated and the well educated. National economic conditions have a direct impact on the vote choice of the less educated. Not so for the well educated: there is no statistically significant, direct connection between national economic conditions and vote choice for those who have some or more college education. This is not to say that their view of national economic conditions has no impact. As Figure 2 shows, it is an indirect consideration influencing the vote by influencing assessments of the candidates and their views on policy. Still, by this standard also, the less educated give direct evidence of retrospective voting, whereas the well educated do not.

Consider now prospective voting. One expression of it is a vote based on policy orientation. There is no evidence for this kind of voting among the less educated. Certainly, there is no significant connection between the policy index and the voting decision for them. One might question whether this is an artifact of measurement; specifically, the less educated—precisely because of their lack of education—are unlikely to organize their opinions on issues in the unidimensional, liberal-conservative fashion the policy index presupposes. Accordingly, we analyzed opinions on individual issues, taken separately and put together in various combinations. These analyses, too, testify to an absence of prospective voting as indicated by policy-driven electoral choice among the less educated.

It is quite different for the well educated. Opinions on major issues are indeed a consideration of direct relevance to their vote. Moreover, the policy opinions of the well educated, but not of the less educated, are rooted in broader political orientations, as indicated by their tendency to put together ideological self-images and issue preferences consistently. This is a difference of no small significance, for it is complex and burdensome to vote prospectively, issue by issue, on an ad hoc basis. Making calculations instead in broad policy tendencies—liberal or conservative—economizes the costs of information required and minimizes the uncertainty of predictions ventured. Finally, the impressions that the well educated form of candidates and rely on in deciding how to vote are grounded in their views on policy in a way that reactions to candidates among the less educated are not. Thus, among the well educated, comparative assessments of the relative competence of the two candidates are, in part, a product of policy opinions. By contrast, among the less educated, judgments of incumbent performance—the crucial aspect of candidate evaluation for them—are not connected to policy stands.

These are some of the particularly salient differences between how the well educated and the less educated decide to vote. There also are points of similarity, for example, the role of party identification. Still, it is worth asking what the differences may amount to that we have observed.

DISCUSSION

Some of our results suggest that the less educated are more likely than the well educated to take advantage of retrospective voting. Fiorina (1981), of course, found just the opposite: that, so far as systematic differences are evident, retrospective voting tends to be the mark of the well educated, not the less educated. It describes the person who is interested and well informed about politics. Why this difference?

Part of the explanation, it seems to us, lies in the properties of (relatively) complex idea systems. It would seem obvious that the person who is well educated, who follows politics closely, who has considerable information about it, should be good at putting ideas together—certainly compared to the person who is not especially educated, attentive, or informed. But what does it mean to say a person is apt at putting together ideas? Among other things, it means that the person sees connections among different considerations—including considerations that may be relatively remotely (or at any rate not immediately or self-evidently) connected. And because of this tendency to see and to make connections among different considerations, decision making tends to be characterized by a broad focus of attention: much is relevant in making up one's mind how to vote. Or, more colloquially, the better-informed voter tends to take account of nearly everything, including the kitchen sink. Hence, the connection between any given consideration and the vote will tend to be strong for the better educated when examined at a bivariate level. This credits the impact of any given consideration, which may be quite small, with some of the impact of all other considerations with which it is correlated, some of which will be quite large. Analyzed at a multivariate level, however, the picture will change because the differential weight of correlated considerations will be evident.

There is another consideration. We have seen evidence of voting based on performance evaluation among the less educated and of voting based on policy direction among the well educated. It is tempting, then, to suggest that the former engage in prospective and the latter in retrospective voting. But this puts the distinction between these two kinds of voting too starkly, or more exactly, overlooks the difference between direct and indirect effects. Thus, the less educated do take account of national economic conditions as a direct consideration in deciding for whom to vote; the well educated do not. But the latter take account of national economic conditions as a consideration in deciding their issue preferences, which in turn they consult in casting their vote. Now, if taking account of the condition of the economy is a mark of retrospective voting, who should be said to be voting retrospectively: the less educated who take account of it directly, or the well educated who take account of it indirectly? It seems to us that it is a false choice.

Still, it seems worthwhile to consider what, more exactly, the notion of prospective voting entails. Consider, therefore, how the well educated make up their minds. On the one side, they take as a prime consideration their views on policy. They also give great weight to how the two candidates stack up when compared to one another. On the other side, they attach less importance to their assessment of the incumbent's performance as an immediate basis for making up their minds. And, consistent with this, they do not take the condition of the economy as a direct consideration in casting their votes.

How, then, might the decision making of the well educated be characterized? It is not uncommon to imagine a Downsian space: voters compare candidate issue positions and pick the one that best matches theirs. The emphasis, here, is on the perception of similarity between the candidate and voter issue positions. But one can look on this space from a different perspective, focusing not on similarities between candidates and voters but instead on dissimilarities between candidates. From this angle, voters compare candidate issue positions with an eye not on minimizing the difference between their views and those of the candidate they support, but rather on maximizing the difference in views between the two candidates. And looking from this angle provides a glimpse of how well-informed voters tend to make up their minds.

Figure 3 displays the positions attributed to the two presidential candidates and the two political parties in 1980 on the issue of gov-

Figure 3. Mean Positions Attributed to Candidates and Parties (1980)

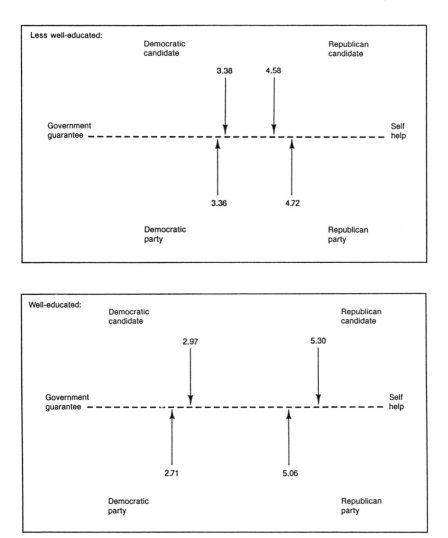

ernment guarantees for jobs. The (mean) positions attributed to the candidates and parties are shown separately for voters with different levels of education—first, the less educated, then the well educated.

The differences between the well educated and the less educated are striking. The well educated see both the Democratic candidate and the Democratic party as farther to the left than do the less educated. Moreover, they see the Republican candidate and the Republican party as farther to the right than do the less educated. The well educated accentuate the differences between the parties and between the candidates, whereas the less educated minimize them.

This tendency to accentuate dissimilarities between candidates or parties seems to us the mark of the well-informed voter. Indeed, it may not be exaggerating to say that the mark of the person who understands American politics is precisely that he or she accentuates—that is, exaggerates—the differences between the parties and the candidates who represent them. This is not to say that it is always right to accentuate such differences. But the person who makes the opposite mistake—who minimizes rather than accentuates the differences between the parties—misunderstands the structure of American politics. He or she supposes that both parties are centrist, which supposes the Republican party to be far less conservative than it in fact is and the Democratic party to be far less liberal than it in fact is. Accentuation enhances the structure of elite issue conflict, while failing to accentuate obscures it.

And accentuation matters because it provides a basis for prospective voting. Even the well-informed voter is sure to lack political information—to lack the information, certainly, to make confident predictions about future actions of successful candidates. Indeed, the very notion of prediction, in the face of the ordinary uncertainties of politics, has been hard to credit. Accordingly, many observers have found it more plausible to suppose instead that the sophisticated voter will engage not in prospective, but retrospective, voting. But in what sense does prospective voting involve a prediction about the future? Only in the sense that one candidate's policy direction is expected to differ from the other's. Now, it would surely be a matter of reading tea leaves to predict the policy choices of the successful candidate except in the context of the issue differences of the political parties. But seen as representatives of their parties, the candidates can be judged comparatively, in context, rather than absolutely, out of context. And, as representatives of their parties, the policy loyalties of the candidates can be predicted, for this prediction is grounded in the dynamic of the American party system. The well-informed voter, operating as a prospective voter, exploits aspects of the record that are as definite, and dependable, as those aspects of the political record on which the retrospective voter relies. The difference between prospective and retrospective voting is not that the former involves a prediction about the future while the latter does not. Both involve a bet that the future will look like the past. They differ only in the aspect of the past on which they focus: the prospective voter takes account of dissimilarities in policy; the retrospective voter looks at the performance of the incumbent.

Insofar as the well informed hinge the voting decision on a comparative assessment of the candidates, including their policy commitments as well as their personal characteristics, they may be thought of as optimizers. What strategy, if any, are the less educated following?

Consider how the less educated make up their minds. They take as a prime consideration the performance of the incumbent, voting for him if they find his performance satisfactory and against him if not. Also, they take into consideration the state of the economy, voting for the incumbent if they find it satisfactory and against him if not. Finally, what the less educated do not take into account counts as well as what they do. Especially notable in this respect is their failure to base their vote on their views on policy issues, even, it seems, on long-standing issues.

How, then, should the decisions of the less-informed voter be characterized? They should not be described as an attempt to calculate the best possible choice based, for example, on a comprehensive survey and evaluation of the full array of possible alternatives. On the contrary, instead of characterizing their strategy as an attempt to identify the best possible choice, it seems more accurate to say that they are attempting to decide whether the way things have been has been good enough. The poorly informed, although not optimizers, may nevertheless be satisficers.

Now, the use of labels like *optimizing* and *satisficing* should certainly be accompanied by a stiff warning. This is partly because the use of labels may invite an inference that the well informed and the poorly informed are making qualitatively different kinds of decisions, and, as a general rule, an empirical analysis that requires demonstration of differences of kind rather than degree has six toes in the grave. So it is important to point out that it is possible to develop a quantitative, and not merely qualitative, account of voting along the lines we have sketched. Such an account would center on voters' focus of attention. Briefly, the better educated and more aware the voter, the broader her focus of attention—that is, the wider the range of considerations she would take into account in casting her vote. Conversely, the less educated and the less aware the voter, the narrower her focus of attention.

But what, more exactly, does it mean to say narrow? What kind of considerations are included? What kind excluded? The less-educated voter, we would suggest, focuses on the terms of the choice narrowly defined. He or she, in a presidential campaign, excludes considerations that are not immediately and obviously relevant. In this sense, the calculations of the less educated involve a strict calculus. By contrast, well-educated and better-informed voters have a wider focus. They take account of considerations at least one step removed from the explicit choice. So they see connections, for example, between their vote and anterior considerations, like policy commitment, that require some imagination and thoughtfulness. They detect anterior considerations, moreover, that are only imperfectly correlated both with one another and with more immediately relevant considerations. In this sense, the calculations of the well educated involve a loosely, rather than strictly, elaborated calculus.

One may object that our line of argument is misguided, if not in its overall objective, then in its specific formulation. After all, many elections have no incumbent to evaluate and hence cannot be accounted for by contrasting alternative forms of evaluation, one serially hinged on the incumbent and the other focused on a flat-footed comparison of incumbent and challenger.

This is a curious objection, self-defeating on its face. Of course, incumbency is not a factor in all elections. But why, in elections pitting an incumbent against a challenger must we refuse on principle to see if incumbency is a factor of importance? What sense does it make to argue that if a variable is not important in all situations it is never important in any?

There is a deeper objection and one more profitable to consider. Elections, in the end, require a comparative judgment. After all, the voters must decide which candidate they prefer. Moreover, in presidential elections that pit an incumbent against a challenger, it would be quite wrong to suggest that large numbers of voters have formed attitudes and impressions only of the former and not of the latter. And, granted that voters have a reaction to both, how do they decide whether to vote for the incumbent or the challenger? Surely, by comparing the two, then casting their vote for the one they prefer. At its root, then, voting is a process of comparative judgment, inevitably and ineluctably so however well or poorly informed the voter.

This view of voting may seem to collide with the view of voting we have urged. Not so. Supposing voters have formed their preferences about candidates, they should choose the one they prefer. Call this their decision rule. Now, this rule is clearly uniform. No one supposes, for example, that it should work one way for the well-informed voter and the other way for the poorly informed voter. It makes no sense to expect that the former, having established his or her preferences, would choose the candidate he or she prefers while the latter would choose the one he or she does not prefer. But—and this is the point to fix on—there is a prior question. How do people arrive at these preferences in the first place? Does the poorly informed voter, in working out his or her preference, give different weights to the same considerations? On our showing, the answers are, respectively, no and yes. The process by which voters make up their minds varies with their informational level. But notice the contention: not that well- and poorly informed voters abide by different decision rules, but that they follow different decision processes. Thus, the less sophisticated voter, in making up his or her mind, tends to fix more on the incumbent and, in evaluating the incumbent, to take account of different considerations than the more sophisticated voter. Once preferences are established, the decision process is, of course, comparative. All the same, the processes by which those preferences are established vary with political awareness, or more broadly, information processing varies with information level.

There is another consideration. Analyses of voting are at risk of being framed in either/or terms, not always, but often. So it is asked, Do citizens vote retrospectively? Or do they vote prospectively? Such choices are false choices. The question is not whether voting is retrospective or prospective, but under which conditions it tends to be the one or the other.

We have tried to illustrate a partial answer to this question. No doubt, it is debatable in part. The measures we used were those at hand, not those we would have devised given a free hand. Moreover, the causal relations among variables may be conceived differently. Our model of vote choice hinges on a contrast between two variables: incumbent approval and comparative competence, both at the end of the causal chain. This is an instructive contrast for a first cut. It is not an obviously optimal approach for subsequent analysis. Part of the difficulty is that the two variables, incumbent approval and comparative competence, are highly intercorrelated, and the causal relations between them have not been specified. It is, of course, possible to overcome this by stipulation. But this is not an appealing strategy, and, indeed, in our judgment, concentrates on quite the wrong end of the causal chain. The point to explore, we think, is the role of party identification at the beginning of the causal sequence, as against candidate images at the end.

This discussion has been an exploratory effort to see what it might mean to say that the structure of choice and the process of choosing are interdependent. We hope that our broad argument is a step in the right direction, for it seems to us unreasonable and unenlightening to insist that the well-informed voter and the poorly informed one make up their minds in quite the same way. And if we are right in this broad argument, it is important to call attention to one of its implications for the study of voting.

That implication concerns the assumption of heterogeneity. To say that voters make up their minds in different ways and, further, that these differences may themselves be systematically accounted for is to say that voters are in some respect systematically heterogeneous. This contention may seem plausible on its face. We certainly think so. But it flies in the face of current analytic practice. Thus, it is customary to elaborate a model of voting for voters taken as a whole. This is the approach that Shanks and Miller take, for instance, and it is the approach that nearly all voting analysts have taken. It entails, of course, the assumption that there is no systematic interaction: how voters decide to vote does not systematically differ depending on some particular characteristic of theirs. And it is precisely this assumption that we believe is wrong. At a minimum, it is unreasonable to insist that a person who is extremely well informed about politics will make his or her voting choice in the same way as a person who habitually ignores public affairs. It is, of course, tempting to suppose that this reduces to a matter of some making up their minds well, and others not. This is a temptation to resist.

Elections organize collective choices. But as we have seen, these choices can typically be organized in two rather different ways. One alternative is to treat the decision as hinging on a comparison of the two candidates; the other, as a judgment to be made about the incumbent. And, as we have also seen, the well-informed voter tends to organize the voting choice the first way; the poorly informed voter, the second.

These are different ways of going about the business of making up one's mind for whom to vote. But the difference between them is not that the well-informed voter who practices the first alternative is making up his or her mind the right way, whereas the poorly informed voter who practices the second is doing it the wrong way. Whether voters are sufficiently informed to behave approximately rationally is a joint product, not just of their capacities for choice, but of the structure of the choice they are making. The well-informed voter is able to locate the candidates against the background of the competing political parties and the points of view they represent, and this ability enables him or her to bring policy preferences to bear. Otherwise, such voters would be at sea, for they are only well informed by comparison with others who know even less about politics. But how about poorly informed voters? Are they incapable of making a rational choice because of their lack of information? Not necessarily, if our analysis is correct. The poorly informed voter may lack the information to make the kind of choice the well-informed voter can, that is, a choice that turns on comparison of the candidates, for instance, with respect to their policy commitments. All the same, the poorly informed voter may have the information needed provided he or she treats the choice as a choice for or against the incumbent; poorly informed or not, the voter is in a position to judge if the incumbent's performance is satisfactory. Satisficing is, after all, the decision strategy par excellence given a lack of information. So, in these alternative ways, the choices of voters can be approximately rational not in spite of—but because of—shortfalls in information.

NOTES

Preparation of this discussion was partly supported by funds from the Survey Research Center at the University of California at Berkeley. We have been the beneficiaries of encouragement and criticism from many—but most particularly from Richard A. Brody, Philip E. Converse, and Bernard Grofman. The data were made available by the Inter-University Consortium for Political and Social Research through the State Data Program of the University of California at Berkeley. The Center for Political Studies of the Institute for Social Research at the University of Michigan collected the data, under a grant from the National Science Foundation, on behalf of the National Election Studies.

1. See, for instance, Page and Brody (1972).

2. See Sniderman, Brody, and Kuklinski (1984); Sniderman, Hagen, Tetlock, and Brady (1986); and Sniderman, Wolfinger, Mutz, and Wiley (1986).

6

A Social-Cognitive Model
of Candidate Appraisal

Wendy M. Rahn
John H. Aldrich
Eugene Borgida
John L. Sullivan

How individuals perceive and think about candidates, issues, and political events has been the focus of considerable research and theoretical development in political cognition (Lau and Sears, 1986). Researchers in political cognition, drawing on theoretical models from cognitive psychology (Hamill, Lodge, and Blake, 1985; Hastie, 1986; Lau, 1986; Lodge and Hamill, 1986), behavioral decision theory (Iyengar, chapter 7, this volume), and social cognition (Conover and Feldman, 1984; Iyengar, Kinder, Peters, and Krosnick, 1984), have conceptualized the domain of political behavior as a particularly rich, naturalistic context in which to examine theoretical issues that are central to an understanding of human cognition. At the same time, these investigations have also begun to contribute new insights to, and perspectives on, long-standing concerns in political science such as the nature of public perceptions and evaluations of political candidates.

Until recently, political scientists, while recognizing the importance of candidate images, have not provided theoretical or rigorous empirical analyses of the role of candidates and their images in electoral choice. In the predominant view presented in *The American Voter* (Campbell, Converse, Miller, and Stokes, 1960), attitudes toward the candidates were seen primarily as projections of partisan bias, although individual candidates could interject dynamism into presidential contests that prompted short-term deviations from normal partisan voting patterns (e.g., Stokes, 1966). In reaction to this view, scholars in the late 1960s began to analyze the impact of short-term forces on the vote, looking especially at the role of issues. The central argument was that issues, instead of being short-term disruptions of otherwise stable partisan choices, could be seen as systematic determinants of voters' decisions (for a review of the issue-voting literature in this period, see Kessel, 1972). One theoretical approach to explain issue voting is the spatial model of electoral competition (see Downs, 1957; Davis, Hinich, and Ordeshook, 1970). Herstein (1981) critiqued this theory, arguing that such spatial-like calculations are too demanding cognitively, and he demonstrated experimentally that people do not employ such a complex reasoning process. One important contribution of the spatial approach, however, was the emphasis on choice as based on a comparison between the two alternative candidates, seen in that case as collections of policy alternatives.

Other models of voter choice posited less demanding calculations than the spatial model, in which summary candidate assessments played a critical role (Brody and Page, 1973; Kelley and Mirer, 1974). Indeed, the decision rule in these models is that individuals vote for the candidate receiving the highest net evaluations. More methodologically complicated models have been developed to examine the causal determinants of these summary assessments (Markus and Converse, 1979; Page and Jones, 1979; Markus, 1982), but they have lacked a systematic theoretical account of the processes that underlie voters' impressions of political candidates. Given these results, scholars of political behavior have recognized for some time that the focus should shift from predicting vote choice per se, as reflected in the component models of voter choice (Stokes, Campbell, and Miller, 1958; Stokes, 1966; Kagay and Caldiera, 1975), to understanding the nature of the candidate appraisal process.

In this chapter we first develop a social-cognitive model of the process of candidate appraisal and then test it using a national survey conducted for the authors by the Gallup poll immediately after the 1984 presidential election. A central part of the theory underlying the model concerns the role of information in forming these assessments. We will argue that the rich and often redundant flow of political information in a presidential election year, combined with the relative simplicity of a choice between two presidential candidates, leads to relatively similar assessment and decisional processes for most individuals. We will test this argument by estimating the model for respondents who are relatively high in political sophistication and those relatively low in sophistication.

CANDIDATE APPRAISAL

Research in political cognition has stimulated renewed interest in the study of candidate images as preeminent factors in the voters' world (Kinder and Sears, 1985). Lau (1986) and Miller, Wattenberg, and Malanchuk (1986), for example, rely on an understanding of information processing based on schema theory (e.g., Taylor and Crocker, 1981) and use responses to the open-ended, like-dislike questions from the University of Michigan Center for Political Studies (CPS) national election surveys to identify "information processing proclivities" among the mass public. Lau argues that individuals appear to rely on four broad classes of schemata, or organized structures of knowledge, to process political information (groups, issues, parties, and candidate personalities). These relatively stable categories, he contends, influence the vote decision. For individuals who possess a well-developed party schema, for example, Lau finds that party identification is nearly twice as important in determining candidate evaluations as it is for individuals without a fully developed schema. Even for the latter voters, however, party identification is relevant to their vote.

Similarly, Miller and his colleagues (1986) categorize citizen responses to the open-ended, like-dislike questions into those dealing with candidates, issues, and groups. They find that candidate-directed comments cluster in five generic dimensions (competence, integrity, reliability, charisma, and personal characteristics) that are stable at the individual level across elections, suggesting that individuals do not respond to candidates as idiosyncratic figures. Both Lau (1986) and Miller, Wattenberg, and Malanchuk (1986) find that higher levels of education are associated with the use of a candidate schema, a finding that Miller and his colleagues attribute to well-educated voters' ability to consider the dispositional qualities of the candidates. Less well-educated voters, by contrast, concentrate on readily observable characteristics of the candidates such as physical attractiveness and background.

Work by Kinder and others (Abelson, Kinder, Peters, and Fiske, 1982; Kinder, 1986; Kinder and Fiske, 1986) has examined the candidate appraisal process. This work has made extensive use of the new CPS candidate appraisal batteries (e.g., asking respondents to rate how well such attributes as "strong leader," "moral," or "inspiring" describe the candidates) to develop a theoretical framework for understanding the perception and evaluation of presidential candidates. In particular, Kinder's analysis (1986) of these measures reveals that individuals think about the candidates in stable, structured ways, following a process that resembles that used to think about ordinary people. Although the assessment of ordinary people and of political candidates is similar, attributions about presidential candidates will be appropriate to the task of assessing presidential character and performance. Judgments of presidential character, therefore, will be structured around particularly central and relevant traits (competence, leadership, integrity, and empathy). Some of these traits (e.g., empathy) can be viewed as germane for assessing any individual, whereas others (e.g., competence and leadership) will receive special emphasis due to the political nature of the task. Moreover, these judgments can be influenced by political predispositions such as ideology, partisanship, and policy preferences.

Thus, in contrast to the early perspectives on vote choice, recent research suggests that the candidate appraisal process does not represent an idiosyncratic response to the vagaries and particular characteristics of a given election contest. Rather, these findings support the notion that, when thinking about political candidates, people tend to rely on the same information processing capabilities that guide their thinking and actions in other, nonpolitical domains (Feldman and Conover, 1983; Kinder and Fiske, 1986; Sullivan, Aldrich, Borgida, and Rahn, forthcoming). When people think about political events and make voting decisions in presidential elections, they first rely on the well-developed set of inferential strategies and processes for assessing character that they use in everyday life (Nisbett and Ross, 1980; Ostrom, 1984; Sherman and Corty, 1984). In this respect, we will argue that individual differences in political expertise or interest (Fiske and Kinder, 1981; Fiske, Kinder, and Larter, 1983) should not result in different candidate appraisal processes because all citizens have sufficient practice in evaluating others in the course of their daily lives. But it is also clear that political expertise affects the processing of information for other political tasks (Zaller, 1986b).

In most elections, as in everyday life, a great deal of information, much of which is complex, becomes available to individuals. Voters are deluged with comparative information, especially in presidential elections, about the candidates' personal characteristics and qualities, their competencies, their stands on various issues that are salient in the campaign, as well as other, nonverbal cues presented by the candidates and their campaigns (see, e.g., Rosenberg, Bohan, McCafferty, and Harris, 1986; Sullivan and Masters, 1988). Research in social cognition suggests that, under such conditions, people perforce simplify the information environment, and, in doing so, they are likely to rely on the familiar cognitive routines that they employ in other decision-making contexts. The presidential campaign itself facilitates impression formation by emphasizing particular personal qualities such as leadership. Media coverage of the campaign may prime individuals to consider such traits in their evaluations of the candidates (Iyengar and Kinder, 1986). Also fortunately for voters, in virtually all presidential election contests, many political cues point in the same direction, reinforcing one another. In other words, the political characteristics of the candidates, including their party affiliations, their ideologies, and their issue positions, are often highly "correlated." This redundancy offers an additional reason for the similarity of the candidate appraisal process across all types of voters, even those with relatively low levels of political sophistication.

More specifically, in the candidate appraisal process, individuals quickly make some basic judgments about the candidates, particularly with respect to their competencies as potential leaders and their individual qualities. In 1984, for example, voters may have learned that there were vast differences between Ronald Reagan and Walter Mondale on the defense spending issue, with Reagan preferring significantly more spending than Mondale. This information could be expected to have an impact on perceptions of the two candidates as differentially strong or weak, depending on the voters' own positions on this issue and on their partisan predispositions. Likewise, other issues and other types of political information feed into judgments of the candidates' characteristics that help to define each candidate as more or less competent in the mind of a particular voter. Thus, although we agree with others (e.g., Hamill, Lodge, and Blake, 1985; Lau, 1986) that different individuals may rely on different types of schemas (e.g., parties, groups, ideology) for processing political information, we suggest that in the electoral context, a wide variety of political cues and other kinds of information are abundantly available to the voters, and potentially all of it can be used when evaluating candidates.[1]

These assessments about personal competencies, in turn, influence how voters feel about each candidate—whether, for example, they feel pride or shame when confronted with a particular candidate, or whether they like or dislike the candidate.[2] In 1984, a voter may have thought that Reagan was very strong based on his positions on defense and other issues, and thus the voter may have concluded that Reagan was competent because of the perceived connection between competence and strength in a political leader. This in turn made the voter feel pride when confronted with the image of Ronald Reagan. Similarly, in 1988, George Bush used the defense and crime issues to dispel his "wimp" image and establish an image of personal weakness for Michael Dukakis. In this fashion, issues can structure candidate images, which in turn influence feelings about the candidates. A person who supports a greater role for the government in helping the poor and destitute, when presented with Reagan's views on welfare, may conclude that Reagan was selfish and politically untrustworthy. Thus issues can affect judgments of personal qualities as well as judgments of political competencies, and, in turn, these judgments influence feelings about the candidates.

The candidate appraisal process, by which personality assessments are made in combination with the electoral campaign that primes certain issues as well as partisanship and ideology, leads to an overall evaluation of presidential candidates' competency and leadership, their personal qualities, and the voters' feelings about the candidates. In a context as complex as a presidential election, candidates portray these qualities in part on the basis of their own personalities, background, and experiences, and in part on features unique to the political arena, such as policy, party, and ideology.

Unlike judgments about people in everyday settings, however, the decision task confronting the voter is ultimately a choice between two candidates. Therefore, the question is not simply whether Mondale was perceived to be competent or not, but whether he was seen to be more or less competent than Reagan.

A MODEL OF CANDIDATE APPRAISAL

The model of candidate appraisal is based on several basic assumptions. First, we assume that images of presidential candidates can be formed in two ways. Images of candidates can be formed by a process similar to that used to form impressions of people encountered in everyday life. The alternative—attending to and processing the large amounts of information available in every new setting—contradicts the assumptions of cognitive economy that characterize normal cognitive functioning (Fiske and Taylor, 1984; Markus and Zajonc, 1985). This assumption therefore leads us to expect that, even for those citizens relatively unconcerned about politics, the formation of candidate images will be a relatively easy task, one not dependent upon a vast store of political awareness and knowledge. Moreover, to the extent that people's initial impressions of and beliefs about candidates are bolstered as they learn more about the candidates during the course of the campaign, new information is often perceived to be largely confirmatory (Lord, Ross, and Lepper, 1979; Ross and Anderson, 1982).

Voters can also derive images of candidates based upon their perceptions of the candidates' stands on key issues, partisanship, and ideology. In this sense, the political context primes political cues that are considered in varying degrees in the development of candidate images. This context creates an appraisal process that can include factors common to everyday appraisals, as well as factors unique to national election campaigns.

A second basic assumption of the model is that most voters are capable of distinguishing between the political characteristics of candidates and the candidates' personal qualities. We make this assumption because in everyday life, in a variety of formal and informal settings, people are called upon to distinguish between the professional and personal qualities of individuals. They notice, for example, that some people are fine human beings, even though they may not be highly competent at their chosen occupations; others are not as personally appealing, but are incredibly competent. In this respect, elections represent a setting in which these types of judgments will come quite naturally to most voters. The electoral process is clearly an arena in which citizens will wish to select leaders who will competently run their government *and* whose personal qualities will evoke trust and confidence in their personal motives.

A third assumption, consistent with recent work in social cognition (Berscheid, 1984; Fiske and Pavelchak, 1986), is that feelings about candidates are developed as a natural part of this candidate appraisal process.[3] These assessments can be conceptualized as an overall, affective summary toward each candidate that has its basis in cognitive appraisal. In presidential elections, of course, feelings toward the candidates will also be grounded in political issues, ideology, and partisanship.

Finally, we assume that, in this context, voting is a relatively uncomplicated decision for most people. It really can be "the simple act of voting" (Kelley and Mirer, 1974). If overall affect about the candidates summarizes judgments and feelings about issues, parties, and the competence and personal qualities of the candidates, it leads in a relatively straightforward fashion to a voting decision. One votes for the candidate one likes best (or dislikes least). It is this assumption in particular that leads us to predict that the process of voting is based on a comparative assessment of the candidates and is similar for people who are heavily involved in politics and those for whom politics is more incidental.

MEASUREMENT

In order to test the preceding theory, we specify a model relating the exogenous variables of partisanship, ideology, and issues to the three dimensions of candidate image that we have discussed—competence, personal qualities, and affect or feelings about candidates. We then need to estimate the parameters in this model separately for people who are heavily involved and those who are less involved in politics. This theoretical model is depicted in Figure 1. A more detailed discussion of measurement follows. The data for estimation of these models are drawn from a postelection survey conducted by the Gallup poll for three of the authors in November 1984. There were 1,509 respondents included in the national sample.

Domestic Issues

In selecting issues for the domestic scale, we initially selected six items that formed a scale as reported in Aldrich, Sullivan, and Borgida (1986). However, because we have argued that the process of deciding for whom to vote is a comparative one, the model could only be tested if we could compare respondents' attitudes on these issues with their perceptions of where each candidate stands on the same issues. Of the original six items in the domestic issues scale, candidate perceptions were solicited on three issues. The domestic issues scale therefore includes these three items—questions measuring respondents' attitudes toward government spending for social services in general, aid to minorities, and jobs and standard of living. The resulting reliability, measured by coefficient alpha, is .60.

Foreign Affairs Issues

The foreign affairs issues scale has two items, one dealing with defense spending and the other measuring respondents' views about whether our government should be strong and tough or flexible and understanding in dealing with other nations. We were limited to these two items because of the requirement that data be available on respondents' perceptions of the two candidates as well as on their own positions.

Candidate Image

As we have conceptualized candidate image, it consists of three components.[4] Two components are cognitive, including respondents' perceptions of the candidates' competence and leadership qualities, and respondents' perceptions of the more personal characteristics of the candidates. The third and final component is affective, referring to how respondents feel about the candidates as people. The first component, competence, represents perceptions of the candidates' personal characteristics that have a strong role component. We measured respondents' perceptions of the candidates' personal charac-

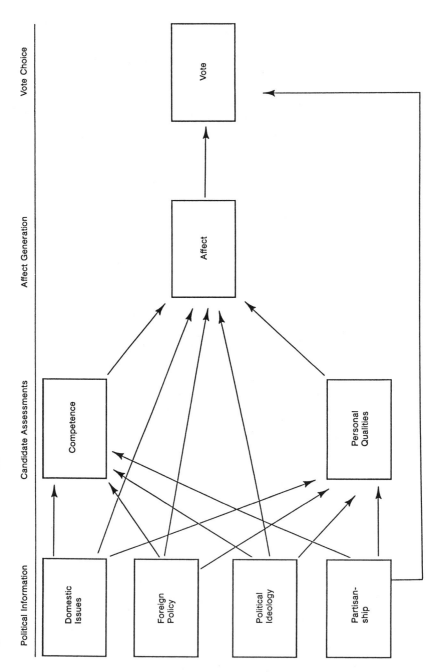

Figure 1. A Model of Candidate Appraisal

teristics that have a clear professional component by asking respondents to evaluate the candidates on three sets of adjective pairs: ineffective-effective, incompetent-competent, and strong-weak.

These adjectives were selected from the basic potency dimension from the original evaluative, potency, and activity (EPA) dimensions of person perception discussed by Osgood, Suci, and Tannenbaum (1957). They were selected because they have obvious connections to perceptions of how personal characteristics translate into professional competencies in high political office in the United States. Respondents undoubtedly react to candidates not only as people, but also as potential (in Reagan's case, actual) occupants of the presidential office. Thus the respondents' reactions to these adjectives represent a mixture of responses to the candidate as a person and more abstract judgments of how this particular candidate might perform in the role of president. Coefficient alpha for this scale, including these three measures, is .76 for Reagan and .78 for Mondale.

The second cognitive component of candidate image is constructed to be more purely personal and character-oriented. Respondents were asked to judge the candidates' personal qualities, measured by the following adjective pairs: trustworthy-untrustworthy, selfish-unselfish, and cool and aloof-warm and friendly. These particular perceptions are less affected by the nature of the political role than are perceptions of competence. We assume that most respondents, when asked to judge whether Reagan or Mondale is cool and aloof or warm and friendly, will react primarily on the basis of their judgments of the candidates' characteristics as persons, not as potential political leaders. Although these judgments are of a more personal nature, they are nonetheless grounded in the information available to the voter, much of which is expressly political. Images of candidates' personal characteristics are almost always created within an expressly political presentation of self and context. Therefore, this component of candidate image is also expected to be influenced by the exogenous, political variables. Coefficient alpha for scales based on these three items is .69 for Reagan and .63 for Mondale.

The last dimension of candidate image is affective. We asked respondents how they felt about each of the two candidates, by inquiring whether thinking about Reagan (and then Mondale) made them feel ashamed or proud, whether it made them feel relaxed and confident or tense and uneasy, and the extent to which they liked or disliked each candidate. These questions represent self-described emotional, or affective, reactions to the candidates as persons. Coefficient alpha for scales based on these three items is .90 for Reagan and .83 for Mondale.[5]

All of the adjective pairs are seven-point scales. Therefore, when combined to form three measures of candidate image, the resulting range of values for each measure is 3–21.

Other Measures

Party identification was measured with the usual seven-point scale, ideology was measured with the seven-point self-identification scale, and the vote was simply "who did you vote for in the 1984 election?"

RESULTS

We have argued that the decision-making process that most voters follow in arriving at a choice for president is comparative. In order to examine that claim, we tested the model illustrated in Figure 1 in several different ways. First, we used the simple values on each item or scale for each respondent and ran separate equations for Reagan and Mondale. In the Reagan equation, for example, the variables measure respondents' positions on domestic and foreign policy issues, their perceptions of Reagan's competence and personal qualities, their feelings toward Reagan, and the respondents' partisan and ideological self-images. The model was estimated first using perceptions of Reagan's character and then using perceptions of Mondale's character. The parameters from these "self-placement" models are not shown, but are available on request. Consistent with the claim that voters cue most heavily on the incumbent, the R^2 for the Reagan equations is generally larger than that for the Mondale equations. Consistent with information processing notions, voters had accumulated more information about Reagan because he was the incumbent.

Respondents' own attitudes on issues, however, are only one potential source of information. The political environment also provides information about the candidates' issue stands, partisanship, ideology, and so on. It is the proximity of the candidates' stands to the individual's own preferences, rather than these preferences per se, that relates the political information environment to individuals' perceptions of the competencies and personal qualities of the candidates. Therefore, we constructed distance measures for each candidate by taking the absolute value of the difference between respondents' own positions and their placements of the candidates on the same issue scales. The same was done for the ideology scale. The differences on issue scales were summed separately across the three domestic and two foreign policy issues and averaged, thus forming

Table 1. Adjusted R^2 for Various Models

| | Candidate Only: | | Full Candidate Comparison*: | | |
| | | | | High Sophisti-cation | Low Sophisti-cation |
	Reagan	Mondale	Whole Sample		
Dependent Variable in Equation†					
Competence:					
Adjusted R^2	.36	.40	.55	.57	.43
N	(1076)	(997)	(974)	(431)	(243)
Personal	.42	.16	.46	.45	.41
qualities:	(1015)	(921)	(897)	(395)	(222)
Affect:	.76	.67	.84	.85	.78
	(969)	(847)	(819)	(360)	(203)
Vote:					
Probit pseudo R^2	.82	.75	.87‡	.85	.88
Regression R^2	.70	.62	.70	.68	.69
	(1009)	(925)	(911)	(406)	(233)

*The last three columns are the results for the comparison scores, presented for the whole sample, the high-sophistication group, and the low-sophistication group.

†See Figure 1 for a listing of independent variables included in each equation.

‡94 percent of the two-candidate vote was correctly predicted by the probit model. The correlation between actual and predicted vote was .88.

two average-distance scales for each candidate. We estimated the model a second time, again separately for each candidate, using the issue and ideology distance scales. The adjusted R^2's for the four equations in these separate-candidate models are reported in Table 1.

We are able to explain a considerable amount of the variance in the competence and personal qualities equations for the two candidates, using the ideology and issue-distance scores as well as party identification (and more variation than when only self-placements were used), with one exception. The R^2 for the Mondale personal qualities equation is quite a bit smaller (.16) than that for the same equation for Reagan (.42). This suggests that the electorate's perceptions of Reagan as a person were structured largely by political predispositions, no doubt due to his status as the incumbent. Images of Mondale as a person, on the other hand, were less rooted in the political variables in our model and apparently derived on the basis of other aspects of the challenger's behavior. Both dimensions of the candidates' images—their professional competence and their personal qualities—were very powerful predictors of respondents' emotional reactions to the candidates, with the political variables explaining some of the remaining variation. For competence, the betas were .26 for Reagan and .31 for Mondale; for personal qualities, .34 for Reagan and .41 for Mondale.

Recall, however, the claim that voters attempt to arrive at a summary judgment of the candidates that in turn provides an efficient basis in deciding for whom to vote. This is, clearly, a comparative judgment, and the separate analysis of each candidate, reported above, is misspecified. Comparisons are made, of course, not only in judgments about issues and ideology, but also in the cognitive images and the feelings that voters develop about the two candidates.

Therefore, we developed a fully comparative model of candidate images. For this model, we constructed issue and ideological distance scores by subtracting the Reagan proximity scores from the Mondale proximity scores. For the ideology, foreign policy, and domestic issue scales, the relative distance scores could range from −6 to +6, with a score of 0 indicating a respondent equally close to the two candidates, a score of +6 indicating maximum distance from Mondale relative to Reagan, and a score of −6 indicating maximum relative distance from Reagan. Our assumption is that the farther individuals perceive themselves from a candidate, the less inclined they are to view him in a favorable light.[6] Similarly, we measured the perceived differences between the two candidates on competence, personal qualities, and affect. The scores were created by taking respondents' perceptions of Mondale on each scale and subtracting them from those of Reagan. The scores therefore represent the degree to which Reagan is perceived as more competent, as possessing more positive personal qualities, and as more affectively appealing than Mondale.[7] Both candidates may be perceived as competent, both as incompetent, or one as competent and the other as incompetent. Which of these conditions occurs most often in a particular election affects the importance of the competence dimension in arriving at feelings about the candidates and in deciding how to vote. A similar logic underlies the other distance and difference measures.

We estimated the model in Figure 1 using comparative differences for all of the variables except party identification and the vote.[8] As the results in Table 1 show, this improved the fit of the model significantly. The R^2's for leadership and for affect are increased the most by conceptualizing the entire decision-making process as a comparative one. Issue distances provide better explanations of perceived differences in competence than do isolated perceptions of Reagan's or Mondale's competence. In turn, perceived differences in competence and in the personal qualities of the candidates provide much better explanations of the differences in feelings toward the candidates than do isolated perceptions and feelings about one particular candidate, even the incumbent. The entire judgmental process appears to be comparative.

We earlier developed an information redundancy argument based on the simplicity of the decision-making task facing the voter. Information about the candidates is abundant and relatively cost-free. It is increasingly presented in formats that are at least marginally entertaining. We therefore do not expect the most highly involved and informed segments of the electorate to process information much differently from the less interested and informed segments. By definition, the more sophisticated are more interested, informed, and politically involved, but they must narrow their focus in roughly the same way that the less sophisticated do in order to cast a ballot. Both groups must arrive at some sort of summary, comparative judgment about how they feel about the two candidates—Do they feel better about Reagan or about Mondale? They then cast their ballots largely on this basis, all else equal. If the process we have outlined is at all characteristic, issues will be summarized and simplified into a series of judgments about the candidates, particularly with respect to their competence and their personal qualities. Regardless of whether these judgments are based on knowledge (or at least perceptions) of one or two key issues, or whether they are based on many issues, the information processing is similar, and the resulting judgments have the same status. It results in a set of summary perceptions that one candidate is more competent or possesses more favorable personal qualities than the other candidate. These in turn are summarized as a set of feelings—strongly defined by a like-dislike judgment—about the candidates, leading finally to a vote choice. The process therefore narrows the relevance for voting behavior of the initial gap in sophistication among voters.

To examine this thesis, we reestimated the four equations of the model for two groups of voters: those highest and those lowest in apparent political sophistication. The estimates for the whole sample and each subgroup are reported in Tables 2–5. The measure of high and low sophistication is based on respondents' levels of education, their knowledge about politics, and their expressed level of interest in politics.[9]

The results are largely supportive of this theoretical approach.[10]

Table 2. Competence Equation—Full Comparative Model

	Whole Sample B	Beta	High Sophistication B	Beta	Low Sophistication B	Beta
Domestic issues	.68 (.11)*	.21	.67 (.15)	.20	.62 (.23)	.18
Foreign issues	.88 (.09)	.29	.82 (.13)	.27	.83 (.19)	.27
Political ideology	.44 (.09)	.16	.49 (.13)	.18	.35† (.18)	.12
Party ID	.72 (.09)	.23	.71 (.13)	.23	.88 (.18)	.28
Constant	−.032‡		.251‡		−1.38‡	
Adj. R^2	.55		.57		.43	
N	974		413		243	

*Standard errors in parentheses
†Significant at .05 level; all other coefficients significant at $p < .05$
‡Not significant at .05 level

Table 3. Personal Qualities Equation—Full Comparative Model

	Whole Sample B	Beta	High Sophistication B	Beta	Low Sophistication B	Beta
Domestic issues	.66 (.10)	.25	.65 (.15)	.25	.85 (.23)	.26
Foreign policy	.45 (.09)	.18	.33 (.13)	.13	.50 (.19)	.18
Political ideology	.41 (.08)	.16	.42 (.13)	.19	.31* (.17)	.12
Party ID	.53 (.08)	.21	.50 (.13)	.20	.74 (.17)	.26
Constant	−1.89		−1.73		−2.98	
Adj. R^2	.46		.45		.41	
N	897		395		222	

*Not significant at .05 level; all other coefficients significant at $p < .05$

Table 4. Affect Equation—Full Comparative Model

	Whole Sample		High Sophistication		Low Sophistication	
	B	Beta	B	Beta	B	Beta
Domestic issues	.56 (.09)	.15	.41 (.13)	.11	.58 (.20)	.14
Foreign policy	.18 (.07)	.05	.22* (.11)	.06	.36 (.17)	.10
Political ideology	.34 (.07)	.11	.31 (.10)	.10	.33 (.14)	.10
Party ID	.47 (.07)	.13	.50 (.11)	.14	.53 (.15)	.15
Competence	.32 (.03)	.28	.36 (.04)	.31	.24 (.06)	.21
Personal qualities	.53 (.03)	.37	.52 (.05)	.36	.51 (.06)	.41
Constant	−1.59		−2.03		−1.64	
Adj. R^2	.84		.85		.78	
N	819		360		203	

*Significant at .05 level; all other coefficients significant at $p < .05$

Table 5. Vote Equation—Full Comparative Model

	Whole Sample		High Sophistication		Low Sophistication	
	B	Beta	B	Beta	B	Beta
Affect	.03 (.001)	.50	.03 (.002)	.48	.03 (.002)	.51
Party ID	.08 (.005)	.41	.08 (.009)	.40	.09 (.010)	.40
Constant	.174		.175		.171	
Adj. R^2	.70		.69		.69	
N	911		406		233	
	Probit Coefficients					
Affect	.22 (.019)	.67	.22 (.028)	.70	.24 (.040)	.69
Party ID	.34 (.040)	.32	.29 (.058)	.27	.43 (.086)	.34
Pseudo R^2	.87		.85		.88	

The unstandardized and standardized coefficients are reported on each variable for the three ways in which the fully comparative model was estimated, that is, for the whole sample and for the low- and high-sophistication groups. Because there are differences between the high- and the low-sophistication subsamples on several of the variances, when we compare the high and low groups, the discussion focuses on the unstandardized coefficients. In comparing the relative impact of one set of variables with another set within any one sample, we will focus on the standardized coefficients.

Examining the results in Table 2, the impact of issues on perceptions of competence is strong for both groups of respondents. The unstandardized coefficients for the high group are .67 for domestic issues and .82 for foreign policy issues; for the low group, these coefficients are .62 and .83. The near equivalence of these coefficients indicates that foreign and domestic issues were important to both groups. As can be seen by the betas, for example, the impact of issues nearly rivals or exceeds that of party identification on the comparative perceptions of candidate competence. The major conclusion to be drawn from these results is that comparative perceptions of candidate competence appear to be equally (and strongly) affected by issues for both groups of respondents.

Perceptions of competence are also affected by partisanship and by perceived differences in political ideology. Partisanship seems to have a somewhat stronger impact for the low group, whereas ideology has a slightly greater impact for the high group. But these differences are not substantial. In fact, comparative judgments of the competence of Reagan and Mondale—for both groups of respondents—appear to be first a function of foreign policy issues, second a projection of partisanship, and third a function of domestic issues. Ideology plays only a minor role. (See the standardized coefficients in Table 2 for these comparisons.) Individuals thus appear to have emphasized how the candidates would conduct themselves as leaders with regard to our nation's foreign and defense policies when they arrived at judgments of the candidates' personal competencies.

In the equation for personal qualities, the unstandardized coefficients for both foreign policy and domestic issues—as well as that for party identification—are greater for the low- than for the high-sophistication group (see Table 3). Thus issues appear to have a marginally greater role in determining the lower group's images of the candidates as people than is true of the higher group's images. But these differences are not as striking as the strong impact issues have for both subgroups, and this underlying similarity is the more important point. The standardized coefficients show that for the high group, domestic issues, ideology, and partisanship have approximately the same impact on comparative perceptions of personal qualities. For the low group, the conclusion is similar except that foreign issues appear to play a somewhat greater role than ideology.

In the affect equation, the impact of competence and of personal qualities, ideology, and partisanship all play a similar role for the high and low groups. Domestic and foreign policy issues have a greater impact in the low group, whereas perceptions of competence are more important to individuals with more political sophistication. Thus, in general, it appears that foreign policy perceptions are more important in the perceptual process for the less sophisticated respondents, in comparison to the more sophisticated group, a somewhat surprising twist. Political ideology is more important to the highly sophisticated respondents in perceptions of the candidates' competencies and personal qualities (see Tables 2 and 3), although the impact of ideology is nearly even for both groups in the affect equation. In 1984, the candidates took clearly distinct positions on foreign policy issues, particularly on the defense spending issue. Our results suggest that less sophisticated voters could readily detect this difference, but that ideological information was less important to them than to the more highly sophisticated members of the electorate. Thus, although the focal point and perspective may differ somewhat between our two groups of respondents, the redundancy in the political information environment makes for a candidate appraisal process that, we argue, is quite similar for the two groups. Note that in Table 4, the relative impact of personal qualities on affect is greater than the impact of competence.[11] This suggests that feelings about the candidates are more firmly grounded in reactions to the candidates as people than they are in reactions to the candidates' competencies. Issues, ideology, and partisanship play little direct role, although they do shape perceptions of competence and personal qualities.

Finally, the vote equations were estimated twice, once using regression analysis and once using probit analysis. These results are presented in Table 5.[12] The impact of affect and partisanship on voting behavior is quite similar for the two groups. Furthermore, within each group, these two variables appear to have very similar impacts on voting, so that partisanship and feelings about candidates (as a summary of perceptions of competence, personal qualities, and issues) are equally important proximal determinants of voting behavior. The correlation between predicted and actual vote was .88, quite high by most standards. Feelings about the candidates appear to be a very powerful summary of other perceptions and attitudes that influence political behavior such as voting.[13]

Our central point is that there are generally small differences in the fit of the model or in individual parameter estimates between the more and less sophisticated respondents. The R^2 values reported in Table 1 show an equally good fit for the four equations in the two groups, with the exception of a somewhat lower R^2 value for the leadership equation for the low-sophistication group. Major individual differences with respect to political sophistication do not generally appear in the assessment of presidential character nor in the relationship between comparative judgments of character and the vote. In both cases, we suggest, complex and redundant information is simplified to make the act of voting a relatively easy task.

SUMMARY

Our theoretical account of the candidate appraisal process is composed of three key elements. First, we have argued that the process of forming assessments of the professional and personal qualities of candidates plays a central role in determining the final vote decision. In our view, person-oriented responses to presidential candidates are neither idiosyncratic nor superficial. Rather, such assessments are grounded in daily processes of impression formation and are, in fact, quite reasonable given the nature of the judgment task and of the information environment. The presidential campaign is, after all, a contest between two highly visible people. The campaign itself and the media that cover the campaign make person-related information easily available and thus highly accessible. This availability, together with the fact that individuals naturally make personality judgments every day, serves to make personal assessments of candidates ubiquitous and unavoidable.

Ordinary processes of impression formation, however, are not directly transferred to the political domain. The political context works, we believe, to modify the process of character assessments in important ways. The use of certain kinds of personality constructs becomes more crucial and more appropriate to the task of choosing the country's leader than it does in assessing character in other daily contexts. In this vein, we have argued that individuals structure their assessments of the candidates' professional qualities in broad terms of political leadership and competence. In turn, these judgments are related to such political variables as partisanship, issue positions, and ideology. Individuals also develop candidate assessments that are more personal in nature. These more personal assessments also are related in part to political variables appropriate to the task of assessing two people running for the presidency, but as our results for Mondale show, they can be derived from other sources as well. The role of these other types of information in character assessments may be more important when candidates are less well known to voters as political figures. Recent research on the presidential nomination campaign (Aldrich, Lin, and Rahn, 1987; Rahn, 1987; Bartels, 1988) has begun to explore this issue.

The political setting of presidential campaigns creates what is fundamentally a choice problem. Thus, the process of impression formation is, from the beginning, a task that must result in a choice between two individuals. This setting means that candidates will be evaluated and comparatively assessed on the key dimensions of competence and personal qualities. We have argued, therefore, not only that the voter must ultimately decide which candidate is the better choice, all things considered, but also that he or she forms assessments of both candidates' leadership abilities and personal qualities. In turn, these assessments lead potential voters to develop feelings about both candidates, and these affective summaries then form the basis for voters' decisions.

We have also suggested that individual differences in political expertise, although important in some kinds of tasks, do not result in different processes of candidate appraisal for two reasons. First, assessment of the personal qualities of individuals occurs naturally and spontaneously in the social world. When confronted with a similar task in politics, individuals will rely on these regularly employed strategies, regardless of their abstract knowledge of or interest in politics. We do not suggest, however, that presidential elections are superficial personality contests. Indeed, the political basis of voters' judgments provides a second rationale for not expecting subgroup differences in the candidate appraisal process. Individuals do have a variety of sources of information to draw upon to make character assessments, information that is explicitly political in nature. Some of this political information, notably partisanship, is conveyed as strong, clear, and simple informational cues. Other information, such as the issue positions of candidates, is quite consistent across issues, especially in 1984. Knowledge of even one or two issue positions would therefore lead most people to the same assessment as would one based on substantial knowledge about many issue positions. An important feature of the full set of information is that much of it is redundant; that is, partisanship, ideology, and the issue positions of the candidates all generally point in the same direction, reinforcing one another and thus the assessments to which they are related. Therefore, individuals may attend to any or all of these sources to guide their assessments and, in many cases, would be led to the same assessments from each source. The result is a candidate assessment process that is remarkably similar across different strata of the electorate.

In this chapter we have placed the candidate appraisal process in a broader theoretical framework by drawing on a perspective derived from research on social cognition. We have extended the work of others in several ways. First, we have argued that the electoral setting makes the candidate appraisal process a comparative one, and we have seen that a model based on comparative judgments outperforms models based on separate assessments of the individual candidates. Second, we have related the model of comparative character assessments to important political variables, illustrating the inherently political nature of such judgments, and we have completed the model by demonstrating its very strong relationship to the vote decision. Finally, in support of our arguments about the repetitiveness of the information environment and about the regularity with which people make character assessments, we have found variations in political expertise to be of strikingly little importance.

NOTES

We would like to thank William Flanigan, Shanto Iyengar, and John Kessel for their comments on an earlier draft of this discussion. This research was supported by a grant from the National Science Foundation, NSF/SES-8410618, to Aldrich, Borgida, and Sullivan. The Foundation and commentators bear no responsibility for the results reported in this paper.

1. Recall that the analyses of both Lau and Miller, Wattenberg, and Malanchuk were based on the open-ended, like-dislike questions. Respondents' comments to these questions may reflect what type of information is most accessible in memory to the individuals at that moment, but may not necessarily reflect the full range of information available to the voters for their judgments about the candidates.

2. At the individual level, the process leading to these affective responses can be understood in terms of several models of social information processing (e.g., Wyer and Srull, 1986). In a general model like the two-stage "schema-triggered affect" model proposed by Fiske and Pavelchak (1986), for example, initial categorization and schematic processing of the target individual is followed by an affect-generation stage. Affective responses to the target may be cued by a broader social category label (e.g., "Democrat" or "conservative"), or they may reflect a summary impression based on an

attribute-by-attribute appraisal of the target's personal qualities and competencies. Affective responses are "category-based" in the former mode and "piecemeal" in the latter mode of processing, according to the schema-triggered affect model. Although the predominant mode of processing may vary by the type of electoral setting, our view of candidate appraisal in presidential elections would suggest that affective responses in this context primarily reflect category-based processing. Thus, successfully categorizing a candidate as competent or trustworthy leads to a quick affective response, rather than this response being based on the sum of the valences associated with each aspect of the candidate's behavior that led to the category-based inferences.

3. Political feelings and emotions are under increasing scrutiny by political scientists, many of whom are beginning to suspect that we have seriously underestimated their role in the understanding of political behavior. See Conover and Feldman (1986), Marcus (1986), and Chubb, Hagen, and Sniderman (1986).

4. Earlier work on the semantic differential by Osgood, Suci, and Tannenbaum (1957) reveals three independent dimensions of person perception: the evaluative (E), potency (P), and activity (A) dimensions. Their research suggests, however, that in the political arena, these dimensions tend to collapse into one overarching perceptual dimension. Watts (1974) shows that the (E) and (A) dimensions converge and are correlated with the (P) dimension when people perceive political objects. This research on the dimensions of perception did not relate the dimensions to voting or to candidate assessment in the way we do, but it did influence our efforts to conceptualize and measure candidate images.

5. We are making a conceptual distinction among the three components of candidate image. The three sets of measures for each candidate are, of course, highly correlated, although they probably share some method covariance which, when partialed out, would reveal greater distinctiveness among the components.

6. Thus, by construction, all signs of the coefficients for the political variables are expected to be positive in the comparative model.

7. Perceptions of candidates' positions on issues and ideology may be subject to misperception bias or a projection effect. If so, the direction of causality assumed here may be questioned. To investigate this possibility we reran our model substituting the sample median placements of the candidates on issues and ideology scales for the respondents' reported perceptions. In estimating this model, the impact of comparative ideological distance was reduced, while that of party identification was increased slightly. The parameter estimates of the two issue variables were essentially unchanged. Overall, the adjusted R^2's were about 10 percent lower in the competence and personal qualities equation. The results can be used to infer some, but relatively minor, amounts of rationalization. Therefore, these results, by themselves, do not seriously contradict the direction of influence specified in our model. With candidates as distinctive as Reagan and Mondale on so many dimensions, we

believe that individuals' perceptions of their positions had a substantial basis in reality, certainly in comparison to, for example, the similarity and ambiguity that characterized Humphrey and Nixon on the Vietnam War in 1968, as analyzed by Page and Brody (1972).

With a cross-sectional (and postelection) "snapshot" of a dynamic process, it is, of course, exceedingly difficult to disentangle empirically what may be the mutually causative nature of our major variables. Nothing in the theory prohibits nonrecursive relationships, but we believe in principle that the process occurs as modeled. If our model is misspecified, it is not in its failure to specify nonrecursive links; rather, the absence of time-series data makes it impossible to include individuals' initially diffuse reactions to candidates, which are then interpreted with political information to form the more abstract and structured judgments of the candidates that are modeled in our equations.

8. The party identification scale already incorporates a comparative judgment because the two parties are implicitly compared. Thus this measure is in fact similar to the others used in our comparative model.

The reliabilities (coefficient alpha) for the difference scores are as follows: domestic policy .60; competence .84; personal qualities .78; and affect .92. Because foreign policy is measured by two variables, coefficient alpha is undefined.

9. A sophistication index was constructed by summing respondents' level of political interest (3-point scale), years of education (8-point scale), and number of correct answers to four general political knowledge questions. Those who scored 8 or less (on the 15-point index) were put into the low-sophistication group (36.2 percent of the sample), while those who scored 11 or higher (39.3 percent of the sample) were put into the high-sophistication group. Although this measure is less than ideal, experimental studies (e.g., Hamill and Lodge, 1986) have shown that cognitive ability and political experience are important components of political sophistication.

10. The four equations were estimated for three groups of respondents: the whole sample and the high- and low-sophistication groups. The number of respondents in the high group ranged from 360 in the affect equation to 431 in the competence equation. The number in the low group ranged from 203 in the affect equation to 222 in the competence equation. The total sample size was 1,509, of which 819 appear in the affect equation and 974 in the competence equation.

The high-sophistication subsample started with 594 respondents and the low-sophistication subsample started with 543 respondents. The number of cases for the low group was reduced considerably because of nonvoting, and also because of missing data on some variables. So the proportion of missing cases is much higher for the low group, and the resulting estimates, which are based on the low group, are not necessarily representative of all low-sophistication voters. They represent the low-sophistication voters able to answer our questions about issues and candidates, and who, in the vote equation, also reported having voted for Reagan or Mondale. In an effort to retain as many cases as possible in order to reduce the possibly unrepresentativeness of the low-sophistication group, the issue distance measures were calculated for all respondents who could place themselves and the candidates on at least one issue. That is, the respondents' distance scores were based on the number of issues on which there was complete information. This procedure helped us to retain cases, although the failure to perceive positions for candidates did eliminate quite a few respondents. In addition, we estimated each equation separately (using listwise deletion for missing data) in order to retain as many cases per equation as possible. Consequently, the results in Tables 2–5 cannot be interpreted in path-analytic terms. We did run the model as a full system, where a case having missing data on any variable in the full system, including vote choice, was eliminated for all equations. The results were virtually identical to those reported here.

11. This difference is underestimated because the reliability for personal qualities is lower than that for competence. A correction for measurement error would therefore undoubtedly increase the importance of personal qualities relative to competence in determining feelings about the candidates.

12. The results from the regression analysis and the probit analysis cannot be directly compared. The standardized and unstandardized regression analogues are reported.

13. The results in Table 5 were initially estimated with an equation that included all possible recursive paths. In the vote equation, ideology had a small impact on the vote for the more sophisticated group, while foreign policy issues had a small effect for the less sophisticated group. However, neither personal qualities nor competence was significant, and thus affective reactions to the candidates fully capture perceptions of professional and personal qualities.

7

Shortcuts to Political Knowledge: The Role of Selective Attention and Accessibility

Shanto Iyengar

How do people understand the world of public affairs and go about choosing among candidates, parties, or policies? To what degree are these choices informed, and on what information do they rest? These questions are basic to theories of citizenship and representative government. In this chapter, I argue that contrary to much conventional wisdom, the average citizen is far from overwhelmed by the issues, events, and personae that enter and leave the political stage. By resorting to various simplifying strategies, people wrestle the "booming, buzzing confusion" of politics into meaningful information and, in so doing, provide themselves with the "intelligence" to formulate their political preferences and decisions.

The argument that individuals cope with complexity by simplifying is hardly novel. From Simon's pioneering work on "satisficing" (1945) to Tversky and Kahneman's "cognitive heuristics" (1974), the common denominator of judgment and decision-making research has been the pervasive use of intuitive and informal over rigorous and systematic solutions to decision or choice problems. People settle for acceptable rather than optimal strategies, strategies that economize effort and are simple to apply (for reviews of the various strands of decision making and judgment research, see Einhorn and Hogarth, 1981; Kahneman, Slovic, and Tversky, 1982; Abelson and Levi, 1985).

So it should be in politics, which, for most of us, is a mere sideshow to the more pressing affairs of daily life. Rather than attempting to monitor the course of public affairs vigilantly, citizens turn to shortcuts that provide them with a more efficient means of making choices and decisions. In this chapter, I focus on two such shortcuts—selective attention and the accessibility bias.

SELECTIVE ATTENTION

To attend to all aspects of public life is physically impossible and would paralyze even the most motivated of citizens. The human organism has the capacity to register only a tiny handful of the stimuli it encounters (for a good description of the limitations of the attentional system, see Dodd and White, 1980). Most aspects of political life pass by unnoticed most of the time. Now and then, some issue or event overshadows all others and is noticed by almost everyone. Under ordinary circumstances, however, political attention is discretionary. Thus, although some people may be highly attentive to news of the stock market, others may be on the lookout for developments in Central America. Information about public affairs is, therefore, likely to be domain-specific; how much one knows (in the factual sense of the term) depends on the particular subject-matter domain. The more relevant some domain is to the individual, the higher the level of information concerning that domain. Stock market analysts may be experts on the state of the economy, yet totally in the dark about Nicaragua. In sum, rather than acquiring information about all things political, individuals specialize in particular domains.

Evidence of Selective Attention to Politics

For evidence concerning selective attention to politics, I turn to a series of experiments into the effects of television newscasts on individuals' perceptions of political issues. Participants in these experiments were residents of New Haven, Connecticut, who responded to newspaper and other advertisements promising payment in return for participation in "media research." In the course of these experiments, we assessed how much our participants knew about various national issues such as unemployment, arms control, pollution, and civil rights. Typically, we asked three or four questions about each issue under investigation and then summed the number of "correct" responses to form indices of issue information. Examination of these indices suggested considerable specificity: individuals relatively informed about a particular issue were not necessarily informed about other issues.[1] How much one knew about national defense, for instance, was not a particularly good predictor of how much one knew about inflation or the environment. As Table 1 reveals, the amount

Table 1. Relationships (r^2) Between Issue Information Indices

Experiment 1			Experiment 2			Experiment 3		
Defense			Unemployment			Arms Race		
Inflation	.14		Civil Rights	.23		Unemployment	.16	
Energy	.06	.16	Social Security	.20	.11	Civil Rights	.35	.36
N	139			111			63	

of shared variance among the various information indices was modest, ranging between .07 and .36, and averaged .20.

For further evidence of selectivity in political attention, I turn to an analysis of what people remember from television news programs. As Converse (1962) demonstrated, old information attracts new information. If the selective attention postulate holds, it follows that people will be more able to remember news accounts of those issues about which they are already relatively informed.

In our three experiments, we exposed participants to either a single newscast or a week-long sequence of daily newscasts into which we inserted a number of news stories covering a particular issue. In the post-test (sometimes administered immediately following the viewing of the newscast and sometimes one day later), we asked participants to list as many news stories as they could from the newscast(s) they had watched. We then counted the number of stories that people recalled bearing on the particular problem emphasized in the news. To the degree that political attention is selective, we should find that individuals who were relatively informed about a particular issue at the outset will recall more news stories about that issue, but not more stories about other issues. As shown in Table 2, with isolated exceptions this is precisely what we found.

Consider the case of the unemployment condition in Experiment 3. Here the effects of unemployment information, civil rights information, and arms control information on recall of unemployment news stories diverged markedly. Although information about unemployment boosted recall of unemployment stories powerfully, neither civil rights nor arms control information had any effect on recall of unemployment news. For eight of the nine experimental conditions, the results were identical: viewers more informed about the problem emphasized in the newscasts retained more information about that issue and that issue alone. In fact, in some instances information about an issue other than that emphasized in the newscasts actually decreased recall of news about the target issue. Thus, viewers

Table 2. Effects of Issue Information on News Recall*

| | | | | | Number of Stories Recalled | | | | | | |
| | Experiment 1 | | | | Experiment 2 | | | | Experiment 3 | | |
	De-fense	Infla-tion	En-ergy		Unem-ploy-ment	Civil Rights	Social Secu-rity		Unem-ploy-ment	Arms Race	Civil Rights
Defense	.09 (.07)	.01 (.12)	.12 (.14)	Unem-ploy-ment	.51 (.19)	.20 (.20)	.10 (.21)	Unem-ploy-ment	.53 (.28)	−.23 (.20)	−.34 (.21)
Inflation	.12 (.08)	.30 (.14)	.31 (.14)	Civil Rights	.41 (.26)	.27 (.14)	.19 (.15)	Arms Race	.10 (.22)	.32 (.15)	.28 (.16)
Energy	.06 (.08)	.12 (.09)	.12 (.12)	Social Security	.12 (.16)	.04 (.15)	.33 (.17)	Civil Rights	.16 (.30)	.08 (.15)	.30 (.22)
N	45	46	48		41	37	33		21	20	22

*Table entries are unstandardized regression coefficients (ols) with their standard errors in parentheses.

who were relatively informed about civil rights in Experiment 2, and who watched a number of stories on social security and unemployment, could recall fewer unemployment and social security stories than viewers who knew less about civil rights. In sum, the evidence is quite strong: people acquire information in domains about which they are already relatively informed.

In addition to these experimental studies, I conducted a random telephone survey of Suffolk County, New York, residents in July 1985. Respondents were asked a battery of information questions on a range of topics including the state of the economy, civil rights, the Middle East, Central America, and the political party affiliation of various social and occupational groups ("group politics"). The specific questions used are listed in the Appendix. A total of 143 individuals were interviewed; for details on the survey design, see Iyengar, 1985.

Information scores corresponding to the number of correct answers were formed for each domain and then regressed against each other. The adjusted R^2's were .13, .27, .43, .44, and .48 for group politics, the economy, Central America, the Middle East, and civil rights information, respectively. The political affiliations of groups were by far the most distinct of the domains. Economic information was also distinct from the other domains, whereas the three remaining domains were more general, with approximately one-half their variation being shared.

More relevant than these R^2's is the extent to which the five indices have common antecedents. A battery of media exposure, social background, and political involvement indicators was used to predict each of the information indices. To the extent that political information is domain-specific, the number of uncommon antecedents should be high. That is, the groups most informed about civil rights should *not* be the groups that are also most informed about the economy. Conversely, to the degree political information is global, the same predictors should apply in each information domain. Table 3 provides the relevant evidence.

Not a single antecedent was common to all five subject-matter domains. The antecedents with the widest reach included attentiveness to media coverage of public affairs and professional occupation, both of which raised the level of information in four of five areas. Males, readers of the *New York Times*, respondents who report discussing politics frequently, Democrats, and Independents all had higher information scores for three of the five indices.

Evidence of domain specificity was considerable. Respondents who watch television news frequently were relatively informed only about the economy. Jews tended to know more about the Middle East, and blacks were more informed than whites about civil rights, a difference that was reversed for information about Central America and the Middle East. Another such reversal occurred with age differences—older respondents knew more about the economy and civil rights, less about group politics.

If one examines the list of antecedents, it is apparent that the two domains with the greatest overlap are Central America and the Middle East, both of which are foreign affairs issues. Similarly, the most distinct index is group partisanship, which is the only domain that does not tap "issue" information. In short, the greater the similarity between any two domains, the more likely individuals are to acquire information about both, and vice versa.

My final evidence bearing on domain-specific versus global political information comes from a national survey of voting-age Americans. The 1985 Pilot Study, conducted by the Center for Political Studies at the University of Michigan between November 1985 and January 1986, included a series of political information questions. The questions fell into four broad domains: foreign affairs, the economy, civil rights, and group politics.

For each domain I computed indices of information and then assessed the degree of overlap. The selectivity argument predicts only modest convergence between levels of information in different subject-matter domains. The adjusted R^2's derived from regressing each information index against the remaining indices were .39, .34,

Table 3. Antecedents of Political Information: Suffolk County Survey*

		Subject-Matter Domain			
	Economy	Central America	Middle East	Racial Discrimination	Group Politics
Attentiveness to public affairs news	—	.37 (.27)	.22 (.08)	.21 (.10)	.19 (.12)
NY Times readers	.77 (.23)	.56 (.22)	.33 (.23)	—	—
Readers of other newspapers	—	—	−.30 (.29)	—	—
News magazine readers	—	.38 (.21)	.26 (.22)	—	—
Regular TV news watchers	.11 (.11)	—	—	—	—
Frequency of political discussion	.28 (.23)	.47 (.21)	.27 (.23)	—	—
Professionals	.59 (.24)	—	.26 (.21)	.67 (.23)	.47 (.28)
Housewives	−.43 (.33)	−.35 (.29)	—	—	—
Clerical workers	—	—	—	.46 (.31)	—
Blue-collar workers	.75 (.34)	—	—	—	—
Protestants	.42 (.22)	—	—	—	—
Jews	—	—	.31 (.20)	—	—
Whites	—	.29 (.24)	.86 (.29)	−.51 (.34)	—
Males	.30 (.23)	—	.43 (.20)	.26 (.22)	—
Age	.01 (.01)	—	—	.02 (.01)	−.02 (.01)
Democrats	.33 (.21)	—	—	.74 (.29)	—
Republicans	—	—	.51 (.21)	—	—
Independents	—	.38 (.21)	.29 (.24)	.91 (.30)	—
Nonpartisans	—	—	—	—	−1.29 (.34)
Level of political activity	—	.27 (.09)	—	—	.16 (.13)

*N = 143. Entries are unstandardized regression coefficients (ols) with standard errors in parentheses.

.28, and .23 for foreign affairs, civil rights, the economy, and group politics, respectively. Clearly, a good bit of the variance in these information measures was specific or unique. I also assessed the relative fit of a one-factor (general information) and four-factor (domain-specific information) model using confirmatory factor analysis (Lisrel VI). Although both models yielded a significant goodness-of-fit (as indexed by $X^2/d.f.$), the fit was clearly superior when four factors were specified. Thus, the $X^2/d.f.$ ratio dropped from 4.45 to 2.12.

Each of the four indices was then examined for traces of common or specific antecedents. If information is the product of selective attention, individuals more informed about a particular issue should not also be more informed about other issues. The best-fitting set of antecedents for each information index is provided in Table 4.

Education and gender differences were common to all four domains, as was liberal self-identification. College graduates, males, and individuals calling themselves liberals were more informed about everything. Individuals who more frequently monitor mass media coverage of political campaigns were more informed about three of the four domains, the exception being civil rights. Respondents' race also affected three indices, with whites being more informed than blacks. On civil rights information, however, this difference was reversed.

Six antecedents—age and level of political participation, and being Catholic, Hispanic, or a housewife, and calling oneself a conservative—predicted two of the four indices. The remaining six differences were specific. Democrats and people more interested in politics were more informed about group politics; Republicans and the more affluent were more informed about foreign affairs; those who discuss politics often were more informed on race; and poor people were significantly less informed on economic matters.

Of all our results, these are the least congruent with the selective attention argument. The more educated, males, and liberals have more information about a variety of political domains. At the same time, a substantial number of antecedents apply to only one or two of the domains. Education is clearly a vital cognitive resource associated with both greater exposure to the information flow and greater ability to assimilate new information. If we exclude education from consideration, the average number of information domains affected by the antecedents is only 1.8.

To summarize, the evidence, although not entirely unequivocal in the case of the 1986 national survey, is generally supportive of the selective attention argument: information holding and recall both reveal traces of subject-matter specificity. Additional evidence bearing,

Table 4. Antecedents of Political Information: NES Pilot Survey*

Predictor	Subject-Matter Domain			
	Foreign Affairs	Economy	Race	Group Politics
Males	.98	.51	.31	.49
	(.13)	(.09)	(.10)	(.14)
College graduates	.90	.46	.98	.41
	(.17)	(.11)	(.12)	(.18)
< 11th grade	−.94	−.69	−.72	−.74
	(.32)	(.23)	(.24)	(.34)
Liberals	.64	.32	.18	.54
	(.18)	(.13)	(.13)	(.22)
Conservatives	—	.38	—	.59
		(.10)		(.16)
Democrats	—	—	—	.49
				(.15)
Republicans	.31	—	—	—
	(.14)			
Political activity[1]	—	.08	—	.12
		(.04)		(.07)
Exposure to media coverage of the campaign[2]	.22	—	.15	.17
	(.07)		(.05)	(.07)
Discusses politics frequently	—	—	.22	—
			(.11)	
Interest in the campaign[3]	—	—	—	.21
				(.15)
Age	.01	.02	—	—
	(.00)	(.00)		
Blacks	−.46	−.61	.46	—
	(.25)	(.18)	(.18)	
Hispanics	—	−.54	—	−.90
		(.25)		(.40)
Catholics	.43	—	—	.42
	(.15)			(.17)
Housewives	.37	—	.26	—
	(.21)		(.16)	
High income (> $35,000)	.34	—	—	—
	(.14)			
Low income (< $10,000)	—	−.40	—	—
		(.12)		
N	343	343	345	345

*Entries are unstandardized regression coefficients, with standard errors in parentheses.
1. Composite index based on V5411-12, V5414-16.
2. Composite index based on exposure to television, radio, magazine, and newspaper coverage of the campaign (V5102, V5104, V5106, and V5108 all scored 1 (yes) and 0 (all others).
3. "Very much interested" versus all others (V101)

albeit indirectly, on the specificity versus generality of political information will be presented in the next section, where I turn from what people know to what they consider when evaluating their president and choosing among political candidates.

Although selective attention is a means of limiting what one takes in, the accessibility bias is a shortcut for retrieving information from memory. Accessibility influences what people take into account and what they ignore when choosing among products, friends, job offers, or political candidates.

Obviously, many different schemes for weighting the factors and criteria go into the making of a decision or choice. The accessibility bias refers to the general tendency of individuals to attach greater weight to considerations that are, for whatever reason, momentarily prominent or salient. More salient cues exert significantly greater effects on choices than equally relevant but less accessible cues, a pattern that has been documented in an impressive range of subject-matter areas (for representative research of this genre, see Taylor and Fiske, 1978; Wyer and Srull, 1981; S. Taylor, 1982; Higgins, Bargh, and Lombardi, 1985).

Accessibility can have many sources. In the world of politics, where citizens are at the mercy of the media, sheer frequency of news coverage would seem to be a critical determinant of what is more or less accessible. To the degree that individuals are fed a steady diet of information about terrorist acts, terrorism will be a relatively accessible issue, and beliefs or opinions about terrorism will be accorded more weight when one thinks about the strengths and weaknesses of political candidates than when terrorism is ignored in media public affairs presentations.

Accessibility may also be determined by individual rather than contextual characteristics. Some individuals may retrieve information about the economy when choosing among candidates, while the threat of war may come to mind more readily for others, irrespective of how much media play the economy and international conflicts receive. One way at getting at such chronic as opposed to sporadic (such as media-induced) differences in accessibility is to return to our indicators of domain-specific information. People particularly attuned to civil rights, for example, not only acquire more information about civil rights, but they are also more likely to use this information when making political judgments or choices. This may be for motivational reasons—they care passionately about equal rights—or because they find civil rights a relatively accessible domain. That is, because they have more stored information about civil rights than other issues, civil rights information is more easily retrieved.

In sum, we have two tests of the accessibility bias. First, individuals will weight issues more heavily when these issues receive considerable media attention. Second, individuals will weight subjects about which they are relatively informed more heavily than subjects about which they know little.

Evidence of Accessibility Effects in Presidential Evaluations and Candidate Preferences

In the course of our experimental investigations of the impact of television news on public opinion, Donald Kinder and I uncovered striking evidence consistent with the first prediction. Generally speaking, we found that sustained news coverage of a particular issue had the effect of boosting the impact of viewers' assessments of how well the president had handled that particular issue on their assessments of the president's overall performance in office, that is, the standard popularity question. We termed this effect *priming*. When people are primed with news about the state of the economy, their economic beliefs, opinions, or policy preferences exert a strengthened impact upon their evaluations of candidates or their voting choices.

I have no wish to burden the reader with the procedural intricacies of our experiments into priming. The manipulations were highly realistic, however. Participants watched one of the network national newscasts each day for a week. The newscasts were unobtrusively edited to provide systematic experimental variation in the coverage accorded particular issues. The news stories making up the "treatment" were themselves actual stories previously broadcast, which had been edited to erase any tell-tale temporal markers. Participants in these experiments represented a fair cross-section of New Haven and were totally innocent of our interventions until we debriefed them following the end of the study (for details on our design and procedures, see Iyengar and Kinder, 1987).

In one such experiment we created three experimental conditions corresponding to heavy coverage of civil rights, unemployment, and the nuclear arms race, respectively. Participants randomly assigned to one condition watched one story on civil rights or racial discrimination each day; a second group watched newscasts that paid special attention to unemployment; the third group received sustained coverage of the spiraling arms race. Each condition was characterized not only by heavy coverage of the target problem, but also by systematic exclusion of news about the two other problems. Thus each condition served as a control group for the others.

One day after the final newscast, participants completed a lengthy post-test in which were embedded several questions probing their assessments of President Ronald Reagan's overall performance in office, his competence and integrity, and his performance with respect to various national issues including those under investigation.

To test for the accessibility bias in evaluations of Reagan's performance, we assessed the degree to which assessments of his performance with respect to each target issue were weighed more heavily by individuals for whom the issue was more accessible, that is, those primed with news coverage of the issue. Thus, people who saw a steady stream of stories about unemployment should weigh their assessments of how well or badly Reagan had dealt with unemployment more heavily when considering his overall performance than should people who saw a steady stream of arms race stories and no stories on issues such as unemployment. We tested this hypothesis by estimating the following equation:

$$
\begin{aligned}
\text{Overall Performance Rating} = a + \\
b_1 \text{Performance Rating on Arms Control)} + \\
b_2 \text{(Performance Rating on Arms Control} \times \\
\text{News Coverage of Arms Control)} + \\
b_3 \text{(Performance Rating on Unemployment)} + \\
b_4 \text{(Performance Rating on Unemployment} \times \\
\text{News Coverage of Unemployment)} + \\
b_5 \text{(Performance Rating on Civil Rights)} + \\
b_6 \text{(Performance Rating on Civil Rights} \times \\
\text{News Coverage of Civil Rights)} + e
\end{aligned}
\tag{1}
$$

News coverage of each target problem is a dummy variable scored 1 for viewers who saw sustained news of the problem and 0 for all others. The coefficient b_1, for example, represents the weight individuals granted the president's performance on arms control under conditions of no news coverage (low accessibility). The interaction coefficient b_2 indicates the weight granted the president's performance on arms control under conditions of heavy coverage (high accessibility). The estimates are provided in Table 5.

As Table 5 shows, the weight accorded assessments of Reagan's performance in civil rights, unemployment, or arms control was much

Table 5. Accessibility Effects in Evaluations of President Reagan's Overall Performance

		Issue Emphasized in Experimental Newscasts		
		Arms Control	Civil Rights	Unemployment
Impact of issue performance ratings on overall performance ratings:				
Low accessibility		.03	.24*	.37†
High accessibility		.49†	.68†	.83†
Adjusted R^2	.71			
N	59			

Table entries are unstandardized regression coefficients, estimated from equation (1); *$p < .05$; †$p < .01$ (reprinted from Iyengar and Kinder, 1987, p. 68).

greater when the news dwelled on these subjects. Among viewers who saw no coverage of arms control, assessments of Reagan's arms control performance were quite irrelevant to assessments of his overall performance ($b_1 = .03$). But among viewers who witnessed several accounts of the spiraling arms race and the Reagan administration's opposition to arms control, assessments of Reagan's arms control performance were highly relevant ($b_2 = .49$). The contrasts are not quite so striking for civil rights and unemployment because these issues are weighed relatively strongly even without the benefit of media priming. Nonetheless, the pattern is impressive: the more prominent an issue in the national information stream, the greater the weight granted that issue when individuals evaluate the president.

The effect was replicated in several of our experiments, with both good news and bad news, for Democratic and Republican presidents, across a wide range of issues, for assessments of the president's overall performance as well as his competence and integrity (although to lesser degrees in the area of personal traits), and in analyses that controlled for the possibility of "halo effects" whereby participants adjust their assessments of the president's performance on some specific issue to be consistent with their overall liking for the president (for details, see Iyengar and Kinder, 1987). In short, the effect is extremely robust.

In the course of our television news research, we also pursued the possibility that voters' preferences for political candidates would similarly be subject to an accessibility bias. One of our experiments was timed to coincide with the 1982 congressional election. This particular study was the brainchild of Roy Behr, who designed and carried it out as part of his Ph.D. dissertation research at Yale University.

In this experiment, participants (all of whom were registered to vote) watched a week-long sequence of local newscasts immediately before the election. The newscasts were edited to vary the degree of coverage accorded the two candidates and the degree of coverage accorded the national economy. More specifically, Behr created three conditions. In the first, participants watched one story each day on the contestants—Bruce Morrison the Democratic challenger and Lawrence DeNardis the Republican incumbent. These stories provided information on the candidates' issue positions, the groups that had endorsed them, their career histories, and personal backgrounds. In the second condition, in place of stories on the candidates, participants watched stories about the national economy. Most of these linked the upcoming election with Ronald Reagan's economic programs. Thus one story featured a speech by the president urging voters to "stay the course," while another suggested that Democrats were anticipating significant victories because of the high level of unemployment nationwide. Finally, participants assigned to a third condition constituted a neutral or baseline comparison group. They watched the same sequence of newscasts, but purged of all reference to the candidates, the economy, or the campaign in general.

The objective of Behr's experiment was to assess the degree to which media attention altered the weights accorded the candidates and the economy as criteria for voting. The prediction was that perceptions of the admirable personal qualities of the two candidates would be accorded more weight when the news highlighted the candidates. Participants were asked, "Is there anything in particular you like about Larry DeNardis? What?" They could list up to three characteristics. The same question was asked with respect to Morrison. The number of positive qualities seen in Morrison was then subtracted from the number of positive qualities seen in DeNardis. Second, we expected that beliefs about the economy would be strengthened as antecedents of candidate evaluations when the news featured the state of the economy. Here we used an index of economic optimism/pessimism that reflects the degree to which participants felt the nation's economy had improved or worsened over the past year, whether they felt it would improve or worsen still further in the year to come, how participants evaluated Reagan's performance in "handling the economy," and finally, whether they felt economic problems could be handled better by Democrats than Republicans. Finally, we hypothesized that viewers given no information about the economy or the candidates would fall back on partisanship and incumbency as criteria: Democrats would prefer Morrison, Republicans would prefer De-Nardis, while those who could name DeNardis but not Morrison (a measure of the incumbency advantage) would vote for the former (for additional details on any of these measures, see Iyengar and Kinder, 1987; for information on the design and procedures, see Behr, 1986).

We assessed participants' candidate preferences by asking them to rate both Morrison and DeNardis on a 100-point "feeling thermometer." The higher the thermometer rating, the more positive the evaluation of the candidate. As a measure of "net" preference, we subtracted the Morrison rating from the DeNardis rating. The thermometer scores are in fact excellent surrogates for voting intention as fifty-five of the fifty-six participants intended to vote for the candidate they rated more positively. We were able to contact twenty-eight of the participants following the election to ask them for whom they had voted. Twenty-six of them voted in line with their thermometer ratings.

The predictions were tested by estimating the following equation:

$$\begin{aligned}
\text{DeNardis Rating} - \text{Morrison Rating} = b_0 + \\
b_1(\text{Party Affiliation}) + \\
b_2(\text{Recognition}) + \\
b_3(\text{Index of Economic Optimism/Pessimism}) + \\
b_4(\# \text{ of "Likes" for DeNardis} - \\
\# \text{ of "Likes" for Morrison}) + \\
b_5(\text{Index of Economic Optimism/Pessimism} \times \\
\text{Economy Condition}) + \\
b_6(\# \text{ of "Likes" for DeNardis} - \\
\# \text{ of "Likes" for Morrison} \times \text{Candidate Condition}) + \\
b_7 \text{ Party Affiliation} \times \text{Control Condition}) + \\
b_8(\text{Recognition} \times \text{Control Condition}) + \\
b_9(\text{Candidate Condition}) + \\
b_{10}(\text{Control Condition}) + e
\end{aligned} \tag{2}$$

In this equation, b_1, b_2, b_3, and b_4 measure the baseline effects of party identification, recognition, economic beliefs, and perceptions of the candidates, respectively. The coefficient b_5 captures the increased weight accorded economic beliefs when the news covers economic conditions. Likewise, b_6 measures the increased weight granted the number of "likes" by participants in the candidate condition. Finally, b_7 and b_8 assess the degree to which partisanship and name recognition are granted more weight among participants in the control condition.

The results, shown in Table 6, provided strong evidence for our first two predictions, but only partial support for the third. Economic beliefs predicted candidate preferences powerfully, regardless of experimental condition. Even when not presented with economic news, voters more optimistic about the economy favored DeNardis by a wider margin than voters who were more pessimistic. However, among participants in the economy condition, the impact of economic beliefs on the difference in the thermometer ratings more than tripled. An even stronger boost emerged with respect to participants' perceptions of the candidates. Those who saw more positive qualities in Morrison than in DeNardis felt less warmly toward the latter, independent of the condition to which they were assigned. But when voters were primed with news about the candidates, this same effect was increased nearly fivefold.

Contrary to our third prediction, incumbency and party did not both exert stronger effects among voters not primed with news about the economy and the candidates. Viewers were influenced by the relative visibility of the candidates; however, this incumbency advantage was not accentuated among viewers who watched no news of the economy or the candidates.[2]

In short, the congressional election experiment demonstrates that the considerations voters take into account when choosing between candidates can be significantly influenced by matters of accessibility. When people are reminded of economic conditions, their perceptions of the economy become more important as criteria; when they see a lot of the candidates, their impressions of the candidates become more important. Depending upon the mix of forces at work in a campaign, effects such as these can prove decisive.

News coverage is but one, albeit a very important, source of information accessibility. Individuals may also invoke a built-in accessibility heuristic by which they consult categories or subject-matters about which they are relatively expert when making their political choices. Put differently, the more one knows about any given political domain, the more accessible that domain for use in making choices or decisions. In short, people use what they know. Individuals relatively informed about economic affairs will rely on economic considerations to a greater degree than individuals relatively informed about foreign affairs or other noneconomic domains. It is possible to test

Table 6. Accessibility Effects in Congressional Vote "Choice"

	DeNardis–Morrison Thermometer Rating
Effects of economic assessments:	
Low accessibility	3.08*
High accessibility	10.49†
Effects of candidate images:	
Low accessibility	6.45†
High accessibility	31.07†
Effects of recognition:	
Low accessibility	10.22†
Adjusted R^2	.63
N	52

Table entries are unstandardized regression coefficients estimated from equation (2); *$p < .05$; †$p < .01$ (reprinted from Iyengar and Kinder, 1987, p. 103).

for such "chronic" differences in accessibility by returning to the measures of domain-specific information incorporated into the 1985 National Election Studies (NES) National Pilot Study (for a discussion of chronic differences in accessibility, see Bargh, 1984).

Recall that the pilot study included measures of economic, foreign affairs, and racial information. In addition, respondents were asked the standard NES knowledge questions concerning the partisan control of the House and Senate before and after the election. I will treat this four-item index as a measure of general political information, information that is not specific to a particular issue.

With these measures of political information in hand, the critical prediction can be stated as follows. Using race as the example, people relatively informed about race will cue off racial considerations when evaluating the president to a greater degree than people less informed about race, and this difference will be greater than that associated with greater and lesser levels of general information. Thus, the effects of one's opinion concerning the role of the federal government in helping minority groups on one's evaluation of Ronald Reagan should be significantly strengthened by the index of racial information, and this opinion-information interaction should be stronger for domain-specific than for general information.

I used respondents' ratings of Reagan on the feeling thermometer as the dependent measure in the analyses that follow. Essentially identical results were obtained using respondents' reports of their vote in the 1984 election (respondents in this survey were a random subset of respondents interviewed in 1984) and using the difference between their 1984 thermometer ratings of Reagan and Mondale. The critical test of the chronic accessibility prediction involves specification of the following two equations:

$$\begin{aligned}
\text{Reagan Evaluation} = b_0 + \\
b_1(\text{Republicans}) + \\
b_2(\text{Democrats}) + \\
b_3(\text{Opinion}_i) + \\
b_4(\text{Information}_i) + \\
b_5(\text{Opinion}_i \times \text{Information}_i) + e
\end{aligned} \tag{3}$$

and

$$\begin{aligned}
\text{Reagan Evaluation} = c_0 + \\
c_1(\text{Republicans}) + \\
c_2(\text{Democrats}) + \\
c_3(\text{Opinion}_i) + \\
c_4(\text{Opinion}_i \times \text{General Information}) + \\
c_5(\text{Opinion}_i \times \text{General Information}) + e
\end{aligned} \tag{4}$$

Subject-matter domains are represented by i and consist of race, the economy, and foreign affairs. Equation (3) thus matches opinions and information within a particular domain, and the coefficient b_5 gauges the domain-specific interaction, for example, the strengthening of the effects of an opinion in some particular domain on evaluations of Reagan induced by information about that domain. The coefficient c_5 measures the same interaction, this time between an opinion within some domain and a measure of general information. The expectation, of course, is that b_5 should consistently exceed c_5.

The value of these comparisons depends, of course, upon the availability of opinions or beliefs within the four information domains. Ideally the test should be carried out with opinions that fall within one and only one of the subject-matter domains. At the very least, the test should be run with opinions/beliefs that are more relevant to one of the domains than the others. I chose the following opinion items to represent the three issue domains. The items are ordered in terms of their "fit" to each domain.

Race

1. A two-item composite index measuring support for affirmative action programs (additional information concerning these and all other items used in this analysis is provided in the Appendix).

2. Respondents' positions on the "help minorities" issue scale.

3. Respondents' approval/disapproval of Ronald Reagan's handling of relations between blacks and whites.

4. A two-item index measuring perceptions of the desirability of federal actions to promote equal rights.

5. Respondents' approval/disapproval of Ronald Reagan's handling of relations with South Africa.

Foreign Affairs

1. Respondents' approval/disapproval of Ronald Reagan's handling of relations with other countries.

2. Respondents' opinions concerning U.S. strength in the world.

3. A two-item index measuring concern over the possibility of war.

4. Respondents' opinions concerning which political party would be more likely to keep the country out of war.

5. Respondents' preferences for internationalism over isolationism (coded 1 for the former and 0 for all others).

6. Respondents' positions on the "get tough" with the USSR issue scale.

7. Respondents' positions on the "U.S. role in Central America" issue scale.

Economy

1. A three-item composite index tapping respondents' perceptions of changes in the health of the national economy over the past year.

2. Respondents' opinions of whether the economic policies of the federal government are responsible for the current state of the economy.

3. Respondents' positions on the "guaranteed jobs" issue scale.

4. Respondents' approval/disapproval of Ronald Reagan's handling of the economy.

5. Respondents' approval/disapproval of Ronald Reagan's handling of the federal budget.

Table 7. "Chronic" Accessibility Effects in Evaluations of President Reagan: Racial Information versus General Information*

	Interaction Effect Associated with:	
Predictor	Racial Information	General Information
Support for affirmative action	1.36 (.39)	.53 (.35)
"Help minorities" issue scale	2.49 (.96)	2.17 (.93)
Approval/disapproval of Reagan's handling of civil rights	1.39 (.68)	1.64 (.64)
Support for federal action to promote equal rights	.85 (.49)	.36 (.43)
Approval/disapproval of Reagan's handling of U.S. relations with S. Africa	1.10 (.68)	.86 (.58)

*Table entries are unstandardized regression coefficients corresponding to b_5 and c_5 in equations (3) and (4). Both information indices scored from 0 to 3 and positive coefficients indicate a strengthening of the effect of the opinion in question. N ranges from 273 to 336.

The results of the domain-specific versus general information tests for race are presented in Table 7. The entries correspond to the interaction coefficients b_5 and c_5 in equations (3) and (4).[3]

Virtually every interaction term is robust, suggesting that racial opinions are generally apt to enter the political calculations of the more informed whatever the measure of information. Note, however, that the domain-specific interactions generally exceed the general information interactions. In the case of support for affirmative action and federal actions on behalf of equal rights, the difference is considerable. The effects of these opinions are significantly strengthened by racial information and only marginally strengthened by general information. On the whole, Table 7 suggests that racial considerations are more influential cues for evaluating President Reagan among both those more informed about racial matters and those more informed about the outcome of the congressional elections, but that the difference between the more and less informed is noticeably greater in the case of racial information.

Turning to foreign affairs (Table 8), the results are mixed. Foreign affairs information wins the interaction contest clearly in only two instances—respondents' concern over war and their belief about

Table 8. "Chronic" Accessibility Effects in Evaluations of President Reagan: Foreign Affairs Information versus General Information*

Predictor	Interaction Effect Associated with:	
	Foreign Affairs Information	General Information
Approval/disapproval of Reagan's handling of foreign policy	.85 (.44)	.96 (.40)
Concern over war	.80 (.27)	.29 (.26)
Perception of party more likely to avoid war	.71 (.47)	.42 (.48)
Internationalism	− 1.16 (1.81)	− 1.14 (1.79)
"Get tough with the Soviets" scale	.41 (.43)	.76 (.48)
"U.S. role in Central America" scale	.05 (.81)	1.15 (.73)

* Table entries are unstandardized regression coefficients; both information indices scored 0–4. N ranges from 250 to 336.

which party is more capable of avoiding war. That is, foreign affairs information boosts the impact of these beliefs on evaluations of Ronald Reagan to a greater degree than does general information. The remaining four comparisons, however, yield no support for the domain-specificity hypothesis. The domain-specific and general interaction terms are roughly equal with respect to respondents' evaluations of Reagan's foreign policy performance. Neither index of information influences how much weight the isolationism question exerts on the Reagan feeling thermometer. Finally, general information tends to be more effective in boosting the effects of the "get tough with the Russians" and "U.S. role in Central America" issue scales.

In considering these results, it must be allowed that foreign affairs is a highly diffuse subject-matter domain. It is difficult for individuals to pay attention to all matters pertaining to foreign affairs. It is more plausible to expect that·some Americans will pay particular attention to particular aspects of foreign policy or world affairs, for example, the Middle East, Central America, and the threat of nuclear war. In the case of respondents' concern over war, for instance, an information index formed by adding responses to the Weinberger and NATO information items (both defense-related) induced significantly stronger interaction effects than those associated with either foreign affairs information or general information. In short, foreign affairs may be too general a subject-matter domain with which to test the domain-specificity argument.

Finally, Table 9 presents the comparisons between domain-specific and general information in the area of economic beliefs. Generally, the results reveal no traces of domain-specificity in evaluations of Ronald Reagan. The degree to which beliefs and opinions regarding the economy affect evaluations of the present are influenced neither by how much respondents know about the economy nor by how much they know generally. In fact, economic information tends to weaken rather than strengthen the impact of economic beliefs on evaluations of Reagan.

Examination of the baseline effects of these economic beliefs/opinions sheds some light on the recalcitrance of these results. In general, the baseline effects are very strong, indicating that all respondents, whatever their level of information about the economy, weighed economic considerations heavily when evaluating the president. Given the degree to which the economy had been the focal point of the Reagan administration's actions and rhetoric, and its prominence in the 1984 presidential campaign, it is plausible to assume that the economy was an accessible subject-matter domain even to respondents with little economic information. That is, the prominence of the economy in the information environment may have neutralized built-in differences in accessibility, thus producing the weak interaction coefficients associated with degree of economic information.[4]

In sum, we find strong chronic accessibility effects associated with racial information, only modest effects associated with foreign affairs information, and none at all in the area of economic information. Foreign affairs may be too broad a domain in which to search for accessibility effects while the prominence of the economy in 1986 made economic beliefs relatively accessible to Americans of all levels of information.

Even allowing for the mixed results from the NES Pilot Study, the balance of evidence presented here indicates that individuals do not consider everything they know that bears on a particular political evaluation or choice. When rating how well the president has performed and when choosing between candidates they rely heavily on factors that happen to be accessible.

Table 9. "Chronic" Accessibility Effects in Evaluations of President Reagan: Economic Information versus General Information*

	Interaction Effect Associated with:	
Predictor	Economic Information	General Information
Perceptions of national	.24	.12
economy	(.32)	(.25)
Blame federal economic	−.59	.59
policies	(.70)	(.63)
Approval/disapproval of	−.28	.63
Reagan's handling of economy	(.63)	(.48)
Approval/disapproval of	−.89	.65
Reagan's handling of budget	(.66)	(.55)
"Guaranteed jobs" scale	−.67	.25
	(.69)	(.55)

*Information indices scored from 0 to 3. N ranges from 309 to 329.

CONCLUSION

Political choice is inherently reductionist. Citizens simply do not have the means to grapple with the full range of contemporary public issues. Yet the exercise of citizenship demands that the complexity of public affairs be somehow overcome. Selective attention and the accessibility bias are two convenient means for doing so. The important question is how well these shortcuts serve citizens' interests and help them realize the "right" choices. Would a voter acting according to selective attention and accessibility arrive at the same result if endowed with perfect information about the choice options?

Selective attention and accessibility would both serve voters' personal interests well to the degree that their attention and information-retrieval processes are need-relevant. If individuals more readily focus on and can retrieve from memory information about issues or subjects that impinge on them directly, or for which they have strong preferences, it would be tantamount to their choices being influenced by issues or subjects about which their concern is greatest.

There is considerable psychological evidence to suggest that attention and memory are indeed enhanced when information is personally relevant (for reviews see Kuiper and Rogers, 1979; Higgins, Kuiper, and Olson, 1981; Ostrom, Pryor, and Simpson, 1981). In this sense, selective attention and accessibility are functional, guiding voters to those domains in which they need information.

When accessibility is determined by factors extraneous to the individual's concerns or needs, as is obviously the case with media-induced accessibility, the possibility that individuals will be deflected from their personal concerns is significant. To the degree the media stress issues or events that individuals are ordinarily unconcerned about, it is likely that these issues will be accorded more weight than they would be, given individuals' natural (e.g., selfish) inclinations and predispositions. Put differently, to the extent accessibility is externally contrived, issues that impinge on personal interests will be less likely to dominate voting choices. This may be the process underlying the "sociotropic" voting phenomenon (see Kinder and Kiewiet, 1979). That is, information about the state of the national economy may prove more accessible to voters during campaigns than information about their personal economic circumstances and is therefore weighed more heavily.

The normative implications of media-induced accessibility effects are unclear. Insofar as voters become less personal and more national in their perspective, the democratic process is enhanced. However, the question of which particular national considerations the media make more accessible is critical here (for a general discussion of this issue, see Behr and Iyengar, 1985). Do the issues raised by the media correspond to the issues raised by the parties and candidates? If this correspondence is loose, the democratic process is distorted. Voters are not only deflected from their personal interests, but are also led down an illusory path, one defined by organizational, commercial, or other such determinants of news coverage.

It would seem desirable that Manichean conceptions of the informed citizen be abandoned. Discussions of the democratic process that assume a citizenry well informed on a multitude of subject-matters are as unrealistic as characterizations of the electorate as political ignoramuses, vulnerable to the most blatant of manipulations. As I have tried to show in this chapter, citizens can live up to their civic obligations, not by totally immersing themselves in politics, but by narrowing their field of vision and allowing their choices to be heavily influenced by considerations that happen to be most accessible.

Appendix

The indices of political information used in my analysis of the 1985 NES Pilot Study are based on items that John Zaller and I developed. Based on preliminary analyses, I constructed indices of racial, foreign affairs, economic, and group politics information. Racial information was measured by asking respondents to identify Thurgood Marshall, the NAACP, and affirmative action. Economic information consisted of questions asking respondents to indicate the current inflation and unemployment rates, and a question on whether the federal deficit had increased or decreased since Reagan was first elected. Foreign affairs information included identification of NATO and questions concerning India, Poland, and the United Nations. Finally, the group politics index was based on respondents' abilities to identify the party usually supported by blacks, poor people, stock brokers, and corporate executives.

In the case of the Suffolk County pre-pilot survey, we included questions tapping information about the Middle East, Central America, race, the economy, and group politics. In the case of the Middle East, respondents were asked to identify Yasser Arafat, Amin Gemayel, and the PLO. The Central America index consisted of three similar identification items with Daniel Ortega, the Contras, and the U.S. position in the Nicaraguan conflict as the targets. The racial, economic, and group politics indices were equivalent to those used in the NES Pilot Survey.

The predictors used in Tables 7–9 were based on the following variables (numbers refer to the NES Codebook identification).

Race

Support for affirmative action (V7423 + V7427)
Help minorities issue scale (V7311)
Approval/disapproval of Reagan's handling of relations between blacks and whites (V8418)
Desirability of federal equal rights action (V7416 + V7418)
Approval/disapproval of Reagan's handling of relations with South Africa (v8420)

Economy

Economic perceptions index (V436 + V424 + V438)
Blame federal economic policies (V441)
Guaranteed jobs issue scale (V5839)
Approval/disapproval of Reagan's handling of the economy (V8414)
Approval/disapproval of Reagan's handling of the budget (V5441)

Foreign Affairs

Approval/disapproval of Reagan's handling of relations with other countries (V8416)

U.S. world strength (V443)
Index of concern of war (V444 + V445)
Which political party will handle the problem of keeping U.S. out of war in the next four years (V446)
Internationalism versus isolationism (V5848)
Get tough with the Soviets issue scale (V740)
U.S. role in Central America issue scale (V7303)

NOTES

The research reported in this chapter was supported by several organizations, including the National Science Foundation, the Board of Overseers of the National Election Studies, the Block Fund of Yale University, and the State University of New York. Portions of this chapter are based on collaborative research. I am grateful to Donald R. Kinder, Roy L. Behr, and the University of Chicago Press for permission to use these results here.

1. In strict terms, how much information individuals have about political issues can reflect not only differences in attention, but differences in information retrieval as well. Those who are relatively expert on the economy may have their information organized to facilitate retrieval. For others this information may be "lost" in long-term memory, even though the information was attended to initially. My use of the term *selective attention* is quite loose and does not distinguish between selective attention and selective memory. To do so would require physiological indicators such as pupil dilation and galvanic skin response found to be associated with attention (e.g., Kahneman, 1973).

2. In addition, we found that party identification had no direct role in shaping candidate preferences. Once we took into account economic beliefs, the image of the candidates, and the relative familiarity of the candidates, viewers' party identifications did not affect their thermometer ratings. Party identification did have strong indirect effects, however, significantly influencing both voters' assessments of economic conditions and their impressions of the candidates. Democrats were much more pessimistic about the economy (the correlation between partisanship and the index of economic optimism/pessimism was r = .55) and had more nice things to say about Morrison than DeNardis (r = .36). Thus party identification did contribute to voting preferences, albeit indirectly. Moreover, these indirect effects were strengthened when the mediating considerations (i.e., economic beliefs and candidate images) were made more accessible.

Thus the effects of party identification on assessments of the economy were greater among participants assigned to the economic condition. Similarly, the partisan differences in viewers' relative appraisals of the candidates increased when the newscasts focused on the candidates. Both these effects can be represented by interaction terms, the first between party identification and assignment to the economic condition, with assessments of the economy being the dependent variable. This interaction approached significance ($t < .18$). The second interaction consists of party identification and assignment to the candidate condition, with the difference in the number of "likes" mentioned being the dependent variable. This interaction was marginally significant ($t < .10$).

3. These results are taken from a more comprehensive analysis that compares the effects of domain-specific and general political information using two different methods of measuring domain-specific information and two measures of general information (see Iyengar, 1986).

4. Whether political knowledge is domain-specific or general is obviously relevant to the measurement of knowledge. Diverging perspectives on this question are provided by Zaller (1986a) and Iyengar (1986).

8

The Cognitive Mediators of Political Choice: Toward a Comprehensive Model of Political Information Processing

Victor C. Ottati
Robert S. Wyer, Jr.

Early approaches to understanding the determinants of voting behavior emphasized the role of global demographic variables. According to the Columbia School (cf. Lazarsfeld, Berelson, and Gaudet, 1944), a person's voting preferences could be adequately predicted from three background characteristics: socioeconomic status, religious affiliation, and residence locale (i.e., urban or rural). As political research continued to develop, political behavior theorists began to focus on the more immediate psychological determinants of political choice. For example, the Michigan School (Campbell, Converse, Miller, and Stokes, 1960) construed the determinants of political choice as a "funnel of causality" in which demographic characteristics (e.g., socioeconomic status) affected people's attitudes toward the candidates and their parties, and these attitudes, in turn, determined their voting intentions. Goldberg (1966) introduced a similar conceptualization.

Major advances have been made in acquiring a fundamental understanding of the dynamic psychological processes that underlie political decision making (e.g., Converse and Markus, 1979; Markus and Converse, 1979; Lodge and Hamill, 1986; Miller, Wattenberg, and Malanchuk, 1986). Many of these advances reflect an interest in the cognitive mechanisms that may underlie the acquisition and use of information in formulating political judgments and decisions. We believe that research stimulated by this concern will ultimately lead to a conceptualization of political decision making that incorporates and substantially elaborates upon both of the earlier approaches.

The shift in emphasis exemplified by the cited work has been accompanied by a corresponding shift in the focus of social psychological research and theorizing over the past decade. Social psychologists have become increasingly dissatisfied with simply identifying the situational and individual difference variables that influence judgment and behavior. This dissatisfaction has stimulated attempts to understand the cognitive processes that mediate the influence of these variables and to determine how these processes may operate in combination to affect behavior and judgments (for reviews of current research and theory in social information processing, see Wyer and Srull, 1984; Sorrentino and Higgins, 1986). These processes include (a) the interpretation and organization of information in terms of previously acquired concepts; (b) the integration of this information with prior knowledge to form a cognitive representation of the person, object, or event to which it is relevant; (c) the storage of this representation in memory; (d) its later retrieval (perhaps along with other cognitive material) for use in making a judgment; (e) a construal of its implications for this judgment; and (f) the generation of an overt response. Much of the previously noted work in political psychology bears directly on several of these processes. To appreciate more fully the importance of this work and the future directions it may take, it is useful to place the phenomena considered in the context of a more general conceptualization that incorporates all of the aforementioned stages of social information processing.

Before embarking on a discussion of specific stages of processing, we should mention three important considerations that come into play at several different stages. First, a person's information-processing capacity is limited. It is often difficult if not impossible for people to think extensively about all of the information they receive, or the prior knowledge they have acquired, that might potentially be relevant to a judgment or decision. And even when it is possible, people are often unmotivated to engage in this extensive cognitive work. Instead, they may employ shortcuts, or cognitive "heuristics," that are likely (although not guaranteed) to produce effective judgments and decisions. The use of heuristics appears to be evident at all stages of processing. For example, people often interpret a stimulus in terms of the first applicable concepts that come to mind, ignoring other possible interpretations. Similarly, people who make a decision or judgment do not usually perform an exhaustive search of memory for all of the decision-relevant knowledge they have accumulated. Instead, they base their judgments on only a small subset of their knowledge that happens to be most accessible. Finally, when people are required to use the knowledge they have recalled to make a judgment, they usually do not perform a rigorous analysis and integration of its various implications. Rather, they employ simplifying rules of thumb to arrive at judgments that may or may not be the same as those they would draw if a more analytic process were used (cf. Sniderman, Griffin, and Glaser, chapter 5 of this volume; for more general discussions of heuristics in judgment, see Kahneman, Slovic, and Tversky, 1982; Sherman and Corty, 1984).

The second consideration takes on particular importance in light of the first. That is, the concepts that people bring to bear on the processing of information they receive, and the cognitive operations they perform on it, may often depend on the purpose for which they expect to use this information. (For a more complete discussion of the role of goals in social information processing, see Srull and Wyer, 1986.) Individuals may respond quite differently to information about a politician's stand on a social issue if their goal is to form an impression of this politician than if they are simply trying to understand what the politician is trying to say or to form a coherent impression of the events and issues being discussed. Under these latter conditions, information may be organized in terms of some politically relevant group or location (e.g., Russia or Nicaragua) or some other politically relevant concept domain (e.g., the state of the economy). These different processing objectives will influence where the information is stored in memory, and therefore whether it is likely to be later recalled at the time a judgment or decision is made. The potential influence of information-processing goals on responses to information and their impact on political judgment will continue to be emphasized throughout this chapter.

The third consideration concerns the possibility that judgments and decisions are influenced not only by the descriptive features of the information one receives about a person or object, but also by the emotional reactions one experiences in the course of processing the information en route to a judgment. This influence may occur at any of several stages. For example, concepts associated with the affect one happens to be experiencing at the time information is received may influence the interpretation of this information. Moreover, one's affective reaction to the information or the person to whom it refers may be included as a feature of the mental representation that is formed on the basis of the information. Finally, the affect one experiences at the time a judgment is made may be used as an indication of how one feels about the object being judged, and therefore it may have a direct, "informational" influence on the judgment. These possibilities will be elaborated in the context of the discussion to follow.

With these considerations in mind, we now turn to a more detailed discussion of the various stages of information processing that underlie the acquisition and use of information to make political decisions. We first identify some of the general phenomena that may occur at each stage and indicate some of their possible implications. Then, we consider a few of the variables often postulated to influence these judgments and decisions and indicate the way in which they may affect processing at several different stages. In doing so, we do not pretend to do justice to the many theoretical and empirical issues that might conceivably be raised. Our objective is simply to show that by considering the factors that may affect political judgment within a general information-processing framework, several additional hypotheses arise concerning the nature of these effects and the conditions in which they occur. More generally, we hope to convey that this conceptual approach, exemplified by much of the previously cited work, may ultimately provide a more complete understanding of the dynamics of political decisions than was possible through the more traditional approaches noted at the beginning of this chapter.

INFORMATION-SEEKING, ENCODING, AND INTERPRETATION

General Considerations

Different people are exposed to different types of political stimulus information. To some extent, the type and amount of political information available to a person are a function of the social milieu in which a person resides. By emphasizing the role of background characteristics, the Columbia School was essentially suggesting that an individual's social environment provides a biased set of political stimulus information. In addition, an individual may either actively seek or avoid exposure to different political environments. Previous research in nonpolitical domains suggests that individuals tend to seek out stimulus information consistent with their prior knowledge and expectations (Snyder and Swann, 1978; Wyer, Strack, and Fuhrman, 1984). This suggests that a Democrat, for example, is likely to seek out pro-Democratic information at the expense of pro-Republican information. This selective information seeking may be the result of behavioral decisions that occur before any information is presented.

Selectivity may also occur at the time information is received. However, the mechanisms underlying it are theoretically somewhat different. The information we actually receive about a political figure can be of several types and is transmitted in a variety of modalities. For example, it may consist of either the politician's statements and behavior or others' reactions to the person. The information may be communicated in a news or magazine article or in a televised speech or press conference. In the latter case, the information is partly non-verbal. That is, it often includes not only what the individual says, but also his or her manner of conveying it, as well as facial expressions. Moreover, information in the latter media is transmitted very quickly, so that the recipient has limited time to think about any particular statement made. In these circumstances, a question arises about what factors determine the particular subset of information that is attended to and how this information is interpreted. There are likely to be few general answers to this question. However, some guidelines may be established that permit one to conceptualize possible contingencies in the conclusions that can be drawn from any particular set of data.

People who receive information about a political figure's issue position must initially interpret it in terms of previously acquired concepts that are applicable to it. These concepts include general trait concepts that are applied to the speaker. Others pertain to the situation or issue to which the speaker's statement or behavior is relevant. Moreover, the interpretation of the information is often ambiguous; that is, more than one concept could potentially be applicable. For example, the stance of a president who announces that he is sending military aid to the government of a third-world country could be interpreted as either "firm" or "belligerent." Alternatively, it could be interpreted as an indication that the country's government is "anti-communist," "weak," or "friendly to American business interests."

As we have noted, however, not all of the possible interpretations of the information are equally likely to be considered. This is particularly true when the total amount of material presented exceeds the individual's processing capacity. In such instances, only a small subset of applicable concepts may be applied, those that happen to come to mind at the time the information is received. This has two, somewhat different, effects:

1. *Selective encoding.* Aspects of the information interpretable in terms of concepts that are easily accessible at the time the information is presented may be encoded in terms of these concepts. In contrast, those aspects that cannot be interpreted in terms of equally accessible concepts are often ignored. Consequently, the particular concepts that happen to be most easily accessible at the time information is presented may bias the subset of this information that is encoded and retained in the mental representation that is formed from it.

2. *Interpretation of ambiguous information.* When a given piece of information can be interpreted in terms of more than one concept,

the applicable concept that is most easily accessible in memory is the most likely one to be applied. Thus, the concepts applied are restricted to those whose features partially match features of the information to be comprehended. When different concepts match equally well, however, the most accessible concept will be used.

Research performed outside the political domain provides evidence of both types of effects. In the first regard, Wyer, Srull, Gordon, and Hartwick (1982) found that when subjects read a description of two boys' activities at one of the boys' homes and had a certain goal in mind (e.g., that of either a potential home buyer or a potential burglar), they later showed better recall of those features particularly relevant to the goal they were assigned. Likewise, Lingle and Ostrom (1979) found that when subjects were given trait adjective descriptions of a person with instructions to decide if the person was suitable for a particular occupation, subjects showed better recall of adjectives that were relevant to the occupation than adjectives that were irrelevant. In a quite different study, Bower, Gilligan, and Monteiro (1981) induced subjects to feel either happy or sad when they read a story about two persons. Subjects later showed relatively better recall of those features of the story that could be interpreted in terms of concepts that were presumably activated at the time the story was received. This selective encoding at the time of input affected the likelihood that the information was retained in long-term memory.

Evidence that ambiguous information is interpreted in terms of whatever concepts happen to be easily accessible in memory at the time the information is received is found in numerous studies of "priming" effects (for reviews, see Higgins and King, 1981; Wyer and Srull, 1981; Bargh, 1984). For example, Srull and Wyer (1979, 1980) initially had subjects perform a sentence construction task that required the use of concepts associated with hostility. Later, in an ostensibly unrelated situation, subjects were asked to form an impression of a person based on descriptions of behaviors that were ambiguous with respect to the hostility (e.g., "refused to pay the rent until his landlord painted his apartment"). Subjects' judgments of the target's hostility increased with the frequency and recency with which they had presumably used this concept in the earlier "priming" task. Although this situation is somewhat artificial, other studies (cf. Higgins and Chaires, 1980; Carver, Ganellen, Froming, and Chambers, 1983) have found analogous effects of activating concepts on subjects' behavior in both problem-solving situations and interpersonal interactions.

It is important to note, however, that these effects occur only when the relevant concepts are activated at the time the information is received. There is little if any evidence that concepts activated *after* information is presented affect either the recall of the information or its interpretation.[1] In the studies by Bower, Gilligan, and Monteiro (1981) and Wyer, Srull, Gordon, and Hartwick (1982), for example, goals and mood states that were induced after subjects read the information had no influence on the type of information they recalled subsequently. Similarly, Srull and Wyer (1980) found that activating trait concepts after ambiguous behavioral information had been presented had no influence on either the interpretation of these behaviors or on judgments of the person who performed them (see also Massad, Hubbard, and Newtson, 1979). These results indicate that the concepts activated at the time information is first received are critical. Once the material is interpreted and stored in memory, information-relevant concepts that are activated subsequently have very little effect.

Determinants of Concept Accessibility

As implied by the research summarized above, the particular concepts that are brought to bear on the encoding of information may be influenced by a variety of situational and individual difference factors. Some of these factors may be fortuitous, as Srull and Wyer (1979, 1980), Martin (1986), and others have found. However, Bargh (1984) and others have found evidence that certain concepts may be "chronically" accessible to some persons by virtue of their backgrounds, goals, or life circumstances, and that these concepts may influence the interpretation of information as well. Wyer and Carlston (1979), for example, describe findings that indicate students' interpretations of an ambiguous social situation were based on concepts that were particularly relevant to their majors in college. Bruner (1951), Klinger (1975), and others have also obtained evidence that persons' goals and values have an influence on the interpretation of the information they receive (for a review of this research, see Srull and Wyer, 1986).

A variety of sociological factors (e.g., socioeconomic status, religion, and residence locale) and individual-difference characteristics may produce chronic differences in accessibility of concepts used to encode political information. Clearly, level of education affects the degree and quality of comprehension. Also, expertise in a given area should enhance category accessibility and comprehension for information that is relevant to this area. Thus, the effects reported by Iyengar (chapter 7, this volume) may be partially rooted in differences in processing that occur at the stage of comprehension and encoding.

More transitory goals that exist at the time people receive information may also influence its encoding into memory. The afore-mentioned studies by Wyer, Srull, Gordon, and Hartwick (1982) and by Lingle and Ostrom (1979) are cases in point. A potentially more important goal from the perspective of political judgment was iden-tified by Higgins and his colleagues (Higgins and Rholes, 1978; Hig-gins and McCann, 1984). That is, people who believe they may be called upon to communicate the information they receive to another may activate concepts that they believe will be particularly useful in attaining this objective. Often, these are concepts that are consistent with the other's assumed point of view. The concepts that people use influence the content and implications of the representation of the information stored in memory. As a result, they come to influence the recipient's own judgments of the person or object to which the information is relevant. In the political arena, people often expect to discuss the information they receive about political candidates with others whose views are either similar or dissimilar to their own. The influence of these expectancies on the recipient's *own* interpretation of the presented information seems worth investigating.

On the other hand, quite fortuitous contextual factors (e.g., ob-jectively irrelevant events mentioned in an earlier television program or a discussion with someone while waiting to hear the speech) may also activate concepts to which the content of the speech is relevant. Such fortuitous experiences may therefore influence both what as-pects of the speech are encoded and retained and how the information is interpreted. In some instances, of course, these contextual factors may be manipulated intentionally as a kind of strategic impression management tactic employed by a political campaign staff. By con-stantly suggesting that a particular personal characteristic is relevant to a candidate's position in one issue domain (e.g., Reagan is firm with drug-users), this personal characteristic is being primed and therefore is more likely to be used when interpreting information relevant to some other domain (e.g., Reagan is firm with Libya). Such a tactic may decrease the likelihood that information in the second domain is encoded in terms of some less desirable trait (e.g., Reagan is reckless with Libya).

The "priming" effects identified in the laboratory seem of par-ticular relevance to the political domain because of one additional finding. Once information has been interpreted in terms of a par-ticular set of concepts, these interpretations are stored in memory, whereas the original information appears to get lost. (For a theoretical discussion of this phenomenon, see Wyer and Srull, 1986.) As a con-sequence, the implications of the interpretation that subjects give to information when it is first received have an increasing influence on information-relevant judgments as time goes on (cf. Higgins, Rholes, and Jones, 1977; Carlston, 1980; Srull and Wyer, 1980). In Srull and Wyer's (1980) study, for example, activating hostility-related concepts had greater effect on judgments of a target person twenty-four hours after the information about the target had been read than on judgments reported immediately afterward. This suggests that if transitory factors influence the interpretation of information about a person, the effects of these factors on judgments and behavior toward the person may be evident for some time, even after the information itself has been forgotten.

ORGANIZATIONAL AND REPRESENTATIONAL PROCESSES

The preceding discussion focused on the interpretation of individual pieces of information in terms of a single concept. Once these encodings have been performed, people may attempt to understand their implications as a whole in light of more general bodies of knowledge they have acquired. This processing often requires thinking about different pieces of information both in relation to one another and in relation to different subsets of prior knowledge. This cognitive activity leads associations to be formed among the different cognitions involved. The result is a configuration of interrelated concepts and knowledge that includes aspects of previously acquired information and encoded features of the new information received.

A variety of factors influence the content and structure of such a configuration. One, of course, is the purpose for which the information is received. If someone hears a candidate's speech for the purpose of forming an impression of the candidate or of deciding whether to vote for the candidate, the recipient may organize the material around a trait or evaluation-based concept of what the person is like. This concept may either have already been formed on the basis of prior knowledge or may be extracted from the information presented. (For specific theoretical formulations of the nature of these representations, see Wyer and Gordon, 1984; Srull, Lichtenstein, and Rothbart, 1985; Srull and Wyer, 1987). Analogous processes operate when one receives information for the purpose of forming an impression of a group (e.g., the Democratic party or Russia). In contrast, a recipient whose objective is to understand the issues or events to which the speaker refers may try to construct a temporally or causally related scenario of the sequence of events being described and to infer their possible consequences (cf. Pennington and Hastie, 1986). This latter representation could include not only events that are explicitly stated in the information, but also other, unmentioned events that were inferred to occur on the basis of prior knowledge about the type of situation being described. The content and structure of these event representations may differ considerably from the content and structure of the person representations postulated by Srull, Lichtenstein, and Rohbart (1985).

Cognitive Responses to Information

The need to understand the nature of the representations formed from information is made salient by the frequent lack of relation between the judgments and decisions that people make and the implications of judgment-relevant information that they can recall. This lack of relation is typical in research on topics ranging from person impression formation (cf. Dreben, Fiske, and Hastie, 1979) to communication and persuasion (Greenwald, 1968; McGuire, 1968a, 1985). Although there are many possible interpretations of this finding (cf. Hastie and Park, 1986; Wyer and Srull, 1986; Lichtenstein and Srull, 1987), the most commonly accepted one is implied by our previous discussion. That is, people who receive information often engage in substantial cognitive activity in the process of understanding it and evaluating its implications in the context of prior knowledge. These cognitive operations may sometimes lead to the addition of unmentioned features of the person or event to which the information refers, and to the deletion of other features that were explicitly stated. At other times, when the presented information conflicts with expectations or with prior knowledge of the referent, people may try to refute its implications. This counterarguing may be done in a variety of ways—by disparaging the source, by identifying logical inconsistencies in the information itself, or by questioning the validity of specific assertions contained in it, based on knowledge of the persons or issues being discussed. (For more detailed discussions of the possible cognitive responses to persuasive messages and their implications, see Petty, Ostrom, and Brock, 1981.) The cognitive representation formed may consist of the results of this cognitive activity, and this representation may provide the basis for later judgments. Empirical support for this possibility was initially obtained by Greenwald (1968), and its implications have since been explored extensively by Petty and Cacioppo (1981).

It follows from this analysis that information will be less influential when recipients have both the ability and the motivation to counterargue the information as it is presented than when they do not. Several studies support this hypothesis. In a classic study by Festinger and Maccoby (1964), subjects listened to a speech advocating a position with which they initially disagreed. They were more influenced by the speech when it was accompanied by a distracting film than when it was accompanied by a film of the speaker. Presumably this is because they engaged in less counterarguing in the former condition than in the latter. (For direct evidence supporting this assumption, see Osterhouse and Brock, 1970.) In a different research paradigm, Freedman and Sears (1965) found that people were less influenced by a speech if they were told that the speaker's intention was to persuade them to adopt the position advocated than if they were not told the speaker's intentions. One interpretation of this difference is that subjects were more motivated to counterargue in the first case than in the second, and so they were relatively less influenced.

If our interpretation of these results is correct, it has obvious implications for the impact of information on political judgments. In fact, the influence of many factors on political judgments may be conceptualized in terms of their mediating influence on people's motivation or ability to counterargue the information they receive about a candidate, and therefore the representations they form on the basis of this information. We will elaborate upon some of these factors later in this chapter.

Affective Responses to Information

Our discussion of both encoding and representational processes has focused on the interpretation and organization of information in terms of semantic concepts of the person or event to which the presented information is relevant and on the descriptive content of the cognitive responses (e.g., counterarguments) to this information. A somewhat different cognitive response may be equally or more important. Specifically, the information we receive often elicits affective or emotional reactions; that is, it makes us angry, afraid, happy, or sad. These reactions may be elicited in part by the descriptive component of the verbal communication. In addition, they may be elicited by nonverbal cues such as the speaker's physical appearance, speech style, or general mannerisms. In both cases, our affective reactions, or concepts associated with them, may be stored in memory as part of our representation of the speaker. In some cases, this may occur even though the specific aspects of the communication that initially gave rise to the reactions are not retained. Thus, for example, we may recall that a particular candidate's speech made us angry (or, alternatively, made us feel good) without being able to remember what specific things the speaker said that gave rise to these reactions.

In this regard, people may not always be clear about the source of the affective reactions they experience. Consequently, they sometimes attribute these reactions in part to things that did not, in fact, produce them (cf. Schachter and Singer, 1962; Schwarz and Clore, 1983). For example, a person who happens to be in a good mood at the time he or she hears a candidate's speech may infer that the candidate is partly responsible for the positive feelings and may store a representation of these feelings in memory at a location pertaining to the candidate. Consequently, the person may later recall that the candidate made him or her feel good, regardless of the reactions that the candidate actually elicited.

STORAGE AND RETRIEVAL

After a representation of a person or event has been formed on the basis of the information one has received, this representation is presumably stored in long-term memory at a location pertaining to its referent. It therefore becomes an available source of knowledge about the person or event to which it pertains. However, the fact that such a representation is available in memory and is relevant to a judgment does not mean that it will actually be retrieved and used. Certainly we acquire large amounts of information about people that we never think of when we are asked to judge these persons, unless someone happens to call the information to our attention. The question is, What determines when and if a particular subset of stored information is retrieved?

Although several conceptualizations of storage and retrieval processes may be applied to the issues of concern in this discussion (cf. Anderson and Bower, 1973), the formulation developed by Wyer and Srull (1986) is particularly useful. In this formulation, long-term memory is conceptualized metaphorically as consisting of a set of content-addressable "storage bins." Each bin is identified by a header whose features specify its referent and thereby circumscribe its contents. The referent of a bin may be a person ("Ronald Reagan"), group ("Republicans"), country ("Russia," "Nicaragua"), event ("the Watergate scandal"), or general concept ("nuclear disarmament"). In each case, the header may contain not only the referent's name, but also other attributes that have become very strongly associated with the referent through learning. (Thus, the header of one's "Nixon" bin may contain the feature "dishonest.") These attributes need not always be semantic. For example, the headers of person bins may often include a visual representation that permits the person to be recognized, as well as representations of emotional reactions that have become strongly associated with them.

According to the model, information (or the representations formed from it) is stored in a bin in the order it is received. Moreover, when a representation has been retrieved from a bin to use in attaining some processing objective, a copy of it is returned to the top of the bin rather than to its original location. This means that more recently acquired and used representations of information are nearer the top of the bin and therefore are more accessible in memory. However, whether information is actually stored in a particular referent bin depends in part on the processing objectives that exist at the time or, more specifically, whether the bin's referent is a focus of these objectives. For example, a man who hears a speech by Ronald Reagan advocating sending arms to Iran may store this information in a "Reagan" bin if his objective at the time is to evaluate Reagan. However, he may store it in an "Iran" bin or a "U.S. foreign policy" bin if his goal is to learn about the troubles in Iran or about American foreign policy.

These considerations become important when considering the likelihood that the information one has received is retrieved and used as a basis for judgments. Although the specific retrieval processes postulated by Wyer and Srull (1986) are somewhat complicated, many of their implications are embodied in three assumptions:

1. When people seek previously acquired information to use in making a judgment or decision, they first compile a set of "probe cues," or features that in combination specify the type of information being sought (e.g., the name of the referent and other associated attributes). Then, they identify a referent bin whose header includes these features.

2. If the judgment or decision can be made on the basis of the small set of features contained in the bin header, these features are used, and a more elaborate search of the bin for judgment-relevant knowledge is not performed.

3. If the header features do *not* provide a sufficient informational basis for making the judgment or decision, a top-down search of the bin contents is performed until a sufficient amount of information has been retrieved to permit a judgment. Thus, when an elaborate search of the bin's contents is necessary, the material nearest

the top of the bin (that is, the material that has been most recently deposited) is most likely to be retrieved and used.

Considered in combination, the storage and retrieval assumptions outlined above have at last three implications for political judgment. First, specific information that people receive about a political candidate will influence their later judgments and voting decisions only if this information was stored in a location (bin) that pertains to this candidate at the time it was first received. In other words, its retrieval depends on whether or not the information was *initially* thought about with reference to the candidate. Therefore, in our earlier example, Reagan's statement about arms to Iran would be retrieved and used as a basis for judging Reagan only if the recipient's goal at the time he received the information had led him to think about Reagan as an object. If he had initially thought about the information only in terms of its implications for Iran, or for American foreign policy, the material would not be stored in his "Reagan" bin, and therefore it would not be later retrieved when information about Reagan was sought.

Second, more general attributes are likely to become associated with a political candidate (and therefore to be contained in the header of the referent bin pertaining to this person) as the candidate becomes better known. Consequently, judgments of the candidate should become relatively more likely to be based on header features rather than the information contained in the bin itself. In other words, the more familiar a political candidate becomes, the more likely it is that general attributes have become associated with him or her, and therefore the less likely it is that new information about the candidate's specific behaviors or issue positions will influence judgments or voting decisions.

It is interesting to consider this hypothesis in the context of research and theory reported by Rahn, Aldrich, Borgida, and Sullivan (chapter 6, this volume). They found evidence that the contribution of "image"-related factors to judgments did not depend on voters' general knowledge of or interest in politics. They concluded that the assessment of a candidate's personal qualities occurred "naturally and spontaneously in the social world," and that voters may rely upon these assessments regardless of any more specific knowledge they have acquired. In effect, this conclusion suggests that people at all levels of expertise form "candidate" bins whose headers contain general attributes of their referent, and that they use these header features as bases for judgments regardless of how much knowledge is stored in the bin itself. A distinction should be made, however, between general political knowledge and candidate familiarity. A voter may become very familiar with a candidate on the basis of photographs and telecasts and may infer attributes of the candidate from the candidate's personal appearance and general mannerisms without retaining much information at all about the person's stands on specific issues. Therefore, the contingency we have hypothesized is not necessarily inconsistent with the conclusions drawn by Rahn et al.

To the extent that specific information in the bin is sought, the third implication of our conceptualization is that information that has been most recently acquired or thought about will be most likely to be retrieved and used as a basis for judgment. In other words, there should be a strong recency effect of information acquisition and use on judgments and decisions. (For evidence supporting this hypothesis in other judgment domains, see Wyer and Hartwick, 1980; Wyer and Srull, 1986.)

In combination, these considerations suggest that the particular information that people retrieve and use as a basis for judgments depends on a variety of factors that influence not only where information is stored at the time it is received, but also the familiarity with the candidate and the recency with which the information about him or her was acquired.

INFERENCE PROCESSES

Our discussion of which information may be most likely to be brought to bear on judgments does not indicate *how* the information is used to arrive at these judgments. We cannot in this chapter do justice to the abundant literature on judgment and decision processes that potentially bears on this question. We will therefore restrict our attention to two general approaches to judgment and decision making and will provide some examples of each.

Heuristic Processes in Judgment

The most common conclusion to emerge from research on social judgment in recent years is that people typically do not engage in complex computational processes in arriving at judgments. Nor do they typically consider a large amount of information in making these judgments. Rather, they typically resort to judgmental *heuristics*, or rules of thumb, that frequently (although not invariably) lead to judgments similar to those they believe they would make on the basis of more extensive considerations. The heuristics that may potentially exist are manifold (cf. Kahneman, Slovic, and Tversky, 1982; Sherman and Corty, 1984), the applicability of which may depend on the type of judgment to be made and the domain of knowledge to which the judgment is relevant. An exhaustive review of the various heuristics that may come into play when formulating social judgments is beyond the scope of this chapter. Therefore, the following discussion will focus on those heuristics most likely to influence political judgments.

Accessibility.   This heuristic is a slight modification of the availability heuristic postulated by Tversky and Kahneman (1973). That is, people may assume that the more easily a particular piece of information comes to mind, the more representative it is of the entire body of information they have acquired and, therefore, the more relevant its implications are for the judgment to be made (Iyengar, chapter 7, this volume). Therefore, they may tend to rely upon this information rather than other, less accessible information. This possibility also provides one explanation of the "recency" effect noted in our discussion of retrieval processes. That is, more recently acquired information is often more accessible in memory. Therefore, it may be considered more representative of one's knowledge as a whole and may be used as a basis for judgments without considering information acquired in the more distant past.

Affect.   As we have already noted, people may use their perceptions of their emotional reactions to a person as an indication of how well they like or dislike the person and may, therefore, use the evaluative implications of these reactions as a basis for judgments. Evidence of an informational influence of affect has been reported in several studies (cf. Griffitt and Veitch, 1971; Clore and Gormly, 1974; Schwarz and Clore, 1983; Strack, Schwarz, and Gschneidinger, 1985; Levine, Wyer, and Schwarz, 1987). In the political domain, this suggests that if the particular subset of information that one recalls about a candidate elicits positive or negative affect, it may lead the candidate to be evaluated positively or negatively independently of the descriptive implications of this information or other knowledge about the candidate's stands on various issues.

An additional implication of the aforementioned research is noteworthy. That is, people are typically unable to distinguish clearly between the affect that is actually elicited by an object they are asked to judge and the affect they happen to be experiencing for other reasons. Consequently, their transitory mood state at the time they make a judgment, or the affect elicited by experiences they have had shortly before judging a political candidate, may be misattributed to the candidate and therefore may affect judgments of the candidate.

Stereotypes.   One of the most commonly recognized heuristic processes that underlies judgments and decisions involves the use of stereotypes (for research on the role of stereotypes in information processing, see Hamilton, 1981). People often form prototypic (stereotypic) representations of ethnic and social groups composed of attributes that they believe to be typical of their members. In doing so, people undoubtedly recognize that the attributes do not apply to every single group member. Nevertheless, in computing judgments and decisions, people may sometimes use these stereotype-related attributes to infer characteristics of individual group members and make judgments based on these characteristics independently of any more specific information they have about the individual being judged (Bodenhausen and Wyer, 1985).

An important contingency in the use of stereotypes as bases for judgments and decisions was identified by Bodenhausen and Lichtenstein (1987). They found that when subjects expected to make a fairly simple judgment of a person on the basis of information they received (e.g., to judge a particular trait of the person, such as aggressiveness), they based their judgments on specific aspects of this information and ignored the person's ethnic group membership. However, when subjects anticipated making a more complex judgment requiring a consideration of many different factors (specifically, a judgment of the person's guilt or innocence of criminal assault), they based their judgments on the group stereotype and ignored the more direct implications of the presented information. In other words, group stereotypes came into play only in complex judgment situations where they were used as a heuristic independently of any more direct judgment information available.

Political judgments are obviously complex in that they potentially require a consideration of several different types of information. To this extent, Bodenhausen and Lichtenstein's results suggest that stereotypes will often come into play in making these judgments. The question is what sorts of stereotypes are likely to be invoked. Ethnic and gender stereotypes undoubtedly may affect political judgments as well as judgments of other types. Perhaps the most common stereotypes employed in political judgment situations, however, are those associated with political party membership, a possibility also noted by Sniderman, Glaser, and Griffin in chapter 5. Specifically, individuals may have stereotyped preconceptions of Republicans and Democrats and may personally agree more with the implications of one stereotype than those of the other. They may therefore use their stereotypic perceptions of these political groups as bases for their voting decisions independently of the candidate's stands on specific issues (with which they may or may not agree).

Although there are undoubtedly other accounts of the influence of party identification on political preference, a conceptualization of these effects within the context of stereotyping research is provocative. For example, Bodenhausen and Lichtenstein (1987) found that the influence of stereotypes was apparent only when subjects were led to believe they would be required to make a complex judgment (a determination of guilt or innocence) *before* they received information about the individual to be judged. When subjects had a simpler judgmental objective in mind at the time they received the information (a trait inference), stereotypes had no influence on the judgments they ultimately made regardless of the actual complexity of these judgments. If this contingency generalizes to the political domain, it suggests that a candidate's party identification (as well as other features that may activate stereotypes) will have its primary influence on people's voting decisions if they have the objective of deciding whether to vote for the candidate at the time they receive information about him or her. If they receive the information with a simpler objective in mind (e.g., deciding whether they agree or disagree with a candidate's statement), the candidate's party identification may have less impact in relation to that of other attributes or to his or her stands on specific issues. These and other contingencies warrant investigation.

Information Integration Rules

Although the use of heuristics in political decision making seems incontrovertible, they are of course not universally applied. Many instances undoubtedly occur in which people are motivated to consider several different pieces of information and to base their judgments on the combined implications of this information. In these instances, what is this combinatorial process? Several alternatives have been proposed, but their applicability is unclear.

Averaging. Anderson (1971, 1981) postulated an algebraic model of information integration in the course of forming a person impression. More specifically, the model assumes that people first consider each piece of information about a person separately and construe its implications. Then they mentally compute an average of these implications, weighting each by its subjective importance. Empirical tests of the validity of this formulation have often provided quite accurate qualitative descriptions of the way in which information combines to influence person judgments (cf. Anderson, 1981). Unfortunately, however, these tests have typically been conducted under very artificial instructional and stimulus presentation conditions, the nature of which may substantially alter the integration process that would occur in less contrived settings (for a detailed discussion of this matter, see Wyer and Carlston, 1979).

Summation. A somewhat different conceptualization has been proposed by Fishbein and Ajzen (1975). They postulate that people's voting decisions (like other behavioral decisions) are based on (a) their attitudes toward performing the behavior (e.g., voting for the candidate) and (b) their normative beliefs that others consider voting for the candidate to be more or less desirable. Attitudes toward voting for the candidate are themselves a summative function of beliefs that voting for the candidate will have various positive and negative consequences.[2] This formulation generates reasonably good predictions among the various model components (Fishbein and Ajzen, 1981). That is, beliefs that voting for a candidate will have desirable or undesirable consequences are significantly correlated with reported attitudes toward voting for the candidate, and these attitudes are correlated with voting intentions. Note that this focus on the consequences of voting for a candidate takes into account one's belief that voting for a candidate will actually have an impact on the outcome of the election. For instance, a voter may like a third-party candidate the most, but may vote for one of the other candidates because he or she recognizes that a vote for the third-party candidate will have no impact.

Nevertheless, there are problems in interpreting both the averaging and summative information integration rules. For one thing, the correlations among components of the Fishbein model, although substantial, are not sufficiently high that one can adequately evaluate whether the combination rule is really averaging, summation, or something else (cf. Birnbaum, 1973).

Party Affiliation, Images, Issues, and Emotions. More general problems arise in using correlation methods to infer the way that information combines to affect judgments. As an example, political judgment research has often considered four possible criteria for evaluating a candidate: the candidate's *party affiliation*, the candidate's *image* (defined in terms of general attributes such as "forceful" or "persuasive," and various physical characteristics), the candidate's stands on specific *issues*, and *emotional reactions* to the candidate. Several researchers (e.g., Abelson, Kinder, Peters, and Fiske, 1982; Rahn, Aldrich, Borgida, and Sullivan, chapter 6, this volume) have attempted to determine which of these types of information constitutes the primary or most immediate basis for formulating one's attitude toward a candidate. Although the question is an important one, correlational approaches to answering it are typically nondiagnostic.

One problem is that the four factors are often highly intercorrelated. Consequently, the contribution of one factor to judgments is difficult to isolate from the contributions of the other three. More importantly, the causal direction of the inferred relations among the factors is unclear a priori and is hard to determine empirically. For instance, a voter may infer that a candidate endorses a given set of issue positions (e.g., favors bombing Libya or favors military intervention in Nicaragua) because he or she believes the candidate has certain personal traits (e.g., assertive) that combine to form the candidate's "image." Conversely, a voter may infer the candidate's personal traits from his or her stands on various issues. Analogously, a voter's perception of a candidate's personal characteristics or issue orientation may elicit emotional responses to the candidate. On the other hand, a voter's assessment of his or her own reactions to the candidate may lead the voter to infer that the candidate has certain personal characteristics or holds issue positions that are evaluatively consistent with these reactions.

Many of these alternative possibilities, which are discussed in other terms by Sniderman, Glaser, and Griffin in chapter 5 can be conceptualized more precisely within the framework of cognitive balance theory (Heider, 1958). Consider a triad consisting of a voter (P), a candidate (O), and a particular concept or issue (X). The relation between each pair of entities (i.e., P's relations to O and to X and P's perception of O's relation to X) may be either positive or negative. According to balance theory, the valences of any two known relations may be used in combination to infer the valence of the third. Thus:

1. P may form a positive attitude toward O on the basis of knowledge that O's stand on an issue X is evaluatively similar to his own. This is consistent with the implications of Downs's (1957) model of voting behavior and is what Sniderman, Glaser, and Griffin label "issue voting."

2. P may infer that O supports or opposes X from the similarity between his attitude toward O and his evaluation of X, based on the assumption that liked persons will agree with him, whereas disliked

persons will disagree. Political scientists have often labeled this a "rationalization effect" (Sniderman, Glaser, and Griffin).

3. *P* may adopt *O*'s position on *X* if he likes *O*, but may adopt the opposite position if he dislikes *O*. This is what Sniderman, Glaser, and Griffin term a "persuasion effect."

Each of these three causal inference processes could produce a positive correlation between a given set of features (e.g., issue perceptions) and attitudes toward the candidate. Correlational approaches alone do not permit these alternative possibilities to be distinguished.

Absolute versus Comparative Judgments

The heuristic and computational processes described above all assume that people make absolute judgments of political candidates before they decide which candidate to support. In other words, they arrive at an overall evaluation of each candidate's merits independently and then compare these evaluations to arrive at a relative preference. An equally, if not more likely, possibility, however, is that people who must decide between two or more candidates first compare them with respect to each characteristic they consider to be important and then choose the candidate that is superior to the others in the greatest number of respects.

The decisions that result from using these two strategies are not always the same. This can be seen from the following simplified example. Assume that three candidates, *A*, *B*, and *C*, are believed to have attributes along three dimensions and that the desirability of each candidate's positions along these dimensions can be measured along a scale from 1 (undesirable) to 5 (desirable). One person's ratings of the three candidates might therefore be those shown in Table 1. Which candidate does the person prefer?

First, suppose the preference for the candidate is determined by subjectively summing evaluations of each candidate along the three attribute dimensions and then comparing these sums. In this case, the person should prefer *C* to both *B* and *A*, and should prefer *B* to *A*.

On the other hand, suppose instead that the person uses a paired-comparison judgment strategy in which two candidates at a time are considered, choosing in each case the one who is superior to the other in the greatest number of ways. In this case, the person should prefer *A* to *B*, *B* to *C*, and *C* to *A*. These pairwise preferences are nontransitive and generally differ from those that would result from an absolute judgment procedure.

Moreover, note that the person's ultimate choice may depend

Table 1. Hypothetical Desirability Ratings of Three Candidates' Attributes along Three Judgment-Relevant Dimensions

	Candidate A	Candidate B	Candidate C
Dimension 1	5	4	3
Dimension 2	2	5	3
Dimension 3	2	1	5
Sum	9	10	11

on the order in which the paired comparisons are performed. Suppose the person first decides between two of the candidates on the basis of the criterion described above, and then, having determined a preference, compares this candidate to the third. If the person happens to consider *A* and *B* first, the ultimate choice should be *C* (as *A* is preferred to *B*, but *C* to *A*). However, if *A* and *C* are considered first, the final choice should be *B* (as *C* is preferred to *A*, but *B* to *C*); if *B* and *C* are considered first, the final choice should be *A* (as *B* is preferred to *C*, but *A* to *B*).

In general, it seems likely that both absolute and comparative judgment strategies are often employed, depending on the circumstances. However, the nature of these circumstances has not been investigated in this judgment domain.

OUTPUT PROCESSES

Once a subjective judgment or inference has been made, a person must transform this subjective judgment into an overt response. In the present domain, for example, one must transform a subjective preference for a candidate into an overt response (i.e., a verbal statement of this preference, a response along a scale provided in a survey questionnaire, or an actual voting decision). A detailed analysis of the processes that underlie these transformations is beyond the scope of the present discussion (for reviews and theoretical analysis, see Ostrom and Upshaw, 1968; Wyer, 1974, 1981; Higgins, 1981; Upshaw, 1984; Strack and Martin, 1987). If the same transformation procedure is applied consistently to all of the candidates one considers, *relative* preferences for the candidates should be similar regardless of the nature of this transformation. However, an additional consideration arises that is of potentially great importance. Specifically, once an overt response has been generated, a cognitive representation of this response is stored in memory at a location pertaining to the object to which the response is relevant (Wyer and Srull, 1986). This representation therefore comes to serve as a source of information that can later be retrieved and used as a basis for other responses. Consequently, factors that affect people's overt responses to a question at one point may have an impact on later judgments and decisions for which the earlier responses have implications.

Several effects of making one response in a questionnaire on later judgments have been identified by Schwarz and his colleagues (cf. Schwarz, Hippler, Deutsch, and Strack, 1985; for a review, see Strack and Martin, 1987). An example of the effects of prior questionnaire responses on behavioral decisions is provided by Sherman, Ahlm, Berman, and Lynn (1978). Here, subjects who were asked to rate the importance of a series of social issues rated recycling as less important when it was presented in the context of other extremely important issues than when it was presented in the context of unimportant ones. This is presumably because the context stimuli affected subjects' assumptions about the range of subjective values to which the response scale provided them was relevant and consequently influenced the numerical value they assigned to the target issue along this scale. (For an elaboration of this interpretation and empirical support for it, see Upshaw, 1965, 1978; Wyer, 1974.) Later, however, subjects were approached by a confederate and asked to help out on a recycling project. Subjects' helping decisions were affected by the context issues in much the same way that their questionnaire ratings had been affected. These effects were not apparent under control conditions in which subjects rated the context issues but did *not* actually rate recycling. Sherman, Ahlm, Berman, and Lynn concluded that subjects' ratings of recycling in experimental conditions were influenced by the context stimuli and that these *ratings*, having been stored in memory, were later retrieved, reinterpreted out of context, and used as a basis for their helping decisions.

If this phenomenon is generalizable, it has clear implications for voting behavior. That is, people who have been asked before an election to report their preferences for a candidate may not yet have made up their minds. Therefore, they may compute a response on the spot depending on what subset of judgment-relevant knowledge comes easily to mind. Later, however, they may retrieve and use this response as a basis for their actual voting decision without recomputing it. Therefore, if contextual and situation-specific factors of the sort we have outlined in this chapter influence the judgments that subjects report in response to a survey, these responses may later be retrieved and used as a basis for voting decisions independently of other considerations. In other words, the questionnaire survey can actually intrude on the decision process it is designed to assess and can *create* the effects it is intended to predict.

SITUATIONAL AND INDIVIDUAL DIFFERENCES
IN POLITICAL DECISION-MAKING

In the context of our discussion, we have alluded to several situational and individual differences variables that influence political judgments through their influence at one or another stage of information processing. However, several variables may influence processing at more than one stage, and the implications of their effect at each stage may differ. An examination of a few variables may convey the potential value of conceptualizing political judgment in terms of the considerations we have proposed.

General Knowledge and Expertise

People obviously differ both in the amount of knowledge they acquire about a political candidate and in their knowledge of political issues in general. This, in turn, may be a result of either their intellectual ability and education level or motivational factors that affect their interest in politics. People's general knowledge of politics could potentially affect the processing of new information about political candidates at several different stages. Both Sniderman, Glaser, and Griffin (chapter 5, this volume) and Rahn, Aldrich, Borgida, and Sullivan (chapter 6, this volume) discuss the effects of expertise on voters' inference strategies. Its potential effects at other stages should also be noted.

1. *Attention and encoding.* People with substantial knowledge about politics are more easily able to encode and organize new information in terms of concepts they have formed on the basis of this knowledge. To this extent, they should be better able to assimilate and retain the information than less knowledgeable persons who have not formed the concepts required to understand it easily (see Sniderman, Glaser, and Griffin, chapter 5). Considered in isolation, this suggests that information should have generally more impact on the judgments of voters if they are high in political expertise than if they are low. In addition, Iyengar notes in chapter 7 that expertise may vary over issue domains. To this extent, people who are expert in some domains but not others may selectively encode information relevant to the domain of their expertise. Consequently, they may be more

likely to retain and be influenced by this subset of information than by information relevant to other domains.

2. *Organization and representational processes.* Politically knowledgeable voters are better able to identify inconsistencies between the presented information and prior knowledge and are better able to counterargue the implications of this information. To the extent that these counterarguments are contained in the representation of the information that they ultimately commit to memory, knowledgeable persons may be *less* influenced by newly presented information than less knowledgeable ones.

The question is how these apparently opposing effects of expertise combine to affect the overall impact of information. A model proposed initially by McGuire (1968b) and slightly modified by Wyer (1974) provides one possible answer. According to this model, the likelihood of being influenced by information (P_I) is a function of the product of (*a*) the probability of receiving the information (P_R) and (*b*) the probability of not counterarguing it effectively given that it is received (i.e., $1 - P_{CA}$, where P_{CA} is the probability of effectively counterarguing the information given that it is received). That is,

$$P_I = P_R(1 - P_{CA}) . \tag{1}$$

.(For a formal derivation of this equation, see Wyer, 1974.) Note that $P_I = 0$ if either $P_R = P_{CA} = 0$ or if $P_R = P_{CA} = 1$, and is maximum when $P_R = P_{CA} = .5$. Thus, suppose the probability of comprehending the information and the probability of counterarguing it effectively both increase monotonically with expertise. Then the impact of the information on judgments will be lower when expertise is either very high or very low than when it is moderate.

3. *Storage and retrieval.* The effects of expertise on storage and retrieval are theoretically somewhat unclear. For example, it might seem intuitively reasonable to suppose that highly knowledgeable persons will be more likely than less knowledgeable ones to construct a referent bin for a candidate whose header contains judgment-relevant features (i.e., general attributes of the candidate that are relevant to political judgments). To this extent, knowledgeable persons may be relatively more likely to base their decisions on header features and correspondingly less apt to base it on the implications of recently acquired specific information about the candidate's behavior and issue positions.

As we noted earlier, however, Rahn, Aldrich, Borgida, and Sullivan argue that both high- and low-expertise individuals use general image-related attributes to judge a candidate. In terms of the "bin" conceptualization we have outlined, this suggests that the headers of "candidate" bins may have similar features regardless of the expertise of the person who constructs them or of the amount of specific knowledge contained in the bins.

4. *Inference processes.* Expertise may influence inference processes in at least two ways. First, as Iyengar states in chapter 7, people may assign greater weight or importance to information about a candidate that pertains to domains in which they have particular interest or expertise, and so this information may have greater influence. Second, high- and low-expertise individuals may use different decision rules to arrive at judgments. Sniderman, Griffin, and Glaser, for example, suggest that low-expertise voters may first consider only the incumbent and, if their evaluation of him or her is sufficiently positive, may make a positive decision without considering the attributes of the challenger. That is, they may consider the challenger only if the incumbent is found wanting. In contrast, voters with high expertise may take a broader view at the outset and may consider the merits of both candidates simultaneously. As Sniderman, Glaser, and Griffin point out, however, it is unclear whether this difference reflects a difference in decision strategy per se or simply a difference in the amount and type of knowledge that high- and low-expertise individuals are able to consider at one time.

In summary, expertise may affect voting behavior at a number of different stages of processing, and the implications of these effects are sometimes opposite in direction. It is hoped that future research will provide additional insight into these various effects and when they occur.

Party Identification

A political candidate's party membership and its similarity to the voter's is known to exert a major influence on voting decisions (Campbell, Gurin, and Miller, 1954; Campbell, Converse, Miller, and Stokes, 1960). This influence, like the influence of expertise, may potentially occur at several different stages of processing. We have already noted the possibility that party identification may be used as a heuristic in making voting decisions. It may also play a role in other types of heuristic-based processing (cf. Sniderman, Glaser, and Griffin). In addition, there are two other possible influences.

1. A candidate's party membership may give rise to expectancies for the person's general orientation and stands on various types of issues and may activate a set of concepts associated with these expectations. The information presented about the candidate, if susceptible

to alternative interpretations, is likely to be interpreted in terms of these expectation-consistent concepts. Moreover, under conditions of high information processing load, the activation of these concepts may lead to selective encoding of the information presented. Thus, for example, a liberal statement may be less apt to be encoded and retained in the representation formed from the information's if the speaker is identified as Republican rather than Democrat. Moreover, an ambiguous statement may be interpreted as more conservative in the first case than in the second.

2. Expectancies induced by a candidate's party membership may affect the selective encoding and interpretation of information independently of the recipient's own party affiliation. In contrast, other cognitive responses to the information are more likely to depend on the recipient's party identification. That is, individuals may expect to agree more strongly with a candidate of their own party than with a candidate of a different party. Therefore, they may be less motivated to counterargue the information conveyed by the former candidate. Consequently, the implications of the representation they form from this information may be more similar to those that the communicator intended to convey, and so the communication may have a more positive influence on their later judgments of both the issue being discussed and the communicator.

The preceding effects on candidate judgments appear similar to the effects of using the candidate's party membership as a heuristic (described in our previous discussion). There is an important distinction, however. The effects of using party membership as a heuristic should occur independently of other available information about the candidate and independently of when this information is presented. In contrast, the effects of party identification on encoding and counterarguing should occur only under conditions in which the candidate's party affiliation is known at the outset, at the time the information is initially presented. If the information has already been encoded and stored in memory by the time the candidate's party membership is learned, the effect of this information on voting decisions should be similar regardless of the party to which the candidate belongs.

Affect and Image

A candidate's "image" may consist of both semantic and nonverbal features. For example, it may include a set of attributes ("liberal," "wishy-washy," "stupid," or "dishonest"). In addition, it may include visual or auditory features pertaining to the candidate's physical appearance, facial expressions, or speech style. These latter features are of particular importance, as they may give rise to trait judgments of the candidate and may elicit positive or negative affective reactions, independently of the specific content of the candidate's speech.

It seems incontrovertible that a candidate's image influences voting decisions (Greenstein, 1960; Kinder and Abelson, 1981). The cognitive mechanisms that underlie its influence are unclear, however. To see the nature of these possible mechanisms, suppose someone watches a telecast of a candidate's speech or news conference. The information transmitted consists, in part, of the content of the speaker's remarks. It also includes nonverbal features that are either stable (e.g., physical attractiveness, age, or articulateness) or transitory (facial expressions, for example). To the extent that the telecast influences the listener's evaluation of the candidate and decision to vote for him or her, this influence could occur for several reasons.

1. The verbal content of a candidate's speech may lead the candidate to be attributed different image-related characteristics, and these characteristics may be stored in memory at a location pertaining to the candidate. To the extent that these features are retrieved at the time the candidate is judged, their evaluative implications should have an impact on these judgments.

2. The nonverbal features associated with the candidate's speech (e.g., physical attractiveness or facial expressions) may also be used as a basis for inferring general attributes of the candidate. These attributes may, in turn, influence evaluations of the candidate in much the same way that the content of the candidate's speech influences these responses.

3. Nonverbal features of a candidate may elicit a positive or negative affective reaction in the viewer and this affect, in turn, may influence the accessibility of semantic features that have previously become associated with the candidate (cf. Isen, Shalker, Clark, and Karp, 1978). For example, positive affective states may increase the accessibility of positive features one has learned about the candidate, whereas negative affective states may increase the accessibility of negative ones. These features, once activated, may be used as a basis for judgments and voting decisions.

4. Emotional responses to the candidate that are elicited by verbal or nonverbal aspects of the speech, or cognitions associated with these reactions, may be included in the representation of the speech stored in memory. To the extent that these emotional responses are retrieved at the time a judgment is made, they may be used as a basis

for this judgment independently of other information (e.g., "Reagan makes me angry; therefore, I don't like him").

Therefore, the features of a candidate's image and affective reactions to the candidate may influence political judgments in numerous ways. A goal of research in this area should be to untangle these alternative effects and to identify the conditions in which they occur.

CONCLUSION

We have barely skimmed the surface of the many theoretical and empirical issues that surround political judgment and decision making. However, our objective has not been to provide a comprehensive analysis of political judgment phenomena. Rather, we have tried to show that a conceptualization of these phenomena from an information-processing perspective can raise new questions and issues that, if answered, may ultimately allow such an analysis to be performed.

We should reiterate a caution we have expressed throughout this discussion, namely the important role of information-processing objectives on the cognitive activity that mediates judgments. Many of the effects of expertise, party membership, and image that we have hypothesized are predicated on the assumption that recipients of the information being presented either by or about a candidate are motivated to evaluate the candidate. In many instances, this motivation may be induced by the information itself. Certainly if a speaker says something we believe to be blatantly untrue or otherwise objectionable, we may, in the course of reconciling this statement, infer that the speaker is either ignorant or deceitful, and these attributes may be stored in memory at a location pertaining to the speaker.

In many instances, however, we may receive information without this objective in mind. This is particularly true when watching television. Here, we are usually exposed to an unending stream of stimulus input, transmitted both visually and auditorally. We often receive this information passively, without any particular goal. In such conditions, many of the effects we have hypothesized may not occur. Specifically, the information may be encoded at a relatively low level of abstractness, without thinking about it extensively in relation to previously acquired information. Moreover, the sort of counterarguing that often occurs when we have a goal of evaluating the candidate and his or her stands on the issues may not be performed. Finally, the information may not always be stored at a memory location pertaining to the candidate. Rather, it may be transmitted to a location in memory pertaining to the issue being discussed, or not stored in any location at all. To this extent, it may not be retrieved and used as a basis for judgment of the candidate when judgment-relevant information is sought.

The processing objectives that exist when a person receives information may depend on both characteristics of the recipient and situational factors. People are clearly more likely to have an objective of evaluating a politician if they are interested in politics than if they are not. In addition, characteristics of the communication and of the context in which it occurs may activate different processing goals. For example, if a president's communication is described as a "campaign speech," recipients may infer that the speech is trying to influence them rather than to inform them. This is likely to activate evaluation goals that may elicit counterarguing or other cognitive processes that would not otherwise occur.

The general implication of these considerations is that one should treat with caution conclusions drawn from both laboratory and field studies of communication impact in assessing their generalizability to situations in which people's processing objectives differ from those that existed in the investigation. This does not mean that generalizability is impossible. Rather, it means that one must be very careful to construct experimental conditions in which subjects are likely to have processing objectives analogous to those that exist outside the laboratory when people receive information about politicians and issues. If this can be done, an information-processing approach to understanding political judgment may provide valuable insights into political behavior. We encourage the continued use of this approach.

NOTES

The writing of this chapter was supported in part by grant MH 3–8585 from the National Institute of Mental Health, and in part by funds provided by the University of Illinois Survey Research Laboratory.

1. Studies using recognition memory procedures have typically found that subjects are more likely to report unmentioned items as having been presented if they are consistent with concepts activated after the information was presented (cf. Dooling and Christiaansen, 1977; Snyder and Uranowitz, 1978). However, this difference may be due to guessing biases that occur at the time recognition items are judged and may not reflect the content of the

representation of the information that is stored in memory (cf. Bellezza and Bower, 1981).

2. The particular index used by Fishbein is $A_b = \sum_{i=1}^{n} b_i e_i$, where A_b is the attitude toward the behavior; b_i is the belief that the behavior will have consequence i, and e_i is the desirability of this consequence.

III

POLITICAL REPRESENTATION AS AN INFORMATION PROBLEM

9

A Positive Theory
of Negative Voting

Morris P. Fiorina
Kenneth A. Shepsle

According to a hoary bit of political folk wisdom, negative evaluations exert a relatively greater impact on electoral behavior than comparable positive evaluations. Key (1966:60) alludes to the "journalistic
supposition that the people only vote against; never, for." In an ap-
posite illustration, journalist Richard Harris (1971:48) reports these
remarks by an observer of the 1970 Tennessee Senate race: "Voters
aren't for Brock, they're against Gore. And a man will stand in line
at the polls a lot longer to vote against somebody than he will to vote
for somebody."

Sentiments like these are somewhat ambiguous, but in more precise if less colorful professional language we take them to mean just
this: given an accomplishment and a transgression of comparable importance, various forms of electoral behavior—in particular, voting—
will bear a stronger relationship to the transgression than to the
achievement.[1]

A number of political scientists have made the negative voting
hypothesis the subject of empirical investigation. In a study of the
electoral impact of national economic conditions, Bloom and Price
(1975) report that the aggregate vote for the congressional candidates
of the in-party bears a significant relationship to deteriorations in
aggregate economic conditions. However, the vote bears no relationship to aggregate improvements. The motive force of negatives apparently exceeds that of positives.

On the individual level, Kernell (1977) compares the relative
importance of presidential approval and disapproval for turnout and

vote choice in the six off-year House elections held between 1946 and 1966 (Gallup samples). He finds that (1) disapproving voters are more likely to turn out than approving voters; (2) out-party identifiers who disapprove are more solidly against the administration than in-party identifiers who are for it; and (3) in-party identifiers who disapprove are more likely to desert their party than out-party identifiers who approve. In each comparison, presidential disapproval shows a stronger effect than presidential approval.

Lau (1982) corroborates Kernell's congressional findings for the 1974 and 1978 American National Election Studies. He also shows that variables representing net negative responses to the open-ended "likes and dislikes" items were stronger predictors of presidential candidate evaluations than were variables representing net positive responses in the 1968, 1972, and 1980 surveys.

Thus, we have a piece of folk wisdom that finds support in systematic empirical analyses.[2] What we do not have, however, is comparably convincing theoretical rationales for negative voting. As Lau (1985:119) observes, "While the literature documenting negativity is quite rich, serious attempts to explain *why* negative information has greater weight than comparable positive information are few." Lau himself presents evidence consistent with two hypotheses grounded in social-psychological theory. The "figure-ground" hypothesis offers a perceptual explanation. It presumes that human beings live in generally positive worlds. Because of its relative infrequency, then, negative information stands out (1985:121). The "cost orientation" hypothesis offers a motivational explanation. It assumes that from an evolutionary standpoint it is more adaptive to avoid losses than to achieve gains (1985:122).

In this discussion, we offer another explanation of negative voting. Although not logically incompatible with explanations grounded in social psychology, ours emerges from an explicitly political model grounded in the economic theory of agency—the theory of the interaction between principals and the agents who must act for them. Our model provides a framework one consequence of which is that citizens (principals) weight the disfavored actions of their leaders (agents) relatively more heavily than the favored actions.

The next section of the chapter exposits the theory of agency as developed in the economics literature and notes several difficulties in applying the existing theory to common political situations. In the third section, we develop an agency model of the representative-constituent relationship and derive the negative voting results.

AN EXPOSITION OF THE ECONOMIC THEORY OF AGENCY

One can think of the economic theory of agency as an analytical characterization of the division and specialization of labor.[3] Put somewhat differently, it is a model of the costs and benefits of delegation and decentralization. In economics this model finds its most important applications in explicating the employment relationship, the organization of firms and industries, and general problems associated with contracting in an uncertain world. After briefly describing the use of the model in economics, we will note certain important features of political settings that differ from the standard economic settings.

The simple agency framework begins with the idea that realizing the enhanced productive possibilities entailed by a division of labor requires overcoming a variety of complications. First, there are asymmetries in information, with some people possessing, or capable of obtaining, more of it than others. Second, the actions of some people may not be observable to others, thereby making it difficult for the former to make promises about their actions and for the latter to accept promises contingent on these actions. Third, there are often direct conflicts of interest among the various parties, creating incentives to cheat, renege, or dissemble when it comes to keeping promises or fulfilling obligations. One can never be certain that another's interests are aligned with one's own, and this uncertainty is compounded by imperfect information and observability.

These imperfections take on special significance when one party (the "principal") hires or delegates responsibility to another party (the "agent"). If one retains a doctor, lawyer, financial advisor, or contractor in order to further some objective (good health, prudent investments) or accomplish some task (draw up a will, remodel the kitchen), how can the principal be assured that the agent will act in the principal's best interest? As Jensen and Meckling (1976:308–309) observe:

> If both parties to the relationship are utility maximizers, there is good reason to believe that the agent will not always act in the best interests of the principal. The principal can limit divergences from his interest by establishing appropriate incentives for the agent and by incurring monitoring costs designed to limit the aberrant activities of the agent. . . . However, it is generally impossible for the principal or the agent at zero cost to ensure that the agent will make optimal decisions from the principal's viewpoint. In most agency relationships, the principal and the agent will incur positive . . . costs (pecuniary and nonpe-

cuniary), and in addition, there will be some divergence between the agent's decisions and those decisions that would maximize the welfare of the principal.

In the economic theory of agency, the problem is seen as the principal's. The agent is simply a utility maximizer; he or she responds mechanically in utility-maximizing fashion to whatever incentives are faced. It is up to the principal to structure the situation, taking the agent's subsequent mechanical response into account. Thus, the theory assumes the principal moves first, choosing a reward structure, fee schedule, or incentive scheme. The agent moves second, maximizing his or her own utility contingent on the payoff promised by the principal.

Consider the simplest possible situation: agent actions are clearly observable, and their impact on the final outcome is unambiguous. Here, only conflict of interest is a problem. A kitchen contractor, for example, might charge for copper pipe while actually using plastic pipe, pocketing the difference in cost and cheating the principal. Given no problems of observability or uncertainty, however, this conflict of interest reduces to a problem in contracting. A "forcing" contract between principal and agent can be written, specifying the precise obligations on the part of each, so long as there are institutions of enforcement—sheriffs and courts—to resolve alleged breaches. In this transaction-cost-free world of neoclassical economics, reliable institutions of exogenous contract enforcement permit the specialization and division of labor to capture economic gains. It is this "frictionless" model upon which the theory of agency seeks to improve.

Most agency theories seek to resolve complications caused by problems of observability and uncertainty. What kinds of institutions might develop to handle these problems? What if there were no easy way for you, the homeowner-principal, to observe directly whether your contractor-agent uses copper or plastic pipes? Perhaps a system of supplier receipts will develop as a monitoring institution. Or the municipality in which the principal resides could require an inspection to certify contract compliance. Or the contractor might post a bond to be forfeited if, the first time a plumbing problem arises, it is ascertained that plastic piping was used. The economic theory of agency, then, is a theory of how principals and agents can avoid the suboptimal consequences of problems that preclude the use of a simple forcing contract.

Political agency shares the aforementioned problems. Citizens retain an agent to serve their political interests. In representative democracies, many of these agents are elected. How can the principals control their agent? There are problems of observability: What deals does the representative enter into, from whom does he or she accept campaign contributions, how does he or she vote in settings of limited public access? There are also problems caused by uncertainty: How can the citizen relate the efforts taken by the agent (assuming these are observable) to those taken by other agents in producing the final outcome? That is, how can the principals determine the veracity of "credit-claiming" (Mayhew, 1974) and "explanations of Washington behavior" (Fenno, 1978)?

But there are other issues with which the standard economic theory of agency does not deal. First, in the economic theory the principal is assumed to have well-defined preferences. In many political settings this cannot be assumed because the principal is a collective, and there are well-known problems involving preference aggregation (Arrow, 1951). Second, the economic theory assumes that only the agent cannot pre-commit (i.e., make credible promises) and that this inability, combined with uncertainty and nonobservability, makes forcing contracts infeasible. The principal, in contrast, is assumed capable of offering a compensation schedule enforceable in a court of law. In political settings, the positions of principal and agent are symmetric. Neither can be held to promises. There is no equivalent of a court of law in which alleged breaches may be adjudicated. Neither the agent's "if elected, I promise. . . . " commitment, nor the principal's "if you do something for me lately. . . . " promise is binding. Either party may renege. Such breaches may or may not be observable, and, in any event, there is no recourse to something like a court of law. In short, there is no exogenous enforcement so that promises, to be credible, must possess self-enforcing properties.

In the next section, we apply the principal-agent approach to legislative elections. We hope to demonstrate that the approach is a useful way to think about the problem of representation and the control of elected officials. The political setting does raise special questions, however, not all of which we can address in a satisfactory manner.

APPLYING THE PRINCIPAL-AGENT MODEL TO LEGISLATIVE ELECTIONS

For purposes of argument, we treat the legislator as the elected agent of constituents who constitute a collective principal. Some varieties of representation theory conceptualize representation in just such terms (Pitkin, 1967, Chapter 6), but whatever one's normative stance, such an approach seems as consistent with empirical reality as any alternative. This principal-agent problem embodies the defining feature of the classic problem: much of what the legislator does is out of the public eye and therefore difficult to monitor. Except for recorded votes, constituents cannot easily determine what their representative is doing. In addition, the collective principal compounds the normal difficulties because each constituent is only one vote of several hundred thousand. Unless they are major donors or prominent group leaders, they have little possibility of exerting an individual effect on the representative's behavior. Thus, a large-scale free-rider problem greatly weakens constituents' incentives to concern themselves with formulation of an optimal reward scheme. Moreover, knowledge that other constituents have conflicting interests and therefore would act in opposition to one's own efforts can only further diminish the already weak individual incentive of constituent-principals. Seemingly, the existence of a collective principal undermines the rationale for applying a principal-agent framework in the first instance. Rather than argue this matter here, we adopt an alternative approach.

In calculating the electoral consequences of their actions, representatives in effect assume that they face reward schemes having various characteristics. We analyze the representative's calculations to see what they implicitly presume about the decisions made by constituent-principals. Then we will return to questions of how and why such behavior might arise. This indirect approach turns out to yield interesting results.

Mayhew argues that U.S. representatives seek reelection by engaging in three broad classes of activities. The first is simple advertising, defined as "any effort to disseminate one's name among constituents in such a fashion as to create a favorable image but in messages having little or no issue content" (1974:49). This form of activity is analogous to the efforts of aspiring agents in fields other than politics—law and medicine, for example. The agent attempts to reach the audience of potential principals—advertising is to a considerable degree a precursor or precondition of the agency relationship he or she hopes to establish. Activities done on behalf of constituent-principals fall into Mayhew's second and third categories. The representative-agent *claims credit* for legislative actions that benefit his or her district. Such credit-claiming is most credible in the allocation of particularized benefits because in that realm individual members of Congress are perceived as prime movers. But Mayhew (1974:59) observes that "the prime mover role is a hard one to play on larger matters. . . . A claim, after all, has to be credible. If a congressman goes before an audience and says, 'I am responsible for passing a bill to curb inflation,' or 'I am responsible for the highway program,' hardly anyone will believe him." Thus, in general, representatives will discount to some degree the electoral consequences of legislation.

Mayhew's third type of activity consists of *position-taking*. To quote him (1974:117–118):

> Would Senators Mark Hatfield and George McGovern have been any the more esteemed by their followers if their antiwar amendment had won rather than lost? Particularized benefits aside, the blunt fact is that congressmen have less of a stake in winning victories than they normally appear to have. Indeed, to look at the point another way, we do not ordinarily think of losses as being politically harmful. We can all point to a good many instances in which congressmen seem to have gotten into trouble by being on the *wrong* side in a roll call vote, but who can think of one where a member got into trouble by being on the *losing* side?

To phrase Mayhew's arguments in decision-theoretic terms, program benefits and costs for which the legislator may claim credit are "state-contingent"—they occur (or not) contingent on the realization of a particular "state of nature," namely, the passage or failure of a bill. In contrast, position-taking consequences are "act-contingent"— they occur (or not) contingent on how the legislator chooses to vote. Figure 1 sets out the basic formulation. If the bill passes, it has an impact on the district regardless of how the legislator voted; if it fails, no such consequences follow (state-contingent—compare the columns). If the legislator votes yea (nay), some issue public will be pleased (displeased) regardless of whether the bill passes or fails (act-contingent—compare the rows).[4] The core of our analysis is an elaboration of the simple schema depicted in Figure 1.

As indicated, we conceptualize the states of nature in the decision problem as a dichotomy—the passage or failure of a particular bill. Assume that the legislator has a subjective probability estimate of passage, but note that such an estimate cannot be independent of the representative's choice of acts.[5] From the structure of majority rule (May, 1952), we know that the probability of the bill's passage must be at least as great if the legislator votes yea than if he or she votes nay. Thus, let w^Y be the conditional probability of the bill's winning given a yea vote, and w^N the conditional probability of the bill's winning given a nay vote. Evidently, $w^Y \geq w^N$.

In order to make the representative's decision problem interesting, assume that an issue partitions his or her constituency into two

Figure 1. Abstract Decision Problem

	States of Nature	
Actions	Bill Passes	Bill Fails
Vote Yea	B, C, PT^Y	PT^Y
Vote Nay	B, C, PT^N	PT^N

where B, C are benefits and costs to groups contingent on bill's passage;
PT^Y are electoral consequences of supporting the bill (voting yea);
PT^N are electoral consequences of opposing the bill (voting nay).

groups with conflicting interests; denote them G_1 and G_2, and assume that G_1 stands to benefit from the proposed legislation, whereas G_2 stands to lose.[6] Thus, we can speak of the representative's voting strategies as simply to support G_1 or oppose G_1.[7]

Denote the net legislative benefits to G_1 as B_1 and the net costs to G_2 as C_2. As noted, a single member of a collective decision-making body should not expect to claim full credit for such benefits, or by symmetry, incur full blame for such losses. We have worked out a version of the model in which legislative benefits and costs are discounted to reflect the imperfections of credit-claiming, but given that inclusion of a credit-claiming discount does not affect our principal results, we omit it here in the interest of simplifying the notation and exposition.

Turning now to position-taking benefits and costs, let A_i and D_i indicate benefits and costs (possibly psychic) that members of G_i feel when the representative casts a vote in *a*greement or *d*isagreement with their interests. Because taking a position is something completely under the control of the individual legislator, no question arises of discounting these consequences.

One final major consideration must be incorporated into the analysis. Most formal models are ahistorical in that they treat the entire electorate as if it were at all times up for grabs. But observers of real-world politics are well aware that the electoral status quo for any officeholder is one of existing political alignments rather than universal lack of commitment. Legislative research in particular emphasizes the importance of the preexisting supporting coalition of the representative. To quote Fenno (1978:9–10):

> In thinking about his reelection constituency, he is helped by a second, more time-related perception—of who voted for him "last time" and

of how well he did overall "last time." Starting with that calculation, he adds or subtracts incrementally on the basis of changes that will have taken place between "last time" and "this time" or "next time." . . . Working back and forth incrementally from "last time" to "this time" or to "next time" helps the congressman to delineate his reelection constituency. It helps because election results provide him with one of the few certainties he operates with. He knows that he won "last time" and by how much. Sometimes that is all he knows.

Both Kingdon (1966:45) and Mayhew (1974:47) express similar ideas. How can such considerations be brought into a simple model of legislator decision making? We employ the following simple formulation. Assume that each group G_i has g_i members, v_i of whom already support the representative. Thus, in those groups that currently support a representative, v_i/g_i is close to 1; in groups that currently oppose him or her, close to 0; and in currently neutral groups, near .5. Depending on existing support patterns, some votes provide a representative with a chance to gain much and lose little, others with a chance to lose much and gain little, and so on. Inasmuch as there is a variety of ways to conceptualize these trade-offs, we must develop a specific model of electoral response before proceeding further.

STANDPATTERS AND SWITCHERS

The model postulates that if the representative votes as G_1 would like, he or she has the potential to capture the votes of the $(g_1 - v_1)$ nonsupporters in G_1, but simultaneously puts at risk the votes of the v_2 supporters he or she has in G_2 who oppose the legislation. The situation is reversed when considering a vote in support of G_2. The votes of present supporters (nonsupporters) are not altered by policy impacts and votes consistent (inconsistent) with their interests. Thus, the v_i supporters in G_i are unaffected by a pro-G_i vote, and the $g_i - v_i$ nonsupporters in G_i are unaffected by an anti-G_i vote. This model recalls the standpatter-switcher formulation of Key (1966) in that voters are assumed to make a standing decision that they reconsider only if they observe behavior inconsistent with that decision. One way to formalize such behavior is to posit a threshold model of individual decision making. Formally, assume that each voter has a utility threshold U^* such that he or she votes for the representative so long as $U_t \geq U^*$, where t is the time of decision, and votes against the representative when $U_t < U^*$. Define S as the set of voters for whom $U_t \geq U^*$, the supporters, and N as the set of voters for whom $U_t < U^*$, the nonsupporters. The consequences of a roll-call vote can drop voter utility levels below or raise them above the support threshold and thereby change their standing decisions. If utility levels do not cross a threshold, previous behavior does not change.

Earlier we skirted a question that we are now in a position to answer. There is a variety of more-or-less objective measures of legislative costs and benefits—money, jobs, and so forth. But the benefits and costs felt by constituents on their representative's expressed agreement and disagreement with their positions appear rather more subjective. In making their voting decisions, constituents must use some common denominator—utility, in short. What about representatives? In calculating their optimal decisions, they too must resort to a common measure. We assume that legislators gauge the consequences of their actions in terms of increments and decrements in their probabilities of support. The latter will naturally be functions of the quantities, B_1, C_2, A_i, D_i. Figure 2 presents the consequence matrix from which we derive vote change matrices as the analysis proceeds.

To explain, there are four (act, state) combinations arising from the two alternative acts (yea, nay) available to the legislator and the two possible outcomes (pass, fail) of the roll-call vote. Four subgroups experience various benefits and costs depending on which of the four (act, state) combinations obtains. If the bill fails (columns 2 and 4), no policy impacts (B_1, C_2) occur, but a position is taken whatever the outcome of the vote, so all columns contain position-taking consequences (A_i, D_i).

For purposes of the analysis, we transform the consequence matrix (Figure 2) into a series of expected vote change matrices (Figures 3a–3d). These matrices have the same entries in columns 1, 2, and 4, but differ in column 3. To illustrate our logic, we will work through the translation of Figure 2 into Figure 3a. First, recall that supporters (v_1, v_2) are those subgroups whose members' utility already exceeds the threshold required to support the representative. Thus, further improvement in their position will not produce additional support: the vote gains associated with consequences in cells (1,1), (1,2), and (3,4) will be zero. Conversely, nonsupporters $(g_1 - v_1, g_2 - v_2)$ are those subgroups whose members' utility presently falls below the threshold required to support the representative. Thus, further deterioration in their position will produce no additional loss of support: the vote losses associated with consequences in cells (4,1), (4,2), and (2,4) will be zero. All other consequences entail the provision of gains to nonsupporters or the imposition of costs on supporters, and hence the possibility of switching votes.

The analysis becomes somewhat complicated because of column

Figure 2. Consequence Matrix

	(1)	(2)	(3)	(4)
Legislator Vote:	Yea	Yea	Nay	Nay
Bill Outcome:	Passes	Fails	Passes	Fails
Constituency Groups				
(1) v_1	B_1, A_1	A_1	$B_1, -D_1$	$-D_1$
(2) $g_1 - v_1$	B_1, A_1	A_1	$B_1, -D_1$	$-D_1$
(3) v_2	$-C_2, -D_2$	$-D_2$	$-C_2, A_2$	A_2
(4) $g_2 - v_2$	$-C_2, -D_2$	$-D_2$	$-C_2, A_2$	A_2

3 of Figure 2. Here, the legislator votes in opposition to group 1 and in favor of group 2, but the legislation passes anyway, providing a benefit to group 1 and imposing a cost on group 2. Thus, the policy impact and position-taking consequences are in conflict, so the nature of the vote switches associated with them depends on the relative importance of the two classes of benefits and costs to the groups. Four cases arise, depending on whether each group views position-taking as more important than policy impact, or vice versa.

To proceed further, we need a numeraire to represent the vote changes associated with the entries of the consequence matrix. We will define a series of probabilities that constitute the legislator's estimates that his or her action and the vote outcome drop a present supporter below the critical threshold or raise a present nonsupporter above the threshold. Thus, for the entries in columns 1, 2, and 4 of Figure 2 we adopt the following definitions:

Probability	*Affected Group*
$p(A_i) = p([U_{jt} + U_j(A_i)] \geqslant U^*)$	$g_1 - v_1, g_2 - v_2$
$p(D_i) = p([U_{jt} + U_j(D_i)] \geqslant U^*)$	v_1, v_2
$p(B_1, A_1) = p([U_{jt} + U_j(B_1) + U_j(A_1)] \geqslant U^*)$	$g_1 - v_1$
$p(C_2, D_2) = p([U_{jt} - U_j(C_2) - U_j(D_2)] < U^*)$	v_2

And for the entries in column 3:

$$p(B_1, D_1) = p([U_{jt} + U_j(B_1) + U_j(D_1)] \geqslant U^*) \qquad g_1 - v_1$$
$$= p([U_{jt} + U_j(B_1) + U_j(D_1)] < U^*) \qquad v_1$$
$$p(C_2, A_2) = p([U_{jt} - U_j(C_2) + U_j(A_2)] < U^*) \qquad v_2$$
$$= p([U_{jt} - U_j(C_2) + U_j(A_2)] \geqslant U^*) \qquad g_2 - v_2$$

When weighted by the number of affected constituents, $(g_i - v_i)$ or v_i, these probabilities permit calculation of the expected vote gains and losses from casting a yea or a nay.

Having developed the preceding concepts and notation, we can now translate the abstract consequence matrix (Figure 2) into matrices suitable for analysis (Figures 3a–3d). At the risk of excessive repetition, we briefly explain again the entries in Figure 3a. In this case, both groups attach greater value to the position-taking consequences than to the policy impact—a case reminiscent of what scholars have called "symbolic politics" (Edelman, 1964; Sears, Lau, Tyler, and Allen, 1980). Thus, a nay vote will produce losses among existing supporters even though they receive the benefits of the legislation's passing (cell 1,3) and will produce gains among present nonsupporters even though they bear the costs of the legislation's passing (cell 4,3). $p(B_1,A_1)$ denotes the increment in likelihood of support from a present nonsupporter in G_1 as a result of claiming credit for the favorable impact, B_1, of a bill the legislator supported. $p(A_1)$ denotes the (smaller) increment from the same group in the event that the bill fails.[8] On the other side of the ledger, $-p(C_2,D_2)$ denotes the decrement in likelihood of support from current supporters in G_2 as a consequence of the passage of unfavorable legislation the representative supported. $-p(D_2)$ denotes the (smaller) decrement in likelihood of support from the same group in the event that the bill fails. All these probabilities are multiplied by the number of group members potentially to be gained or lost. In effect, the legislator somehow combines constituents' reactions to real benefits and costs, B_1 and C_2, and (possibly) psychic benefits and costs, A_i and D_i. This may sound difficult, but politicians must engage in some such estimation procedure when they balance off support and opposition.

The representative will vote yea (support G_1) if the expected vote gain from that action exceeds the expected vote gain from voting nay. Algebraically,

$$E(\text{yea}) = w^Y[p(B_1,A_1)\,(g_1 - v_1) - v_2 p(C_2,D_2)] + $$
$$(1 - w^Y)\,[(g_1 - v_1)p(A_1) - v_2 p(D_2)]$$

$$E(\text{nay}) = w^N[p(C_2,A_2)\,(g_2 - v_2) - v_1 p(B_1,D_1)] + $$
$$(1 - w^N)\,[(g_2 - v_2)p(A_2) - v_1 p(D_1)]$$

Subtracting, let $\Delta = E(\text{yea}) - E(\text{nay}) =$

$$w^Y(g_1 - v_1)\,[p(B_1,A_1) - p(A_1)] - w^Y v_2[p(C_2,D_2) - p(D_2)] + $$
$$w^N(g_2 - v_2)\,[p(A_2) - p(C_2,A_2)] - w^N v_1[p(D_1) - p(B_1,D_1)] + $$
$$(g_1 - v_1)p(A_1) - v_2 p(D_2) - (g_2 - v_2)p(A_2) + v_1 p(D_1) \qquad (1)$$

If (1) is positive, a vote-maximizing representative will cast a vote in the interest of G_1, and if negative, in the interest of G_2. Even if one is hesitant to posit pure vote-maximizing, it still seems a very plausible proposition that as (1) gets larger, a representative is relatively more likely to support G_1, and as (1) gets smaller, relatively more likely to support G_2.

What substantive propositions follow from roll-call behavior in accord with condition (1)? A number of them are quite common-sensical. For example, the more numerous a group, other things equal, the more likely will a representative take their side. This obvious proposition holds in all four cases, as one certainly would hope. Likewise, so long as the probabilities of crossing the critical threshold rise and fall monotonically with utility increases and decreases, respectively, the probability that the legislator takes a group's side of a conflict increases directly with the magnitude of the benefits and costs (both policy impacts and position-taking) at stake in the conflict. Some of the implications of (1) are more surprising, however, and these constitute the contribution of the model.

Recall that one of the major notions underlying the model is that of electoral history: existing support patterns should have an impact on the legislator's voting decisions. Consider then the responsiveness of the representative's voting decision to the v_i, the existing levels of support for him or her in the two groups. Surprisingly, the likelihood that a representative will support a group's interest does not necessarily increase with the level of the group's support for the representative. To put it another way, the legislator's calculus does not guarantee reciprocity—group support may not be repaid by responsiveness, for an increase in v_i can lead to an increase, decrease, or no change in the likelihood that a legislator votes to advance the group's interest. The conditions that restrict the direction of responsiveness are easy to specify, however, and interestingly, they yield negative voting as their substantive implication.

Take the special cases of (1) in which $w^Y = 0$, that is, the bill is doomed regardless of how the legislator chooses to vote. This is a common real-world situation, of course. In this case, the legislator's calculation reduces purely to a matter of taking the right position: (1) simplifies to (1'):

$$(1') \; \Delta = E(\text{yea}) - E(\text{nay}) = p(A_1) \, (g_1 - v_1) - p(D_2)v_2$$
$$- \, p(A_2) \, (g_2 - v_2) + p(D_1)v_1$$

Then:

$$\partial\Delta/\partial v_1 = p(D_1) - p(A_1), \text{ (positive if } p(D_1) > p(A_1))$$
$$\partial\Delta/\partial v_2 = p(A_2) - p(D_2), \text{ (negative if } p(A_2) < p(D_2))$$

Figure 3a. $u(B_1) < u(D_1)$; $u(C_2) < u(A_2)$ (Symbolic?)

		(1)	(2)	(3)	(4)
Contingency:		P/Y	F/Y	P/N	F/N
Probability:		$\underline{w^Y}$	$(1 - w^Y)$	$\underline{w^N}$	$(1 - w^N)$
Groups					
(1) v_1		0	0	$-p(B_1, D_1)$	$-p(D_1)$
(2) $g_1 - v_1$		$p(B_1, A_1)$	$p(A_1)$	0	0
(3) v_2		$-p(C_2, D_2)$	$-p(D_2)$	0	0
(4) $g_2 - v_2$		0	0	$p(C_2, A_2)$	$p(A_2)$

Note: $p(B_1, A_1) \geqslant p(A_1)$; $p(B_1, D_1) \leqslant p(D_1)$; $p(C_2, D_2) \geqslant p(D_2)$; $p(C_2, A_2) \leqslant p(A_2)$ (See note 7)

Thus, in this special case the condition that guarantees that group electoral support produces representational responsiveness is simply that unfriendly votes displease group members more than friendly votes please them—negative voting.

In the general case, the result is only slightly different. Looking at (1):

$$\partial\Delta/\partial v_1 = w^Y[-p(B_1, A_1) + p(A_1)]$$
$$- p(A_1) - w^N[-p(B_1, D_1) + p(D_1)] + p(D_1)$$
$$\partial\Delta/\partial v_2 = w^Y[-p(C_2, D_2) + p(D_2)] - p(D_2)$$
$$- W^N[-p(C_2, A_2) + p(A_2)] + p(A_2)$$

In each case, the first bracketed term is non-positive and the second bracketed term is positive (see the inequalities below the case 1 matrix in Figure 3a). Thus, for $\partial\Delta/\partial v_1$ to be positive (which G_1 wishes), it is *necessary* that $p(D_1) > p(A_1)$. Conversely, for $\partial\Delta/\partial v_2$ to be negative (which G_2 wishes), it is *sufficient* that $p(A_2) < p(D_2)$. Thus, the two sufficient conditions of the special case become one sufficient condition and one necessary condition in the general case: negative voting emerges as a means for constituents to insure the responsiveness of their representative.

The preceding analysis holds for case 1—position-taking consequences matter more to constituents than legislative impacts. What of the other cases, where this condition is reversed for one or both of the groups? Although the conclusions weaken somewhat, negative voting nevertheless appears to be a desirable behavioral pattern for constituents in the other cases as well. Consider case 2 (Figure 3b), where both groups now regard the policy impact of the legislation as more important than the legislator's positions. This case is more reminiscent of tangible or "pocketbook" legislative impacts.

Note how the entries in column 3 of Figure 3b differ from those in the corresponding column of Figure 3a. Proceeding as before,

$$E(\text{yea}) = w^Y[p(B_1,A_1)\,(g_1 - v_1) - v_2 p(C_2,D_2)] +$$
$$(1 - w^Y)\,[p(A_1)\,(g_1 - v_1) - v_2 p(D_2)]$$
$$E(\text{nay}) = w^N[p(B_1,D_1)\,(g_1 - v_1) - v_2 p(C_2,A_2)] +$$
$$(1 - w_N)\,[p(A_2)\,(g_2 - v_2) - v_1 p(D_1)]$$

Letting $\Delta = E(\text{yea}) - E(\text{nay})$

$$(2a)\quad \partial\Delta\partial v_1 = w^Y[p(A_1) - p(B_1,D_1)]$$
$$- w^N[p(D_1) - p(B_1,D_1)] - p(A_1) + p(D_1)$$
$$(2b)\quad \partial\Delta/\partial v_2 = w^Y[p(D_2) - p(C_2,D_2)]$$
$$- w^N[p(A_2) - p(C_2,A_2)] - p(D_2) + p(A_2)$$

First, note that the special case, $w^Y = 0$, yields the same results as previously—negative voting guarantees the positive responsiveness of the legislator to the level of group support. Because the special case is based only on columns 2 and 4, which are identical in Figures 3a–3d, all four cases generate the same implications when $w^Y = 0$.

In the general case, the first bracketed term in (2a) and (2b) is always negative, but the second bracketed term can be positive, negative, or zero. If it is non-negative, the results are as before: negative voting is a necessary (group 1) or sufficient (group 2) condition for roll-call responsiveness. If the second term is negative, however, no conclusion can be drawn about the necessity or sufficiency of negative voting. Inspection of the conditions, however, shows that even when negative voting is not necessary for roll-call responsiveness, its existence increases the magnitudes of $\partial\Delta/\partial v_1$ and $\partial\Delta/\partial v_2$, thus heightening the responsiveness of the representative to the previous support of his or her constituents. So, although the logical implications of the case 2 analysis are not as definitive as those of case 1, their substantive thrust remains the same.

Cases 3 and 4 (Appendix) are asymmetric in that one group values the representative's position more than the legislative impact, whereas the other group holds the opposite valuation. Thus, one group's situation is the same as in case 1, while the other group's situation is the same as in case 2. Not surprisingly, then, the results are a mixture of cases 1 and 2. In case 3, negative voting is sufficient for responsiveness to group 2, but may only intensify responsiveness to group 1. In case 4, negative voting is necessary for responsiveness to group 1, but may only intensify responsiveness to group 2.

Figure 3b. $u(B_1) \geq u(D_1)$; $u(C_2) \geq u(A_2)$ (Pocketbook?)

	(1)	(2)	(3)	(4)
Contingency:	P/Y	F/Y	P/N	F/N
Probability:	$\underline{w^Y}$	$(1 - w^Y)$	$\underline{w^N}$	$(1 - w^N)$
Groups				
(1) v_1	0	0	0	$-p(D_1)$
(2) $g_1 - v_1$	$p(B_1, A_1)$	$p(A_1)$	$p(B_1, D_1)$	0
(3) v_2	$-p(C_2, D_2)$	$-p(D_2)$	$-p(C_2, A_2)$	0
(4) $g_2 - v_2$	0	0	0	$p(A_2)$

Note: $p(B_1,A_1) \geq p(A_1)$; $p(B_1,A_1) \geq p(B_1,D_1)$; $p(C_2,D_2) \geq p(D_2)$; $p(C_2,D_2) \geq p(C_2,A_2)$ (See note 7)

CONCLUSION

Any common-sense notion of faithful representation would presume that increasing group support for a representative should produce increasing attention by the representative to group interests. But the foregoing analysis suggests that such a plausible proposition hinges on the presence of a special kind of asymmetric sentiment among constituents. Whatever its value in some religions, forgiveness appears to have little value in a representational context—at least in the simple sense of representation as roll-call responsiveness. If high responsiveness is desired, constituents should husband their gratitude but freely bestow their resentment: they should engage in negative voting.

The preceding conclusion is the main implication of our model of the implicit reward scheme faced by representatives: constituents engage in negative voting in order to insure that their representative reciprocates their previous electoral support. The model elevates negative voting above the status of casual observation, empirical generalization, and ad hoc assumption, and "endogenizes" this behavior by showing that it operates as a means to an intelligible end—exerting control over representatives.

Although we believe that the analysis developed in the preceding pages is extremely suggestive of a rational basis for negative voting, we recognize that important theoretical questions remain. First, nothing yet said provides an answer to the collective goods objection—even if negative voting is in the collective interest of a group, why would any individual member have sufficient incentive to negative vote as a means of insuring the larger group interest? Of course, the unified leadership of a well-organized group would have the incentive and the ability to enforce such a support pattern, so we have a comparative statics result associating negative voting with group organization. But unorganized issue publics, demographic categories, and so forth are still not accounted for. One could appeal to an evolutionary argument—groups whose members do not negative vote do not have their interests furthered and gradually lose their political influence to groups that do negative vote—but this seems a rather strained argument. To be sure, "multiple principals problems" have not been adequately treated in any principal-agent model with which we are familiar, and economic models generally have never yet explained why people vote at all—the ultimate collective action objection. So perhaps we are overly concerned with the rationality of individual behavior in this context.

A second unanswered theoretical question arises from the implicit assumption that groups want their representatives to further their interests by voting sincerely on each issue. If that is the case, then negative voting contributes to that outcome. But why should constituents have such a desire? Should they not wish their representatives to logroll? To vote strategically? Perhaps the answer to these queries is that logrolling and various forms of strategic behavior are too difficult for mass constituencies to monitor. Consider this question, Does the average constituent trust her representative sufficiently to believe that a vote ostensibly opposed to the constituent's interest reflects a secret deal that will pay off with interest somewhere down the line, or that it reflects an attempt to carry off a complicated parliamentary maneuver? That seems like a great deal to ask. Such considerations lead us to suggest that groups with substantial monitoring capacity (e.g., groups with full-time representation in Washington) will be more likely to tolerate or even encourage strategic behavior, vote trading, and so forth, while those without it (e.g., "mass publics") will opt for sincere voting and adopt strategies such as negative voting that will insure it.[9]

More positively, our analysis sheds some light on the "enforcement-commitment problem" described earlier. Although we do not attempt to establish it rigorously here, the negative voting/responsiveness relationship appears to have a self-enforcing quality to it, so that commitments are credible. Given negative voting by constituents, legislators appear to have a reduced incentive to cheat on roll calls by being nonresponsive. This proposition is straightforward inasmuch as responsiveness constitutes the legislator's "best response" to the reward scheme he or she faces. On the principal's side, given responsiveness by the legislator, constituents appear to have no incentive to renege on the negative voting reward schedule. If they fail to inflict disproportionate punishment on unresponsive agents, the latter will be less likely to find responsiveness on roll-call votes to be the "best response" to constituent behavior. Of course, the collective action problem discussed above weakens somewhat the force of this argument.

Our standpatter-switcher model of principal behavior is one member of a family of models. Specifically, the utility threshold idea underlying this model and reflected in Figures 3a–3d assumes that some act/state contingencies have no effect on some classes of citizens. For example, in contingency (1)—bill passes and agent votes yea— neither current supporters who applaud the agent's act, (v_1), nor current opponents who decry it, $(g_2 - v_2)$, are affected. But consider a less deterministic world in which supporters and opponents are distinguished in terms of their *likelihood* of supporting the agent next time rather than in terms of deterministic categories. For example, in contingency (1) category v_1 constituents, already supportive of the agent and approving of both his or her act and the outcome of the vote, might be assumed to be *even more* supportive ex post. The opposite sort of effect would be predicted for the category $(g_2 - v_2)$ constituents. This alternative model suggests that negative voting is an artifact. In other words, a pattern of negative voting may be observed in the data, but it is without substantive significance.[10] Thus, this discussion is not the final word on negative voting. What we have done is to offer one explanation for the phenomenon, an explanation that demonstrates that even seemingly "psychological" phenomena are by no means inconsistent with models of rational behavior in politics.[11]

Appendix

Case 3.
$$u(B_1) > u(D_1); \ u(C_2) < u(A_2)$$
$$\partial\Delta/\partial v_1 = w^Y(\leq 0) - w^N(> \ = \ < 0) - p(A_1) + p(D_1)$$

When the term multiplied by w^N is non-negative, $p(D_1) > p(A_1)$ is necessary for responsiveness. When the term is negative, no implication follows.

$$\partial\Delta/\partial v_2 = w^Y(\leq 0) - w^N(\geq 0) - p(D_2) + p(A_2)$$

$p(D_2) > p(A_2)$ is sufficient for responsiveness.

Figure 3c. $u(B_1) \geq u(D_1)$; $u(C_2) < u(A_2)$ (Case 3)

	(1)	(2)	(3)	(4)
Contingency:	P/Y	F/Y	P/N	F/N
Probability:	$\underline{w^Y}$	$\underline{(1 - w^Y)}$	$\underline{w^N}$	$\underline{(1 - w^N)}$
Groups				
(1) v_1	0	0	0	$-p(D_1)$
(2) $g_1 - v_1$	$p(B_1, A_1)$	$p(A_1)$	$p(B_1, D_1)$	0
(3) v_2	$-p(C_2, D_2)$	$-p(D_2)$	0	0
(4) $g_2 - v_2$	0	0	$-p(C_2, A_2)$	$p(A_2)$

Note: $p(B_1,A_1) \geq p(A_1)$; $p(B_1,A_1) \geq p(B_1,D_1)$; $p(C_2,D_2) \geq p(D_2)$; $p(C_2,A_2) \leq p(A_2)$

Figure 3d. $u(B_1) < u(D_1)$; $u(C_2) \geq u(A_2)$ (Case 4)

	(1)	(2)	(3)	(4)
Contingency:	P/Y	F/Y	P/N	F/N
Probability:	$\underline{w^Y}$	$\underline{(1 - w^Y)}$	$\underline{w^N}$	$\underline{(1 - w^N)}$
Groups				
(1) v_1	0	0	$p(B_1, D_1)$	$-p(D_1)$
(2) $g_1 - v_1$	$p(B_1, A_1)$	$p(A_1)$	0	0
(3) v_2	$-p(C_2, D_2)$	$-p(D_2)$	$-p(C_2, A_2)$	0
(4) $g_2 - v_2$	0	0	0	$p(A_2)$

Note: $p(B_1,A_1) \geq p(A_1)$; $p(C_2,D_2) \geq p(D_2)$; $p(C_2,D_2) \geq p(C_2,A_2)$; $p(B_1,D_1) \leq p(D_1)$

Case 4.

$$u(B_1) < u(D_1); \quad u(C_2) > u(A_2)$$
$$\partial\Delta/\partial v_1 = w^Y(\leq 0) - w^N(\geq 0) - p(A_1) + p(D_1)$$

$p(D_1) > p(A_1)$ is necessary for responsiveness.

$$\partial\Delta/\partial v_2 = w^Y(\leq 0) - w^N(> = < 0) - p(D_2) + p(A_2)$$

When the term multiplied by w^N is non-negative, $p(D_2) > p(A_2)$ is sufficient for responsiveness. When the term is negative, no implication follows.

NOTES

We wish to thank Samuel Kernell and Richard Lau for their comments on an earlier version of this chapter.

1. More generally, "A 'negativity effect' refers to the greater weight given to negative information relative to equally extreme and equally likely positive information in a variety of information-processing tasks" (Lau, 1985:119).

2. We do not wish to imply that empirical support for negative voting is unqualified. In an individual-level study of the effects of economic judgments on electoral behavior, for example, Kiewiet (1983) finds little support for negative voting. In an aggregate study forecasting the presidential vote in each state, Rosenstone (1985) reports no indication of negative voting. Both studies estimated models with many variables. Thus, the findings of the studies cited in the text may be spurious. On the other hand, minor or time-variant effects may not survive the competition of numerous more powerful or more systematic effects in large multivariate models. The reader should bear in mind that the models developed below identify conditions under which negative voting should be more or less strong.

3. Although of relatively recent development, the literature on agency theory is voluminous. For a general survey written for political scientists, see Moe (1984). For a more specialized survey of the technical literature, see Levinthal (1984).

4. More exactly, state-contingent consequences vary necessarily with the states of nature and possibly with the choice of acts as well. Act-contingent consequences vary necessarily with the choice of acts and possibly with the states of nature as well. State-contingent consequences often are called simply contingent consequences (the states of the world often being termed *contingencies*), and act-contingent consequences often are called simply *noncontingent consequences.* We use alternative terminology because in practice what is act-contingent and what is state-contingent depends on how one formulates the problem. For example, in the formulation of this discussion, position-taking consequences are act-contingent because the states of nature are posited as passage and failure of the bill. But in Fiorina's (1974) formulation, position-taking consequences are state-contingent because he defines the states as whether the groups care about the issue.

5. For a thoughtful discussion of the proper formulation and interpretation of decision problems in such circumstances, see Gibbard and Harper (1978).

6. This is not to say that all constituents necessarily care about or are affected by the issue, but only to say that among the concerned or affected there are two sides.

7. Evidently, other formulations could allow abstention (e.g., Fiorina, 1974, chapter 4). For now, we stick with the simplest possible model.

8. That is, the probability that a nonsupporter's utility rises above the threshold is at least as great if the legislator supports his or her position *and*

favorable legislation passes than if the legislation fails. Similarly, we assume that the probability a supporter's utility drops below the threshold is at least as great if the legislator opposes his or her position *and* unfavorable legislation passes than if the legislation fails. In short, we are making the natural assumption that the likelihoods of voter support at the least do not vary inversely with any component of voter utility.

9. For an elaboration of this argument, see Denzau, Riker, and Shepsle (1985).

10. If a constituent's probability of support were a concave function of his or her utility from agent actions and legislative outcomes, then what appears to be negative voting is actually a consequence of the mathematical properties of probabilities. See Fiorina and Shepsle (1989).

11. There are other explanations, of course. For example, suppose constituents reward *first* (by electing an agent), expecting subsequent responsiveness. If that responsiveness is forthcoming, then there will be little change in constituent voting; if it is not forthcoming, then constituents "throw the rascal out" for reneging. This may *appear* to be negative voting if one focuses only on subsequent constituent reactions and does not factor into the account the initial constituent "payment." We thank Barry Weingast for suggesting this possibility.

10

Incentives, Opportunities, and the Logic of Public Opinion in American Political Representation

Edward G. Carmines
James H. Kuklinski

Public opinion holds an exalted position in American society. Polling organizations report it, scholars study it, and political pundits kneel at its altar. Even Walter Lippmann, public opinion's most outspoken critic, could not refrain from writing three volumes about it (1913, 1922, 1925).

Empirical reports of public opinion's place in American politics fall into two distinct camps. One line of inquiry, heavily psychological in orientation, seeks to ascertain how "ordinary folks" (Kinder and Mebane's term [1983]) think about politics. Do they make a connection between their own life circumstances and government policies? Do they deduce specific opinions from ideological predispositions or other core values? Do they display stability in their attitudes over time and consistency at any one particular time? Is their response to political issues and actors principally affective or cognitive? And do they show evidence of "schematic" thinking about politics? Kinder (1983:390) summarizes the conclusions of this work: "Americans are in fact indifferent to much that transpires in politics, hazy about many of its principal players, lackadaisical regarding debates that preoccupy Washington, ignorant of basic facts that the well-informed take for granted, and unsure about . . . policies." He concludes (1983:390) that "We are left with the mystery of how people arrive at those political opinions they do hold."

Those working in the second tradition take these same individual preferences as given and aggregate them to the level of the congressional district or nation. They pose the now familiar question, Do members of Congress—individually or collectively—follow popular sentiments when they decide policy? Although subsequent work improved Miller and Stokes's (1963) original design and examined other data, their conclusion that public opinion influences what national legislators do, sometimes substantially, remains intact. As Page and Shapiro (1983:189; see also Kuklinski, 1978) put it twenty years later, "Opinion changes are important causes of policy change. When Americans' policy preferences shift, it is likely that congruent changes in policy will follow."

Consider now the view that emerges when the two sets of conclusions become one: Elected officials often heed the opinions of citizens who are ill-informed about and espouse little interest in governmental affairs. In stark terms, the blind and unknowledgeable lead the way, largely, albeit indirectly, determining their nation's policies. It is a portrayal that even staunch supporters of government-by-public opinion will find unsettling. Disturbing or not, it presumably describes modern-day governance.

Or does it? The following pages offer a more encouraging view of government-by-public opinion than does extant empirical work. Assuming that institutional actors respond to mass preferences in some fashion, given the variety of studies that point to this conclusion (e.g., Miller and Stokes, 1963; Kingdon, 1973; Wright and Berkman, 1986), we argue that democratic governance can be relatively "informed" governance.

But how can this be, given the conclusions just noted? We part from most previous research by not beginning with survey-generated data and the accompanying (implicit) assumption that public opinion is "natural," something to be taken for granted if not understood. The widespread use of surveys both reflects this assumption (interviewing is possible because people hold preferences) and reinforces it (after all, most people do express their opinions when asked). Rather, we set forth a logic of public opinion in American governance that explicitly recognizes the constraints that preclude an informed citizenry and, in light of them, propose a mechanism by which individuals can still make meaningful political judgments.

THE INFORMED CITIZEN: STRUCTURE AS A CONSTRAINT ON THE IDEAL

In the mid-fifties, Berelson, Lazarsfeld, and McPhee (1954:308) set forth a standard for the democratic citizen that political scientists came to cite routinely: "The democratic citizen is expected to be well informed about political affairs. He is supposed to know what the issues are, what their history is, what the relevant facts are, what alternatives are proposed . . . what the likely consequences are." One might reasonably ask, How else could it be? No one would advocate that uninformed citizens—who know little or nothing about alternatives, their probable consequences, and the like—should determine the direction of governmental policy.

Desirable and plausible as the Berelson strictures may appear, and widely held as they are, they do not represent the historically dominant view in the study of democracy and political representation. Eighteenth-century writers especially, who more thoroughly and systematically contemplated the nature of governance than anyone since, expressed little expectation of an informed electorate. To the contrary, they shared a basic belief that citizens would fall far short of the standard Berelson later imposed. Not blind to the intellectual limitations of ordinary men and women, these architects also saw a large-scale central government as inherently in conflict with the idea of a highly informed citizenry. The anti-Federalists, while most attuned to the antidemocratic consequences of a republic, did not stand alone in their concern. On more than one occasion, the Federalists acknowledged that ordinary people could not provide the kind of enlightened guidance on national issues that they often gave on local ones, even though they recognized the potentially negative consequences of such an admission on their efforts to implement a new government.

So why have modern scholars routinely overlooked the very thing that early writers felt would indelibly shape the workings of American politics? For one thing, once the structure that the Founders heatedly debated was put into place, students of American politics deemed it self-evident and therefore assumed it could be ignored; political scientists presumably can do better than to dwell on the familiar. For another, an unprecedented availability of survey data encouraged scholars to concentrate almost exclusively on individual cognitive capacities—and consistently reach dismal conclusions—without taking the structure of governance into account. Microanalysis became the sport of the day.

There is much to recommend this national pastime, which has greatly expanded the horizons of our knowledge. We also believe that explicitly recognizing the constraints a republic imposes on its citizens, and the possibilities for becoming informed that it allows, can help to unravel the puzzle set out earlier, Does uninformed public opinion truly shape congressional policy making?

DIMENSIONS OF THE CITIZEN'S PLIGHT

The Complexity of Policymaking

Governmental affairs are complex. Indeed so obvious is this complexity that drawing attention to it hardly seems necessary. Let us nonetheless see where stating the unexceptional leads.

Take a typical situation where Congress is considering two alternative unemployment policies between which citizens are asked to choose. In principle, reaching a sound choice should first of all entail identifying the major components of each alternative. Do the proposed programs, each designed to curb unemployment, include tax reforms? Blueprints to prime the housing industry? Job programs? Intricate monetary and fiscal incentives? Moreover, which societal groups does each policy initiative explicitly target? What are the projected overall costs, monetary and otherwise?

In addition to becoming familiar with the proposals themselves, citizens in principle will also need to assess the context within which they are made. What is the general state of economic affairs, and in which direction are the various indicators moving? Does the nation's unemployment picture look weaker in some sectors than others? Finally, did earlier sessions of Congress pass legislation similar to the proposals now being considered and, if so, what were their effects?

Having stated the citizen's task in its extreme should in no way take away from the basic point: Anyone wishing to make a wholly informed judgment about policy alternatives could clearly spend many years in preparation, by which time a new Congress would be deliberating a new agenda.

Ascertaining Cause and Effect and the Problem of Indeterminacy

Citizens make causal judgments and inferences every day of their lives. What caused the dramatic reduction in this year's heating bills, the relatively warm weather or the newly installed furnace? Are a child's poor grades due to lack of ability or to a poorly trained teaching staff that does not motivate students? Is the growing neighborhood crime rate a result of a deteriorating city economy, an inadequate police force, or both?

Determining the causal link is more difficult in some of these everyday situations than others, of course, but even the most trying example pales in comparison to the task facing the citizen-as-political-evaluator. The inflation rate dropped considerably during the Reagan administration's first term. Why? Perhaps the answer lies with the so-called supply-side economic policies that Ronald Reagan purportedly implemented early in his tenure. If so, was one specific program more responsible than others? Or is the change in oil prices, over which Reagan had little control, a more plausible explanation? After all, the decline in per-barrel cost of oil was precipitous and substantial.

National politics is a world in which many forces work simultaneously and indirectly and, consequently, one in which ascertaining cause and effect borders on the impossible. As we argue shortly, this essentially indeterminate nature of policymaking affords elected officials a valuable opportunity to interpret national affairs to their advantage. But it also limits ordinary citizens' efforts to reason from cause to consequence quite independently of any inherent intellectual shortcomings they may have. Recognizing the essentially indeterminate nature of politics should give pause to those who attribute citizens' inabilities to think causally about politics only to their individual weaknesses.

Citizens as "Outsiders"

Political complexity and the indeterminacy that accompanies it are not uniquely the citizen's problem. Professional economists disagree among themselves over what has caused what and what will lead to what. A more telling constraint on the citizen, and one that exacerbates the preceding problems, is that large-scale governments by their very nature limit people's access to the kind of original information that comes with direct participation in the proverbial town meeting. The very act of voting representatives into Congress places citizens outside the national policy process and thus severely limits what they can know about policy alternatives and their possible consequences.

Ironically, although people may be unable to obtain much primary information about public policy, they hear more about national affairs than any human can possibly comprehend, and certainly more than ever before. Witness, for example, the proliferation of news broadcasts, press conferences, and public addresses, let alone national newspapers such as *U.S.A. Today*. And herein lies the citizen's fundamental dilemma: Although besieged with secondary, piecemeal, and incomplete information about policy activities in Washington, enough to confuse rather than enlighten, rarely can he or she go directly to the "facts." The typical citizen faces a perplexing and seemingly unavoidable plight as an "outsider."

Government by public opinion is an appealing concept in American political thought, but one that, in practice, seemingly places an undue if not overwhelming burden on the individual. By all counts, citizens lack an adequate informational base on which to form policy preferences.

Add to this that people admit to lacking the motivation necessary even to approach the ideal citizen standard, as research has amply documented. It is the rare individual indeed who actively collects and threads together what information there is; most people prefer that it come to them, and in a readily consumable form. Given the structure of American politics, let alone the demands of daily life, who would question this posture? Most successful political scientists, we venture to guess, devote considerably more time to their research and teaching than to the details of the latest policy initiative in Washington.

We have arrived at nagging questions such as these: Given the complexity and indeterminacy of public policymaking, citizens' status as "outsiders" to the legislative process, and their passive stance toward the collection of information, is it not unrealistic to expect them to make informed political judgments? What is one to think about people favoring or opposing a complex economic or nuclear deterrence package when they do not actively search out information about it, and when they would be limited in what they could find if they did? On what conceivable basis can citizens conclude that an earlier program has worked or failed? Perhaps the question should no longer be, How informed are citizens? but, given the context within which they find themselves, How can people become even minimally informed?

HEURISTICS: A SHORTCUT TO POLITICAL INFORMATION

The foregoing discussion would seem to suggest, simply enough, that citizens have little or no informational basis on which to form preferences about the major policy debates of the day. And yet plainly most citizens do have opinions. Indeed, most citizens express them on a vast array of political issues, from national defense to social welfare to abortion. Moreover, although these attitudes may not represent reasoned judgments logically derived from full-blown and well-articulated philosophical premises, neither are they capricious or whimsical. Most people seemingly know why they prefer one policy position over another. How is this possible, given their lack of attention to politics and their paucity of information about national affairs?

Anthony Downs (1957) was the first political analyst to give serious attention to the problem of political information in modern mass democracies. Reasoning that the costs of becoming informed about the details of political issues generally outweigh the relative benefits to be derived from voting on an informed basis, he argues that it is irrational for most citizens to become fully knowledgeable about affairs in Washington. Downs (1957:210) identifies three types of costs involved in becoming informed:

1. *Procurement costs* are the costs of gathering, selecting, and transmitting data.
2. *Analysis costs* are the costs of undertaking a factual analysis of data.
3. *Evaluative costs* are the costs of relating data or factual analyses to specific goals, i.e., of evaluating them.

Together, these costs constitute a formidable barrier to becoming politically informed—too formidable, Downs argues, for most citizens rationally to invest the time, attention, and resources needed to meet the Berelson standard. Rather, rational citizens have strong incentives to develop methods of avoiding the substantial costs of information acquisition. They do so by developing a variety of shortcuts in the gathering and use of information. These shortcuts allow citizens to make political decisions and form political preferences without becoming fully informed about the context and details of the issues in question. In short, their use leads to the minimally informed—but informed nonetheless—citizenry mentioned previously.

There are two fundamental questions that need to be considered with respect to the use of informational shortcuts: what are the particular strategies employed, and how rational are they? Downs gave more attention to the latter issue than the former. He argues that reducing information costs is rational if it leads to approximately the same decision as that reached through a much more exhaustive and time-consuming process. After all, if the final decision derived from the two information strategies is approximately the same, why not employ the one that requires less time, attention, and resources? This is the essential logic underlying Downs's account of information in mass democracies.

Downs uses this logic to explain why most citizens adopt a long-term party identification. In his words (1957:100):

> some rational men habitually vote for the same party in every election. In several preceding elections, they carefully informed themselves about all of the competing parties, and all the issues of the moment; yet they always came to the same conclusion about how to vote. Therefore they have resolved to repeat this decision automatically without becoming well-informed, unless some catastrophe makes them realize it no longer expresses their best interests. Like all habits, this one saves resources, since it keeps voters from investing in information which would not alter their behavior. Thus it is a rational habit.

Since Downs wrote so insightfully about the rational basis of political ignorance, a large literature in cognitive and social psychology focusing on decision making under conditions of complexity and uncertainty has emerged (for a comprehensive review, see Ottati and Wyer, chapter 8, this volume). Beginning with Tversky and Kahneman's highly influential paper (1974), this work (see especially Kahneman, Slovic, and Tversky, 1982) has disclosed that individuals use a wide variety of heuristics—that is, shortcuts that reduce complex problem solving to more simple judgmental operations—to make social decisions.

Political scientists have begun to investigate heuristics that may be especially useful in making political judgments and evaluations. Brady and Sniderman (1985) suggest that citizens use a likability heuristic to estimate the issue positions of politically salient groups. By combining two pieces of information—their own position on an issue and their feelings toward opposing groups—people are able to estimate quite accurately the group's issue positions. Iyengar's experimental research (chapter 7, this volume) into the effects of television newscasts on viewers' perceptions of political issues shows that individuals use two major shortcuts—selective attention and an accessibility bias—to simplify and make sense of the "booming, buzzing confusion" of politics.

And in a recent study that is most relevant to our purposes, Sniderman, Hagen, Tetlock, and Brady (1986) examine three heuristics that supposedly allow citizens to figure out positions on complex political issues without knowing very much about the specific content and details of them. The three issue heuristics are affect (likes and dislikes), ideology (liberalism and conservatism), and attributions of responsibility (the so-called desert heuristic). Thus, to take the example that Sniderman and his colleagues use, citizens may oppose governmental assistance for blacks and other minorities because they are conservative in political outlook, because they dislike blacks, or because they don't believe blacks deserve governmental assistance. Conversely, individuals may support governmental assistance because they are liberals, like blacks, or believe blacks deserve assistance due to their unfortunate but unavoidable situation.

While people undoubtedly use these heuristics when making political decisions and evaluations, they may have more limited applicability than Sniderman and his colleagues suggest. For one thing, as the authors recognize, highly educated citizens, a fairly small proportion of the population, are the primary users of the ideology heuristic. For another, the affect and desert heuristics would seem to be mostly relevant to issue domains dominated by highly salient and controversial groups that generate powerful public reactions. The use of these heuristics depends, in other words, upon the easy designation of "bad guys/good guys."

In this chapter, we propose and consider the logic underlying another heuristic, one we see as uniquely attuned to recent developments in American politics: Citizens take policy cues from "insiders," specifically, members of Congress.[1] That is, they look to the very representatives whose decisions their opinions are supposed to guide.

It is not difficult to see why "political signals" could play a significant role in citizen decision making. By simply turning on the evening network news, people can ascertain "who is for what," a piece of information that is digestible and easily recalled. As we have pointed out, moreover, the citizen's plight is not a lack of information but an overabundance of the "wrong" type of information (i.e., secondary, piecemeal, incomplete, too general). Not so with information derived from key members of the U.S. Congress. Knowing how Senator Kennedy feels about a particular social welfare proposal would seem to be a crucially relevant piece of information for many citizens, one that brings them as close as they can come to being insiders themselves. Readily accessible, easily processible, crucially relevant—these are the characteristics that make congressionally based information fundamental to citizen decision making.

For the political signaling process to function as we have suggested requires, first, that congressional members have the opportunities, incentives, and resources to act as effective signalers and, second, that citizens use inside information to form policy preferences. Let us now turn to a consideration of the first question. To answer it affirmatively requires a theory of institutional behavior that differs markedly from the currently predominant one.

POLICY ENTREPRENEURSHIP AND REPUTATION IN CONGRESS

The dominant theory of institutional behavior—developed mainly to explain candidate election strategies but intended to apply to politicians more generally—argues that office holders and seekers should and do avoid taking clear and unambiguous positions on major policy issues (Downs, 1957; Shepsle, 1972; Page, 1976, 1978). Page has spelled out in greatest detail the argument's underlying logic. Politicians do not emphasize specific policy stands, according to Page, because to do so is costly. Appeals to liberals will alienate conservatives, while appeals to conservatives will estrange liberals. Clinging to the median position, he argues, will alienate both liberals and conservatives. Under these conditions, "the candidate's best strategy is to avoid issues of a divisive sort, and place (as nearly as possible) *no* emphasis on them, but devote all his time, money, and energy to matters of consensus (e.g., progress, prosperity, and peace)" (Page, 1978). Thus, Page argues, issue ambiguity—that is, vagueness and low emphasis—is a function of politicians' incentives. Because they are not penalized for making consensual appeals, but can find it costly to take clear and consistent positions on divisive policy issues, politicians have no reason to speak out clearly and forcefully on matters of public policy.

Should this argument apply to all politicians in all situations, it would not make sense to consider Congress as a source of valuable information to citizens. Pronouncements that peace is a good thing may comfort but will not inform people. However, there are reasons to doubt the general applicability of ambiguity theory. The argument presumes that citizens have well-defined issue preferences that—and this is a critical point—are not open to politicians' attempts at persuasion. But research indicates that people do respond to political messages, sometimes affectively, sometimes cognitively, in either case unmistakably (for a summary of this work see Lau and Sears, 1986). The malleability of public preferences leaves the door open to politicians' efforts to change them.

Ambiguity theory also assumes, implicitly, that constituencies are ideologically divided and socioeconomically heterogeneous. If constituencies are strongly divided over issues of public policy—not just over the importance of different issues but over what to do in given policy areas—then it may make sense for elected representatives to deemphasize policy entrepreneurship and concentrate solely on constituency service and narrow reelection activities. In this situation, taking a strong stand on one side of a policy dispute may very well incur the wrath of those on the other side and thus dim one's prospect of continued support and reelection. But this seems a far cry from a common situation in which socioeconomic and ideological homogeneity characterize electoral districts and states. For Senator Dole to champion farmers' interests or Senator Kennedy to articulate the liberal strain of opinion found in Massachusetts is hardly a strategy that courts electoral disaster.

Nothing thus far indicates that members of Congress function as policy entrepreneurs who advocate definite policy positions. We have only tried to demonstrate that the nature of individual attitudes and the distribution of preferences within some electoral constituencies leave open the possibility. To understand why legislators become policy entrepreneurs—clearly we think at least some of them do—we need to identify the incentives and opportunities associated with such an institutional strategy.

Incentives, Opportunities, and Policy Entrepreneurship in Congress

The most immediate goal of members of Congress is to gain reelection and, more generally, to become electorally secure (Mayhew, 1974). But consider this familiar, within-institution, scene:

> A policy initiative gets on the congressional docket; some members applaud it, others note its shortcomings and propose alternatives. Proponents and opponents alike predict the program's likely impact on various segments of the populace—blacks, working people, the middle class, elderly people. Each side, led by one or more champions of the cause, puts forth its best case. At times debate becomes so intense as to bring proceedings to a grinding halt—or so it seems.

Political competition in Congress—that is what this sketch describes.[2] With predictable regularity, factions form around a proposed policy, some legislators favoring it, others opposing it, all purporting to do "what the American people want."

Now if one takes political competition as a fact of congressional life, then policy leadership must be taken as given as well. The essence of political competition is winning, and the critical element in winning is strong leadership. Yet ambiguity theory says politicians have little incentive to become policy entrepreneurs, so where do the incentives and opportunities lie?

Focusing on electoral reprisals, as the predominant theory does, slights the institutional prestige (as well as the influence within the Washington community) that comes with policy entrepreneurship. Just as the label "leading political scientist," a title earned by one's research, carries with it honor and deference (let alone a healthy salary) among one's peers, so does effective policy leadership bring its share of rewards, including respect from fellow members. Risk always accompanies entrepreneurship, to be sure, but internal incentives alone should compel many congressional members to act as policy leaders.

Two other factors—one institutional, the other external—require explicit policy statements from congressional members. The institutional factor is obvious but often overlooked. Voting in committees and on the floor is a regular and time-consuming activity that results in congressional members staking out public positions on the controversial issues of the day, even when they would prefer otherwise. The external factor has to do with the electoral circumstances that surround candidates for Congress. Although issues of public policy may not be the dominant concern of the general election constituency, they often represent the central motivating force for party activists, financial contributors, and campaign workers. To maintain the support of these key political actors, congressional candidates are often forced to adopt specific issue positions, even when these positions might dim their general election prospects (Wright, 1978). So institutional and external factors reinforce internal incentives in encouraging policy entrepreneurial activity among members of Congress.

While both the Senate and the House have witnessed increased entrepreneurial activity during recent decades, it is the former chamber that has experienced the more substantial transformation. For a variety of reasons the Senate has become a hotbed of policy initiation and development (Carmines and Dodd, 1985; Polsby, 1971; Sinclair, 1986). Most obviously, the Senate stands as the principal incubator of presidential candidates (Peabody, Ornstein, and Rhode, 1976). Those who run for the presidency are expected to develop a full range of policy proposals to deal with the nation's problems. Therefore, to be taken seriously as presidential aspirants, senators must not only appear to be interested in and knowledgeable about salient problems, but they must also develop policy initiatives to deal with them. Policy leadership, in short, goes hand in hand with the Senate's role as presidential incubator.

Not only do senators have strong incentives for engaging in entrepreneurial activity, but they also have the resources to do so. Most important, the personal staffs of senators tend to be large and professional, which allows the staffs to do extensive research in a number of policy areas. Senators can select from a large number of policy domains, become knowledgeable, and then work to gain national recognition.

Finally, all the attention the national media lavish on senators encourages and facilitates policy leadership (Hess, 1986). The publicity associated with national media coverage is there to be used and exploited. But this is only the case if individual senators provide "good" news. If dull and unappealing, even senators will be of little interest to newsmakers. Given this situation, what better way for senators to gain and retain the attention of the national media than to become identified with—and perhaps even become policy advocates for—salient national concerns? Policy initiation and development provide senators with a viable means for both gaining media attention and shaping the positive content of the news.

Institutional prestige, a need to win the policy battle, and thoughts about a possible run at the highest office are, we think, the incentives that drive congressional members to act as policy leaders. Large professional staffs and extensive national media attention comprise a structure that greatly facilitates entrepreneurial activity within Congress. The combination of incentives and opportunities has led to the emergence of the Senate as a major source of policy initiation and development.

From Policy Leadership to Reputation

We have argued that it is rational for at least some senators and (to a lesser extent) House members to be policy entrepreneurs—to initiate and develop specific programs, to argue for or against proposed policies, and to criticize or applaud past policies. Many legislators probably act as policy leaders at one time or another in their careers. What interests us here are those congressional members who do so over and over again, for with repeated entrepreneurship come policy *reputations*. Consider three names—Edward Kennedy, Jesse Helms, and Claude Pepper—and three labels, "advocate of liberal policy," "generalist conservative," and "champion of the elderly." Many school children could correctly associate names and labels, given the legislators' national reputations. The reputations of these three legislators may be firmly established now, but only as the result of continued leadership within and outside Congress.

Establishment of a reputation, then, is a dynamic process, driven by the representative's ongoing policy activities. The reputations that congressional members earn may be general, as in the case of archrivals Kennedy and Helms, or policy-specific, as in the case of Pepper. Moreover, they may change over time. To be able to say precisely when legislators do and do not have policy reputations and how they change requires an elaborate theory of reputation that is beyond the scope of this chapter (see Calvert, 1986). That policy reputations exist is beyond dispute.

Now entrepreneurial activity only makes sense in a world of imperfect information. If all consequences of various policy options were perfectly observable before legislative deliberation, senators' and House members' statements and actions would be superfluous. Not only does imperfect information open the door to policy entrepreneurship and reputation-building, but it also allows entrepreneurs to claim success. A legislator who initiated a new jobs program, for example, can usually "prove" success even though others see failure. Who is to say, finally, what has and has not worked? The indeterminate nature of politics enhances reputation-building.

Analytically, we can distinguish among three types of congressional signalers. The first—and surely the most visible—are those congressional members with general and well-defined political ideologies. In the contemporary Senate, the prototypes of the ideological signal-giver are Kennedy on the left and Helms on the right. Session in and session out, across a wide range of specific issues, Kennedy and Helms help define what it means to be a liberal and conservative.

A second type of congressional signal-giver is the policy specialist. These signalers do not provide salient information and policy cues across the full congressional agenda, but only within specific policy domains. Prominent contemporary examples include Congressman Pepper on issues associated with the elderly, Senator Nunn on defense matters, and Senator Bradley on taxes. Because of their expertise, visibility, and reputations, these members have become highly effective policy signalers within their areas of specialization.

There is a third type of congressional signal-giver, more diffuse and less well defined than the previous two. These are members whose signal-giving capacity derives neither from their general ideology nor their policy expertise. Instead, they are seen as well-informed political leaders who have reached reasoned judgments on difficult and complex political matters. It is no coincidence that this type of signaler, of which former Senator Baker and Senator Byrd are examples, often holds positions of formal authority within the legislature. Like the electorate-at-large, their congressional colleagues see them as moderate, well-informed, trusted—that is, having precisely those qualities that lead others to entrust them with substantial power and authority.

Although it is possible to distinguish among these types of signal-givers analytically, these categories are tentative and flexible and may be neither exhaustive nor mutually exclusive. Senator Dole, for example, cuts across all three types, being a conservative ideologue at an earlier point in his congressional career, then a trusted party leader, and always an expert on agricultural issues. His example also reminds us that a legislative role as signal-giver can evolve through time in response to changing career patterns and political circumstances.

Entrepreneurial activities are largely internal to Congress, but mass communications give them currency and influence well beyond the national centers of government. Consequently, a congressional member's leadership efforts accumulate into a policy reputation not only among colleagues, but also among citizens. Policy reputations are common knowledge, public information that is widely disseminated to ordinary people. It is reasonable to assume, therefore, that they are a critical link between citizens and their national institutions and a key to understanding how the former reach policy judgments.

BECOMING INFORMED: ON THE LOGIC OF USING INSIDE INFORMATION

Reflect momentarily on a scene familiar to any viewer of network news. After briefly introducing the dimensions of an emerging policy dispute in Congress, the newscaster identifies Senators A, B, and C as proponents and Senators X, Y, and Z as opponents of a recently considered initiative. In addition, the network interviews one leading and well-known spokesperson on each side of the debate. Over the next three months, the network continues to air the views and statements of the central congressional actors, including comments on an alternative program that emerges as part of the deliberations.

By simply watching these newscasts, people can gain considerable insight into a policy debate in which they are not directly involved. On the one hand, they learn *who* are the staunchest supporters and opponents of the policy proposal. And, as we argued previously, with the "who" usually come political reputations, the culminations of past activities that give citizens a basis on which to decide whether they do or do not trust the legislator to do the right thing. On the other hand, the public statements that these policy entrepreneurs make, and the media convey, tell a citizen *what* positions they hold in the specific proposals.

Each message alone—the "who" and the "what"—has limited value, but together they represent a potentially useful and readily interpretable piece of information. In the simple (and perhaps common) case where trusted congressional members take one side of the policy debate and untrusted legislators the other, the institutionally generated information is reinforcing and gives citizens a firm basis on which to form an opinion. To know that legislators whom one trusts favor—and those one distrusts oppose—a policy should move an individual toward a positive but not a negative judgment about it (or should have little effect at all). An opposite configuration presumably will lead to a very different result.

The effect of this "insider-to-outsider" communication need not be limited to the *direction* of an individual's policy preference. It is no secret that congressional leaders try to frame policy debates to their advantage, about which Schattschneider (1960) wrote so eloquently. Is an import fee on Japanese goods a question of international trade and maintaining good relationships with foreign countries, or a matter of protecting the American worker? Should the imposition of pollution controls be seen mainly as an environmental or as an economic concern? If legislative entrepreneurs, through a combination of their reputations and public positions, can "inform" citizens about the "proper" direction of their preferences, so should they be able to "inform" them about the "right" way to construe the debate itself.

Two citizens may hold the same position on a proposed legislative program, and view the policy debate in similar terms, yet hold qualitatively different opinions: One expresses confidence in her preference, whereas the other is unsure of his. Why the greater confidence in one instance? At least in principle, the availability and use of "inside" information can affect the certainty with which people hold and express preferences. To know that Senator Edward Kennedy, for example, opposes the latest tax reform plan gives people a definite "step up" on those blind to the configuration of national legislators involved in the policy debate.

The logic just outlined, although admittedly simple, is a natural derivation given the structure of contemporary American politics. By using summary information that emerges from the legislative struggle—information that by no means is complete or unbiased, but represents the single best inside source available to citizens-at-large—people can compensate for an inaccessibility to original information and simultaneously deal with the overload of secondary political messages that characterize contemporary society. Downs (1957:233) captures the essential logic underlying this process of information-seeking among ordinary citizens when he observes:

> S cannot be expert in all the fields of policy that are relevant to his decision. Therefore, he will seek assistance from men who are experts in those fields, have the same political goals he does, and have good judgment. Furthermore, if S knows that T, whom he trusts, has general political goals similar to his own and better judgment than S himself, then it is rational for S to delegate the final decision to T if the latter has information equal to S's. . . . In this case the returns from information are very large indeed. . . .

What will increase people's willingness to use reputationally based information? Legislators who have accumulated a "track record" over a long duration, and who tend to be consistent in their statements and behaviors, should be more attractive inside sources than unknown lawmakers; in the latter case, reputations may be non-existent. Similarly, people familiar with the congressional members' long-term performances should be especially disposed toward a role as signal-taker. In other words, the process we have been describing presumably is most operative between well-established legislators on the one hand and politically aware citizens on the other. Conversely, logic dictates that the total absence of either factor—reputation or awareness—precludes signal-taking as a means of becoming informed (Table 1).

An interesting case—it applies to a large segment of the population—exists when people pay only fleeting attention to national affairs. Do the public statements that legislators make as part of major policy debates still influence how individuals think about the controversy? We believe they do, especially when media coverage of the deliberations continues over time. Even the most casual observers of network news programs cannot avoid discussions of a president's economic initiatives, disagreements over the advisability of U.S. aid to the Contras, or, earlier, heated exchanges on President Carter's proposed energy program. Modern technology almost ensures the penetration of national debates into the public consciousness.

Finally, people should find inside information more valuable on emerging than on established issues. When not familiar with the dimensions of the controversy, citizens presumably will be especially inclined to look for help.

Earlier, we proposed three types of congressional signalers—the ideologue, the policy specialist, and the trusted generalist. Corresponding to these would seem to be three types of signal-takers. The first type are ideologically motivated citizens—citizens with well-defined, consistent, "extreme" political views—who presumably look to ideological congressional signalers for their primary political cues. The second type of signal-taker focuses attention on a specific policy area, such as mass transportation or health. Not interested in obtaining information and taking cues across the full policy agenda, these citizens eschew ideological signalers in favor of policy specialists within Congress. The third group are those individuals who neither display a strong ideological orientation nor focus exclusively on a single policy area. These citizens lack a passion for politics and tend to be moderate in their views. They place their faith principally in national legislators who espouse a balanced view and function as brokers within Congress.

FROM LOGIC TO SUGGESTIVE EVIDENCE

No matter how active and influential within the institution, members of Congress can serve as inside sources of information only if the media afford them extensive and prolonged coverage; the establishment and communication of policy reputations require no less. A question, therefore, is whether television news programs, the principal source of political information for most people, regularly report the activities and policy statements of at least a subset of all national legislators.

Since 1972, the Vanderbilt Television Archive has published, by year, the number of times the three major networks mentioned each member of Congress on its nightly broadcasts. These counts reveal great discrepancies in the coverage that House members and senators received during the period 1972–84. In 1979, for example, the average senator warranted 17.1 network mentions, but the range ran all the way from 0 to 407, with the most-covered senator, Kennedy, accounting for one-quarter of all citations. And by no means is 1979 exceptional: In every year for which data are available, a select group of national lawmakers monopolized the news while many others remained anonymous to citizens across the land.

Extensive coverage does not necessarily translate into *prolonged* coverage. Sam Ervin, for example, became a media phenomenon during the Watergate hearings and for a short time thereafter, but otherwise rarely appeared on nightly news programs. Similarly, Thomas Eagleton's controversial bid for the Democratic vice-presidential nomination catapulted him into national prominence in 1972, but the media literally forgot about him in the following years. These and similar examples aside, some lawmakers have maintained high levels of coverage over time. Kennedy, Baker, Dole, Goldwater, Cranston, O'Neill, and Helms head the list, which comports with casual observations of "who's who" in American politics.

Note that all but one of the media's favored legislators reside in the Senate. Generally speaking, senators stand more equal than their House counterparts in the national policy process, a reality to which the media apparently are sensitive. The relatively greater influence of senators within the institution translates into greater media attractiveness, which in turn represents a potential advantage in shaping mass preferences.

If adequate media coverage of national legislators is one necessary condition for signal-taking as a means to gain information and

Table 1. Likelihood of Signal-taking, Given Level of Political Awareness and Nature of Legislator's Policy Reputation

Legislator's Policy Reputation*

		Well Known	Not Well Known
Citizen's level of political awareness	High	High	Low/Moderate
	Low	Moderate	Low

* Entries indicate likelihood that an individual will act as a signal-taker.

form judgments, that people use inside information is the other. Logically they should; whether they in fact do begs empirical analysis. Although the data we report fall considerably short of conclusive, they suggest a congruence between logic and reality.

In two separate surveys, one of California adults and another of University of Illinois students, we asked respondents whether any national legislators worked for (and against) their interests. Despite the difficulty of the recall questions, nearly 60 percent of the adult and 55 percent of the student sample identified at least one incumbent lawmaker (Table 2). Equally interesting, respondents in both samples tended to identify congressional members who had championed one or more causes, and thanks to the media, had established reputations. It is no coincidence that Senators Dole, Helms, Kennedy, and Cranston and House Speaker O'Neill both dominated nightly news programs *and* became political lightning rods for citizens-at-large.

Well-educated people and people with a fairly strong interest in politics, we argued earlier, will be most inclined to look to insiders. To the extent that association of legislators with one's interests is a measure of that inclination, our expectation is well founded. Both education and interest in politics correlate positively with the naming of at least one member of Congress as working for or against the individual's interests. In the former case, the relationship is linear, in the latter nonlinear: the discrepancy between people with little and much political interest outdistances that between the poorly and well educated. Reputation, cognitive ability, and interest seemingly work

Table 2. Most Frequently Named U.S. Senators and House Members

Member of Congress Named	Number of Times Named	
	California Sample	Illinois Sample
Howard Baker	19	5
Philip Burton	14	0
Dan Crane	0	12*
Alan Cranston	123*	6
Alan Dixon	0	7
Robert Dole	12	4
Barry Goldwater	12	3
Gary Hart	11	6
Mark Hatfield	10	0
Sam Hayakawa	85*	3
Jesse Helms	38	13
Jack Kemp	12	4
Edward Kennedy	89	19
Tom Lantos	136*	0
Paul Laxalt	10	0
Pete McCloskey	121	0
Tip O'Neill	40	7
Claude Pepper	16	0
Charles Percy	6	13*
Strom Thurmond	11	3
Other U.S. senators	20	21
Other House members	23	16

*Respondent's own representative or U.S. senator

in tandem to link representatives and citizens. By no means does the linkage involve all members of Congress or all ordinary people.

Thus far we have said little more than that some people outside the national policy process identify their interests with one or more legislators, from which we infer that the latter's reputations allow people to make the connection. We still lack concrete evidence that members' publicly stated stands influence what and how people think about matters of public policy. The following results suggest that when people directly receive information about legislators' policy positions, it influences their judgments and opinions.

As we noted previously, 55 percent of the University of Illinois sample identified one or more members of Congress as working either for or against their interests when asked an open-ended question to that effect. We used and manipulated this information in a second questionnaire that the students completed two months later. Among the many items that the second survey asked were two on economic policy. The first reads: "Would you say, as do ( ), that the overall state of affairs in the United States today is good, or would you say, as do ( ), that the overall state of affairs in the United States today is not very good?" Letting (+) designate a positively and (−) a negatively viewed legislator, as ascertained in the first questionnaire, many combinations within the parentheses are possible, although we concentrated on two: (1) + for, − against; (2) − for, + against. In essence, varying responses to the first questionnaire in the second allowed us to employ a classical experimental design.

The difference in means indicates that the positions legislators take can influence respondents' general economic evaluations, indeed strongly so (Figure 1). It is a long leap from a manipulated survey item to the real world, of course, but perhaps not so great as one might first think. Admittedly, people do not give evening newscasts or morning newspapers the immediate and sustained attention they presumably give questionnaires, but many do watch and read; in the process they consciously or unconsciously consume valuable "inside" information.

At least on the basis of our small survey, individuals also respond to the way legislators define the scope of a policy debate. A second question asked about acid rain, which at the time of the survey had not yet become an issue in the United States.

> Acid rain results from power plants burning high sulfur coal to generate electricity. Research indicates that it is killing fish populations in the United States and Canada, causing plants and trees to die, and leading to the deterioration of buildings and highways. The question is what to do about it. On one hand are those—(, for example)—who argue that legislation greatly reducing the sulfur emissions of power plants will drive up energy costs, cause many people in the coal industry to lose their jobs, and cost millions of dollars. In other words, they oppose legislation at this time on *economic* grounds. On the other hand are those—(, for example)—who say that unless tough legislation is passed soon, the environment will be damaged beyond repair. In other words, they favor legislation at this time on *environmental* grounds. Obviously deciding what to do is no easy task. Put yourself in the position of a member of Congress. If you had to choose, would you, like ( ), oppose acid rain legislation on *economic* grounds or, like ( ), favor it on *environmental* grounds.

In this instance, we randomly assigned respondents to one of two categories: (1) + construe the legislation as economic, − construe it as

Figure 1. Relationship between Political Signals and Evaluation of Overall State of Economic Affairs*

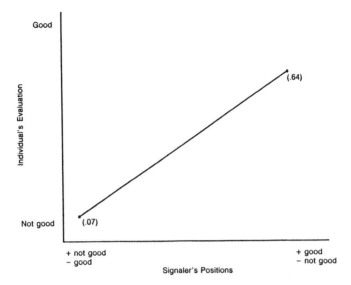

* + indicates positive signal given, − negative signal given; figures in parentheses are means of responses, where not good = 0, good = 1

environmental; (2) − construe the legislation as economic, + construe it as environmental.

Figure 2 indicates a relationship between the type of information respondents received and their interpretations of the policy debate, although it is not as strong as the immediately preceding results. When told that trusted legislators define the issue as economic and untrusted as environmental, respondents showed a greater inclination to construe the issue in economic terms than when given the opposite information.

We used a different pool of students to ascertain whether the kind of "inside" information we have been exploring affects the certainty with which people hold their preferences. The specific question we posed is, Do people who know both the "facts" about the policy debate and the positions of prominent U.S. senators express higher levels of certainty than those who know only the former?

Using Carmines and Stimson's (1980) distinction between "easy" and "hard" issues, we asked students to indicate their own preferences and their level of confidence in those preferences on two policy debates. The "easy" issue took this form:

Figure 2. Relationship between Signalers' Constructions and Individuals' Conceptions of Policy

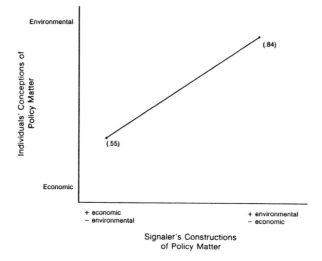

+ indicates positive signal-givers, − negative signal-givers; figures in parentheses are means of responses, where + economic, − environmental = 0, + environmental, − economic = 1

> Congress is considering a bill that would monetarily compensate black steel workers, who, according to determinations reached by the U.S. Civil Rights Commission, received less pay than white steel workers in equivalent jobs. The amount of compensation would depend on the alleged number of years of discrimination. In no case would the amount exceed $200,000.

The "hard" issue read:

> Congress is considering a bill that would replace much of the existing arsenal of U.S. missiles with a new system. Nearly all intermediate-range missiles would be dismantled and replaced with short-range missiles having a maximum range of 600 miles and a new type of tactical nuclear weapon that can reach its destination in one-half the time the existing cruise missile can. The proposed system is largely designed to counter the Soviet SS-20s and SS-4s.

On each hypothetical bill, one-half of the students read only the two descriptions. The other half were also told that Senator Edward Kennedy was a leading proponent and Senator Jesse Helms a strong opponent of the bill.

The results in Figure 3 indicate that knowing the two senators' positions increased respondents' confidence in their own stated preferences. On both types of issues, individuals who were given the two senators' positions expressed greater levels of certainty than those who were not. Even more telling are the differential effects across the two issue types. Knowing where two well-known legislators stood increased certainty much more on the hard than the easy issue. It would appear that "inside" information becomes especially valuable when people cannot easily respond to a policy debate "from the gut," a fact that takes on added significance if one assumes that firmly held opinions are preferable to loosely held ones in democratic societies.

Figure 3. Relationship between Type of Information and Certainty of Expressed Preference

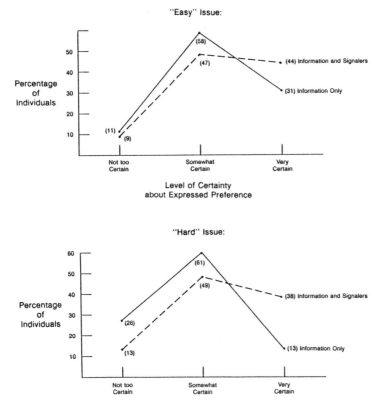

CAVEATS AND IMPLICATIONS

From the inception of systematic empirical analysis in political science, the demand-compliance model of political representation has dominated thinking about the linkage between mass opinions and congressional policymaking. Not only can researchers readily test it empirically—collect a (often indirect) measure of district opinion and tabulate relevant roll call votes—but the model also reflects the popular normative position that government *should* respond to its citizens' wishes. Unfortunately, its central assumption, that people form and communicate policy demands to elected representatives, who in turn comply to a greater or lesser extent, ignores some basic facts of political life. These include the complexity of public policymaking, which renders easy judgments next to impossible, an asymmetry in accessibility to information that gives elected representatives an undeniable advantage over the citizens who elect them, and, finally, the demands of private life that preclude most people from actively becoming informed about the major policy debates of the moment. In short, the demand-compliance model begins with an unrealistic portrayal of the citizen and fails to recognize the structural features of American representative democracy that limit citizens' abilities to become politically informed.

Taking the realities of modern representative democracies into account, we have argued, raises a question that earlier investigations have often overlooked: Given the constraints upon them, how do private citizens arrive at the political judgments that presumably guide congressional decision making? The same realities point to signal-taking as an answer. Prominent members of Congress, engaged in the competition of everyday legislative life, transfer "inside" information to citizens-at-large. These political messages, in turn, condition how and what people who receive and use them think.

While we derived the idea of signal-taking from the structure of contemporary representative democracies, it is satisfying to know that the concept comports with prevailing perspectives on the individual. Signal-takers are both prototypical Downsian rational actors and what psychologists call "cognitive misers" (Fiske and Taylor, 1984; Nisbett and Ross, 1980): they find a way to make political decisions without upsetting or altering their daily lives. An academic researcher striving to win a Nobel Prize probably will not sacrifice precious laboratory time to reach a well-informed judgment about the placement of a new missile system in Europe. But by viewing nightly news programs, he or she can readily obtain critical baseline information—who favors what and why.

Although a rational mode of decision making, citizen reliance on legislators' signals often begins with affect. Indeed, what binds the citizen-outsider to members of Congress is one of the most basic feelings of all—trust. Even the most ardent devotees of the "individual-as-cold-calculator" perspective now acknowledge feelings and emotions as critical components in all types of judgment.

Before turning to the implications of our argument for the workings of American politics, we would be remiss not to acknowledge its limitations. Most important, political signals in the real world are not as direct and clear as we have perhaps implied, and considerably less so than those presented in the experimental surveys. Our empirical analyses show that unambiguous messages from members of Congress condition people's judgments. How much influence actual signals have, and under what conditions, given the substantial amount of "noise" that accompanies them, remain open questions. In the same vein, we did not examine how people react to potentially conflicting signals—Jesse Helms and Edward Kennedy both supporting a civil rights initiative, for example.

Nor did we explicitly address the matter of availability. What if, on any given policy debate in Congress, the national legislators to whom a citizen has historically looked do not emerge as visible spokespersons for one side or the other? Does this unavailability not undermine the very logic of signal-taking as a means by which individuals form preferences? Perhaps not. As we noted earlier, a select group of congressional members have consistently garnered disproportionate amounts of network coverage, at least during the years for which we have data. Not coincidentally, these are the same members with whom most people associate their political interests. Moreover, during any given legislative session, only a few issues emerge and endure. As time passes and the media concentrate on the leading actors in the debates, ordinary citizens likely form impressions of them: Do they appear trustworthy and competent? Are they generally known as liberals or conservatives? All this notwithstanding, availability is the *sine qua non* of the signaling process, and thus it warrants fuller treatment than we have given it here.

Of course, people can draw on environmental sources of information other than legislators' political statements. Interest groups and the president also convey signals, and apparently people heed them (Kuklinski, Metlay, and Kay, 1982; McKelvey and Ordeshook, chapter 12, this volume; Page, Shapiro, and Dempsey, 1987). We initially focused on members of Congress because they truly are the "ultimate insiders." By focusing more narrowly, moreover, we avoided what otherwise might have been an insurmountable task. In fact, despite our initial decision, we have been left with annoying questions for which we have no answers. This said, a full-blown conception of representative democracy from an informational perspective will need to take other political actors into account.

Given that political signals emanate naturally from the legislative process, and assuming that people use them as a primary source of political information, what are the implications for the nature of democratic representation in the United States? We end our discussion with four conjectures with which the reader may disagree and, in any event, whose validity future research must test.

1. Contrary to populist conceptions of political representation, American politics is elite-driven. The division of labor between those whose primary business is governing the nation and those for whom politics is secondary dictates that the former will, under most circumstances, set the agenda, define the parameters of major debates, and bring deliberations to their conclusion. We are not demoting public opinion to a place of insignificance in American politics; some issues begin at the grass-roots level, Vietnam and abortion being cases in point, and it is the rare legislator who ignores the pulse of his or her district when casting a visible roll-call vote. But the fact remains: "insiders," be they in politics or business, occupy the driver's seat.

Note our use of the term *elite-driven,* as opposed to *elite-dominated* or *manipulated* (but see Ginsberg, 1986). The latter implicitly assume an elite monolith. By its very nature, the competitive legislative process ensures alternative voices and signals from which citizens can choose. Moreover, most congressional members intend to remain in the "market," which greatly reduces—although, unfortunately, does not eliminate—the likelihood of their betraying or pulling the wool over the public's eye. Facing reelection and internal competition supposedly collars the potentially recalcitrant and/or deceitful legislator.

2. On any policy debate before Congress, a very few members disproportionately influence public opinion. In recent years, a select group of U.S. senators, led by the likes of Edward Kennedy and Jesse Helms, have constantly served as the principal conveyors of inside information. How certain members emerge as policy leaders and darlings of the media we cannot say. But once they do, their influence on citizen attitudes extends well beyond their own states.

Members recognize that the Senate, especially, affords an opportunity for them to become national leaders of public opinion. Consider the case of Senator John D. Rockefeller from West Virginia. In an interview (Cohen, 1987), he and senior members of his staff openly discussed plans to establish the senator as a leading expert on international competitiveness on the assumption that this policy domain will become increasingly salient to citizens-at-large in future years. Congressional members recognize that signaling is an integral part of the legislative process, and therefore of political representation, and some establish long-term plans to become leading participants in the game.

3. The citizen-as-signal-taker participates in two distinct "markets." On one hand is the *information market,* that pool of legislators who provide political signals. Although in principle the pool consists of all congressional members, in practice it consists of the select few who emerge as policy leaders. The single House member and the two U.S. senators for whom the individual citizen can cast ballots, on the other hand, comprise the much smaller *election market.*

Now institutional actors to whom many people look for information may not be part of their election markets. Two implications follow. First, voting turnout in many districts and states may be suboptimal in that people who reside in them lack an opportunity to express preferences for those national legislators with whom they associate their interests. An election in which Kennedy and Helms face each other, for example, should stimulate greater interest among Illinois voters than one that pits Alan Dixon against an unknown Republican.

Second, congressional members who do not function as policy leaders within the institution and as major signalers to the outside world, and who come from districts where public opinion is unpredictable, face an especially challenging task as decision makers. Not knowing who will emerge as political signalers, and thus as framers of the debate for citizens-at-large, let alone which side will more successfully sway public attitudes, these legislators may have no option but to wait. In other words, not being a policy entrepreneur *within* the institution, for whatever reasons, relegates them to a delegate role with regard to their constituents. This situation should be most prevalent on new and emerging issues, such as euthanasia or mandatory AIDS testing.

4. Although signals exist in both markets and politics, they differ considerably in the nature of the information they convey and thus in their effectiveness as communication mechanisms. Price, the principal signal in the marketplace, represents a concrete, precise, and unambiguous piece of information that consumers and suppliers alike see. Alternatively, according to a "rational expectations" perspective (cf. Muth, 1961) the signal is the behavior of market "insiders" who

are akin to policy entrepreneurs in Congress. Even in the latter case, the signal sends a clear message about an objective reality. When individuals privy to a corporation's internal decisions unload its stock, all brokers witness the act.

Consider, in contrast, the political signals that emanate from Congress. People almost invariably receive different messages at the same time: a program has worked or it has not worked; a policy initiative to stimulate the economy will burden the average taxpayer or it will increase corporate activity and ultimately add to the individual's purchasing power; the Contras represent a critical bastion against communist infiltration and therefore warrant United States support or the United States should eliminate all foreign aid to groups such as the Contras who flagrantly violate human rights. Even when the government reports objective indicators, such as the change in unemployment, conflicting statements attributing cause and responsibility abound.

In short, political signals lack the concreteness, simplicity, and precision of market signals. At the same time, they are more complex and ambiguous. Political signaling greatly reduces the "booming, buzzing confusion" that surrounds politics for the average citizen, but it does not eliminate it altogether.

More than half a century ago, Lippmann (1925:64) captured the essence of the citizen's plight when he wrote:

> We must assume that the members of a public will not anticipate a problem much before its crisis has become obvious, nor stay with the problem long after its crisis is past. They will not know the antecedent events, will not have seen the issue as it developed, will not have thought out or willed a program, and will not be able to predict the consequences of acting on that program.
>
> The public will arrive in the middle of the third act and will leave before the last curtain, having stayed just long enough perhaps to decide who is the hero and who the villain of the piece.

As we have seen, this is all that is required of citizens for political signaling to function in American representative democracy.

NOTES

1. The classic work on cue-taking within Congress is, of course, Matthews and Stimson (1975).

2. For a more fully developed treatment of political competition within Congress, see Kuklinski (1988).

11

Agency and the Role of Political Institutions

Pablo T. Spiller

Political markets are plagued with agency problems; voters elect their representatives under substantial uncertainty about what the representatives' objectives are. The same representatives are re-elected, although voters do not know exactly what the representatives did during their tenures and how their actions relate to the voters' well-being. Representatives, in turn, delegate much of the work of their offices to committees or to subcommittees, again with substantial uncertainty about their colleagues' actions. Furthermore, Congress delegates regulatory power to regulatory agencies and to the courts, and again, agency problems abound in the resulting interface.

Politics, then, can be seen as a hierarchy of principal-agent relationships. On top of the pyramid are the voters representing the ultimate principals. At the bottom of the pyramid are, perhaps, the government bureaucrats. In between is a series of layers in which multiple principals and multiple agents interact.

This depiction of the political arena may provide the impression that agents may be free to pursue their own objectives almost independently of the interest of the ultimate principals (the voters). Hence, the agency relationship would not result in an efficient allocation of political resources. The preceding two chapters, as well as the literature dealing with agency problems in politics, suggest otherwise. Instead of claiming that agency problems allow agents total freedom to pursue their own objectives, the modern theory of agency suggests that the rationale for most political institutions is to make agents' choices closer to those that would maximize total political surplus. In many cases this would imply choices closer to those preferred by the principals.

The agency approach to political institutions, then, analyzes what principals and agents can do to solve the inefficiencies that delegation naturally creates. There are several differences in the application of the agency approach to political and economic issues. First, the usual agency relationship derived from the economics literature takes the principal as the one that can commit to a specific contract form (i.e., to a specific institution). This assumption does not reflect all possible agency relationships in economics and certainly not in politics. The client-lawyer relationship, for example, does not satisfy that assumption. Lawyers usually set the terms and conditions of the contract. In politics, the passive agent is even less frequent; consider, for example, the voter-legislator relationship. Although voters may be seen as the ultimate principals, the legislators themselves may be able to impose restrictions on voters' abilities to punish legislators. Hence, I would expect that agents in political environments will have a larger strategic role in determining institutions than is assumed in most of the economics literature.

A second difference is that, although most economic models assume a single principal, multiple principals seem to be the norm in politics. Consider, for example, the voter-legislator relationship. A legislator is the agent for a multiplicity of voters. Even when several voters may have common interests, the potential for free-riding is obvious. Even if free-riding can be avoided, multiple voting groups imply that the legislator will have to satisfy conflicting interests. Similar problems arise when dealing with the Congress-regulator relationship. Although congressional oversight committees are more homogeneous than is Congress at large, there are still differences among committee members. Hence, regulators may play committee members against each other. As will be seen, however, these differences, although important, do not make the application of the agency approach to political issues substantially different from its applications in economics.

Agency literature has been applied to political science in three main areas: elections, congressional institutions, and regulatory control. The chapters in this volume by Fiorina and Shepsle and Carmines and Kuklinski focus on elections and so constitute a natural place to begin my discussion.

AGENCY AND ELECTORAL INSTITUTIONS

The seeming lack of information that characterizes the electoral process makes it, in principle, subject to potentially large agency problems. On the one hand, the basic question in political science—why people bother to vote at all—still remains to be answered. Because the probability of an individual's vote being the decisive one is as close to zero as a human mind can assess, voters motivated exclusively by an expected economic payoff calculation will find the costs of voting above their expected gains. Hence, economically motivated voters will not vote, and those who do must pursue some other objectives.

Consider now those voters who (for whatever reason) do want to vote. They have to gather and process information about the candidates. Because information gathering and processing are costly and have substantial externalities, a free-rider problem will develop so that, in the absence of coordination or the development of other institutions, no information will be gathered and processed. Again, voters are left in the dark, and in the absence of information, no voting would take place.

The problem with the preceding argument is that it misses the potential gains from the creation of institutions that reduce, on the one hand, the need for information gathering and, on the other hand, the cost of information gathering and processing.

Among the institutions that reduce the need for information gathering is retrospective voting. Ferejohn's (1986) retrospective voting model is one of the first to develop formally an agency voting model requiring no information gathering by voters. Essentially, the voters' problem is to find a threshold utility level so that if their current utility is below that level, they will vote against the incumbent; if their current utility is above the threshold, they will reelect the incumbent.

Fiorina and Shepsle's discussion is in the same spirit as Ferejohn's. They use retrospective voting to show that negative voting can be a rational response of voters facing uncertainty about the incumbent's actions. Negative voting develops when the probability of voting against the incumbent among voters facing a reduction in their well-being is larger than the probability of voting in favor of the incumbent among those facing an increase in their well-being. Fiorina and Shepsle present the conditions for negative voting, which they define as a "means for constituents to insure the responsiveness of their representative" (232).

Fiorina and Shepsle start from a set of axioms about voting behavior. That is, voting behavior is not derived from utility maximization, but instead it is assumed. Thus, their result remains to be shown as an optimal outcome to joint decision making by different groups of voters. In particular, the choice of the utility threshold (U^*) is a strategic decision by each voters' group that should take into account the optimal response of the legislator.

I believe that the result of the Fiorina and Shepsle model could be developed from a game with multiple principals and a single agent. The multiple principals are the different groups of voters, and the agent is each legislator. The strategies of each group of voters are the choice of U^* and of the probability of voting in favor depending on whether the voters' utility level exceeds or falls below U^*. The legislator strategy, in turn, is a voting pattern. The optimal strategy of each group is chosen as a best response to the other group and to legislator strategies. Likewise, the legislator strategy has to be a best response to the different voter group strategies. Such a model may provide negative voting as an outcome. If it does, as I conjecture, then Fiorina and Shepsle's result would be strengthened substantially.

Carmines and Kuklinski analyze a problem related to other chapters in this volume: how does a democracy function when voters seemingly lack information about issues and about how candidates' positions will affect the voters' welfare? Implicitly using an agency framework, they develop a theory of institutions that tends to ameliorate the agency problems between voters and legislators. Their major contribution is the suggestion that legislators' signaling may be used by voters in forming expectations about future welfare.

The Carmines and Kuklinski model could also be represented as a game between two sets of players. On the one hand, the voters are "besieged with secondary, piecemeal, and incomplete information. . . . The typical citizen faces a perplexing and seemingly unavoidable plight as an 'outsider' " (244). On the other hand, there are the legislators, the "insiders" to Washington politics. The insiders' strategies are to send signals to the "perplexed" voters and, in turn, the outsiders' strategies are to decide to whose signal to listen. The signals that the insiders send about the potential impact of a policy on their constituents may or may not reflect the "truth." For signaling to be an equilibrium, then, reputation for truth-telling has to develop. Such a game may have multiple equilibria. One is a signaling equilibrium in which a legislator with a truth-telling reputation sends signals, and voters follow him or her. This equilibrium has to be enforced by a punishment strategy in case the legislator is found "cheating." That is, voters may find that the legislator's signal does not represent the truth. Such a punishment may consist of voting for another candidate in the next election.

Signaling equilibrium and retrospective voting are thus complementary institutions. Signaling provides a second dimension to voters' decision making. Not only will voters now ask the question, Am I better off than expected?, but they will also base their predictions about future welfare on signals their legislator sends. Carmines and Kuklinski's reputation model is related to other reputation models developed in economics and applied to the analysis of congressional institutions, in particular by Calvert (1986).

The electoral connection (Mayhew, 1974), then, is not agency problem-free. Moreover, the models analyzed in this chapter, as well as elsewhere in the literature, suggest that electoral institutions will develop to make it work, at least to some extent. Among other issues that could be analyzed from an agency perspective are the design of electoral processes (e.g., primaries), the role of legislative tenure, and the reduction in legislators' turnover.

Whether the electoral connection works has been the subject of substantial empirical scrutiny, especially among economists (e.g., Kau and Rubin, 1979; Kalt and Zupan, 1984; Peltzman, 1984). Because the implications of agency theory for the development of electoral institutions remain to be explored fully, the extant empirical evidence should be seen primarily as suggesting stylized facts rather than providing tests of the agency theory of politics.

AGENCY AND CONGRESSIONAL INSTITUTIONS

The agency approach to congressional institutions is represented in a body of research that analyzes congressional institutions as solving contracting problems between different parties, in particular, voters and legislators. Because legislators' actions take place in—and are subject to the institutions that govern—Congress, this approach complements and is related to the discussion of the previous section.

Shepsle and Weingast (1987) and Weingast and Marshall (1987) have proposed contracting frameworks to analyze congressional institutions. While Shepsle and Weingast deal with the importance of committees, Weingast and Marshall analyze, in a consistent contracting framework, other aspects of Congress as well. Legislative leadership is another institution that has received attention from an agency perspective (Calvert, 1986), and is closely related to the electoral aspects of agency discussed previously.

Calvert considers a model in which an exogenously given congressional leader tries to impose his or her desire on the rest of the legislature. The leader has some ability to punish those followers who deviate (i.e., who do not vote accordingly). The leader's ability to punish determines as well the limit to his or her demands from the rest of the legislators. If the leader's demands are "too large," it may pay the legislators not to follow. Thus, an equilibrium is a set of demands, a punishment strategy, and a decision whether to follow so that each is a best response to the other players' equilibrium strategies.

There is a feasible, and I think interesting, combination of Calvert's and Carmines and Kuklinski's frameworks. Consider the case in which one of the leader's strategies is to endorse an incumbent legislator. Then, by Carmines and Kuklinski's model, such an endorsement provides voters with a valuable signal that they will follow if they believe it to be credible. Thus, in making their voting decisions, voters will look at what their congressional leaders say about the current candidates. There are then several layers of leadership. On the one hand, there are the congressional leaders who command power in Congress at large, and who use their power to punish in order to obtain legislation for a wider array of interests. This type of leader is not only followed by the members of Congress, but also by a sect of voters. On the other hand, there is the congressional leader who may enforce collaboration from fellow legislators through signaling whether or not to support a candidate to his or her (perhaps ideological) constituency-at-large. Thus, Carmines and Kuklinski's signaling model and Calvert's leadership models can be embedded in a general framework of congressional behavior.

Congressional signaling and reputation, then, may be understood as manifestations of institutions arising to solve information and coordination problems. Further research along these lines should be useful in understanding the role of other political institutions like parties (for a game-theoretic formulation see Baron, 1987), congressional caucuses, or different legislative rules and procedures (see Krehbiel, Shepsle, and Weingast, 1987; Baron and Ferejohn, 1987).

AGENCY AND REGULATORY INSTITUTIONS

The role of agency problems in the design of regulatory institutions has attracted perhaps the most attention among political scientists and economists. There may be good reasons for such emphasis; regulations are congressional creatures, but Congress does not directly implement them.

The basic question of why Congress delegates regulatory authority is at the core of the agency approach to regulatory institutions. Fiorina (1982, 1985) raised the question, and it still remains to be answered fully. Dismissing (perhaps as too simplistic) the "complexity" rationale, Fiorina theorizes that group concentration and shifting responsibility are at the core of a theory of congressional delegation of regulatory authority. His theory, although not formally developed in agency terms, has all the necessary ingredients for an agency theory. First, voters cannot fully observe what legislators do and, hence, must act in a retrospective way. Second, if regulators design regulatory implementation, subject to congressional oversight, then voters' retrospective strategies may be attenuated. The ability of voters to punish each individual legislator is even further reduced when courts administer the regulations. Hence, Fiorina postulates a three-level regulatory framework in which voters are on top of the hierarchy, congressmen are in the middle, and regulators are on the bottom. The interesting feature of this pyramid, however, is that legislators may change the nature of information transmission and thereby the ability of the ultimate principals (i.e., voters) to control the immediate agents (legislators). For a similar structure, see Spiller (1988).

The idea that Congress designs regulatory institutions to improve its ability to regulate regulators is at the core of several papers by McCubbins and Schwartz (1984), Calvert, McCubbins, and Weingast (1987), and Spiller (1988), as well as others. The thrust of this line of research is that delegation of regulatory authority to regulatory commissions creates an agency problem. Congress, then, will develop institutions to control its regulators. For example, McCubbins and Schwartz (1984) suggest that members of Congress will use their constituencies to control regulators through the "fire alarm" process. That is, they will institute a review of the regulatory agency only after receiving enough complaints from their constituencies. Thus, there is no need for a continuous oversight (policing) of the agency. Even though there does not seem to be any oversight, the agency is under control.

McCubbins and Schwartz's fire alarm idea could be developed from the following formal agency model. Consider a congressional committee in charge of a regulatory agency. The regulatory agency takes actions, x (e.g., effort), unobservable to the committee. The committee observes the realized output, y. Let y be a binary variable, with $y = l,h$. The probability of $y = l$ is given by $f(x)$, $f'(x) > 0$, $f''(x) < 0$. Let the committee prefer to observe $y = l$ rather than $y = h$. If the committee observes h, it does not know if h was realized because of low effort by the regulator, or purely bad luck. Upon observing the realized outcome, the committee may undertake a regulatory review. The review, however, would take time and be costly for the committee.

Let the direct cost be R. There is also an indirect cost to the review because of the reduction in the agency's regulatory effectiveness during the review. The review will also be costly for the regulator, with regulator's cost given by T. The review will provide the committee with some information about the regulator's actions. That is, the committee will observe a signal, s, with s being correlated with x. The equilibrium to the game, then, is a contract between the committee and the regulator, such that (a) with probability p the committee starts a regulatory review if $y = h$ (reviews will not be undertaken when $y = 1$); (b) there is a threshold level for the signal s, such that if $s < s^*$, then the committee will impose the maximum feasible penalty upon the regulator P (i.e., may reduce its budget). If $s > s^*$, the committee imposes no extra penalty. In any case, upon realization of $y = h$, the regulator's expected utility is reduced to its minimum level. In turn, the regulator undertakes regulatory actions. Regulatory effort, however, most often will not be first best. Regulatory reviews play a role similar to auditing in buyer-supplier relationships (see Demski, Sappington, and Spiller, 1987).

Because of the discreteness nature of the model, it has an extreme fire alarm feature. Whenever $y = h$, a regulatory review is undertaken. Alternatively, when y is a continuous variable, the equilibrium will specify a y^* such that if the observed $y > y^*$, the committee will institute a regulatory review, while none will be undertaken as long as $y < y^*$. The fire alarm, however, is not triggered by constituents.

McCubbins and Schwartz's fire alarm, however, is triggered by constituents. To institute such a fire alarm, consider the case in which the committee receives monthly letters from the relevant constituency complaining about the workings of the regulatory agency. Constituents here play the role of a continuous monitoring device. That is, legislators receive continuous signals (z) that are correlated with x. The higher the level of the constituents' complaints, the higher the probability that the regulator was not undertaking sufficient effort. Thus, the equilibrium now is going to consist of a threshold z^*, such that if $z > z^*$ a regulatory review is undertaken, and a threshold s^*, such that if $s < s^*$ an additional penalty P is imposed upon the regulatory agency.

Thus, McCubbins and Schwartz's constituent-generated fire alarm notion becomes almost indistinguishable from one in which constituents play no role, but Congress directly observes the output but not the actual regulatory actions.

The role of allowing interest groups to monitor the regulators was further explored by McCubbins, Noll, and Weingast (1987). Here, administrative procedures are organized such that interested parties are assured participation. By allowing constituents to participate in the hearings and procedures of the regulatory agencies, Congress increases the correlation between interest groups' monitoring signals and actual regulatory actions. Thus, the efficiency of the fire alarm system is increased, and regulatory reviews may now be undertaken less often.

A different role for interest groups is analyzed in Spiller (1988), where interest groups are allowed to compete directly with Congress for the regulator's favors. Interest groups' influence on regulators has several implications for the design of regulatory institutions. First, it implies that, apart from corner solutions, regulatory effort will not be at the optimal level (for Congress). Second, regulatory implementation will take several interest groups into account, even when the congressional oversight committee may be dominated by a single interest group. Third, because of the competition between members of Congress and interest groups, regulators will usually command rents. Dissipation of rents may take the form of patronage appointments, and appointed regulators will come from a pool of individuals who have paid their dues to the relevant legislators. Finally, congressional and interest group rewards (or punishments) are negatively correlated. Congressional rewards may take the form of increasing the agency's budget, reappointing the regulator, promoting the regulator to a more senior administrative job, or allowing the regulator access to members of Congress once the regulator leaves the office. On the other hand, interest group rewards may take the form of direct (but illegal) cash transfers or directly or indirectly hiring the regulator (indirect hiring takes place when the regulator goes to work for a private company, usually a law firm, and Congress funnels business to that private company). Another form of rewarding regulators may be cooperating with the regulatory agency on the normal regulatory proceedings of the agency.

The framework developed in Spiller (1988) can be combined with the monitoring one described previously. Consider again the case in which the regulatory output is discrete, $y = l,h$, with Congress preferring $y = l$ over $y = h$. Again, x represents the regulator's effort and is unobservable. In the absence of monitoring, Congress will set a low (high) budget, while the interest group will set a high (zero) transfer when $y = h$ ($y = l$). Assume now that there is monitoring of the regulator's actions through constituency participation in the regulatory process. Now, instead of reducing budgets whenever $y = h$, a regulatory review will be undertaken when the signal from the constituents (z) exceeds a threshold level (z^*). Following the regulatory review, if the observed signal $s < s^*$, then the regulatory agency's budget may be further reduced. If $s > s^*$, no additional penalty is imposed on the regulator. The advantage of using the monitoring system is that while the regulator's expected utility when $y = h$ is reduced to the minimum feasible by Congress's future actions, once monitoring is called upon, the regulator faces a lottery. Because s is correlated with x, a further reduction in budgets following a low s increases the incentives for the regulator to undertake a relatively higher x. Likewise, by not reducing budgets when s is large, operating (regulatory) performance is not hurt in some cases, even when $y = h$.

The employment implications of Spiller are of a different nature than those derived in Calvert, McCubbins, and Weingast (1987), which analyzes the appointment game between Congress and the president. Although in Spiller all potential regulators are alike, Calvert, McCubbins, and Weingast allow regulators to differ in their taste. Extending Spiller's framework to allow taste differences among regulators implies that regulators will usually be chosen from those closer to the oversight committee's preferences. Thus, interest groups will have to make larger transfer offers to be able to achieve influence. The rest of the results may not differ.

When the regulatory actions or policies are multidimensional, and the committee members' preferences are not identical, the regulator may have substantial discretion (see Hammond, Hill, and Miller [1985] for a deterministic framework). An agency framework with multidimensional outputs and multiple principals may provide good insights into the extent to which congressional committees may regulate regulators.

SUMMARY

Agency problems arise whenever there is delegation and imperfect information, natural characteristics of the political process. Although the agency approach only recently has been applied formally to political science, the substantial discussion of agency issues in politics should serve as a guide to further formal explorations of those topics.

IV

SYSTEMIC
PERSPECTIVES ON
THE RATIONALITY OF
AMERICAN POLITICS

12

Information and Elections: Retrospective Voting and Rational Expectations

Richard D. McKelvey
Peter C. Ordeshook

There are wide discrepancies between the assumptions of voter knowledge embodied in the classical spatial theory of elections, on the one hand, and the empirical facts on levels of voter political awareness revealed by survey research and public opinion polls, on the other. The assumptions that voters know the candidates' positions on salient issues, that they know their own preferences on these issues, and even that they conceptualize election outcomes in terms of well-defined policy dimensions seem fundamentally at odds with the findings of decades of public opinion research.

Empirical research reveals an electorate that varies considerably in its level of concern over political events and in the amounts and sources of its political information. But the average level of information is appallingly low by the standards of traditional democratic theory. A large portion of the electorate is unaware of basic facts of political discourse such as the number of senators from their state or the names of their representatives (Almond and Verba, 1963; Kinder and Sears, 1985). Few voters can correctly identify candidate positions on the most broadly defined issues, and large numbers of voters have trouble identifying their own preferences on these same issues (Berelson, Lazarsfeld, and McPhee, 1954; Campbell, Converse, Miller, and Stokes, 1960). Candidates and parties contribute to voter confusion through their success in generating ambiguity in their policy pronouncements (Page, 1978). Only a fraction of the electorate conceptualizes politics in the ideological terms taken for granted by politicians and academics (Campbell, Converse, Miller, and Stokes, 1960; Converse, 1964). To the extent that voters have issue concerns, the electorate seems to be divided into issue publics concerned only over issues that have direct and immediate bearing on those voters' welfare (Repass, 1971). When it comes to making decisions in such a sparse information environment, uninformed voters apparently base their voting decisions on historical and retrospective considerations (Key, 1966; Kramer, 1971; Fiorina, 1981) and take cues from reference groups and other cheap information sources (Popkin, Gorman, Phillips, and Smith, 1976; Kuklinski, Metlay, and Kay, 1982). In light of these facts, with apparent justification, some political scientists do not view the Downsian approach as providing an adequate understanding of democratic processes and institutions (Ferguson, 1983).

Born of the simple economic view that individuals seek to maximize their individual welfare, and based on information assumptions substantially at variance with the above picture, the Downsian models derive a general result (first noted by Black, 1958): the Median Voter Theorem. This theorem asserts that in a one-dimensional policy space, when voters have single-peaked preferences, two candidates seeking to win an election will converge to the ideal point of the median voter. These models have been modified to incorporate multiple dimensions, statistical uncertainty, variations in turnout, dichotomous issues, alternative objectives for candidates, campaign activists, preferences that do not yield Condorcet winners, and mechanisms whereby voters simplify their perceptions of issues. But even with such modifications, the general finding of this research is that there is a central tendency in simple two-candidate elections (for a comprehensive survey, see Enelow and Hinich, 1984).

The above models have all been developed under the assumptions of full information. But are the discrepancies between data and assumptions so great as to render spatial theory incapable of shedding any light on how democratic processes operate in the absence of complete information? Does the lack of information on the part of the voters mean that the forces of political competition, if they exist at all, are wholly removed from the electoral arena? Does the neo-Marxist critique of representative democracy, which resurrects the hypothesis of public policy dictated by monopolistic "elites," offer a more appropriate paradigm than the Downsian approach, which implicitly emphasizes competition and popular control of public policy?

Although answers to such questions are beyond the scope of this discussion, our research is relevant to these broad and important issues. Specifically, we will review a series of experimental results that study voting in the absence of complete information. These experiments are designed to evaluate how well voters perform under incomplete information and to address the question whether the main inference of the Downsian models—the convergence of candidates to median voter or core outcomes—still holds in the presence of incomplete information. We consider several different experimental designs differing in the quality and amount of information available to the voters and candidates. We find encouraging results regarding the ability of voters to make "informed" decisions in the presence of incomplete information. Regarding candidates, we find some degree of median voter convergence by the candidates in all the experiments, with the speed and accuracy of convergence related to the quality and amount of information available to the voters.

Our conclusion is that the pervasiveness of imperfect or incomplete information found in empirical research is not a sufficient condition for ineffective popular control. It is possible for voters to make informed choices and for candidates to converge toward policies that would prevail if everybody's information were complete.

Our analysis may also have implications for why voters seem to have such low levels of information about politics. Popkin, Gorman, Phillips, and Smith (1976) hypothesize that information is an investment and that voters rationally fail to make costly investments in political information. Both our theory and our experimental data would tend to support this argument in the sense that we find that a variety of cheap information sources can inform the decisions of voters almost as well as expensive sources can. These sources include the historical record of the candidates and their parties (both in terms of the voter's perception of his or her welfare and in terms of observed policy positions), interest group endorsements of candidates, public opinion polls, and the opinions of friends and other associates.

The experiments concern three distinct designs that differ in terms of the amount and the source of information that voters and candidates possess. In the first experimental design, reported in detail in Collier, McKelvey, Ordeshook, and Williams (1987) and Gray, McKelvey, and Ordeshook (1986), and which models the traditional hypothesis of retrospective voting, we provide voters and candidates with virtually no information about the structure of the situation that confronts them. Voters observe historical information about their payoffs (real income) derived from the policies (spatial positions) of previous incumbents, but they do not observe these policies directly. Further, to model the situation in which voters do not even conceptualize elections in terms of issues, the voters in our experiments are uninformed about the specific relationship (payoff function) between an incumbent's policies and their welfare. Nor do they know that an incumbent's strategy concerns the selection of positions in some policy space. Candidates observe the aggregate vote in each election, and although they know the form of the policy space (its dimensionality), they do not observe voter payoff functions, the distribution of voter ideal points, or even the votes of specific voters.

The following section of this chapter, then, concerns an electorate in which voters are unable to identify the positions of candidates on issues and where contemporaneous events, including prospective policy positions of the candidates, endorsements, or campaign rhetoric, are not available to the voters. Despite the minimal information supplied to subjects in this design, we find that incumbents converge (albeit slowly) toward the electorate's median preference. Moreover, the attractiveness of the median persists even if the underlying preferences of the electorate change in unanticipated ways, if incumbents can only imperfectly control policy, or if candidates themselves hold policy preferences at odds with the preferences of the electorate.

Although we see convergence in the above design, it is slow. Even after twenty-five election periods, there is still considerable variation in the candidate positions around the core point. Further, because candidates do not adopt prospective policy positions, it is not possible to evaluate the voters' strategies in terms of how they compare with a full information benchmark.

We next review a second design, reported in McKelvey and Ordeshook (1985b and 1986b), that supplies voters with some additional historical and contemporaneous information in such a way that the design models the Downsian view of retrospective voting (for the distinction between traditional and Downsian views, see Fiorina, 1981). Here, voters know of the existence of an issue space and know their own utility functions in that space. Voters observe the historical record of incumbents in terms of actual issue positions (rather than just payoffs) that incumbent candidates have adopted in previous periods. In addition, both candidates, the incumbent and the challenger, take prospective policy positions. Voters do not observe these policy positions, but they do observe an endorsement of the candidate in the current election campaign based on the policy positions adopted by the candidates. Candidates do not know anything about voter preferences aside from what they can infer on the basis of the margins of victory in each election. In these experiments, we are now able to evaluate the voting strategies in comparison with what would occur under full information, and we find that more than 80 percent of the voters vote for the correct candidate. Regarding candidate behavior, we again find convergence of the candidates toward the median. However, the convergence does not appear to be significantly faster than in the previous experiments.

In a third design, reported in McKelvey and Ordeshook (1984, 1985a, 1987), voters, instead of having access to historical policy positions, are supplied with some indirect information about the candidates' policy positions in the current campaign. In these experiments, a subset of the voters are informed and the remaining voters are uninformed. The informed voters know the current policy positions of the candidates, whereas the uninformed voters do not. Uninformed voters, on the other hand, have some information about the electorate's distribution of preferences (or at least about some identifiable subgroups within the electorate) and information about endorsements and public opinion polls where these polls provide (possibly contaminated) information about the decisions of informed voters. Candidates observe this same endorsement and poll information. We now find, in addition to "informed" voter behavior, quite rapid convergence of the candidates to positions near the electorate's median preference.

TRADITIONAL RETROSPECTIVE VOTING

Our first experimental design is modeled after the view of voters, labeled "traditional retrospective voting," that the following quote from Key (1966) best summarizes: "The patterns of flow of the major streams of shifting voters graphically reflect the electorate in its great, and perhaps principal, role as an appraiser of past events, past performance, and past actions. It judges retrospectively: it commands prospectively only insofar as it expresses either approval or disapproval of that which has happened before."

Key's observation does not address the question of what kind of retrospective information voters possess, that is, are they informed about past candidate policy positions (the Downsian version), or are they only aware of their own welfare (the traditional version)? In this section we consider the traditional perspective, whereas in the next section we consider the Downsian view.

Our intention was to design an experiment in which the only information voters had access to was retrospective—historical information on their own welfare from past incumbents. To see how we experimentally examine traditional retrospective voting, let us review our experimental structure (see Collier, McKelvey, Ordeshook, and Williams, 1987, and Gray, McKelvey, and Ordeshook, 1986 for more details). Briefly, these experiments incorporate the following procedures: Two subjects are assigned to be candidates, and the remaining subjects are voters. Voters are assigned payoff functions in either a one- or two-dimensional issue space. In the one-dimensional experiments, the space is the interval (0,100), and preferences are symmetric and single-peaked. In the two-dimensional experiments, the space is a grid (0,1000) × (0,1000), preferences are described by circular indifference contours, and ideal points are located to insure a median in all directions (and hence a complete information equilibrium for candidates at this median). Voters are not informed about the form of their payoff functions or even about the existence of an issue space, and candidates, although aware of the issue space, are similarly uninformed about the voters' payoff functions, as well as the payoffs themselves. Candidates know of the existence of issues because they must choose positions on them, but the only information they learn as the experiment proceeds is which candidate won and by how much. At the beginning of an experiment, one candidate is randomly selected as the initial incumbent. He or she earns a fixed salary ($1) for being the incumbent, during which time he or she must choose a position in the issue space as the incumbent's policy while in office. This position determines a payoff for each voter based on that voter's assigned payoff function. The voters are told their payoffs, but not the actual position adopted by the incumbent, and they must vote whether to reelect the incumbent or to elect the challenger. The result of the election is tallied and announced, the winner becomes the new incumbent, and the process is repeated. This continues for a predetermined number of periods (forty periods in the two-dimensional experiments), or until time expires (twenty-five to forty-five periods over two hours in the one-dimensional experiments). This procedure, by making it impossible for voters to secure any contemporaneous information about candidates, models the situation in which voters, unaware or unconcerned with contemporary issues and campaign rhetoric, must vote on the basis of the historical stream of benefits they associate with incumbents or the incumbents' parties.

In addition to this basic structure, we also consider the following three modifications, each of which tests the robustness of our experimental results.

Modification 1: In this modification, which we use only in the one-dimensional experiments, incumbents, instead of earning a fixed salary for their term in office, earn a salary that is on a linear scale that varies from 50 cents to $2, depending on the positions they adopt. In the "unidirectional" version, both candidates' scales are maximized at the same point, 0 or 100, depending on which is farthest from the median. In the "bidirectional" version, the scales are maximized at opposite ends of the issue dimension. Hence, in both versions, incumbents are free to choose their salary (in the range 50 cents to $2).

Modification 2: After the incumbent selects a position, it is perturbed by a random error. Candidates are informed of the perturbed position, and the perturbed position is used to calculate the overt payoffs. Two distributions are considered in the one-dimensional case, one with a low variance and one with a high variance: The first permits a perturbation of up to five units and the second permits perturbations of up to ten units. This modification is the only one that we have yet considered in the two-dimensional case, and here we have only one error distribution, which follows a normal distribution with $\sigma = 25$ units (on the 1000-unit scale).

Modification 3: In the final modification, which applies only to the one-dimensional experiments, each experiment is conducted exactly like an unmodified version except that in period 21 all voter preferences are shifted in one direction by thirty-five units.

Modification 1 deals with the situation where candidates have policy preferences, modification 2 deals with the situation when candidates do not have complete control over policy outcomes, and modification 3 deals with the case where voter preferences change. In a complete information environment, where both candidates adopt prospective policy positions before the election and fully informed voters vote on the basis of these positions, one would predict convergence to the median voter outcome not only in the unmodified experiments, but also in all three of the above modifications.

A total of forty-three one-dimensional experiments and twenty two-dimensional experiments were run. In these experiments' unstructured environments it is difficult to speculate on what decision problem voters and candidates believe they are confronting and, thus, on the decision rules subjects use. In lieu of a formal treatment, then, we proceed directly to the data to assess (1) whether voters use their information in "reasonable" ways, and (2) whether the incumbents converge to the unknown median.

With respect to (1), we evaluate two simple voting models consistent with the traditional retrospective voting hypothesis. The first model supposes that each voter looks at all previous incumbents, and on the basis of a discounted weighting of the past, chooses the incumbent if the value of the incumbent's current position equals or exceeds the discounted past. This model fits the description of voters who ask, Am I better off today than I was four years ago? An alternative model that permits the development of party loyalty supposes that each voter estimates separate discounted benefit streams for each candidate or party. If the current incumbent's stream equals or exceeds the stream associated with the challenger, then the voter votes to reelect the incumbent.

In each experiment and for each voter we do a grid search over the discount rate and initial expectation, finding the best fits to the data for each voter (see Gray, McKelvey, and Ordeshook, 1986 and Collier, McKelvey, Ordeshook, and Williams, 1987 for details). We find that, in the one-dimensional experiments, 87 percent of all voter decisions are consistent with the first model, and 80 percent are consistent with the second model. And, recognizing the possibility that different subjects might use different criteria, if we choose the model that best fits each subject in an experiment, then 88 percent of all decisions are consistent with the best-fitting model. Of the 255 subject observations, the first model fits best 182 times, the second fits best 50 times, and both fit equally well 23 times. In the two-dimensional experiments, the first model is consistent with 88 percent of all voter decisions, the second model is consistent with 84 percent of these decisions, and the best-fitting model is consistent with 90 percent of all decisions. If voting were random, one would only expect to predict 56 percent of the voting behavior. Hence, despite the limited information possessed by voters about the experiment's structure, they appear to act in coherent ways. Of course, we cannot compare this behavior to any complete information benchmark because the non-incumbent candidate does not adopt a strategy in these experiments, and it is not clear what an optimal voting strategy for an informed voter should be.

With respect to (2), it is more difficult to identify a model of how candidates should use the signals that voters generate because they are uninformed about the shape of voter utility functions on the issues. Nevertheless, the general pattern that summarizes all experiments is the convergence of incumbent strategies toward positions near the electorate's median preference.

Ignoring differences occasioned by the various modifications for the moment, one way to assess the degree to which candidates converge to the median is to regress the true median against the position of the incumbent in each period using the equation,

$$IP = a + b\,Med \qquad (1)$$

where IP is the incumbent's position and Med is the true median (in the two-dimensional experiments, we treat the data from each dimension as a separate observation). If incumbents know the location

Table 1. Estimates of Regressions (1) and (2) for Design 1*

	Regression Eq. (1)			Regression Eq. (2)†			
	a	b	R^2	$ln(\alpha)$	β	ρ/DW	n
One Dimension				2.39	$-.014$	.543	1108
				(.110)	(.007)	1.657	
Periods 1–5	39.3	.21	.06				185
	(2.91)	(.05)	(15.5)				
Periods 11–15	22.0	.59	.37				185
	(2.75)	(.05)	(14.6)				
Periods 21–25	17.0	.69	.52				182
	(2.67)	(.05)	(12.5)				
Two Dimensions				3.33	$-.026$	.637	480
				(.139)	(.008)	1.933	
Periods 1–5	45.4	.06	.00				200
	(4.14)	(.07)	(21.7)				
Periods 11–15	15.8	.64	.56				200
	(2.46)	(.04)	(13.0)				
Periods 21–25	15.8	.67	.56				200
	(2.58)	(.04)	(13.5)				
Periods 35–40	11.2	.77	.66				200
	(2.38)	(.04)	(12.5)				

* Standard errors are in parentheses.

† All data from the two-dimensional experiments are normalized to correspond to a (100) × (100) issue space for comparability with the one-dimensional data.

of the median and converge to it, then we should find that $a = 0$ and $b = 1$. Combining all data (except those with a median shift—modification 3), Table 1 reports the results of this regression using data from the first five periods, periods 11–15, periods 21–25, and periods 35–40.

Alternatively, because the hypothesis is that candidates will diverge less from the median as the experiments proceed, if we let *Dist* equal the distance between the true median and the position of the incumbent (plus 1 to avoid log(0)), we can estimate the following regression (to equalize scales, *Dist* is divided by 10 in the two-dimensional experiments):

$$Dist = \alpha e^{\beta t} \tag{2}$$

where t is the period, and α and β are parameters to be estimated. The results of estimating this equation, assuming a log-normal error structure, are also presented in Table 1. These estimates exhibited a significant serial correlation, so the equations were estimated using the Cohrane-Orcutt iterative method to estimate the serial correlation. The final values of p and the Durbin-Watson statistic are included in Table 1. Estimates of equation (2) are based only on the first twenty-five periods, so the estimates are comparable to those in the next section. Experiments with a median shift are treated as two separate experiments, with the periods before the shift comprising the first experiment, and those after the shift comprising the second.

The regression estimates in Table 1 bear out the general hypothesis that candidates move closer to the median on average as the experiments proceed. First, in equation (2), the estimates of β for both the one-dimensional and two-dimensional cases are negative and are significantly less than zero at the .05 level. Second, the estimate of a in equation (1) generally decreases as the experiment proceeds, and the estimate of b, although not approaching one, increases. Third, with respect to the differences between the one- and two-dimensional experiments, notice that the magnitude of the estimates of both $ln(\alpha)$ and β are greater with two issues than with one. It appears from Table 1 that the rate of convergence of the two-dimensional experiments may be slightly faster than the one-dimensional experiments. However, the difference is not statistically significant. The differences in the constant are significant and indicate that the candidates began considerably further from the median in the two-dimensional case and, thus, never converged as close to the median as in the one-dimensional case. Figure 1 plots the average distance from the median of the one- and two-dimensional experiments.

The data in Table 1 do not reveal variations across experimental modifications. Hence, Table 2 presents some simple summary data about the average distance of incumbents' positions from the median in periods 1–5, 11–15, and 21–25 of each unidimensional experiment. Table 3 reports similar data for the two-dimensional experiments and the single modification considered there. Also, both tables report the average number of times incumbents chose policies within ten units from the median in each interval.

Notice first that, regardless of the modification considered or whether no modification is considered at all, and regardless of whether we look at Table 2 or 3, the candidates are considerably closer to the median at the end of an experiment than at the beginning. Second, if we look across the several modifications, we might detect various patterns, but none is striking or statistically significant. Indeed, the most striking pattern is that there is not much difference among the

Figure 1. Comparison of One- and Two-Dimensional Experiments, Downsian Retrospective Voting

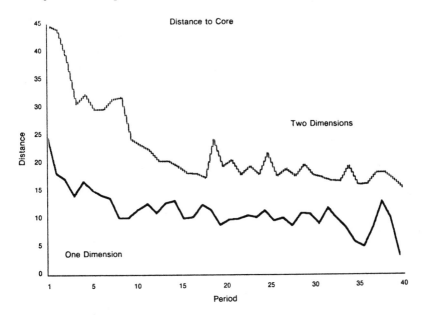

several experimental varieties. Hence, not only is there evidence of convergence, which is the implication of the estimates in Table 1, but these experiments also suggest that this pattern is robust: Paying incumbents to move from the median (modification 1) and random perturbations of incumbents' policies (modification 2) fail to dampen this pattern, and incumbents can track changing voter preferences (modification 3).

Although we cannot statistically detect differences among the various modifications, there appears to be considerable variation in the patterns that we observe across experiments. Figures 2–9 show the candidate positions for particular experiments. Focusing on the one-dimensional case, in some experiments (Figure 2) the candidates initially adopted positions near the median and did not stray far except for what appears to be an occasional experimental shift (the dashed horizontal line denotes the median, *x*'s and *o*'s, the identity of the incumbent). In other experiments (Figure 3), the candidates' initial choices are far from the median, but adjustments are made quickly. Figure 4 describes an experiment in which convergence to the median is slow owing to very conservative adjustments by incumbents, whereas Figure 5 depicts slow convergence owing to a different considera-

Table 2. Summary of Outcomes for Design 1, One-Dimensional Experiments

		Avg. Dist. from Med.			% within 10 of Med.				Avg. Number
		1–5	11–15	21–25	1–5	11–15	21–25	n	Periods
Mod. 1	Unidirectional	25.6	16.9	13.8	17%	40%	33%	6	35.6
	Bidirectional	10.1	9.7	5.4	57	63	100	6	28.0
Mod. 2	Low noise	16.4	10.1	9.4	33	73	64	6	30.0
	High noise	16.8	13.9	9.2	50	63	60	6	33.0
Mod. 3	Before shift	19.2	10.4		20	53		6	20.0
	After shift*	22.7	6.7		20	93			19.9
No modification		15.4	13.3	11.4	46	60	66	13	31.6
Overall		16.9	12.5	10.1	39	59	65	43	32.8

* Periods 21–25 and 31–35

Table 3. Summary of Outcomes for Design 1, Two-Dimensional Experiments

		Avg. Dist. from Med.				% within 10 of Med.				n	Avg. Number Periods
Periods:	1–5	11–15	21–25	35–40		1–5	11–15	21–25	35–40		
Mod. 2	34.4	19.5	17.6	12.4		14	14	30	60	10	40
No mod.	39.8	20.3	18.5	18.0		8	20	30	30	10	40
Overall	37.1	19.9	18.1	15.2		11	17	30	45	20	40

tion—the incumbents' apparent desire to maximize payoffs with extreme positions. Figure 6 describes an experiment in which incumbents rarely changed a successful strategy, but by occasionally "testing the waters" with the election of the challenger, voters conveyed information to both candidates about preferred directions of change. Figure 7, on the other hand, illustrates what happens if voters continually reelect the incumbent and thereby fail to convey appropriate information to candidates. Figure 8 dramatically illustrates the attractiveness of the median even when one candidate's payoff is maximized when he or she adopts positions at 0, while the other's payoff is maximized when he or she adopts positions at 100. It should be evident from this figure which candidate is paid to move in which direction. Finally, Figure 9 illustrates the tracking of the median that

Table 1 documents. Although the shift in preferences after period 20 seems to confuse candidates for awhile, incumbents quickly converge to the new median.

DOWNSIAN RETROSPECTIVE VOTING

In the preceding analysis, voters are unaware of issues and of the relationship between their payoffs and the issue positions of candidates. An alternative view of retrospective voting (which we refer to as Downsian retrospective voting) sees voters as aware of issues, with an understanding of their preferences on those issues. In this view, voters are still uninformed of the issue positions of incumbents and challengers in the current campaign, and they instead make inferences about policy positions based on the candidates' historical records (or the records of their parties). We now ask whether such historical information is sufficient for voters to cast an informed vote and whether this "issue awareness" accelerates convergence to a median.

Theoretical Background

As in the previous portrayal of retrospective voting, we study Downsian retrospection with a sequence of elections, but now we give voters access to one additional piece of information, the historical policy positions of incumbents. In addition, before each election, both candidates A and B adopt issue positions that represent the position of the candidates. The position of the losing candidate is never revealed to voters, and voters must choose between A and B before the position of either candidate is revealed. In addition to this historical information about the policy positions of past incumbents, we suppose that voters observe one contemporaneous piece of information: an endorsement that indicates which candidate is farthest to the left or right on the issue. Finally, we suppose that candidates also are uninformed in that they do not know the distribution of ideal points in the electorate. Like the voters, they have access only to the historical record of incumbents (together with the positions they adopt in the current campaign).

Notice the important differences between this experimental design and that of the last section. In the traditional retrospective view modeled by the previous design, voters are unaware of issues and their preferences on issues, whereas exactly the opposite is true here. For the experiments that we discussed previously, voters know only their historical stream of benefits, whereas here they know the exact

Figure 2. Unmodified

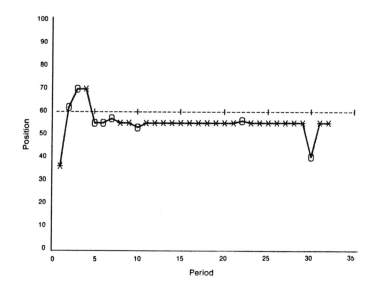

Figure 3. Unmodified

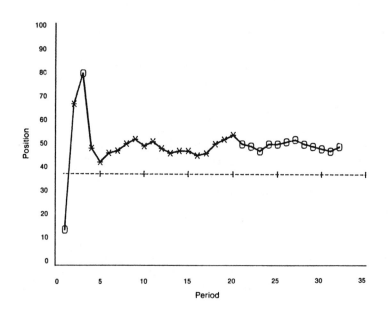

Figure 4. Modification 1

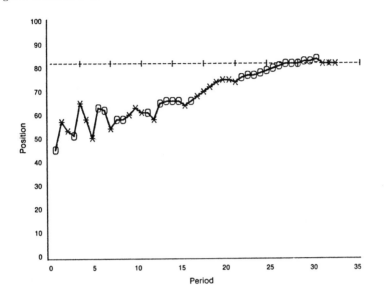

Figure 5. Modification 1

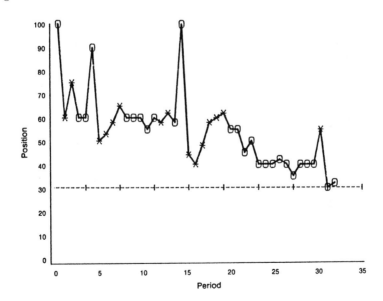

Figure 6. Unmodified

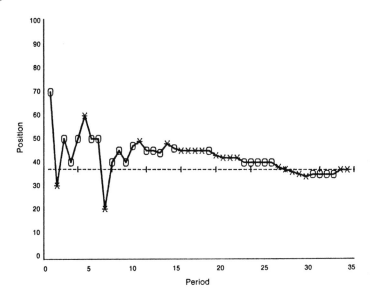

Figure 7. Unmodified

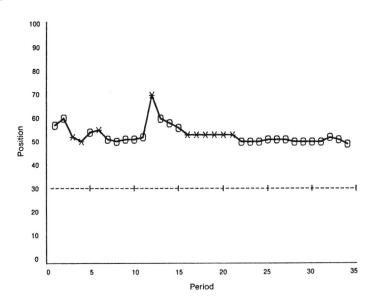

Figure 8. Modification 1 (Bipolar)

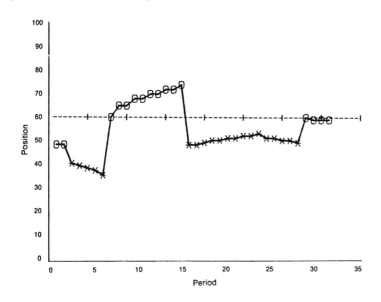

Figure 9: Modification 3

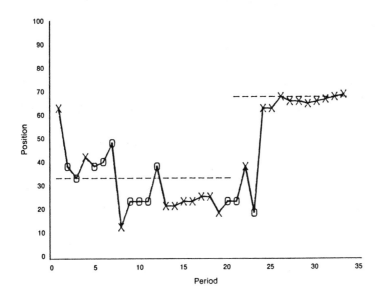

policies implemented by previous administrations. And whereas the traditional hypothesis supposes that voters act on whether the current incumbent is performing "adequately," the Downsian view supposes that voters form beliefs about the actual positions of candidates in the current campaign.

In a formal model that incorporates the information conditions of this experimental design, we define a rational expectations equilibrium and ascertain the conditions under which such an equilibrium exists and when it would yield the same outcomes that prevail when everyone is perfectly informed (McKelvey and Ordeshook, 1986b). In that model, we let g_A and g_B be the probability density functions that candidates A and B use to select their positions (in which case it may be more accurate to think of each election as a competition between parties that must nominate candidates). Letting $s = (s_1, \ldots, s_n)$ denote the votes of voters 1 through n, then (s, g_A, g_B) is a *Stationary Rational Expectations Equilibrium* (SREE) if (1) for all i, s_i is an optimal strategy given i's beliefs about g_A and g_B (voters choose ballots that maximize their expected utility); (2) each voter's belief is consistent with the observed history of the two parties or candidates; and (3) the parties adopt strategies that correspond to the distribution of their past winning positions. An SREE is *stable* if neither candidate can change the distribution of winning outcomes by changing his or her strategy. We then prove the following result: *If the number of voters is odd, if the election concerns a single issue, and if voters have symmetric single-peaked utility functions, then a unique stable SREE exists such that both candidates converge to the electorate's median ideal point.*

Experimental Results

Turning now to the data obtained from our second experimental design, we discuss here the results of eleven unidimensional and three two-dimensional experiments structured to correspond to the informational setting of the model (McKelvey and Ordeshook 1985b). These experiments are run almost exactly like those of the previous section except that (1) both candidates adopt a position in each period; (2) voters are given a candidate "endorsement," that is, they are told which candidate is farthest to the left (but not the actual policy positions) before they vote; and (3) voters are told the policy positions of the winning candidate after his or her term in office.

We begin with an analysis of the extent to which the voters vote as if they possess complete information. Looking at the first row in Table 4, we see that over all periods of all experiments, excluding the initial period of each experiment, 82 percent of the voters vote for

Table 4. Voting Behavior in Design 2, Percent Correct

	First Five (%)	Trials 11–15 (%)	Last Five (%)	All Trials (%)
Full information	76	84	83	82
Partial information	78	88	87	85

Table 5. Estimates of Regressions (1) and (2) for Design 2*

	Regression Eq. (1)			Regression Eq. (2)			
	a	b	R^2	$ln(\alpha)$	β	ρ/DW	n
One Dimension				2.43 (.271)	−.033 (.018)	.014 1.289	225
Trials 1–5	17.3 (12.4)	.55 (.19)	.12 (21.9)				55
Trials 11–15	1.7 (6.0)	.95 (.09)	.65 (10.6)				55
Trials 21–25	8.2 (6.4)	.79 (.10)	.73 (8.2)				27
Two Dimensions				2.88 (.281)	−.024 (.019)	.613 1.739	61

*Standard errors are in parentheses.

Table 6. Summary of Outcomes for Design 2

	Avg. Dist. from Med.			% within 10 of Med.		
Periods:	1–5	11–15	21–25	1–5	11–15	21–25
One dimension	20.7	7.7	8.1	19.2	33	71
Two dimensions	19.2	14.2	10.6	33	13	17

the candidate offering them the highest utility, that is, these voters vote as if they possess complete information. This correspondence increases, moreover, from 76 percent in the first five periods to 83 percent in the last five.

How is it that uninformed voters are able to achieve this degree of accuracy in their voting behavior? It appears that voters follow a fairly simple decision rule that can be deduced from the theory outlined previously: From the historical information, voters are able to get a good idea of the general area in which the candidates are likely to adopt positions. But with this information, the endorsement is sufficient information to tell the voter *exactly* how to vote. Voters with ideal points to the left of the expected candidate positions should vote for the endorsed candidate, and those with ideal points to the right should vote for the unendorsed candidate. It is only voters with ideal points in the general vicinity of the expected positions who should have difficulty deciding which candidate for whom to vote.

The second row of Table 4 shows the result of estimating such a model of voting behavior. We assume that in each period, voters estimate the expected candidate position by doing a regression on the past positions of the candidates using a discount rate to weight the more recent observations more heavily than the past ones. The discount rate is estimated to maximize the number of correct predictions across all voters, yielding a best-fitting discount rate of 18.9. This means that data from period t-2 are assigned a standard deviation of $(18.9)^{1/2} = 4.16$ that of period t-1, implying that it is weighted only .23 times as heavily as the more recent period. As can be seen from the second row of Table 4, this model explains approximately 85 percent of the voter behavior.

Turning now to the candidates, Tables 5 and 6 reproduce Tables 1 and 2 using the data from the current experiments. Notice that for the one-dimensional experiments, the data in this table tell a story quite similar to that told by Tables 1 and 2: Candidates converge closer to the (unknown) median as the experiments proceed. However, because of the smaller number of experiments for the Downsian retrospective voting experiments, the standard errors tend to be larger, and we are less confident of the results. A comparison of the one-dimensional Downsian experiments with the experiments of the previous section suggests that the convergence in the Downsian experiments may be somewhat faster than that for the traditional retrospective voting experiments. Table 2 shows that for the traditional retrospective voting experiments, candidates start at an average distance of 16.9 units from the median, and that by period 11–15, they are within 12.5 units of the median. Correspondingly, the proportion within ten units of the median changes from 39 percent to 59 percent. Table 5, on the other hand, shows that in the Downsian retrospective voting experiments, the winning candidates begin an average of 20.7 units from the core, and converge to within 7.7 units by periods 11–15. Likewise, the percentages within ten units change from 33 percent to 71 percent. The data using regression equations (1) and (2) tell the same story. Table 1 shows that, although the estimated intercept, a, for equation (1) is 22.0 overall in trials 11–15, it more closely approximates the theoretical prediction of zero in the second series (1.7 for winning candidates). Similarly, the slope coefficient b is .59 overall in Table 1, but it is far closer to one (.95) in Table 5. Finally, with respect to equation (2), the magnitude of the estimated rate at which candidates converge to the median, β, is approximately twice as high in the second series as it is in the first (.59 in Table 1 versus .95 in Table 5). Because of the smaller number of experiments, we cannot say even that the estimate of β is significant, much less that the differences are.

Figures 10–13 illustrate some of the more extreme patterns in the one-dimensional experiments, and they, in addition to the experiments that we illustrate elsewhere (McKelvey and Ordeshook, 1985b), can be compared with Figures 2–9 (here we plot the positions of both candidates, and we circle the winning candidate's position). In Figure 10, the unendorsed candidate wins in trials 1–8, and the candidates correctly interpret this as a signal to move up on the issue, but after the endorsed candidate wins in trial 9, the candidates never stray far from the median. Figure 11 illustrates two candidates who initially move past the median after the unendorsed candidate wins four times in succession. But after period 5, the unendorsed candidate always wins, which causes the candidates to move below the median after period 11. These victories are caused by one voter (number 6) voting incorrectly nearly every time, thereby leading the candidates to believe incorrectly that the median is less than 60. Figure 12 shows raid convergence to the median made interesting by an occasional attempt on the part of one candidate to win by securing or by avoiding the endorsement. Figure 13 shows an especially interesting and unique pattern. Here the candidates converge quickly to the median, but then begin jockeying to try and obtain or avoid the endorsement. This causes them to escalate their oscillations about the median, and we can only speculate about eventual outcomes had time permitted the experiment to proceed.

In addition to eleven one-dimensional experiments, we also ran three two-dimensional experiments designed so that a total median existed. There was no variation in the actual core point between these three experiments, so we cannot run the equivalent of regression (1) on these experiments. However, Table 5 presents the results of running regression equation (2) on the two-dimensional experiments. There is evident convergence of the candidates toward the median here as well. However, two of the experiments converged to points about twelve units away from the median, which accounts for the fact that the percentage within ten units of the median decreases while the average distance to the median decreases. Although we would

Figure 10

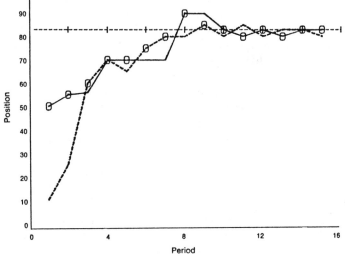

Figure 11

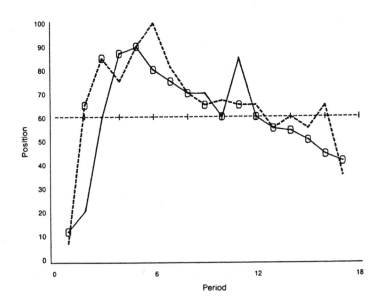

Figure 12

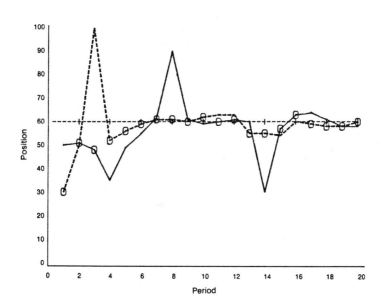

Figure 13

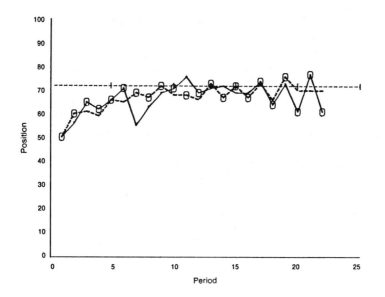

require more than three experiments to make definitive judgments, the evidence suggests that, under the imposed limited information conditions, candidates can operate in a two-dimensional environment and will converge toward the median, although possibly with greater difficulty than in a one-dimensional environment.

SINGLE PERIOD MODEL

To this point we have studied situations where, with the exception of an endorsement, voters receive only historical information and candidates know only the outcomes of previous contests and the strategies of the opponents in those contests. Although such information seems to be adequate for voters to make relatively informed decisions, it does not seem sufficient to yield very rapid candidate convergence to core points. In this section, we consider the effect of further indirect contemporaneous information—public opinion information—on candidate behavior.

Theoretical Background

To see the potential value of poll data, consider a voter who regards himself or herself as preferring policies to the "right of center" on a given issue, and who, based on the histories of the candidates' parties and current interest group endorsements, knows that A is more conservative than the opponent. Suppose initial polls reveal that A and his opponent split about evenly among those voters with a preference. If the voter assumes that the poll contains some information, then at least two hypotheses are consistent with the poll: (1) A and his opponent are both moderates on opposite sides of, but near, the ideological center, or (2) A and his opponent are both extremists on opposite sides of the political spectrum. In either of these cases, if the voter believes that some voters are informed, then the voter can conclude that it is best to vote for A. In case (1), the voter is close to both candidates but probably closer to A because the voter regards himself or herself as being not far from the "center." In case (2), the voter is far from both candidates, but, because the voter sees himself or herself as being slightly to the "right of center," he or she is again probably closer to A. In fact, a careful analysis of this example shows that regardless of the positions of A and B, the poll information is enough for the voter to conclude that he or she should vote for A over B.

This example reveals how voters can use some low-cost contemporaneous information—a poll and an awareness of the relative positions of the candidates—to choose between candidates. Notice that in this scenario the voter never learns the candidates' actual positions. Rather, the poll indicates the midpoint between the candidates relative to the voter's ideal preference. With an even split, the positions of the two candidates must be balanced around the median. If the poll reflects accurate (but perhaps noisy) data, then the hypothesis that one candidate but not the other is an extremist is inconsistent with the poll result. An estimate of the midpoint between the candidates, an assessment of one's own position relative to the electorate, and a belief about which candidate is to the left permit a voter to infer which candidate is closest to his or her ideal.

It might seem that the unreliability of early polls can mislead voters. But polls are not static: they are taken sequentially during an election campaign, and we cannot assume that they are independent. Instead, we should explore the possibility that beliefs about candidates derived from early polls affect later polls, which affect still later polls and so on, and we should establish the nature of an equilibrium to this serial process.

A formal model of the above process is developed in McKelvey and Ordeshook (1985a), which we review briefly here. In the one-dimensional case, we assume that all voters have symmetric single-peaked preferences. In addition, we suppose that the electorate, is comprised of informed and uninformed voters. Informed voters know the true candidate positions, whereas uninformed voters must rely on indirect cues such as endorsements and public opinion polls. Further, it is assumed that the distribution of preferences of the rest of the electorate is known to the voters. Although this seems a strong assumption, there is empirical reason to believe that even uninformed voters may have good information about interest groups and other reference groups in society (see e.g., Kuklinski, Metlay, and Kay, 1982). Both the voters and the candidates are assumed to have beliefs about parameters that are utility-relevant to them. However, rather than assuming, as we did in the previous section, that voters have beliefs about the actual strategies of candidates, we assume instead that these beliefs are about the midpoint between the candidates. With respect to candidates, we assume that they do not know which voters are informed and which are uninformed and, thus, they do not know which voters will vote on the basis of their actual campaign strategies and which will vote either randomly or on the basis of unknown considerations. Hence, they cannot ascertain the relevant median voter to which they should target their strategies. Instead, they observe only the same poll data as voters, and they must infer the relevant voters to which they should appeal on the basis of these data. The candidates' relevant beliefs thus concern the location of the total median of voter ideal points (assuming that such a median exists).

In the scenario, an equilibrium to the election game is a vector of candidate and voter strategies and beliefs that satisfy the following conditions: (V1) Each voter votes for the candidate who is on the same side of the candidate midpoint as his or her ideal point. (C1) Each candidate chooses a policy that maximizes his or her expected payoff given his or her belief about the location of the informed media. (V2) For each informed voter, his or her belief about the candidate midpoint corresponds to that defined by the actual candidate positions, whereas for each uniformed voter, this belief is a best fit to the poll data—the voter picks an estimate of this midpoint that generates the observed poll. (C2) Each candidate believes that the true median is on the same side of the true candidate midpoint as is the winner. It is also useful to identify situations in which the voters are in equilibrium for a fixed pair of candidate strategies. Hence, given the candidates' positions, a *voter equilibrium* conditional on these positions is a vector of strategies and beliefs for the electorate that satisfy conditions (V1) and (V2).

Elsewhere, we prove the following result (see McKelvey and Ordeshook, 1986a): *Assume that the cumulative density functions of the ideal points for the informed and uninformed voters are invertible, and that some positive fraction of the voters are informed. Then, for every pair of candidate positions in which the candidates choose distinct policies, there is a voter equilibrium. Any voter equilibrium entails all voters voting for the correct candidates. Further, there is "full" equilibrium (for candidates and voters), and the unique stable equilibrium consists of candidates converging to the median ideal point.*

One can also define an iterative process by which uninformed voters might adjust their strategies and beliefs over time. Specifically, uninformed voters initially vote randomly. After observing the first poll, they obtain an estimate of the candidate midpoint on the basis of that poll, assuming that other voters except themselves are informed. This leads to a new poll result. Uninformed voters revise their beliefs based on this new poll, etc. It can be shown that this process converges to the equilibrium.

These results also can be extended to a multidimensional context (see McKelvey and Ordeshook, 1985a). In this case, the voter needs to observe poll information broken down by subgroups of the population (e.g., socioeconomic or ethnic groups). To guarantee an equilibrium, there needs to be at least as many subgroups as the number of dimensions of the space plus one. These subgroups need not partition the space, and one could think of these subgroups as various reference groups from which the voters take cues.

Experimental Results

The experiments to test the preceding model require large numbers of voters in order to generate useful poll results, and hence they are expensive to run. Consequently, our analysis of the preceding one-dimensional model is based on only two experiments (reported in McKelvey and Ordeshook, 1985a). Although this generates substantial data for voters, the data on candidates must be regarded as tentative. The one-dimensional experiments are designed to match exactly the theoretical structure described previously. Between forty and fifty subjects were voters in each of these two experiments that were run as follows: two subjects were selected as candidates, and the remaining subjects were divided randomly into informed and uninformed voters. Each experiment consists of a series of election periods. In each period the two candidates first adopt policy positions on a line between 0 and 100. Candidate positions are fixed for the duration of the period, after which the candidates are free to adopt new positions. Once these positions are selected, the endorsement is announced, and a sequence of two polls is taken, followed by a final election vote. In each poll, voters are asked how they would vote if the election were held now. Informed voters (half the sample) are told the positions of the candidates, while uninformed voters are never told the positions—only the endorsement in that period. Thus, unlike the experiments in the previous section, but like the ones that test the traditional retrospective hypothesis, there is no possibility for uninformed voters to make inferences about candidate positions from any historical record. Uninformed voters, however, are told the location of their ideal point relative to the full electorate (i.e., whether they are in the 10th percentile, etc.). This information, in conjunction with the poll, is sufficient for the formation of a belief about the location of the candidates' midpoint relative to their ideal (whether that midpoint is to the left or the right) that, with the endorsement, permits voters to estimate a preferred candidate.

All voters must participate in the poll, and all are told the poll results. As in all earlier experiments, voters are paid on the basis of a single-peaked utility function and the position of the winning candidate, whereas candidates are paid on the basis of how many elections they win. In both of the experiments, the median of informed voters is set at 75, of uninformed voters at 45 and 48, and the overall median at 60.

Looking first at voters, we find that, overall, 79.2 percent of all final vote decisions by uninformed voters correspond to the decisions they ought to make if they possessed complete information (informed voters vote correctly 97.2 percent of the time). To the extent that a poll contains error, however, a correct decision given the information supplied by a poll need not be identical to a complete information decision. Adjusting our predictions for this error, the percentage of voters who use the polls according to the model is 84.9.

Regarding candidate behavior, Figures 14a and 14b plot candidate positions in the two one-dimensional experiments (circled positions denote the winning candidate), and they dramatically document a rapid convergence to the median. Indeed, the candidates appear to converge in as few as two or three election periods. However, because the distribution of informed and uninformed is different, and only about three-fourths of the uninformed voters vote correctly, the candidates converge to a point slightly away from the total median in the direction of the informed median. Hence, these data support the hypothesis that the voters' evaluations of candidates' use of this same data yield a convergence rate that exceeds the rate observed when voters are given historical information about incumbents' actual policy positions—at least for unidimensional contests. Figure 15 gives a graphic comparison of the convergence rates for the one-dimensional experiments under all three designs.

In addition to the one-dimensional experiments, we have run three two-dimensional experiments (see McKelvey and Ordeshook, 1984) to test the multidimensional extension. These two-dimensional experiments are somewhat more complicated and less conclusive. In these experiments, the electorate is divided into three groups, and each group is divided into informed and uninformed sub-parts. All voters know their own utility functions, which have circular indifference contours, decreasing from an ideal point, and they know that other voters have similarly shaped utility functions, with possibly differing ideal points. Voters do not know the ideal points of other voters, but they are told the mean ideal point for each of the groups. The experiments are run like the one-dimensional experiments, except that the poll information voters receive is broken down by subgroups. Thus, after each poll, the voters learn the proportion of each group supporting each candidate. The experiments consist of six, nine, and seven periods and use from fifty-three to eighty-nine subjects as voters.

Figure 14a

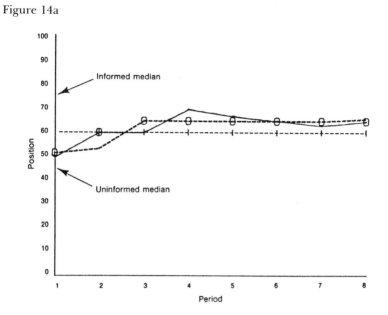

Figure 14b

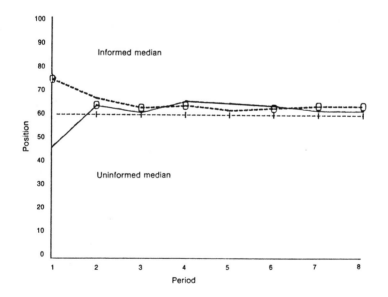

Figure 15. Comparison of One-Dimensional Experiments

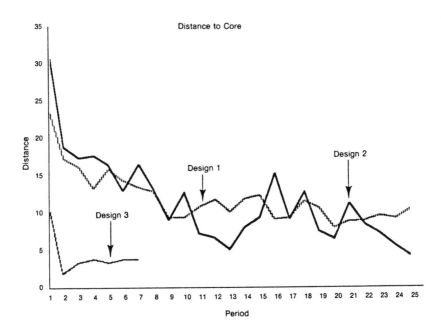

Overall, 81.1 percent of all final vote decisions cast by uninformed voters in these two-dimensional experiments correspond to correct decisions under complete information, and 85.5 percent are "correct," given the poll information voters possess. Note though that, although we cannot reject the hypothesis that voters process information as our theoretical structure assumes, we also cannot reject the hypothesis of some simplifying heuristic such as voting the majority preference of the group whose median is closest to one's ideal (86.2 percent consistent). Nevertheless, the behavior of voters in the two-dimensional models seems consistent with what we find in the one-dimensional experiments in terms of the overall absolute error rate for voters.

The implications of the three two-dimensional experiments regarding candidate behavior, on the other hand, are less clear. Owing to the required size of each experiment, no less than three hours is required to conduct an experiment consisting of nine election periods, which precludes any assurances that the candidates have attained or even approached an equilibrium. Indeed, in the actual data, only three of six candidates can be said to have converged to positions close to the overall median. But in one experiment that does not evidence convergence, one candidate confused the x and y axes, and hence misinterpreted all data. Hence, we cannot say whether the additional data supplied to candidates by the polls in two-dimensional elections cause them to converge faster than the rates we observe in the purely retrospective experiments. Certainly, these two-dimensional experiments, like the previous ones, present candidates with a more difficult task than do elections with a single issue, and convergence, if it occurs at all, is slower in multidimensional elections than it is in elections that concern a single issue.

CONCLUSIONS

Our experiments suggest that, in principle, it is possible for voters to vote as if they are informed and for the electoral process to be responsive to voter preferences even in very sparse informational environments. The voters are able to make relatively informed choices on the basis of contemporaneous endorsements together with either historical data on past policies of incumbents or contemporaneous poll data (the second and third designs). The candidates exhibit some degree of convergence to the median position in all our experiments. However, the rates of convergence of the candidates in the traditional retrospective voting experiments seem to be fairly slow. Adding more information in the form of knowledge of past policy positions and current endorsements may lead to marginal improvement, but the change is not dramatic. On the other hand, if voters have contemporaneous information—such as might be conveyed by public opinion polls—about the opinions of other portions of the electorate whose preferences they know, this can lead to substantial improvement in the speed of convergence. One might draw the further inference, then, that if voters have information of both varieties simultaneously—historical and contemporaneous—then candidates would converge even more rapidly to a full information equilibrium. Thus, there appear to be a number of ways in which voters can shortcut the requirement of complete information imposed in traditional spatial models of elections and still exercise some degree of popular control on the policies of the government.

A final comment on what one can learn from experimental studies of voting behavior is in order. We do not suggest that our experiments in any way mirror or simulate the real world. In the real world, different voters have widely different sources and amounts of information, events take place over years rather than over hours, and there are innumerable complexities that we completely ignore in the laboratory. One cannot conclude on the basis of our experimental results that, in the real world, candidates must converge to the median outcome at the rate we predict because there are many variables for which we have not controlled.

Our experiments are intended instead to address certain issues in democratic theory. We ask the question whether it is *possible* for democratic systems to make informed choices in the presence of incomplete information. We thus set up, in the laboratory, situations in which we enforce very specific and idealized information regimes much more rigorously than they would occur in the real world. The advantage of an experimental study is precisely the experimental control we have over these variables of interest. If, under the severe restrictions on information that we place on subjects in the laboratory, we still see behavior similar to the full information expectation, then we feel confident in concluding that lack of information, by itself, does not necessarily preclude the democratic process from being attracted to full information outcomes. We also feel confident (although somewhat less so) in concluding that, all else being equal, more information, or information settings closer to what we might find in the real world, would not lead to worse results. If outcomes in the real world do differ systematically from full information outcomes, there must be other reasons besides lack of information. The experiments also lead us to suspect that there should be theoretical models explaining the results we find.

NOTE

This research was supported by NSF grants to the University of Texas at Austin and to the California Institute of Technology.

13

Citizen Information, Rationality, and the Politics of Macroeconomic Policy

Henry W. Chappell, Jr.
William R. Keech

How and how well does American representative democracy work given conditions of limited and decentralized information? And what role do the information and rationality of citizens play in the performance of such a government? We investigate these topics in the context of macroeconomic policy because macroeconomics allows us to be relatively precise and objective in assessing the performance of a political system.

The issue of citizen information and rationality recalls a theme prominent in political science of the 1950s and 1960s: the possibility of a disjuncture between the demands of citizenship delineated in "classical" democratic theory and the actual behavior of the American electorate (Berelson, Lazarsfeld, and McPhee, 1954). In fact the requirements of informed citizenship were not delineated clearly in classical democratic theory (Keech, 1962), and neither normative theory nor subsequent empirical work has generated clear statements of what level of information or rationality is to be expected of democratic citizens, at least from the viewpoint of system performance.[1]

DEFINING AND ATTACKING THE PROBLEM OF CITIZEN BEHAVIOR AND MACROECONOMIC PERFORMANCE

Macroeconomic issues permit us to evaluate collective "citizen rationality" from the viewpoint of system performance because this is an area in which theory and empirical work enable us to link citizen behavior to such performance. In discussing these issues, we shall consider the macroeconomy as what Simon calls an "artificial system," a system that "adapts to an outer environment subject only to the goal defined by its inner environment" (1981:32). In the case of the economy, "the outer environment is defined by available technologies and the behavior of other economic actors, other markets, or other economies. The inner environment is defined by the system's goals and by its capabilities for rational, adaptive behavior" (1981:31).

More specifically, the macroeconomic outer environment might be represented by a system of empirical relationships among the prices and quantities of goods and services defined by a model or theory of the macroeconomy. There is considerable disagreement about the exact nature of this outer environment and the degree to which it responds to human control, and we will make use of this fact in our analysis.

The inner environment for our purposes is the system of policymaking used to choose the values of those macroeconomic variables subject to control, such as the instruments of fiscal and monetary policy. For most of the half century in which macroeconomics has been an identifiable field within economics, this "inner environment" has been conceived as a policymaker who pursues the public good without constraint by political pressures. Such a welfare-maximizing social planner is familiar in economic theory.

It has been recognized that policymaking is decentralized and that policymakers may need to adapt to another outer environment besides the macroeconomy itself, specifically that of the political system that gives them their authority. Lindbeck (1976:11), for example, has observed that although politicians may be well-informed and idealistic "guardians of the general good," they may also be "concerned with their own welfare, obtained by seizing and staying in power, rather than the welfare of society as a whole." For years this complication was considered so insignificant that it could safely be ignored (Buchanan and Wagner, 1977: chapter 6). The political environment of macroeconomic policymaking was not considered relevant enough to receive systematic attention.

There is of course some irony in considering the behavior of citizens, their information, and rationality as an outer environment to which policymakers may need to adapt. Consideration of the public welfare presumably should help define the nature of the goals that guide adaptation to the macroeconomic outer environment. Indeed, we might expect the public to be the main source of incentives for policymakers to maximize public welfare. But as we will show, there is a possibility that the electorate may provide perverse incentives for elected policymakers, that is, incentives to undermine public well-being.

Our benchmark for evaluating the information and rationality of citizens, then, is the possibility that these citizens would obstruct an "appropriate" adaptation of the policymaking system to the macroeconomic environment. We will use macroeconomic theories to identify the kinds of choices by policymakers to be deemed appropriate. As we show in the next section, there is not one single macroeconomic theory with an invariant set of recommendations, and we make use of this fact in our analysis.

Although macroeconomic theories do suggest some ways citizens might obstruct appropriate policymaking, we do not find robust or convincing evidence that citizens in fact do so. By extension we suggest that citizens are well informed and rational enough by this standard, which is not a very demanding one.[2]

MACROECONOMIC THEORY: CHARACTERIZING THE OUTER ENVIRONMENT

Because macroeconomic theory has changed so much in recent decades, there is not one authoritative statement of the kinds of choices that are appropriate. Therefore, the implications for citizen rationality we derive from any of the theories must be considered tentative and conditional. This fact has important implications for citizen rationality, to which we return after reviewing existing theories. We would not expect citizens to be more sophisticated than economic theorists, but the presumed requisites for citizen behavior may change as the theory changes. What then should be our standards of citizen information and rationality?

The ensuing review of macroeconomic theories contains only two examples with explicit possibilities for citizen "irrationality" in the sense we are using. That is, in two cases presumed citizen behavior patterns obstruct appropriate adaptation by policymakers to the macroeconomic outer environment. Nonetheless, we will review other theories and make use of their implications for citizen rationality, and we will also make some observations on their theoretical and empirical strength.

The Classical System

While macroeconomics has been an identifiable field only since the 1930s, the *classical system* was the term used for the macroeconomic ideas in economic theory up until that time. In the classical theory, there was no room for macroeconomic policymaking. Supply was seen as creating its own demand, according to Say's Law. There was no role for fiscal policy as a way to influence macroeconomic performance. Although there was monetary theory, there was no theory of monetary policy as a way in which public officials could stabilize the economy. Political incentives were irrelevant in the absence of a theory of meaningful policy choices. No standard of citizen information and rationality was directly implied.

The Keynesian System

In the first chapter of *The General Theory . . .* , Keynes (1936:3) argued that "the postulates of the classical theory are applicable to a special case only, and not to the general case." The special case to which he referred was one in which "supply creates its own demand." Keynes's theory of aggregate demand showed that effective demand could fluctuate according to variations in income and in business expectations. Keynesian models provided a rationale for government to compensate for fluctuations in demand by increasing public spending without compensating increases in taxes. Because available resources are slack in times of insufficient demand, this policy implies a costless welfare improvement.

As Buchanan and Wagner (1977:102) have pointed out, there are political implications for such a policy choice. "In a democratic society, there would be no political obstacles to budget deficits in an economy with genuine Keynesian unemployment. Budget deficits make it possible to spend without taxing." Breaking the norm of annually balanced budgets was necessary to justify a Keynesian response to unemployment, but, once past that hurdle, the response is easy to sell to an electorate.

Here, then, is the first example of macroeconomic theory suggesting an appropriate policy response to an economic situation and the first clear possibility that voters might support or obstruct appropriate policy. In the Keynesian view, public support for a balanced budget under conditions of insufficient aggregate demand would be inappropriate, just as support for deficits would be in conditions of sufficient or of excess demand.

If the choice between deficits and balanced budgets never became an electoral issue, citizen information and rationality would have no bearing on appropriate adaptation to the macroeconomic environment. However, because competitors for elective office differ on such issues, this simple Keynesian theory gives us a way of saying what kinds of citizen behavior are appropriate and, by extension, a standard of information and rationality.

In this theoretical setting, the question becomes whether citizens know enough to distinguish between situations in which budget deficits are appropriate and those in which they are not. Buchanan and Wagner argue that citizens do not know enough to do this. They argue that before roughly 1960, citizens did not have to know so much because the balanced budget norm was so strong. After it was broken, however, what was left was an unconstrained preference for the increase in current consumption that is implied by increased government spending or reduced taxes, regardless of the economic situation. Buchanan and Wagner surely feel that citizens are not sufficiently rational and informed, and the consequences they see are inflation, indebtedness, and a bloated public sector. They propose a constitutional balanced budget amendment as a solution.

The Phillips Curve

For a period beginning in the late 1950s and lasting into the 1970s, it was widely believed that there was a stable trade-off between inflation and unemployment, represented by a "Phillips curve." In one well-known formulation, Samuelson and Solow (1960) suggested that the United States faced a "menu" of choices between roughly 5-1/2 percent unemployment and zero inflation on the one hand, and 3 percent unemployment and 4-1/2 percent inflation on the other. They expected that "the tug of war of politics will end us up in the next few years somewhere between these selected points" (1960:192–193).

Although Samuelson and Solow explicitly recognized that the trade-off they identified could shift due to a variety of factors, it was implied that positions on the curve were not inherently unstable. Moreover, no choice on the trade-off was presented as being inherently superior. The possibility that the political process would decide was not shown to be one that threatened any irrationality.

Hibbs's work has elaborated the political implications of this view of the nature of economic policy choices. Hibbs (1979, 1987) has provided evidence that different socioeconomic groups in the society have different preferences for inflation and unemployment. Although both are seen as "bads" to be minimized, different groups have different marginal rates of substitution between them, implying choices of different locations on the Phillips curve. These different choices correspond to different objective consequences of inflation and unemployment for the groups in question (Hibbs, 1977, 1987), implying that the subgroups of the public accurately perceive their interests. Finally, different parties reflect the interests of different class groups, so that the political process allows each group to implement its preferences when in office (Hibbs, 1977, 1987).

There was no explicit risk of irrationality in this process because groups accurately perceived their interests and because the consequences of their choices were not hidden or postponed. There is no adaptation to the macroeconomic environment that this model of public choice would obstruct.

The Natural Rate of Unemployment

As early as 1968, Milton Friedman undermined the idea of a stable trade-off, observing that "at any moment of time there is some level of unemployment which has the property that it is consistent with equilibrium in the structure of *real* wages rates," in other words, a "natural rate of unemployment" (1968:8). The Phillips curve as analyzed previously reflects a short-run trade-off, resulting, in Friedman's view, from the fact that a stimulus to demand will lead to an increase in output and employment before an increase in prices. But once the increase in prices catches up, unemployment will return to its former level because workers will have seen that their real wages have not increased with their nominal wages. The Phillips curve contained a basic defect, the failure to distinguish between nominal and real wages, and therefore it represents a temporary but not a permanent trade-off (Friedman, 1968:7–11; see also Friedman, 1977: 454–459).

This view of the macroeconomic outer environment did have implications for the rationality of the political process. It suggested that policymakers could not sustain unemployment rates below the "natural rate" without accelerating inflation. To keep inflation constant, unemployment would have to return to the natural rate. To reduce inflation, unemployment would have to rise (temporarily) above the natural rate. An appropriate short-run adaptation to the macroeconomic outer environment would be to maintain unemployment at its natural rate. The stable menu of choices described previously broke down.

If policymakers were to understand this limitation on their ability to reduce unemployment rates through demand management, they might not try. However, if they had to appeal to voters in order to maintain their offices, voters' expectations might lead them to inappropriate choices. Specifically, if voters rewarded unemployment below the natural rate or punished unemployment as high as the natural rate, policymakers might be tempted to induce an inappropriate policy response.

Nordhaus (1975) formulated a model that had just these features. An elected official who controlled the unemployment rate maximized votes by stimulating the economy just before elections. Because voters were presumed to have short memories of economic conditions early in a term, the reelected politician could induce a recession after the election to bring the associated inflation rate back down in time to face the next election in the same way. Such activity might create a "political business cycle," and in the long run it might be associated with a higher rate of inflation and a lower rate of unemployment "than is optimal" (Nordhaus, 1975:178).

Nordhaus shows that in this view of the macroeconomic outer environment, the presumed goals of politicians and the presumed behavior of voters led to an inappropriate adaptation to the environment. Here, then, is another standard of voter information and rationality derived from a view of the outer environment. The Nordhaus model of the political business cycle is very explicit about the costs and consequences of political manipulation. But if our standard of rationality is merely avoidance of inappropriate adaptations to the macroeconomic environment, the Nordhaus model does not imply a very demanding standard of voter behavior. Voter rationality in this context might be no more than satisfaction with unemployment at the natural rate or a failure to punish politicians for high unemployment.[3] No particular information level or cognitive process is required.

In this view, voters would not have to make the distinctions between occasions for deficit or balanced budgets, as implied by Buchanan and Wagner (1977), in order to be rational and informed. It would be sufficient for them to ignore economic policy. This is a model in which voter ignorance may be compatible with an appropriate adaptation to the macroeconomic outer environment. We may consider this rationality under the circumstances, whereas repeatedly rewarding politicians for inducing political business cycles might be considered otherwise.

Each of the two models of voter irrationality identified thus far has both simple and complex solutions. The complex solutions would demand essentially that voters understand the model and the consequences of their behavior. Because politicians and economists do not seem always to recognize and agree on these models, it would be quite extraordinary to expect so much of voters. The simple solution to Buchanan and Wagner's model of pathology is to return to the norm of annually balanced budgets by passing a constitutional amendment. A simple solution to Nordhaus's model of pathology is for voters to ignore unemployment rates or simply to be inflation averse.

The Theory of Economic Policy

The models described above are all partial and limited. The Buchanan and Wagner (1977) model of the political implications of Keynesian economics focuses on long-term consequences not addressed in the short-term models of the Phillips curve. Similarly, such short-term models do not deal with the longer-term effects of deficit spending. And although the natural rate models have a longer time horizon than the simple Phillips curve models, they typically ignore the secondary consequences of the fiscal or monetary policies that may be used to control the changes.

Most such issues can be incorporated into a large-scale macroeconometric model that includes equations for all of the features of interest. These models, which may be as small as three or four equations or as large as eight hundred equations, relate a vector of state variables, such as unemployment, to a vector of exogenous control variables, such as government spending or money growth. These models can be used to forecast future values of state variables given the values of the controls, and they can be used to simulate the consequences of alternative policy choices.[4] Such models can be adapted to the features of virtually any of the views discussed previously.

Fair (1978b) has shown that such macroeconometric models can be used to evaluate the economic performance of administrations. Such evaluation depends on the formulation of a welfare or loss function that is additive across time. Fair postulates welfare loss as a function of inflation and of deviations of output growth from its target value. He evaluates the performance of five postwar administrations by comparing their actual performance to the control theory solutions to the optimizing problems they faced. Elsewhere (1978a), Fair has estimated "The Effect of Economic Events on Votes for President," and, in principle, the two enterprises might be combined.

Specifically, one might simulate the effects of vote-maximizing economic policies on economic performance. For example, Chappell and Keech (1983) simulate the effects of such a political motivation in a macroeconometric model that has the essential features of the Nordhaus political business cycle model. We show that the amount of welfare loss depends on the length of voters' memories, the time horizon of the policymaker, and the length of the electoral terms.

Rational Expectations

In his summary of the essential features of the theory of economic policy, Lucas points out that comparison of alternative policies under a model of the economy presumes that the parameters relating choices to outcomes not vary systematically with the choices of policy. However, he says, "Everything we know about dynamic economic theory indicates that this presumption is unjustified" (1981:110–111).

The idea is that economic agents will incorporate into their expectations and decisions the policies made by government. For example, in terms of the natural rate argument above, government might reduce unemployment below the natural rate by an expansion of the money supply. According to the logic sketched previously, this works temporarily because of a confusion between nominal and real wages. It works because the government has surprised the economic agents. But having done so once, the agents may be less likely to respond to a second such stimulus. Coupled with the assumption that markets clear, such logic leads quickly to the proposition that systematic government stabilization policy is impossible, and that the government can affect real economic variables only by surprising people.

The rational expectations view is by no means universally accepted in economics, but it has had an enormous impact on macroeconomic thinking. Full acceptance of the policy ineffectiveness proposition certainly undermines political business cycle models because these models depend crucially on the government being able to manipulate the economy in systematic ways that rational expectations theory denies. Insofar as this theory holds true, citizens would seem to be invulnerable to pathological political manipulation.

However, rational expectations theory is based on some assumptions about the rationality of economic agents (otherwise citizens and voters) that are far more demanding than those typically made in political science. For example, economic agents are expected to make decisions using expectations for the future that "are essentially the same as the predictions of the relevant economic theory" (Muth, 1961:316). In one strong formulation, "Rational expectations are the expectations that an economic agent would have if he had a complete and correct model of the economy in which he was functioning and used all information available to him in conjunction with this model to predict what would happen in the economy" (Schotter, 1985:102). But what should be considered the relevant economic theory? If the models in the textbooks of the 1960s or 1970s are now considered incorrect, what would rational expectations assume regarding citizens?[5] And if citizens are so "rational" as economic agents, why should we worry about anything less from them in their role as citizens?

CITIZEN INFORMATION AND RATIONALITY
IN A CHANGING ENVIRONMENT

Our review of macroeconomic theories has had the manifest purpose of identifying models of the macroeconomic outer environment that could be used as a basis for identifying standards of citizen information and rationality. All of these theories have involved what Simon calls "substantive rationality," that is, behavior that is "appropriate to the achievement of given goals within the limits imposed by given conditions and constraints" (1982:425). When the nature of the outer environment is well understood, when goals are clear, and when human cognitive capacities are adequate, substantive rationality is quite appropriate. None of these conditions may hold for the macroeconomic outer environment.

A secondary implication of the review is that there is no single, authoritative macroeconomic theory. None of the theories approaches the status of, for example, Newtonian physics for the settings to which it is relevant. This is a situation in which "procedural rationality" is required because "the adaptation process itself is problematic" (Simon, 1981:32). "Behavior is procedurally rational when it is the outcome of appropriate deliberation" (Simon, 1982:426). Macroeconomic theory itself may be seen as a procedurally rational, adaptive, or evolutionary process, which changes as the environment itself changes beyond the situations to which existing theory spoke. Economic theorists themselves seem not always to have had the understanding of the relevant economic theory that can be rationally expected of citizens. Empirical studies suggest that even policymakers themselves "satisfice" rather than follow substantive rationality postulates of maximizing subject to constraint (Frey, 1983; Mosley, 1984). We expect no more of citizens.

We have used substantive rationality in terms of a series of theories to identify the risks of inappropriate deliberation. However, our review of macroeconomic theories makes clear that judgments about appropriate adaptation depend on theory that is itself adaptive to changing environments. With these considerations in mind, our question about citizen information and rationality can now be addressed in terms of empirical studies of cognition and behavior. We will review several studies that have implications for the ways in which citizens would react to economic policymaking and performance and for the ways in which policymakers adapt to the macroeconomic outer environment.

Ordinary Economic Theory

We consider first what Kinder and Mebane (1983:141) call "ordinary economic theory," the beliefs people have about the causes and responsibilities for their own and the country's economic circumstances. First, there is abundant evidence that in many situations narrowly conceived self-interest has very little impact on political attitudes and voting. (See Sears and Citrin, 1982, especially p. 160, for an important exception.) Sears, Lau, Tyler, and Allen (1980) find that measures of personal exposure to a variety of economic and noneconomic problems have a remarkably small impact on attitudes toward policies dealing with those problems. With respect to economic problems like unemployment and personal financial well-being, the evidence is consistent and clear. Schlozman and Verba (1979), Feldman (1982), and Kiewiet (1983) find that personal experience of such problems is not blamed on government, translated into support for governmental solutions to those problems, or seen as an important influence on voter choice. Government is not seen as a cause of these personal problems, nor is it seen as morally accountable for them.

Instead, the idea that individuals are responsible for their own well-being and for coping with their own problems is alive and well. Sniderman and Brody (1977:505–508) find that large majorities of those who identified a personal economic problem felt that they should work it out themselves and well under a third felt that government should help. This finding is echoed in Scholzman and Verba (1979: chapter 5) regarding belief in the individualism of "The American Dream" and in Feldman (1982) regarding beliefs in equal opportunity and the work ethic.

Thus, much of personal economic experience seems not to constrain government's ability to adapt to the macroeconomic outer environment. Policymakers seem remarkably free to be responsible and sensible in economic policymaking, and there is little evidence that patterns of citizen cognition or behavior stand in the way of appropriate choices by public officials.

Yet Kiewiet finds that perceptions of government responsibility for personal problems varied according to the type of problem. In particular, inflation was seen as a government responsibility. If prices are going up for a respondent, they are going up for everybody. This personal problem is "symptomatic of a problem affecting the entire economy. . . . Consequently, most people who felt their worst economic problem was inflation believed the government should be trying to curb it" (1983:75–76).

Moreover, there is abundant evidence that citizens hold government responsible for national (as opposed to personal) economic problems. For example, Kinder and Mebane (1983:149–154) find that government is very prominent in popular accounts of the causes of inflation. Yet national economic assessments are not simply surrogates for personal problems. Kiewiet (1983:88–95) shows that the two are only weakly related, and that assessments of national conditions are much more volatile than personal conditions.

Kiewiet finds that individual assessments of national economic conditions did significantly affect voting for president and for Congress. Positive assessments of national business conditions were associated with support for incumbents regardless of party, while there was intermittent evidence of support for a policy-oriented voting hypothesis. Specifically, there was some evidence that perception of unemployment as a national problem was associated with voting Democratic and that perception of inflation as a national problem was associated with voting for Republicans (Kiewiet, 1983: chapter 6).

Ordinary economic theory is not always wise from the standpoint of the economist. There is abundant evidence of popular support for price controls in spite of strong views of economists that controls have many undesirable consequences (Blinder, 1979:110–116). Similarly, public opinion about the balance of the federal budget has always been conventional and at odds with Keynesian views (Blinder and Holtz-Eakin, 1984).

Aggregated Time-Series Studies of Political Support

The studies just reported investigated behavior and cognition measured on the individual level and without special attention to variations in objectively measured economic conditions. Dozens of studies have estimated the relationship between economic conditions and popular support for public officials using aggregated time-series data. These studies have used dependent variables such as congressional and presidential vote and, most commonly, presidential popularity. Typically, they use economic independent variables such as inflation, unemployment, and income growth. These variables are objective measures of national economic conditions measured over time; they thereby incorporate a large range of economic experience. The economic variables are almost always entered in an additive fashion, wherein the expected signs for inflation and unemployment are negative, and those for income growth are positive. The relationship between the coefficients on target variables such as inflation and unemployment can be used to infer marginal rates of substitution between them, and these rates may vary among social, economic, and political groups (Hibbs, 1982a:326–330).

The models that can be so described are compatible with a view of the macroeconomic outer environment characterized by a static Phillips curve. The marginal rates of substitution can be drawn in the same unemployment-inflation space used to represent such a presumably inverse, stable relationship between unemployment and inflation. The tangency between the Phillips curve and a curve representing a voter's marginal rate of substitution would be a constrained optimum for that voter. Models of rational collective choice contingent on these assumptions are only a short step away (Keech, 1980:350–353; McCubbins and Schwartz, 1985). That is, if the macroeconomic outer environment is accurately represented by a static Phillips curve, the fact that voters are seen as having target values of zero for unemployment and inflation does not imply irrationality. Policy in such a world does not have unforeseen consequences, and present choices do not foreclose later options.

However, as our review of macroeconomic theory indicated, this view of the economic world is no longer widely accepted. More modern and sophisticated views suggest that the kind of voter behavior implied by most support models may not be sensible. Specifically, most of these models assume that voters not only reward public officials the lower the unemployment rate is, but also that they do so with a memory that is very short. That is, most of the models assume voters are like those that Nordhaus (1975) showed were vulnerable to political manipulation. They reward unemployment below the natural rate, and they pay attention only to recent events.

In spite of the existence and rather wide citation of the Nordhaus (1975) model, virtually none of the support studies with these features took note of the implications of their findings in view of this model, although Alt and Chrystal (1983:52) refer to such voters as myopic and amnesic. Hibbs (1982a:319–321) argues that memories are long enough to discourage political business cycles, but in fact his measure of these memories is a geometrically declining weight that falls to less than .2 two years before an election. In general, the implications of these models for voter vulnerability to political business cycles were largely ignored.[6]

Chappell and Keech (1985a) show that, insofar as these models imply that voters are vulnerable to cynical manipulation, they are not robust. Specifically, we formulated alternative models of the way in which voters respond to economic performance. One is a conventional model, which implies naiveté about achievable economic goals. It includes an empirically estimated short memory and a reward for higher GNP without regard to potential output or inflationary consequences. The other is designed to incorporate a sophisticated decision rule regarding economic performance. Essentially, it punishes deviations from potential output regardless of whether they are above or below, but it tolerates slack in the economy in inflationary times.

In empirical tests, the sophisticated voter model worked in general at least as well as the naive voter model, and in many respects better. We do not conclude that there is robust evidence that voters are sophisticated any more than we can conclude that there is solid evidence that they are not. What we do conclude is that voting behavior is as consistent with the view that voters are economically sophisticated as with the view that they are not. Aggregated evidence such as this certainly does not make a robust case that voters would punish politicians for following sensible economic policies, or that they offer irresistible incentives to do so. In general, the aggregated evidence linking voter support for incumbents to economic conditions does not make a convincing case that voters are vulnerable to this particular pathology.

Similar results followed from incorporating a sophisticated rule for control of monetary policy into a political support function that was compared with a standard, naive formulation. Here, too, the model with the sophisticated decision rule performed as well as the model with the naive decision rule (Chappell and Keech, 1985b). Once again, our inference is not that voters actually operate with such sophisticated decision rules, but rather that politicians would not be punished by voters for following sensible as opposed to short-sighted policies.

CONCLUSIONS

This discussion has been based on the presumption that citizen information and rationality can be evaluated in terms of their consequences. We have chosen to focus on consequences for macroeconomic policy because this field has the richest set of theories and models with which to explore the implications of different patterns of information and rationality. Some of the theories make startling assumptions, for example, that "economic agents form their expectations as if they know the process which will ultimately generate the actual outcomes in question" (Friedman, 1979:23). But our review has shown that economists' own understanding of these processes is continuously adapting. Regardless of public levels of information, or of evaluations of the substantive rationality of the electorate, it is by no means clear that robust patterns of citizen behavior obstruct the ability of policymakers to adapt to the macroeconomic environment according to the best economic advice of the day.

Our study has brought us full circle back toward a view of policymaking that predated the more cynical views of the 1970s and 1980s. A leading model of a politically induced pathology in macroeconomic policy depended on the assumption that politicians maximize votes that were a naive function of economic variables under full control of the public officials (Nordhaus, 1975). Few contemporary views envision anything approaching such precision of control, and subsequent studies of the long-term properties of the model showed it to be self-defeating for the politicians as well as for the public in some respects (Chappell and Keech, 1983; Keech and Simon, 1985).

There is progress in macroeconomic theory. Each step builds upon and subsumes previous steps. The advances in theory help us to understand how to adapt to a changing macroeconomic environment, and they help us to define reasonable aspiration levels. They also help us to infer appropriate or inappropriate patterns of citizen response.

The task of this discussion has been to relate these inferences to observed patterns of public information and rationality. In two cases, we found models of potential voter irrationality or of politically induced pathologies. Each had a simple and a complex solution. The complex solutions demanded a degree of voter information and rationality that we are unlikely to find among politicians, let alone voters. The simple solutions demanded far less. An aversion to deficits and a desire for a balanced federal budget is a simple solution to the problems identified by Buchanan and Wagner (1977). An aversion to inflation that dominates the aversion to unemployment is a simple solution to the problem identified by Nordhaus.

Our implication is that the prevalence of aversion to deficits and to inflation among the electorate is not a wholly unhealthy state of affairs in spite of the fact that both views have occasionally been pronounced as irrational by observers persuaded by the sophistication of the day. The resilience of such conventional wisdom may be a healthy sign. We also imply that politicians who try to be "guardians of the general good" can also prevail in spite of the imperfections in their understanding of the world and perhaps even in competition with those who maximize naive voting functions.

NOTES

1. There is a tradition of democratic theory based on Rousseau and Mill that stresses that informed citizenship and participation contribute to the personal development of individuals (see Pateman, 1970). Our analysis will consider instead the part that citizen behavior plays in the overall macroeconomic performance of the nation.

2. Our use of a performance standard should not be taken to suggest that poor system performance implies citizen irrationality. Poor performance might be due to a great variety of causes, including external shocks, politicians' failings, and a disjuncture between individual and collective rationality.

3. As Chappell and Keech (1983) point out, a longer memory also helps, but does not totally avoid the incentive to induce cycles.

4. For one of the most economical statements of the nature of such models, see Lucas (1981:106–108). For descriptions of recent and prominent examples, see Eckstein (1983), Fair (1984), and Elliott (1985).

5. Edward Gramlich (1983:162–163) has found that citizen expectations of inflation fit rational expectations hypotheses somewhat better than those of economists.

6. The issue of rationality that received the most discussion regarded whether or not there was *any* informational basis to the dynamics of presidential popularity (see Monroe, 1984:194–196).

14

Information and Rationality in Elections

Morris P. Fiorina

Since the early seventies, two of the most active and exciting areas of research on the electoral process have been spatial models of electoral competition and models of economic voting. However, these lines of research have evolved in quite different directions. Like two trains traveling in opposite directions on parallel tracks, at first they moved closer together, at some point they passed, and now they seem to be proceeding in opposite directions.

Consider these quotations from a younger Ordeshook and collaborators (Davis, Hinich, and Ordeshook, 1970:430–431):

> First, *we assume that citizens act as if they estimate a preferred position for every dimension*. Thus, we ignore the possibility that citizens frequently do not or cannot evaluate alternative proposals for many issues. Second, *we assume that all citizens use the same indices to measure any given policy . . . all citizens make identical estimates of* θ_j [the vector of candidate positions].
> . . . Thus, we ignore such problems as cognitive balance, imperfect information, and candidates' attempts to have different citizens believe different things about them. [emphasis in original]

At approximately the same time, the seminal figure in the economic voting literature advanced an alternative perspective (Kramer, 1971:133–134):

> One might picture the voter as a rational, information-processing individual who proceeds by collecting information of various kinds— party platforms and policy pronouncements, legislative voting records, and perhaps expert or authoritative opinions on these matters. Such a

voter analyzes this information in light of his own self-interest and decides which party presents the "best" package of positions. . . .

In a more realistic setting, however, a voter—even a rational self-interested voter—may not find it practical or efficient to proceed in this manner. . . .

we shall, therefore, assume that a decision rule of the following type is operative: if the performance of the incumbent party is "satisfactory" according to some simple standard, the voter votes to retain the incumbent party in office. . . .

By the late 1970s, some movement in both literatures was apparent. Hinich and his collaborators developed variations on spatial models that were less demanding of voters (Hinich and Pollard, 1981; Enelow and Hinich 1982). Meanwhile, on the economic voting front, Kramer shifted his stance while launching a major methodological critique constructed around a revised model of economic voting (Kramer, 1983:97):

we assume that the relevant financial impacts on voter i can be represented as a change in his real income, and that i's vote in election t is determined by the following simple, purely deterministic relation:

$$v_{it} = a_i + Bg_{it}$$

where g_{it} is the government-induced change in i's income over the period preceding the election. . . .

The assumption that the voter differentiates between government-induced and nongovernment-induced changes in financial condition departs considerably from the spirit of Kramer's earlier work. One imagines the following colloquy:

CPS interviewer: During the past year would you say that your financial situation has gotten better, gotten worse, or has it stayed about the same?
Respondent: Worse.
Interviewer: How is that?
Respondent: Well, I'd attribute 40 percent of it to the Reagan deficit, 25 percent to poor management in my industry, and the remainder to personal illness, though I'll blame the government for half of that because of their failure to contain health care costs. Of course, all these figures are net of the gains produced by the collapse of OPEC.

Caricature aside, the original broad gulf between the two literatures evidently had narrowed considerably.

Today, the gulf has reappeared, but the original positions are reversed. McKelvey and an older Ordeshook (chapter 12, this vol-

ume), now model "an electorate that does not necessarily conceptualize competition in terms of specific issues, where voters do not
attempt to identify the positions of candidates on issues, where contemporaneous events including campaign rhetoric are ignored, and
where instinct and habit are permitted to be the dominant imperatives
of electoral choice." Moreover, "Although candidates observe the aggregate vote in each election, and they know the form of the policy
space . . . candidates cannot observe voter payoff functions, the distribution of voter ideal points, or even the votes of specific voters."
Meanwhile, the successors to Kramer

> assume that the president, through fiscal and monetary policies, controls
> real output, Q. We then define the variable Z_t to serve as an indicator
> of policy stance, where
>
> $$Z_t = Q_t/Qn_t - 1$$
>
> and Qn is natural real gross national product. . . . A simple linear feed-
> back rule relating Z_t to the lagged rate of inflation, P_{t-1}, is used to define
> desirable policies:
>
> $$Z_{t*} = dP_{t-1}, d < 0$$
>
> Z_{t*} denotes the optimal value of Z_t as perceived by sophisticated vot-
> ers. . . .
>   To measure economic performance, then, it is appropriate to
> judge policymakers on the basis of how far they deviate from the op-
> timum policy, Z_{t*} (Chappell and Keech, 1985a:13).

Undoubtedly there is a lesson to be drawn from examining these
intellectual movements, although I do not know what it is. As for the
relationship of information to the rationality of voting behavior and
elections, when the leaders of the rational choice school find satisfaction in fairly primitive forms of political behavior, and advanced students of economic voting flirt with rational expectations (Williams,
1986), it is apparent that scholars have reached no consensus. Still,
some of the issues have become clearer, and we can better appreciate
the arguments. Elsewhere (1981:193) I have questioned the value of
arguments about voter rationality, but in the present context that is
the obvious place to begin. The next section of this chapter discusses
the concept of rationality and its relationship to information. The
third section discusses the application of the concept to elections and
concludes that information and rationality are independent concepts;
linking them only confuses matters. A fourth section takes up the
question of why all citizens are not rationally ignorant. And the final

section considers whether there are any research areas where information and rationality might usefully be discussed together.

Election studies of the 1950s and 1960s typically viewed information as a prerequisite of rationality. To be rational a voter must know certain things (where "things" pertains to issues) and rely on that knowledge. A well-known illustration appears in *The American Voter*, where the authors report a "test" of issue-based voting, a test most of the American public fails (Campbell, Converse, Miller, and Stokes, 1960: chapter 8). According to this traditional view, rationality is a measurable, more-or-less continuous variable, and information is a major indicator of rationality. The more information people possess, the greater the potential for rationality, although the analyst must still ascertain whether that potential is realized by a vote cast on the basis of the pertinent information.

Microeconomics, a discipline based on the notion of rationality, relies on a concept much less substantive than that common in the earlier political science literature. Economists view rational behavior as maximizing behavior. But the import of that assumption varies from context to context. In some contexts, maximizing might entail the possession of a great deal of highly specialized information, and a great deal of expense in processing it, whereas in other contexts ignorance would be rational. In the electoral context, Downs introduced this mode of thought to political science when he observed that consideration of the costs of information makes it unreasonable to expect that most citizens will be well informed: "Any concept of democracy based on an electorate of equally well informed citizens is irrational; i.e., it presupposes that citizens behave irrationally" (1957:236). The essence of Downs's argument is that the analyst consider what is reasonable for an ordinary citizen to do in a given context.

Such arguments have had an impact on contemporary political scientists. Page and Brody (1972), for example, note that the quality of information held by citizens depends at least in part on the nature of the electoral process. Politicians who obfuscate, equivocate, and collude are unlikely to generate the kind of information that would produce the fully informed citizens of some idealistic political theories.[1] But if that is the case, must we then conclude that elections are inherently flawed as collective choice methods?

Leaving aside the question of flawed relative to what, some research has suggested that even taking voters and politicians as they apparently are, elections may nevertheless have certain "good" properties. Specifically, retrospective accountability demands relatively little of the voter and has the potential to induce elected officials to engage in socially desirable behavior (Fiorina, 1981; Ferejohn, 1986). The McKelvey-Ordeshook discussion in this volume fits about here. To put their model and evidence in a nutshell, even without classically rational (i.e., informed) voters, electoral processes function well in the sense that they produce the perfect information equilibrium. Aside from rehabilitating the voter's image, the contribution of the economic concept of rationality is that it severs the connection between an informed electorate and an informed outcome: an outcome that exhausts all available information does not require exhaustively informed (and exhausted) voters.

The Chappell-Keech chapter of this book pursues a different notion of rationality. Rather than specifying the meaning of rationality, then working out the relation between individual rationality and system performance, Chappell and Keech "evaluate citizen information and rationality in terms of their consequences for public policymaking". Whereas McKelvey and Ordeshook suggest that even without classically rational citizens, system performance may still be okay, Chappell and Keech appear to suggest that one way to judge citizen rationality is whether system performance is satisfactory.

Chappell and Keech make a useful, probably incontestable, argument that the economic welfare implications of elections hinge on whether the electorate's political behavior "would obstruct an 'appropriate' adaptation of the policymaking system to the macroeconomic environment" (315). But I am hesitant to make nonobstructive citizen behavior a criterion or component of rational behavior. First, the concept becomes hostage to each successive revolution in macroeconomics, a difficulty Chappell and Keech recognize. When one model holds sway, voters are rational, but if the orthodoxy changes, voters become irrational, even if nothing about their adaptation to their situation changes at all.

A second problem with a "by the outcome they shall be judged" formulation is that it puts more of the onus for behaving rationally on voters than I think appropriate. The behavior of voters and candidates together interacting in a specific institutional framework determines the electoral outcome. We should not single out voters as especially responsible for political outcomes, especially when stylized accounts of the electoral game suggest that voters are more in the position of Stackelberg followers.[2] Under the economic conception, voters are rational if they choose maximizing actions in a nonstrategic environment, or their equilibrium strategies in a strategic environment. Whether the outcome/equilibrium is optimal is a question that is independent of the rationality of the actions of individuals.

One of the central insights of modern choice theory is the distinction between individual and collective rationality, more exactly, the distinction between the rationality of behavior and the optimality of outcomes. The Prisoner's Dilemma game is the quintessential example. Applied to that game, the Chappell and Keech line of argument would question the rationality of players who adopt dominant strategies and thereby fail to achieve the Pareto optimal outcome. But, of course, it is precisely the disjunction between individual and collective rationality that gives the game its significance.

Whether or not the Chappell and Keech treatment of rationality wins adherents should make little difference to them, for the questions they pose can be posed and examined just as easily without taking a position on rationality one way or the other. Does or does not voter behavior obstruct an appropriate macroeconomic response? Whatever the answer, the term *rationality* is not needed to provide it.

Of course, to reaffirm the appropriateness of the traditional economic conception of rationality is not to say that the former has no problems. In fact, when scholars apply the concept in the context of mass elections they encounter major difficulties. Although these have been recognized for years, if not decades, in the absence of superior theories we continue to tiptoe around them.

PUZZLES OF INFORMATION AND RATIONALITY IN MASS ELECTIONS

By way of introduction let us briefly consider what has been called the puzzle of participation in mass elections. As various analysts have noted, standard conceptions of rational behavior do not explain why anyone bothers to vote in a mass election. There have been any number of minor debates—is the probability of a tied election 10^{-15} or 10^{-12} and so forth—but the bottom line remains: no individual's impact on the election outcome is sufficiently great that his or her expected benefit from voting exceeds his or her cost. There appears to be no escaping this result.[3] In one appearance of the paradox that ate rational choice theory, Ledyard (1984) carries out a fully strategic analysis of a two-candidate election. He proves that in equilibrium turnout levels are zero, a theoretically intriguing, if empirically somewhat disconcerting, result.

Informed citizens pose the same type of problem for rational choice arguments as do citizens who incomprehensibly insist on voting.

Just as most people regard high participation as a collective good, so most people regard a well-informed electorate as a collective good. But just as citizens have no apparent personal incentive to vote, so they appear to have no apparent personal incentive to be informed. With virtually no chance of affecting the election outcome, it matters not whether one's vote is informed or uninformed. Just as nonparticipation is rational, so is ignorance (Downs, 1957; Becker, 1958). This line of thinking suggests that scholarly evaluations of voters in the 1960s were accurate enough, but for the wrong reason. Voters are irrational—not because they have so little information, but because they have so much!

Why should Everyman know where the candidates stand on the issues? Why should Everyman know what the government is currently doing in a given policy area? Why should Everyman have an opinion about the future course of public policy? With an electorate numbering in the millions, why should Everyman rationally know anything? The simple fact is that in a mass election, no rational citizen should be informed. From the standpoint of the economic conception of means-ends rationality, informed citizens are the anomaly that requires explanation. Of course, it may be that more complex conceptions of individual rationality can support better-informed voters, a possibility to be discussed in the next section. It is unlikely, however, that any conception of means-ends rationality can support an electorate that registers higher ratings for *Meet the Press* than for *Dallas*.

If current models do not suggest any positive relationship between information and individual rationality in elections, then for the time being we should take voters as they are and attempt to trace the consequences of their behavior, however "rational" or not it might seem to be. This is the line of thinking pursued by McKelvey and Ordeshook, with encouraging results. Building on empirical portraits of the voter, they prove that under specific conditions an electorate of relatively uninformed voters choosing between relatively uninformed candidates will generate the same electoral outcome as an electorate of perfectly informed voters choosing between perfectly informed candidates. It is not clear whether we should call the outcome "collectively rational," although it is Pareto optimal, but if we do, we also break the connection between information and collective rationality, for the theoretical results show that the choices of poorly informed voters and candidates will generate a collectively rational outcome.[4]

In sum, current thinking suggests that there is no necessary relationship between information and rationality in mass elections, whether we view rationality in individual terms, or in terms of collective consistency or optimality properties. From the arguments reviewed, the existence of highly informed voters cannot be explained in terms of individual rationality. From the generic nonexistence of electoral equilibria (McKelvey, 1979), we may conclude that highly informed voters are not sufficient to produce collectively rational outcomes.[5] And from the McKelvey-Ordeshook line of research, we may conclude that highly informed voters are not generally necessary for collectively rational outcomes. Seemingly, somewhere in the literature one can find arguments for every possible combination of high and low information levels and individual and collective rationality. Is it time to abandon the discussion?

THE PUZZLE OF INFORMED CITIZENS

If one's vote has no discernible impact on the outcome of the election, why should one bear any cost in order to cast an informed vote? The answer is clear—one shouldn't. But whatever the logic, the suggestion that discussion now cease almost certainly will fall on deaf ears. As with the puzzle of participation, the puzzle of information will continue to fascinate scholars. Real people can be found at every level of the information continuum. A little thought suggests that there are plenty of reasons for people to procure information; it is just that none of these reasons has anything to do with enhancing people's prospects of gain from casting an informed vote in a mass election.

The Duty to Be Informed

Riker and Ordeshook (1968) attempt to save the rationality of political participation by embracing the Michigan School's findings that people vote out of a sense of duty. Although Barry (1970) correctly observes that this is a rather desperate attempt to save an unsatisfactory model, there is no doubt that many citizens do vote out of duty. This observation seems equally plausible as an explanation of why some people are informed. Classical accounts (e.g., Mill) of one's responsibilities as a citizen do not demand just casting a vote, they demand casting an informed vote. Some people struggle with voter information pamphlets, read newspaper endorsements, and even attend candidate meetings simply because they feel they should.

Duties and obligations obviously play an important role in human behavior, but their relationship to individual rationality is not clear. In fact, dutifully informed citizens probably underlie the past confusion about the relationship between information levels and individual rationality. If the more highly educated are more strongly socialized into the norms of citizenship, then we would expect to find higher information levels among those casually viewed as more "rational." But as the argument in the preceding section shows, such a conclusion is the opposite of the correct one. The more highly educated, better-informed citizen is actually an illustration of how arational factors can override the dictates of individual rationality. The poorly educated, uninformed citizens are the individually rational ones. Of course, one can make an argument that good citizenship illustrates a higher form of rationality (Meehl, 1977), but that claim extends beyond the scope of this discussion.

Informed Citizens as Fans

Voting has been likened to spectator sport (Brennan and Buchanan, 1984). Millions of citizens buy tickets, cable connections, and satellite dishes so that they may cheer on their favored teams. Do they believe that their investment will increase the probability of a favorable outcome for their team? Of course not.[6] Nevertheless, they continue to engage in fan behavior, often with great enthusiasm, and rational choice theorists do not regard this behavior as irrational, or even curious. Why, then, should we regard the analogous behavior in politics—vote—as an anomaly?

The same argument extends quite easily to the realm of information. Fans often become quite knowledgeable about their teams. I live among thousands of benighted people who clutter their memory banks with useless trivia about "Kevin," "DJ," and, of course, "Larry." (Certainly these people are crazy—rational people would store information about "Magic" and Worthy.) If human beings choose to gather great stores of information about competitions and contests of all manner, where no investment motive seems remotely plausible, why should it come as any great surprise when some people are well informed about politics? Is rooting on the Republicans inherently more puzzling or interesting than rooting on the Lakers? Notice that the spectator sport explanation does not suggest that the well informed are either more or less individually rational than the uninformed. Some people are serious fans, some are not.

This line of argument does have some implications for the types of information that people will have. Knowledge of the state of the contest probably would be most widespread. Next would come familiarity with the particular tactics adopted by the contestants, along with errors, clutch plays, and chokes. Last would come details about the internal operation of the league—its organizational structure, its business operations, and so forth. In addition, we might expect that in general people would have higher levels of information about close contests than about blow-outs. Evidently, patterns of political information among real voters bear some resemblance to these speculations.

Accidental and Incidental Exposure

Workers playing a radio for entertainment are inevitably exposed to the day's headlines every hour on the hour. A relaxed citizen watching the "Bill Cosby Show" involuntarily sees the previews of the late-night news. Feeling sociable, an office-worker sits down at the lunch table and joins an ongoing political conversation (of course, one might ask why anyone else at the table had information, but this is not a general equilibrium argument). One could proliferate examples like these without end, but the point is clear. Citizens often receive information in the course of doing other things. There is no question of information costs, no question of deciding to gather information as opposed to doing something else. Just as exposed portions of skin get tanned by the sun when people walk around out of doors, so people become informed as they go about their daily business. Neither phenomenon is especially noteworthy, and the second has no more relation to individual rationality than the first.

It Was the Best Alternative at the Time

Every reader of this volume surely has read some unfamiliar material while seated in a dentist's office, an auto repair shop, or on a transcontinental flight. The sweating commuter stuck in traffic listens to public affairs radio rather than submit to still another round of the top 40. The pre-pubescent struggles through the late-night news rather than go to bed. Such decisions arouse no one's curiosity. Although gathering and processing information is costly, individuals sometimes find themselves in situations where one costly activity diminishes or substitutes for other, higher costs inherent in the situation—physical fear in the dentist's office, economic fear in the auto repair shop, the boredom of traveling, the nothingness of sleep.

A rational model of individual information accumulation starts from the presumption that the individual chooses to gather information rather than perform any of a wide variety of other possible acts. But in the real world, citizens may be put in situations where their actions are severely constrained, where bearing the costs of gathering information is preferable to enduring other costs that are the sole alternative. Focus on a dull article is sometimes preferable to focus on the pain of a broken tooth and the fear gnawing at one's stomach.

This fourth consideration is somewhat related to the third, in that information is accumulated not for its own value but as a by-product of another choice. The arguments differ, however, in that the third focuses on the lack of actual choice when information gathering incidentally accompanies other activities, while the fourth argument focuses on the choice of a less costly activity when the alternative appears to be a more costly one.

Information as a Collector's Item

Neatly arranged in our family room are more than three hundred comic books, each lovingly encased in a protective plastic wrapper by my twelve-year-old son. Once, long ago, I registered mild disapproval of the amount of financial and other resources invested in this useless activity. That parental judgment elicited a disrespectful observation about the six hundred bottles of Bordeaux in the basement. Given the child's youth and undeveloped sense of values, one can forgive his inappropriate analogy between comic books and wine, but there is no denying that multitudes of people collect multitudes of objects and quantities, many of which have no apparent instrumental value.

One of the editors of this volume collects artificial flies. He may say they are instrumental in catching trout, but his friends know better. The sober New Englander, Richard Fenno, reportedly has a campaign button collection numbering more than six thousand. Other colleagues collect stamps, coins, T-shirts, and beer bottle caps. In many cases, large collections held for a length of time can develop real economic value. Often we rationalize our holdings in such fashion, but deep down we know it isn't true. And it is easy enough to think of collectibles with no economic value—string, rubber bands, and so forth.

Intangibles like information can be a collector's object just as easily as tangibles. Many children collect information on dinosaurs, although they can never hope to own one. Adults focus on more serious subjects—works of art, astronomy, baseball—although they too can never hope to own a Raphael, Halley's comet, or the Pittsburgh Pirates. Here again one might argue that information specialists—experts—have an economic motive. They can deliver speeches, write newsletters, and in other ways capitalize on their collection of information. But most do not, and at any rate we can cite examples of people who collect information about things of no earthly value. One colleague, who shall remain nameless, is a bona fide expert on Doris Day movies.

Collecting information about the Democrats, Ronald Reagan, or American economic policy does not seem inherently more unreasonable than collecting information about art, wine, or baseball, although it is understandable why more people collect information about baseball than about economic policy (recall the spectator sport argument above). Whatever quality in the make-up of humanity that leads people to collect anything leads at least some people to collect information about politics. Of course, in the absence of an explanation of such behavior, we cannot say whether it is rational or irrational, but it has no apparent relation to gains expected from casting a vote.

Information as Social Definition

Driving a Porsche makes a social statement: it identifies the driver as a certain kind of person. A Mondale-Ferraro sticker on the bumper made another statement. To sip white wine at a cocktail party makes a social statement. To decline Gallo makes another statement. For whatever reason, people accumulate political information and communicate it in order to make statements about themselves (perhaps *to* themselves). Opposition to a tax limitation initiative identifies you as a person different from the selfish and callous bourgeois who favor it. Opposition to a gun control initiative establishes you as a person different from the wimpy liberals who support it. People's political stances are part of their self-definition. Western literature is replete with works about people trying to find out who they are. One way to figure it out is to see where you stand on the issues, which groups you sympathize with, and what candidates you support. Political psychologists have discussed such ideas, but I am not aware of any suggestion that information procured in the process of self-definition has any special relation to individual calculations about the value of casting an informed vote.

Social scientists attuned to everyday life will have no difficulty proliferating motives for becoming informed. Individually, none of these may account for much of the variation in information levels in the mass public. But cumulatively, their sheer variety would be expected to produce considerable variation across the continuum from complete ignorance to very well informed. From the standpoint of the earlier discussion, most of these reasons can be summarized with the simple observation that many people attach an inherent value to political information, they treat it as a consumption good rather than an investment. But that summarization concedes the argument. Well-informed voters have not gathered information in order to cast an informed vote; rather, they are able to cast an informed vote because they have accumulated information for other unrelated reasons.

RATIONAL CHOICE MODELS AND INFORMATION IN ELECTIONS

If information levels have nothing to do with individual rationality in a mass electoral setting, and if informed voters are neither necessary nor sufficient for collectively rational election outcomes, do proponents of rational choice models have anything to say about the subject of information and elections? I believe we do, but the focus of our attention should shift away from ordinary citizens to elites.

If people are informed principally because of the sorts of considerations discussed in the preceding section, then we may think of them as akin to an "environment" in which elites rationally attempt to maximize the achievement of their various goals. The media, for example, are in the business of selling information. It is not surprising that the media treat politics as sport. Because media elites are concerned with selling information as a commodity rather than with communicating the content of that information, they naturally concentrate on the entertainment value of the information.

Candidates wish to convey favorable information about themselves. Some candidates may feel they lack entertainment value and so attempt to capitalize on accidental/incidental exposure. They buy radio spots, stand at plant gates, and in other ways insinuate themselves into the consciousness of the electorate. Other candidates link themselves to an issue, group, or another public figure with symbolic value and thereby reach voters through the self-definition avenue. Likewise, racial and ethnic groups and some single-issue groups capitalize on the self-definition motive of people. General interest groups also appeal to people's sense of self (the independent, thoughtful citizen), and in addition they work the duty angle ("people like you have an obligation to give the nation the benefit of your exceptional qualities").

Disseminating information is only one subject of study. Elites also shape the information they communicate. They have beliefs about what matters, about how to sell an idea or person. As Riker (1984) argues, this is virgin territory for rational choice analysis, but as he also demonstrates, it is an area amenable to rational analysis.

In sum, electoral processes involve numerous actors other than the mass public. Many of these actors have compelling personal motives to fabricate, accumulate, and disseminate information. Various factors lead them to adopt some informational strategies rather than others. What are these factors and how do they affect elite calculations? Here is the most fruitful ground for rational analysis of information in elections. As for information in the mass public, the political psychologists have done an acceptable job. Those of us who share the rational choice persuasion need only correct their interpretations now and then.

NOTES

Henry Brady, Gary Cox, William Keech, and R. Douglas Rivers provided constructive comments on this chapter.

1. As Key (1966:7) remarked, "Fed a steady diet of buncombe, the people may come to expect and to respond with highest probability to buncombe."

2. We should note, however, that in their footnote 2, Chappell and Keech disavow any intent to place the entire burden of system performance on the backs of individual voters.

3. More correctly, there is one known escape, the possibility that voters behave as minimax regretters (Ferejohn and Fiorina, 1974, 1975). While philosophers of science have been quite enthusiastic about this proposal (Moon, 1975; Ball, 1976), political theorists stubbornly refuse to consider it seriously.

4. The principal reason for skepticism about the otherwise impressive theoretical and experimental results reported by McKelvey and Ordeshook is that they ignore the large n problem discussed in the text. Their theoretical results assume that all citizens vote, eliminating the puzzle of participation by fiat. Their experimental results are based on a small group situation, and thus lack validity as examples of mass elections. The experimental electorates are sufficiently small that voters have some personal incentive to glean what little information they can out of the setting. What incentive exists if the electors number in the millions?

5. Results on the uncovered set may amend this conclusion. Apparently this set of alternatives is Pareto optimal, and sophisticated voters will produce an outcome in the set (Shepsle and Weingast, 1984b).

6. In the aggregate, the mood created by thousands of cheering fans may affect the course of play. But the contribution of each individual fan remains trivial in exactly the same sense as the contribution of each individual voter in a mass election.

V

FROM INDIVIDUAL TO AGGREGATE AND THE REDUCTION OF "NOISE" IN REPRESENTATIONAL SYSTEMS

15

A Macro Theory of
Information Flow

James A. Stimson

Voters seem to act with a decent understanding of the essential issues that separate parties and candidates from one another. That is naturally the case for those who pay a good deal of attention to political life. But it is also the case for those who profess little interest in politics, claim to spend almost no time and effort attending to political affairs, and have a generally impoverished storehouse of knowledge about the basic facts of American politics. Because the electorate consists primarily of the inattentive, we are left to wonder how it comes to have that decent understanding of party and candidate issue positions. That is the question that motivates this work. How, given general ignorance of things political, does the American electorate come to be informed of the policy choices it confronts?

We shall survey some evidence of what the electorate does and does not know, ponder some proposed explanations of the conflict between inattention and knowledge, and suggest an explanation in the intermediary role of citizen political activists. The model to be developed presumes the social transmission of political knowledge, that the inattentive segment of the electorate makes inferences about who stands for what by projecting the views of citizen activists onto the parties and candidates the activists support. This mediated cognitions model is then used to account for the anomalously high level of policy position information in the electorate.

MODELING MASS COGNITION: HOW ELECTORATES PERCEIVE
THE DYNAMICS OF POLICY IMAGES IN PARTY BEHAVIOR

Voters repeatedly tell us that they don't follow public affairs, have little interest in politics or policy, view government as relatively remote from their lives, and have little concern over which particular set of public officials ought to be in charge. But yet, in the aggregate, these same voters seem surprisingly well informed about the choices they make. One of the longest-running conflicts in the study of mass electorates, this contradictory set of facts presents no easy way out. We can deny one or the other set of facts, but after two decades of argument between the "voters don't pay attention" and "voters are not fools" schools of thought, the evidence marshaled on both sides is impressive. It seems to be the case that most citizens do not pay enough attention to public affairs to have a decent understanding of the issues with which they must come to grip to make informed choices. And yet it also seems to be the case that choices are informed by a decent understanding.

As Brady and Sniderman (1985:1061) put the issue, "Citizens, it turns out, are remarkably accurate in estimating the issue positions of strategic groups in politics, including groups like liberals and conservatives about which one might well suppose the mass public to be ignorant. Given how much citizens do not know about politics, it is worthwhile establishing that there is an aspect of politics—and an important one—about which they are knowledgeable."

The realm of macroeconomic policymaking provides a stark contrast between ignorant citizens and informed electorates. We have long learned to expect citizen ignorance of the basic facts of government economic policymaking. Issues so simple as the equation relating expenditures, revenues, and deficits seem to elude most. And we can imagine the result of a survey pop quiz on Keynesian policy adaptations or on monetarism. But Chappell and Keech (1985a) demonstrate that electoral support for government economic policy is sophisticated, that it rewards neither full employment policies nor anti-inflationary restraints, but rather the right policy at the right time, given the national economic circumstances of the moment.

Public officials such as members of Congress repeatedly tell us, in a similar vein, that the public is almost wholly unaware of their official behavior, often despite their own best efforts to inform. But these same officials worry, and not just a little, about the electoral consequences of their acts. Are they irrationally fearful, ignorant of the true level of public information? Or is there some way in which a public that does not know about a single individual act, such as a roll-call vote, somehow comes to understand a pattern of behavior?

Electoral history provides many examples of voter perceptions of a singularly interesting variety, perceptions of facts at variance with the truth, as best as it can be objectively observed, and yet from the point of view of the relative choice between parties or candidates, perceptions that provide the basis for a sound expression of the voter's preferences. How may we come to terms with the probably common perception that George McGovern in 1972 stood for "acid, amnesty, and abortion," for example, when McGovern in fact had a mixed (and largely private) view of the abortion issue and certainly did not favor illegal drug use or the legalization of "acid." But in the two-candidate choice of that year, inaccurate as those assertions are, they do capture the notion that McGovern was the one who would be likely to be sympathetic to the left counter-culture to which these themes were tied.

Even more contrary to fact was the widespread belief, of no small consequence to the election outcome, that Jimmy Carter was weak on defense (meaning specifically defense spending) in 1980. The fact of the matter was that Carter instigated the first defense spending increase in real terms since the Vietnam buildup and at the time perhaps the most impressive peacetime buildup since the onset of the cold war era. But applied to the choice between Carter and Ronald Reagan, the public's misperception of Carter was the basis of an accurate relative assessment of which candidate would likely spend more.

If we inquire closely into public policy as debated in the policy-conscious environment of Washington, we must be impressed with how truly difficult most policy disputes are. When interesting policy debates arise, they are only rarely of the for or against variety readily communicated for mass consumption. More often they are complicated, specific, and involve disputes over facts and assumptions, not basic values. Values and ideologies do have a role, almost invariably, but that role is often so subtle that only the day-to-day experts in a particular policy area correctly know which side is which. Question after question presents issues of great complexity. But voters do at least sometimes seem to be making choices on issues they can't reasonably understand, yet they make relative choices that accurately reflect their underlying preferences.

These contradictions and many more can be resolved if we abandon the notion of individual citizens as atomistic fact collectors and decision makers. If instead we view the collection of factual information as a social process in the same way that Berelson, Lazarsfeld, and McPhee (1954) long ago characterized the formation of voting intentions as a two-step flow of communication, then we can come to terms with how millions of inattentive citizens somehow acquire reasonably accurate information about policy positions and policy choices. All we need do is to assume that the normal economics of specialization and division of labor are applicable also to the collection of political information, and then both an account of information flow and a resolution of otherwise contradictory facts are at hand.

Inattentive citizens are likely to collect facts from the more politically attentive people with whom they have personal contact. That is something we have long known, but we keep forgetting it. Probably owing to both the norms of popular democratic theory that idealizes the individual citizen as decision maker and our intellectual dependence upon survey research as a method of observing the world, and one that constantly directs our focus to the individual as unit of analysis, our tendency always is to think of the psychology of individual cognition as if it occurred in a social vacuum, the lonely contest of the individual citizen and his or her television set.

Consider the economy of fact-gathering about policy choices. The citizen who would express personal preferences in choices between alternative candidates and parties must know what are the relevant choices (and the relevant set is always much smaller, more applied, more specific, and more technical than the set of general preference questions to which it is related), who stands for what, how large is the relative difference between alternatives, and so forth.

Two barriers stand in the way of individual fact-gathering about policy choices: (1) the activity is extremely expensive; it requires an attentiveness to government and politics considerably beyond what most citizens seem willing to consider, and (2) having paid the high price of attentiveness to public affairs, the individual citizen gathering his or her own facts still is very likely to be wrong, to take a position contrary to what he or she would espouse given more expert knowledge on the matter.

The citizen who prefers to be inattentive to politics—and we tend to underestimate the reasonableness of that preference—could choose to bypass both costs and errors by simply looking to someone in his or her personal environment for evidence of the relevant facts, someone with known views (often, perhaps without wishing to). The inference is simple and accurate enough on average to make it a reasonable guide: Joe Blow supports candidate *X;* therefore *X* probably stands for the same things as Joe Blow. Fill in television's "Archie Bunker" for Joe Blow and Richard Nixon for *X*, and an inference that follows, for example, is that Nixon is not warmly disposed toward black Americans.

It is likely that this sort of reasoning is very common. It allows a simple and impressively accurate means of making sense of political stands, and it can proceed without necessity of translating complicated policy pronouncements into the more relevant project of position with regard to other candidates and parties. Indeed, one of the more interesting properties of this sort of political reasoning is that it can proceed without the candidate or party saying anything at all about the policy in question. That suggests that widespread mediated cognitions may deprive the candidate of much of the control of his or her own position that is commonly presumed by rational choice projections of candidate policy positioning.

Who would be those of known views in the individual's environment? Citizen political activists, those relatively ordinary people who take up the opportunities to participate that most shun, would seem to be prime candidates. They are the specialists who pay attention when others do not. Their views are public, on display from lawn signs, campaign pins, and bumper stickers. Sometimes their views are known, and they give direct coloration to the parties and candidates they support. Sometimes their views on issues are not known but are advertised along with candidate support: a peace symbol and McGovern sticker on the same bumper told a story in 1972. Sometimes the association of political support with a subculture or life-style is the basis of inferences about candidate views: if the McGovern sticker appeared on the bumper of an aging Volkswagen van of a certain distinctive type, the symbolic association of candidate and a cluster of left political views could be inferred.

The process of inferring candidate and party views from the views of the activist supports would be most direct and powerful for members of primary groups, including an activist cue-giver. There the constellation of issue positions associated with political support would generally be well known from direct conversation over a lengthy period. That maybe supplemented, and in some cases replaced, by figures who are impersonally "known," such as politicians and movie stars—a Jane Fonda endorsement in the 1970s and 1980s could tell us a good deal about a politician's likely set of views—as well as by the altogether anonymous mechanisms such as the bumper sticker.

One way to inquire what a party stands for—a theme to be developed in detail below—is to aggregate the positions of its "members," those who express a sense of identification with the party and presumably also with its goals. But however correct this strategy may be as accounting, it overlooks the fact that policy views for most citizens are a private matter. Looking at the policy views of the mass electorate permits the measurement in the context of survey research of views whose only public expression is in the survey interview. If we ask instead what a party visibly stands for, then we need to focus on those viewpoints that might reasonably be expected to be expressed, to be seen and heard in the neighborhood, workplace, or wherever government and politics are discussed.

We assume for this analysis that one of the things that distinguishes activists from typical citizens is the public expression of political views. Indeed, "talking about politics" is one of the items employed to define activism. If we assume, furthermore, that the visibility of a citizen's views is in rough proportion to his or her activity—a matter of degree, not kind—then a method of examining visible party positions suggests itself. The logical extension of a simple accounting of identifier positions, equally weighted for all, is to weight views by the degree to which they are publicly expressed, made operational in this case by activism. Thus the citizen who reports no activity beyond voting is altogether removed from this "public" opinion analysis, whereas the more active are weighted by degree of activism.[1]

COGNITION OF PARTY AND CANDIDATE POLICY POSITIONS: HOW MUCH DOES THE ELECTORATE KNOW?

We begin the analysis with evidence of what the public knows. Respondents have been asked in the NES national surveys where the two parties position themselves on some of the same issues where respondent preferences are surveyed. Since 1972, similar information has been obtained about candidate positions. Presented without objective standard of where the parties should be located (but see Brady and Sniderman, 1985, where such standards are developed), the party position cognitions of Table 1 are nonetheless a close fit to commentaries on the party issue positions of the period. Not only do the voters uniformly perceive the Democrats to be more liberal on most policies in most elections—and the exceptions on racial issues in the 1950s and early 1960s are consistent with the actual positions of the parties at that time—but they also appear sensitive to variations in party position from election to election. Aggregate perceptions expand party issue differentiation in years of contentious policy candidacies (1964, 1972, and 1980) and contract it in other years. In cases where a new party differentiation appeared during the period (race in the

1960s or women's role around 1980), citizen cognitions follow sharply and closely.

For all who have read appalling stories of the elementary facts about political life that citizens should know but don't, perhaps more for those who have seen that reality first hand, it should come as some surprise that this truly essential information about policy choices is perceived with commendable accuracy. Table 1 suggests that American citizens saw little confusion or randomness in the political world.

The candidate position perceptions (Table 2) tell a similar story. Available for a shorter time period, the candidate perceptions are even stronger evidence. The presidential candidates are primarily new figures on the political scene, with images less tied to party histories than the parties themselves and potentially much harder to gauge. What can be said about both tables is this: although we lack an objective standard that can validate the accuracy of these perceptions, it is clear that the perceptual data make a very bad case for the confused, random, or ignorant electorate. Although we can locate ignorance, confusion, and misperception among individual respondents, there is none to be seen in the macro phenomenon of electoral policy perception. The American electorate as an organic entity knows the positions contending parties and candidates take.

Part of this riddle is a matter of perspective. To look at individuals is to be impressed by ignorance. No matter how low a standard of reasonable information levels is put forward, we manage always to find numerous survey respondents who fail it. When we look at aggregates, individual ignorance takes on a random appearance and the knowledge of the better-informed elements of the electorate then dominates collective measures of issue perception. Thus we see central tendencies in mass cognitions of party and candidate issue positions that, particularly in longitudinal context, appear highly perceptive.

But aggregation alone cannot fully account for the quality of issue (and ideology) perceptions. Everything we know about American and other electorates suggests that they are inattentive to public affairs. The logic of rationally self-interested choice suggests moreover that they should be. What we know about the central debates over public policy, as raised by the professionals in governing, suggests that only an extremely attentive public has a decent chance to keep abreast of the nuances of alternative policy choices. We are left then with a riddle, an inattentive electorate that possesses an aggregate quality of policy information that inattentive electorates cannot possess.

Most will readily concede that looking upon sophistication, issue awareness, ideology, and the way each is or is not rationally related

Table 1. Positions of Party Activists and Perceptions of Party Positions

Issue	Party Activist Positions			Perceived Party Positions		
	Democrats	Repub-licans	Difference	Democrats Liberal	Repub-licans Liberal	Difference
Women's Role:						
1972	52.86	49.86	3.00	30.4	9.6	20.8
1976	52.01	49.22	2.79	34.2	8.2	26.0
1980	58.89	56.04	2.85	60.4	8.6	51.8
1984	53.11	46.58	6.53	59.3	13.2	46.1
Minority Aid:						
1956	49.72	49.83	−.11	20.1	22.1	−2.0
1960	51.52	50.28	1.24	22.7	21.4	1.3
1964	52.69	45.10	7.59	60.4	7.3	53.1
1968	53.64	48.29	5.35	51.0	10.8	40.2
1972	53.95	47.97	5.98	53.3	11.3	40.0
1976	51.63	49.24	2.39	53.3	14.5	38.8
1980	52.41	47.63	4.78	76.2	9.4	66.8
1984	52.31	46.52	5.79	63.1	17.7	45.4
Jobs and Standard of Living:						
1956	51.32	46.83	4.49	34.8	15.9	18.9
1960	50.38	45.82	4.56	51.2	12.5	38.7
1964	50.93	44.95	5.98	60.8	8.1	52.7
1968	54.06	48.12	3.94	53.0	13.1	39.9
1972	52.92	45.48	7.44	69.6	11.7	57.9
1976	52.84	45.91	6.93	62.8	12.5	50.3
1980	45.43	38.08	7.35	72.5	9.3	63.2
1984	53.09	44.53	8.56	65.8	10.6	55.2
Education: Aid:						
1956	51.70	48.13	3.57	29.7	14.9	14.8
1960	51.85	44.81	7.04	41.9	13.1	28.8
1964	52.41	43.75	8.66	52.9	11.7	41.2
1968	52.97	45.38	6.59	43.3	15.8	27.5
School Desegregation:						
1956	49.61	50.80	−1.19	22.8	25.0	−2.2
1960	50.71	49.88	.93	15.7	20.4	−4.7
1964	52.03	47.70	4.33	56.4	6.9	49.5
1968	52.59	49.44	3.15	51.7	8.7	43.0

* The item used for 1956 through 1968 refers to "fair treatment in jobs and housing" for minorities.

353   *James A. Stimson*

Table 2. Positions of Candidate Activists* and Perceptions of Candidate
Positions

Issue	Candidate Activist Positions			Perceived Candidate Positions		
	Democrats	Repub-licans	Difference	Democrat More Liberal	Repub-lican More Liberal	Difference
Liberal/Conservative:						
1972	60.62	44.20	16.42	84.0	9.2	74.8
1976	56.92	42.55	14.37	74.7	13.1	61.6
1980	57.32	40.85	16.47	71.1	22.2	48.9
1984	56.65	42.12	14.53	68.9	20.5	48.4
Women's Role:						
1972	55.48	51.05	4.43	36.4	12.7	23.7
1976	50.72	49.51	1.21	25.6	16.6	9.0
1980	58.76	54.15	4.61	65.0	10.3	54.7
1984	55.24	46.00	9.24	65.5	14.8	50.7
Defense Spending:						
1972	50.18	38.82	11.36			
1976	51.17	46.81	4.36			
1980	47.61	42.68	4.93	77.8	13.5	64.3
1984	56.29	44.80	11.49	82.2	8.5	73.7
Minority Aid:						
1972	58.02	47.90	10.12	65.2	11.5	53.7
1976	51.77	46.81	4.96	46.0	16.5	29.5
1980	47.61	42.68	4.93	76.4	12.0	64.4
1984	53.60	46.37	7.23	63.6	17.9	45.7
Jobs and Standard of Living:						
1972	55.89	45.55	10.44	79.6	10.8	68.8
1976	54.76	44.59	10.17	58.5	16.5	42.0
1980	47.81	38.08	9.73	71.1	12.9	58.2
1984	54.81	44.26	10.55	69.3	10.0	59.3

* "Candidate Activists" are party identifiers who report voting for their party's presidential candidate.

to behavior gives us different answers at individual and aggregate levels of analysis. Then which of the contrary answers is correct? Is the electorate a collection of ignorant, unsophisticated, nonideological individuals, or is it a single, sophisticated, aware, ideological body? The answer must depend upon whether theory directs our interests to people or to electorates. The psychology of voting dictates the former. Many—and I am inclined to think, most—political questions dictate the latter. As Converse notes in chapter 16 of this volume, many electoral questions in a representative democracy involve representation of one or another kind, and representation is aggregation.

It will be useful to digress from the main line of exposition on the role of citizen activists in mediated cognition to a focus on the attributes of the activists.

CITIZEN ACTIVISTS: WHO? WHAT? AND WHY?

Citizen activists are the crucial link in the proposed model of political learning. They are the (by and large) normally situated people whose one atypical attribute is unusually intense involvement in politics. Although they are clearly nothing like a cross-section of the electorate, they also have very little in common with professionals in the world of politics. They do not hold or seek office, and their intense involvement in politics, counted in minutes, hours, and at most, days, is intense only relative to an uninvolved mass electorate.

Coming to terms with the attributes, behaviors, and institutional roles of the activists is our task here. It is challenging, for the literature offers hints but little guidance on the topic. The activists fall between the well-studied mass electorate on the one hand and the professional politician on the other. The activists' atypicality suggests that established theory and research on mass behavior will be of little help. And those whom Nexon (1971) labeled "occasional activists" are also unlikely to resemble full-time professional politicians. To play the "game" of politics for sport and good citizenship cannot be much similar to the grim business of protecting a livelihood.

Activism is occasional in American politics. Button-wearing and doorbell-ringing are intermittent activities, dated by the electoral calendar. So too is activism occasional on a longer time scale. Different individuals become active in successive campaign seasons. Each campaign faces anew the problem of recruiting its foot soldiers. Political campaigns need citizens with the personal attributes of good salesmen, for selling is what the campaign is all about. What the campaign needs from the citizen activist—his or her time, energy, and emotional involvement—is costly. What it has to offer in compensation is a sense of good citizenship and, sometimes, the opportunity to advance a personal ideology. Because what the campaign needs is costly and it needs citizens who have plenty to do with their time, and inducements to political activity are limited at best, failure to recruit adequate numbers of workers is a normal attribute of political campaigns. Such failure is nearly universal in campaigns for state and congressional offices. It is frequent even in presidential contests where campaign-induced press hype about "armies of volunteers" usually describes mere patrols, led, often as not, by mercenaries.

Sometimes a presidential campaign succeeds in inducing widespread political activity. And this, unlike Nexon's usage, is a second sense in which activism is "occasional." The pool of potential activists is evidently much larger than the number of activists in any given year. All activists are "occasional activists" in Nexon's sense in that they are active only "in season." But quite a number participate in some seasons and skip others. They are "occasional" on a larger time scale. Generalizations about activists and activism are accordingly hazardous. Activists are always present, but they are not necessarily the same people from one election to the next. This chameleon coloring is unkind to hypotheses derived from single elections or even from a short series of them. Among the more prominent casualties (Beck and Jennings, 1979) is the staple hypothesis to political commentators: "Activists in both parties are more extreme than the mass parties, Republican activists more conservative, Democratic activists more liberal." Democratic activists are sometimes more liberal than their party, Republican activists are sometimes more conservative. But neither is always the case, and it is rare that the activists of both parties deviate from their party norm in the same year.

Nexon's asymmetry variation of the hypothesis (Republican activists, but not their Democratic counterparts, are more extreme than their party) was a nice adaptation of the staple hypothesis to the 1956–1964 period he studied—and particularly to 1964. But it was no sooner written than the asymmetrical extremism disappeared from the Republican party only to reappear on the Democratic side (Beck and Jennings, 1979).

The Verba and Nie (1972) thesis that middle-age produces peak participation rates was disconfirmed by an influx of young adult activists in the very year *Participation in America* went to press. And as soon as commentators became accustomed to associating "activist" with "youthful," the pattern quickly reverted to its pre-1972 norm (Beck and Jennings, 1979).

What is important in establishing who are the citizen activists is that they are not by and large the same people from one election to the next. Although activists as a group have generally similar attributes from year to year, they are rarely the same people. That fact opens up the large possibility that their coloration may be highly responsive to the stimuli that induce activity in a given contest, most particularly to variation in candidate policy positions and ideology. This ability to respond very quickly to changes in political context makes the citizen activists the most variable set of actors in the system. That in turn suggests an important role for them in any account of the dynamics of political change.

To accommodate contextual variability in the attributes of political foot soldiers and the motivations to political activity, we must examine the phenomenon over time. Before we take up that task, we digress to a brief discourse on data and method. Then we may go on to a portrait of activism.

DATA AND METHOD

The basic data resource is the National Election Series (NES) for all presidential elections, 1956 through 1984. The eight studies provide a pool of more than fifteen thousand citizens who were interviewed during the period. From this very large—and largely inert—pool it is possible to isolate that tiny fraction of citizens who report active involvement in politics. Depending upon the rigor of criteria for determining who is an activist, it is possible to extract a thirty-year activist subsample of a bit less than a thousand citizens, about one out of every twenty respondents interviewed. Thus, although the samples of activists in any particular election (averaging around a hundred) are too small for any but the most perfunctory analyses, the thirty-year pool allows considerable leverage, particularly for over-time analyses.

The citizen activists we study, as Nexon and others before us, are quite different from others (e.g., delegates to national political conventions) who have been lumped under the same rubric. It is worth emphasizing that they are citizens, different in degree of political commitment than ordinary citizens, but not in kind.

The citizen activists share many of the characteristics of the national mass samples of which they are a selection. They differ principally in taking up the opportunities to become involved in politics that others shun. They are in many regards the "opinion" leaders" identified in the early voting studies (Berelson, Lazarsfeld, and McPhee, 1954), citizens situated in their diverse settings who become disproportionately influential because they care more about political affairs than their friends, family, and co-workers.

Two overlapping sets of activists can be isolated from the election study samples. The first, and most important for subsequent analysis, are campaign activists, identified by self-report of engaging in multiple common political activities such as attending political rallies, wearing buttons, donating money, and the like. Our measurement technique is a simple summary count of the number of acts performed.[2] The activities, all behavioral, are (1) voting, which discriminates only at the passive end of the continuum; (2) attending political rallies or meetings; (3) wearing a campaign button or displaying a bumper sticker; (4) working for a party or candidate; (5) attempting to influence others; and (6) donating money (not including the $1 federal income tax check-off). Where we classify into an activist/nonactivist dichotomy, the criterion for activist classification is four or more acts, which isolates the most active 5 or 6 percent of the electorate.[3]

"Informational activism," a second measurement approach, is based upon respondent reports of paying attention to the campaign through various media (newspapers, magazines, radio, and television). Not activism at all in a behavioral sense, informational activism measures passive involvement in the world of politics. Informational activism is a less rigorous standard of involvement than behavioral activism. The merely well informed can become so in their living rooms. Because the overlap between informational and behavioral involvement is modest, we shall make limited use of the informational measure. Its greatest contribution indeed is to the point that actually doing something is very different from psychological or intellectual involvement.

We return now to some preliminary specifications of the fundamental thesis that mass issue cognition is driven by projection of activists' positions and party support.

NOTES ON DESIGN AND ANALYSIS

The basic data are measures of personal issue position and beliefs about where the parties and candidates stand for the fifteen thousand respondents of the NES presidential election studies. The data on respondent positions are used to estimate the true positions of party activists. The perceptions data estimate, as intended, the party and candidate positions. For the analysis to come the dependent perceptions data are aggregated by year and by region (employing the ICPSR standard eight-region scheme). The activist position data are aggregated both nationally and separately by region.

The regional activist subsamples present some severe sampling variation problems. Annual national samples of about a hundred activists cannot be divided eight ways without becoming dangerously small. To counteract the small sample problem, activist position is measured by using all respondents, rather than just those who cross the arbitrary numerical threshold (more than three activities) into "activism." Responses are then weighted by activity level. The weighting scheme counts up to five activities not including the relatively passive act of voting. Thus, respondents who vote and do nothing else do not contribute to the measure. Those who go beyond voting are weighted in proportion to the number of their activities. The procedure effectively highlights the positions of true activists and takes advantage of the more numerous semiactive respondents to bolster the number of cases used for measurement.

Whether the regional activists should be more highly associated with citizen perceptions of the national parties than similar national groups is unknown. That depends upon what respondents have in mind when they estimate where parties and candidates position themselves. We shall see that the regional activist estimates do not perform well in contrast to national measures. Whether that is a matter of substantive significance (pointing to the nationalization of party image) or merely a reflection of the fact that small sample estimates are unreliable is beyond the scope of this discussion.

The data on both activist position and mass perceptions, when merged, are a cross-section of time series. We shall estimate the presumed causal effect of activist positions on mass cognitions using pooled regression modeling. Error properties in these analyses sometimes, but not always, satisfy ordinary least squares assumptions, and so we will alternate between simple and more complex modeling procedures.

All activist position measures are transformed into a standard metric with mean of 50 and standard deviation 10 for the full national cross-sections for each election. That allows the splicing together across time of differently formatted questions that tap a common dimension. All measures are interpretable relative to the electorate; positions greater than 50 indicating relative liberalism and the reverse conservatism for the activist groups. For regression modeling, Republican activist positions are subtracted from Democratic positions to produce a net party (or candidate) difference measure. In the norm positive, these scores indicate the degree to which Democratic activists are more liberal than their Republican counterparts.

Mass perceptions are transformed into a trichotomy that is interpretable for each issue as the proportions indicating greater Democratic liberalism, no party difference, or greater Republican liberalism. When aggregated, the interpretation shifts to net preponderance of those giving the conventional party positions over those giving the unconventional.

ESTIMATING THE MEDIATED PERCEPTIONS MODEL

If the mass electorate projects party and candidate positions from the actual positions of the activists who support them, then the sort of statistical model appropriate to estimate the effect is simple indeed. We expect a bivariate relationship between (aggregated) activist position and (aggregated) party or candidate position perceptions. Additional effects, for example, dummy variables for particular regions or particular years, are employed to clean up specifications. They become essentially indicators of ignorance, systematic effects that should have been predicted by the activist positions and were not.

The chief focus will be upon two issue domains: policies related to federal intervention to assure full employment and Federal efforts to promote the rights of minority groups that can reasonably be constructed across the full span of the NES series. With an effective sample size of sixty-four (eight regions for eight elections), the present maximum leverage for modeling is a long enough span of time to observe systematic change in party position. Other issues are available for a maximum of four consecutive elections and will be ignored in this preliminary effort.[4]

A commentary on the nature of variation in perceptions of party position is a useful beginning to the analysis. Two aspects of the variation are notable. One is that there is no substantial regional variation in perceptions. On no issue (racial issues included) is the cross-region variation significant in the aggregated data. Equally striking is the fact that every single issue presents significant, usually highly significant, variation over time in the same data. The dynamics of position perception are clearly the phenomenon in need of explanation. Such significant over-time variation is another piece of evidence in support of the accuracy of citizen perceptions. If perceptions were not sensitive to real changes in political context, we would not expect to see year-to-year change in them, and particularly not striking year-to-year change.

GOVERNMENT RESPONSIBILITY FOR JOBS AND STANDARD OF LIVING

Arguably the central issue of the New Deal party system, the question of the degree to which government ought to intervene in the private economy to secure full employment conditions, steadily differentiates the two parties of American national politics. Through the period 1956–1984, the Democrats are perceived as the party more

Figure 1. Jobs and Standard of Living

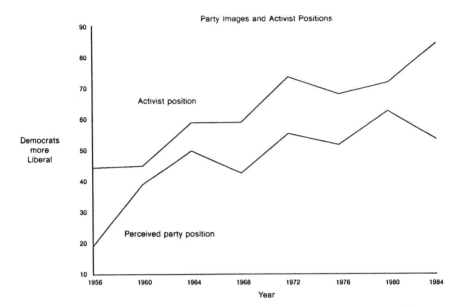

likely to pursue an active federal role. But Figure 1 shows that party perceptions on this old and stable issue have fluctuated considerably over the span. The high points of party differentiation in 1964, 1972, and 1980 correspond with the ideological candidacies of Barry Goldwater, George McGovern, and Ronald Reagan. In each of the three cases, the old, settled issue was unsettled by new position-taking (Goldwater and Reagan frontal challenges to the New Deal and McGovern's attempted extension of it) and the electorate's perception of them. Perhaps the most anomalous point in the series is 1984, where the same Ronald Reagan matched with the liberal Walter Mondale produces less-than-expected party differentiation.[5]

Figure 1 also graphs the position of party activists in each campaign (in a scale modified to project into the same space). The strong similarity of the two series, differing in direction only in 1984, suggests what we shall soon see in regression models; mass perceptions map neatly onto activist positions. Table 3 shows three regression models of the relationship. The first, a simple bivariate prediction of party perceptions from activist positions, tells most of the story. The aggregated activist positions are very strongly related to party perceptions. The relationship is highly significant ($t = 7.4$), and the single

Table 3. Perceptions of Party Positions on "Jobs" Predicted by Party Activist Positions; Regression Coefficients and Standard Errors in Parentheses

Variable	Model 1: Bivariate	Model 2: 1984 Dummy Added	Model 3: First Differences
Net activist positions	7.78[a]	10.33[a]	6.67[c]
(national)	(1.05)	(1.22)	(2.98)
1984 dummy	—	− 17.00[b]	− 21.36[b]
		(4.94)	(6.27)
Intercept	− 2.25	− 16.43[c]	4.41
	(6.88)	(7.57)	(2.64)
N	64	64	56
R^2	.47	.56	.20

a. $p < .001$ b. $p < .01$ c. $p < .05$

independent variable accounts for almost 50 percent of the variance in perceptions.

As could be predicted from Figure 1, the bivariate model fails to account well for 1984. In a second analysis in Table 3, a dummy variable for 1984 is introduced to clean up the specification. The increase in R^2 of this second model over the first essentially capitalizes on our ignorance of what occurred in 1984, of why activists reached a peak of differentiation in that year and perceptions did not. But it permits an efficient estimation of the activist coefficient of interest. That coefficient becomes significantly stronger in the presence of the 1984 dummy.

It is no trivial matter that the electorate seems to know where the parties stand on matters of central electoral importance. But it is also not a very difficult feat. If some respondents just know from history that the Democrats are more consistently liberal, activist, and interventionist and others don't know at all, then aggregate perceptions of the level of party differences will be reasonably accurate in lieu of any current knowledge of party or candidate issue postures. A more demanding kind of knowledge is the perception of year-to-year change. Such knowledge implies that the electorate is—by some unknown means—following current political debate, that it is sensitive to movement in the policy sphere. Even knowledge of the level of relative positions implies electoral mandates stronger than those often argued in the voting behavior literature. But quite clearly, electoral sensitivity to policy movements could imply striking policy mandates. A rough and ready test of the perception of change is the regression of the first difference of party issue perceptions (how far apart are they this time compared to last time?) on the similar first difference activist positions. That regression, reported in the last column of Table 3, provides yet additional evidence for the mediated perceptions model. Much weaker in statistical fit than the "levels" regressions (as is normally the case with different data), the coefficient associated with activist policy movement is still significant and of approximately the same magnitude as before.

FEDERAL TREATMENT OF MINORITIES

Mass perceptions of party positions on questions of treatment of and aid to minority groups is in many regards a more interesting policy domain than the jobs arena. In the racial area, the parties have dramatically shifted positions, moving from a very slight net Republican liberalism at the beginning of the period to a dramatic leftward movement of the Democrats beginning in 1964 and increasing since then (see Carmines and Stimson [1986, 1988]) for a detailed causal mapping of issue evolution in the racial case). Unlike the jobs case where the parties have always been ordered in the same direction and differentiation merely expands or contracts from election to election, the racial case in Figure 2 presents movement of perceptions across a major portion of the possible issue space.

Because race presents more movement in cognitions, it is a greater challenge and opportunity to the mediated cognitions model, which responds very well. The simple prediction of party perceptions from activist positions (in Table 4) is stronger than the jobs case, with a t ratio approaching 10 and $R^2 = .57$. Adding a dummy variable to specify our ignorance (this time for 1980) modestly reduces the coefficient for activist position and strengthens its significance. Most important, reducing the data to first differences for both variables leaves the order of magnitude of the coefficient unchanged with an exceptionally good fit for differenced data. What we can assert from Table 4 and Figure 2 is that mass perceptions track activist positions.

BUT IS THE ASSOCIATION SPURIOUS?

A last matter remains. All the evidence that the mass electorate tracks party activist positions in its perceptions of where the parties stand could be swept away with the assertion that the association

Figure 2. Treatment of Minorities

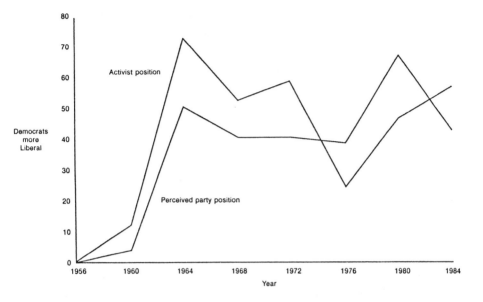

is spurious. Activists after all are expected to be an unusually well informed subset of partisans. Might the close association between activists' positions and mass perceptions be due simply to the fact that activist positions conform closely to objective party positions? Might not the association exist even if no member of the mass electorate ever noticed a citizen activist position?

Leverage on this spuriousness challenge can be had by replicating the analysis for groups like the activists who are unusually well informed, but who lack the activists' visibility. Those earlier referred to as "informational activists" are a nearly ideal control for such an analysis. Operationally defined as those who report paying attention to the campaign through all four of the possible media (radio, TV, newspapers, and magazines), the informational activists should be unusually well-informed citizens. Unlike the activists, their media attentive behavior is a private activity (except of course for that not insubstantial subset who are both informational and behavioral activists). What the informational activists do in politics is visible only in their living rooms. "Paying attention" emits no cues.

The regressions on jobs and minority treatment perceptions are replicated in Table 5, using the informational activists' positions as

Table 4. Perceptions of Positions on Minority Aid Predicted by Activist Positions; Regression Coefficients and Standard Errors in Parentheses

Variable	Model 1: Bivariate	Model 2: 1980 Dummy Added	Model 3: First Differences
Net activist positions	7.07[a]	6.63[a]	5.82[a]
(national)	(.78)	(.57)	(.57)
1980 dummy	—	32.78[a]	—
		(4.25)	
Intercept	6.93	4.62	1.17
	(3.78)	(2.72)	(2.74)
N	64	64	56
R^2	.57	.78	.45

a. $p < .001$ b. $p < .01$ c. $p < .05$

the predictors of mass perceptions. If the mediated cognitions thesis has substance, the informational activists' positions ought not to be as potent a predictor as those of the behavioral activists. That is indeed what can be seen in Table 5, where the regressions are performed both on the regular variables ("Levels") and on first differences.

In one case, the level of jobs cognitions, the informational activists predict very nearly as well as the behavioral. But because the dependent series trends upward, without any sharp reversals, it would be well predicted by any time series that also trends. The much more rigorous test is whether the first differences in one series predict the other. That test is unmistakably failed; the coefficient is insignificant, in the wrong direction, and with very nearly a zero fit. The racial case produces different results but a similar conclusion. There the coefficients are significant in the expected direction in both regressions, but both the magnitude of the coefficients and the quality of model fit are considerably reduced from the comparable regression of Table 4. If the subset of behavioral activists were removed from the ranks of the informational activists, the fit quite probably would be reduced still further.[6]

SO WHAT? THE IMPLICATIONS OF MEDIATED COGNITION

If the thesis advanced here is correct—that electorates derive knowledge of party issue positions by projecting positions of better-

Table 5. Predicting Party Positions on Jobs and Treatment of Minorities from the Positions of Informational Activists

Variable	Jobs and Standard of Living		Treatment of Minorities	
	"Levels"	Differences	"Levels"	Differences
Informational	5.47[a]	− 1.40	6.55[a]	4.43[a]
activist position	(.74)	(2.03)	(1.19)	(1.21)
Intercept	13.92[b]	6.57[c]	6.85	4.82
	(4.80)	(2.98)	(5.85)	(3.19)
N	64	56	64	56
R^2	.465	.009	.327	.198

a. $p < .001$ b. $p < .01$ c. $p < .05$

known activist figures—does it matter? Does it affect our view of the normal flow of American political life? It does.

What matters most about the thesis is that it accounts for the riddle of inattentive electorates who seem to know much of what they need to know to make policy-informed choices. It suggests that electorates are policy-conscious bodies even though made up in the main of individually ignorant citizens. It suggests that study after study demonstrating the ignorance of the individual citizen will have no consequence for the phenomenon central to applied democracy, whether electorates make policy-conscious decisions at the polls. It suggests that electoral mandates are real, not fictions of the overactive imaginations of successful candidates for public office.

The dynamics of group behavior and the political culture of cognitions are very different phenomena than the psychological processes we normally study. A question arising from this riddle of individual and group behaviors is what it is we should be studying when we seek to account for consequential political behavior. More by tradition and convention than by self-conscious choice, arising from the initial successes of survey research and from the psychological orientations of early survey analysts, the dominant—if implicit—answer to that query is individual behavior. Individual behavior, in practice, often means individual psychological processes. Indeed, we have learned a great deal from the study of individual psychological processes. But the presumption that motivates this work, stated without defense, is that many of the things that matter in political life, essential political behaviors, have very little to do with individual psychological processes. They are macro behaviors, such as mediated cognitions, that require for understanding a focus on "between" rather than "within" individual effects.

TOWARD A MACRO THEORY OF BEHAVIOR: A RESEARCH PROGRAM

Micro political behavior is quite probably the area of greatest achievement of new knowledge in political science in the last few decades. But an unintended consequence is the relative neglect of the study of the collective behavior of electorates. Sometimes we can safely aggregate our knowledge of individual behavior upward to groups. Often we cannot. Group behaviors have emergent properties that arise from context and interaction.

It is far from controversial to assert that macro behavior is important; it is a truism. But when we turn to the analysis of most political behaviors, almost invariably we conceptualize the problem exclusively as a matter of individual behaviors. Many questions can be addressed by either micro and macro analyses, with one or the other usually more direct and therefore superior. The voting decision is a clear case of micro-level superiority; its importance has much to do with the micro dominance of political behavior research.

It will often be the case that micro phenomena will appear mainly as noisy variation around a small, but vastly more important, macro central tendency. Such an assertion does not defy micro political behavior research but is indeed based upon the best of it. One of the key findings of three decades of analysis of individual political behavior is that much of it appears random. Response set and "nonattitudes," often presented as methodological issues, have an important substantive implication. They tell us to expect large proportions of an electorate to behave in a manner that will often be indistinguishable from randomness. And in an electorate where "Ideologues" are few and "Nature of the Times" and "No Issue Content" responses are many (Campbell, Converse, Miller, and Stokes, 1960), opinions of majorities may be quite inconsequential. But collective opinion—an emergent macro phenomenon, not the mere summation of individuals' opinions—may at the same time be of striking consequence. In those cases our exclusive reliance on micro thinking threatens to make us experts in noise.

Macro analyses offer far more leverage on questions such as electoral movements and mandates, matters not notable successes in the micro behavior tradition. We currently have very limited understanding of them, in part because our micro behavior paradigm gives them more an air of mystery than of simple explanatory problems. We simply cannot deal with movements of opinion or trends in behavior, although we know full well that herding behavior is not unknown to the human species because these matters require focus on emergent collective behaviors. They are misfit to micro theory and research.

One pays a price for macro analysis—the ability to use individual-level knowledge to sort out competing causal influences. But there is an important gain as well in perspective on the meaning of electoral events and currents that can only come from longitudinal comparison. Those small central tendencies that can be lost in the noise of individual cross-sectional data stand out starkly in macro time series. They give one a very different perspective on the question of what particular behavioral variation is consequential for political life.

NOTES

I would like to acknowledge the assistance of Carolyn Lewis in undertaking the massive data manipulations that are a necessary precursor to aggregated longitudinal and cross-section analyses of the National Election Study series and of Mark Hartray who assisted in the task. The chapter is beneficiary of the critical wisdom of Chris Achen, Lee Epstein, Carolyn Lewis, Bob Luskin, Paul Sniderman, Aaron Wildavsky, and of the editors. None but the last will have to bear the consequences of my mistakes. The data used in this chapter were made available by the Inter-University Consortium for Political and Social Research. The data were collected under a grant from the National Science Foundation. Neither the original collectors of the data nor the Consortium bear any responsibility for the analyses or interpretations presented here.

1. This weighting by visibility technique is a borrowing from Converse, Clausen, and Miller (1965).

2. See Verba and Nie (1972:68) and Beck and Jennings (1979:738–739) for validation of similar scales.

3. Necessarily excluded by the design of the election studies are the sizable number of young people who become campaign activists before attaining the right to vote. This exclusion is no doubt more serious in the years before 1972, when the national eligibility age was lowered to eighteen.

4. An alternative approach would be to shift the time period to 1972–1984 and employ the off-year studies that present activism measures and continuous seven-point scales for that but not the earlier period. Superior for continuity of measurement, this strategy does not allow study of the 1960s when much of the most interesting change in perceptions of party position occurred.

5. The Reagan 1984 appeal is probably moderated over that of 1980

by the campaign focus on retrospective evaluation of economic performance—"Morning in America"—in contrast to the sharper prospective policy
differentiation of the earlier year. Like Adlai Stevenson thirty years earlier,
it may also be the case that the Mondale policy positions were relatively non-
salient, with the dominant theme of Mondale perceptions being that he was
a likely loser.

   6. It is also the case that in multivariate specifications, where the two
kinds of activist positions compete to predict mass cognitions, the behavioral
activists always dominate.

16

Popular Representation and the Distribution of Information

Philip E. Converse

As radical doctrines of social contract and the consent of the governed began to have their impact on Western thought and political institutions toward the end of the eighteenth century, one of the chief lines of resistance was of course the view that the common "subject" or, in the more radical vocabulary, the common "citizen" simply lacked the information necessary for any sensible contribution to debates over the grand policies of state.

There can be no doubt that some of the well placed used such arguments out of sheer panic that the new ideas were a dangerous threat to their entrenched privileges. But even for those well-placed persons who were attracted to the new ideals of egalitarianism, the information argument was a troubling one. Good decision making requires good information. And while the common citizen might be expected to be a fair judge of matters close to his or her ken, such as how a minister's pay was best raised or how much repair must be done on the local bridge, good information about national and international affairs was exactly what most citizens, preoccupied by their daily subsistence rounds, conspicuously lacked.

There is little mystery in the fact that these radical notions first took vigorous root—in practice, not merely theory—in America. Most obviously, the "first new nation" was less bound up in a set of traditional institutions than were the parent countries of Europe and at the time of the Revolution was searching for a set of governmental forms that might remedy the dysfunctions of monarchies abroad. The democratic, or at least republican, ideas also recommended themselves because they were a reasonably direct extension of many of the local

governmental arrangements that had grown up over several genera-
tions to handle policy questions too fine-grained for colonial administrations in London or Paris to worry about.

A second reason, more arguable but more crucial to our purposes here, is the likelihood that the information barrier to democratic
forms, while still of frightening magnitude, was as low in the New
England colonies of America as it would have been anywhere else in
the world of that day. Although the truth lies beyond reconstruction,
it is possible to believe that the rates of functional literacy among the
New England settlers as of 1660 was at least as high, and perhaps
higher, than that in England in the same period or, for that matter,
any other natural population of comparable size and geographic distribution of the era. And the northern colonies, even in the earliest
period, may well have been more endowed than what we now call the
Third World as recently as 1940. For this population, the notion of
lateral exchanges of information and opinion among the citizenry who
were congenial to democratic forms, while still unsettling in its radi-
calism, was at least less than absurd.

Nonetheless, the information problem was sufficiently daunting,
even in the nearly liberated American colonies, that the new forms
were hedged in the most gingerly fashion. It was not a democracy,
but a republic. It was representative government, not populism. The
most important elections were indirect, not direct. And even those
who labored from the outset to open the system more widely to full
popular sovereignty recognized the precariousness of the experiment.
One of the most articulate spokesmen, Thomas Jefferson, made his
Bill for the More General Diffusion of Knowledge a centerpiece of
his proposed reforms for Virginia in appreciation of the fact that his
"faith in freedom and self-government was at bottom a faith in education" (Peterson, 1975) and the conviction that state responsibility
for the rapid promotion of the education of the populace was the best
hedge against democracy, indeed leading to tyranny by the straight-
line method.

Two centuries have changed this landscape where information
and democracy cohabit in numerous ways. We may not have gone
much beyond Jefferson's comprehensive plan for public education
through the university level, but the proportion of the population
following this route has advanced almost majestically over the full
span of this period. What this "more general diffusion of knowledge"
may have done for democracy is more arguable although we certainly
feel safer with democratic forms somewhat more direct than envisioned in the original design for the United States. And with fingers

crossed we may imagine that the electorate is at least mildly inoculated against the cruder forms of demagoguery and other perversions that carry the risk of regime derailment.

Nonetheless, few of us would want to claim that the "information problem" is solved. Yet a series of other changes in the intervening centuries have placed this problem in different perspectives. More dramatic, perhaps, than the advance of education levels, and surely less foreseen, has been staggering change in the accessibility of political information to a quasi-totality of the modern electorate. Two hundred years ago the problem was one of scarcity of information and how to get it to the voter. Today the problem is rather one of superabundance. The voter is bombarded with political information. This is especially true for information at the national level and, paradoxically, it is now easier to keep up with federal government issues and performance than with one's own ward or community. The strategic problem at the national level often seems less one of an information search than how to protect oneself from being inundated with information. In this vein we have titles such as Graber's (1984) *Processing the News: How People Tame the Information Tide.*

A cognate development of recent years involves the notions of satisficing and bounded rationality associated originally with Herbert Simon (1945). Some versions of the bounded rationality theme—those emphasizing information costs as a limit to full optimization—fit poorly with doctrines of superabundance of information. However, it is easy to restore a fit by either of two sensible routes. One argues that although unassorted information may seem superabundant, "good" information (meaning not only accurate but also decision relevant and incisive) these days continues to be hard to find so that information costs cannot be disregarded. The other route seizes upon the fact that large quantities of incoming information are difficult to order and analyze in the mind and that although the raw materials may have dropped enormously in price over the past two centuries, meaningful processing in the mind is as costly as ever. Even these residual processing limits may be becoming obsolescent with the advance of computing and artificial intelligence, but that is for the future.

For now, a tide of work goes forward in cognitive psychology as to the ways in which individuals ingest, process, and store information for different time frames of later retrieval. In equal good health is work upon decision making with imperfect information. If any of these lines of inquiry needed blessing, which they do not, I would vote that they receive such. But I shall largely, if not completely, bypass work at this micro level, and devote my discussion instead to issues that emerge in political systems at the aggregate level. In particular, I would like to consider first some simple truths about the distribution of political information in current electorates and then go on to draw an observation or two as to the implications of these truths for the nature of popular representation in modern democracies.

THE DISTRIBUTION OF POLITICAL INFORMATION

It is no small impediment to my discussion that we lack any suitable consensual unit of measurement for information in this context. The notion of "bits" of information, however clever and profoundly useful in some settings, simply will not help us here. This is true for several reasons including the fact that with a lot of other things constant, some types of information are vastly more valuable than others. It was no accident that Jefferson's bill referred to knowledge and not merely information. The distinction is one that current work in cognitive psychology may help to put on a firmer footing. But for the time being I shall proceed as though varying amounts of information could be measured and compared in some general case.

The two simplest truths I know about the distribution of political information in modern electorates are that the mean is low and the variance high. Relative to what, given our lack of units of measurement? Relative merely to naive expectation.

I call these two observations "truths," although now and again they are challenged. While the distribution of pure information is rarely a target for measurement in representative adult samples, we now have several decades in which at least sporadic measurement of the sort has taken place. Almost invariably, what stuns naive observers about the results are the low "scores."

It is important not to leap from these low scores, as is often done, to an assumption that substantial portions of the electorate know virtually nothing about current national politics. This is not true either. A chemical trace of absolute know-nothings undoubtedly exists in the electorate, but for the most part, even those who would fall persistently in the bottom decile of political information tests still may have a substantial set of apperceptions about the national political world, such that with proper interviewer probing they could talk nonrepetitively about it for significant spans of time. There is no paradox here: the combination of some political knowledge with scores approaching zero on information tests simply attests to the astronomical size of the potential universe of political information.

I am more interested here in the high variance of the distribution of information in electorates as we move from the least informed to the most informed. Although it is a matter of common observation that some people know vastly more about politics than others, it is my belief that most of us rather underestimate just how great the differences actually are. They are not just "differences." They are orders of magnitudes of differences and, conceivably in a real way, orders of magnitudes of orders of magnitudes. (This may be true, as we have just seen, without playing games that hinge on denominators approaching absolute zero.)

A little reflection helps us to understand how such astronomical differences arise. Those who study active political elites, especially those political by occupation, such as legislators or other government officials, are aware that their subjects live and breathe politics for very large fractions of their waking hours and do so over long periods of time. At the other end of the spectrum, we need not go to outliers in chemical-trace proportions to find significant fractions of the population whose time spent actively processing political information in the mind probably averages less than five minutes a day over equally long spans of time. Just in attention time alone, we are into orders of magnitude of difference.

But this is just the beginning of differentiation. There is ample evidence from both field and experimental settings that it takes past information successfully stored to make larger amounts of incoming information storable. With information as with wealth, "them what has gets," and there is no comforting system of progressive taxation on information to help redress the drift toward glaring inequalities.

Among others, Graber (1984) has documented many of these processes. Even though her information measures had ceiling problems, she found that her panelists with high prior information in an area showed higher learning rates for subsequent information in that area than did respondents who brought little information to the subject. They also showed high rates on adjacent political topics covered in the same sources. In addition, they retained information for longer times and accessed it more effectively. It is as though information already organized as schemata in the mind acts as information-catchers when they are numerous and already densely filled. In minds where such schemata are few and sparsely populated with past information, new information streams in one ear and out the other. In short, we are dealing here with a positive-feedback system of a kind where initial inequalities feed upon themselves, and differences best described in orders of magnitude of orders of magnitude are quite conceivable indeed.

What determines who rises to the upper levels of these political information hierarchies? The strongest individual-level correlate is embarrassingly obvious: the quickest learners and the most broadly informed are the most highly interested. Here again it is best to imagine a two-way causal nexus: not only does interest speed up learning, but also past knowledge, successfully stored, makes new information much more meaningful and hence interesting. Graber (1984:118) describes the process more clinically: while the interested members of her panel focused their attention and successfully learned,

> By contrast, panelists whose interest was low also were unable to focus their attention. Since they did not know what information they wanted, their learning was passive and haphazard rather than active. Consequently, they learned little, even when they spent considerable time watching the debates on television, and felt that they needed more information. Many of them conceded that their lack of motivation to learn would prevent them from learning even if more information became available in a format and at a time ideally suited to their tastes.

While the motivational basis for the monstrous maldistribution of information in the electorate is in one sense obvious, it has substantial theoretical significance. After all, a variety of diagnoses of the information problem in the electorate have been put forward over the years, including cognitive limitations in information processing of some individuals or highly differential access to information from one stratum of the electorate to another. Strong motivational differences, especially when found in an environment as information-rich as our own, carry their own obvious message. They do not rule out other diagnoses as making some possible contribution. On the other hand, they suggest strongly that these other diagnoses are probably not central to the maldistribution phenomenon.

The steep stratification of the electorate jointly in terms of both information possession and information receptivity is well worth keeping in mind in analyzing electoral data. I think of it often when I see coefficients bearing on information processes that are calculated for the electorate as a whole. Such coefficients are not uninteresting even as mere averages. But averages calculated over heterogeneity as vast as this miss important parts of the story, and partitioning the electorate into strata in terms of information or involvement is often more revealing.

For studies of mass media impact, for example, the metaphor of a stratified electorate can be useful. Thus we can imagine that information about politics penetrates these layers from the top down, as it were, and does so at different speeds and to different depths, depending on the nature of the information. Some nuggets of information, such as the news that the Democrats had nominated a woman for vice president, or the fact that Nixon was resigning in the face of an impeachment threat, undoubtedly penetrate from top to bottom almost instantaneously, but most information penetrates more slowly. MacKuen (1981) has shown nonetheless that the more attentive strata of the electorate are most rapidly responsive to what the media are defining as current salient problems. If we move beyond this great agenda-setting power to questions of influence exerted over prior issue positions, more complicated models may be required. However, what Carmines and Stimson (1980) have called "easy" and "hard" issues would undoubtedly reflect differences in this kind of penetration outcome as well.

The metaphor of a general-purpose stratification of this sort may turn out to be overly simplified because there are many fragments of evidence suggesting that the public is also best thought of as at least partially differentiated into "issue publics" that have somewhat specialized interests and hence motivations to attend to incoming information. This is not, however, an enormous complication on the metaphor. What is important is that seeing the electorate in this stratified way remains particularly heuristic and illuminating.

Among other things, it renders vivid one paradox of the aggregate information process in electorates: while people near the bottom of the information stratification tend to ingest rather little of the information with which the society is bombarded, when information does succeed in penetrating to these levels it probably has an impact on thought and behavior that is very disproportionate, if perhaps admittedly transient, relative to the impact of the same information ingested "higher up," where it simply is absorbed into a much greater leaven of organized information from the past.

RATIONAL VOTERS VERSUS RATIONAL SYSTEMS

Whatever metaphors we use, the maldistribution of information has a crucial bearing, in several distinct senses of the word, on electoral systems as representation mechanisms. The main goal of the remaining discussion is to examine a few of the ways in which this impact runs its course.

The first and grandest impact, of course, is the obvious way in which the maldistribution of information helps to generate representation systems to begin with. Elementary civics textbooks often point out that a system of indirect representation had to supplant the more directly democratic town meeting at the national level because of physical limits on the numbers of citizens that could conceivably be packed within earshot of one another. Whatever contribution such physical limits ever made, it is clear that they have become obsolete. We now have the electronic technology for direct plenary democracy on all major policy issues of the day if we cared to develop it in that direction.

The suggestion is not a very lively one, however, and in large measure because the maldistribution of information portends poorly for any such arrangement. If good decisions require good information as input, and if the decisions are relatively complex ones requiring that large amounts of information be properly digested by the actual decision makers, then it is almost inevitable that some division of labor must invade the political process and partition the actors into a small group of experts who sift policy information on more or less a full-time basis and those who are doing other things with their time.

This description of an information distribution of labor is not meant in any way to conceal the other great reason for representation, which undoubtedly has to do with power and the control of the few by the many. Politics is not, of course, the only arena in which divisions of labor exist in some fundamental tension with egalitarian ideologies: the same tension can often engulf the home among other sites of human activity. But while indeed representation systems involve an information division of labor accompanied by strong power differentials, the touchstone of the democratic ethic requires that not all power be given over to the specialists. It is, of course, this part of the process that most occupies us here.

Through popular elections, referenda, and other means, a modicum of gross control over the system is reserved for the nonspecialists, the governed. Some forms of participation, as Verba and Nie (1972) have emphasized, are capable of carrying relatively fine-grain messages upward (cf. Kuklinski and Stanga, 1979). The steering mechanism most central in terms of the clarity of its institutionalization and scope of population involved—the popular election—is obviously a gross mechanism that is slow, ambiguous, and innocent of much detail (Converse, 1975). But popular elections do suffice to throw rascals out of office if events surrounding their administrations are insufferable. And perhaps more potently if less visibly, as a long line of literature has demonstrated repeatedly, representative concern about reelection undoubtedly maintains a running bonus of further substantive accountability among elected officials (Friedrich, 1941; Mayhew, 1974; Kuklinski, 1978).

At least this is the democratic blueprint. Exactly what happens within the large numbers of governed nonspecialists is not detailed in the usual editions of the blueprint although electoral colleges are one way in which a further layer of more local notables has been recognized. Once past such small top layers, however, the blueprint is largely unspecified. Information is treated as if it were adequate in amount, and no further formal note is taken of the possibility that information may be vastly maldistributed among constituents.

How does the representation system actually work given such maldistribution? After the advent of sample surveys demonstrated the low overall levels of information across most of the electorate, it was initially hard to see the voter as making any very rational contribution to democracy or to the representation process, at least if rationality is defined in more than a very pallid or tautological sense. Yet it soon developed that keen observers could come away with quite different impressions of the overall performance of both the electoral system and the representation system. Both, looked at in a certain light, seemed to show very clear signs of a kind of rational responsiveness of voters to political and economic conditions that was hard to reconcile with other evidence of low information and endemic confusions about many features of the process specialists take for granted.

I have always assumed that it was more than coincidence that most of these revised looks focused upon change in voting at the margin or dealt only with aggregate data or, as has been most common, were a combination of the two. On the survey side, for example, Key's (1966) *The Responsible Electorate* relentlessly pursued the "changers"—those citizens who fore or aft had been sufficiently exercised by current conditions to move out of their normal continuities of party voting. He showed that their changes were indeed responsive to contemporary conditions and policy debates. Whether this made individual voters "rational" or not depends mightily, as always, on how we might want to define that famous term. If "issue voting" suffices to qualify one as rational, then the case was made. Key himself did not go that far. Responsiveness was a safer description, because his materials were stained with changers motivated by a variety of wild beliefs that could not conceivably survive without the insulation of remarkable ignorance. To cope with these facts, he coined the metaphor of the "echo chamber": if people were only fed election buncombe, they could do no more than parrot it back. But responsive, and hence responsible, they were.

The important point here is much less any argument over terms like *rationality* than the fact that Key was not attempting to account for voting in general but rather for *change* in voting. These are not, obviously, unrelated tasks. But they are also very far from identical. Accounting for voting in general must deal with both stability and change. Accounting for change alone deals with a minority of voters, usually quite small, who are by definition atypical of citizens at that time and place. Understanding their changes is noble work. There is no other subset of voters as important. But this accounting alone is different from that of accounting for voting in general, and obviously so.

The same signs, "responsive" if not necessarily rational, come through handsomely in aggregate data analyses of voting such as those provided by Burnham (1970) in one vineyard and Kramer (1971) or Tufte (1975) or Hibbs (1982b) in another. In these studies, voters are not merely responsive or even ideological. They are almost exquisitely so, down to short-term changes in conditions and meaningful response variations measured in fractions of percentage points. On the other hand, we are here looking not only at change at the margin exclusively, but—unlike even Key—we are also looking at net change rather than gross change.

Does it matter that we look at voting through these lenses rather than the lens of the sample survey? It is my belief that it matters and matters powerfully. The key proposition to illuminate the difference is a very simple one and obvious to all: the process of aggregation drives out noise, and noise is what most vividly roars to attention with the total disaggregation of the sample survey. The quickest "fix" for a poor signal-to-noise ratio is to aggregate your data, and if you are looking for what remains a tiny signal numerically, such as one involving a percentage point or two, you may still be in trouble with the sample survey because small case numbers make the detection of small signals chancy. With the same small signal and large case numbers, as in analyses of official vote totals, the signal comes through loud and clear.

There are in fact a variety of controversies in the field of electoral studies that resist deflation primarily because the power of aggregation in tidying up messy data is so unappreciated. It may illuminate our subsequent argument if we examine a more detailed example.

Many years ago we presented data suggesting that ideological understandings of politics were remarkably underdeveloped in the American electorate, at least in the 1950s (Campbell, Converse, Miller, and Stokes, 1960; Converse, 1964). A very large fraction of the electorate—one-third to one-half—was unable to supply any meaning for such common ideological terms as *liberal* or *conservative*. And only a small fraction of the electorate—one in ten or so, depending on definitions—seemed to display active use of ideological standards of comparison in forming political perceptions and evaluations.

One of the empirical challenges to these conclusions arose from data that we and others began to collect in Europe in the late 1960s and early 1970s, involving ideological labels such as *left* and *right*. It was found in several countries that as many as 80–90 percent of voters were willing to describe locations for themselves on a left-right dimension. More impressive still, when these electorates were asked to place the multiple parties of their systems on the same left-right scale, the mean values assigned gave an ordering and spacing of the system's parties from left to right that seemed essentially that which journalists or practicing politicians would generate (Barnes, 1971; Sani, 1974). Thus it was not only true that almost all of these European voters felt well anchored in an ideological firmament, but they also could use these frames of reference with deadly accuracy to measure out relative positions of the parties in their systems. These data seemed flatly contradictory to ours from the United States: either European voters were much more ideologically sensitive than their counterparts in America, or the American conclusions themselves were wrong, being based probably on inadequate data.

As it turns out, however, there is no incompatibility whatever between the American and European phenomena in this example. This is best documented by the fact that both streams of findings coexist with complete comfort in the study of political representation in France that my colleague Roy Pierce and I have reported (Converse and Pierce, 1986).

In these data, collected in multiple waves in the late 1960s, nearly 80 percent of French respondents were willing to place themselves on a left-right scale from zero to one hundred. Moreover, when asked to assign locations on the left-right continuum to the ten most prominent party groups in the political system of the time, they did so with what seems to be remarkable accuracy. In this case, we have a benchmark for accuracy, inasmuch as we also posed the same party location question of nearly three hundred politicians who were candidates for the French National Assembly at the time. It turns out that the mean locations from party to party assigned by the mass public correlate at a level of $r = .97$ with the same means as estimated by our elite "experts." Thus all the findings that hinted at great voter sensitivity to the ideological are very sharply mirrored in these data.

If we delve more deeply, however, we soon find that these signs are superficial and underneath them the French voter seems about as insensitive ideologically as the American counterpart. There are some differences: the left-right vocabulary is much more constantly used in the French press than is the corresponding liberal-conservative vocabulary in the United States, and thus it has higher recognition value in France. About 13 percent fewer French than Americans simply say they do not know what these ideological terms mean. Nonetheless, about one-quarter of French respondents say straight out that they do not know what these terms signify politically. And further analyses of meaning suggest that if anything, a greater proportion of American voters has a sophisticated grasp of the implications of such ideological differences. The safest conclusion, however, is that the two electorates do not really differ much from one another in these regards. And these results seem to extend elsewhere in Europe as well (Klingemann, 1979a, 1979b, 1979c).

But how can it be true that more French are willing to locate themselves on the scale than are willing to guess at some meaning for the polar terms? The answer here is simple. Of those who locate themselves at all, virtually one-third place themselves at the exact middle of the scale. Indeed, "50" is the modal response to the self-location question and by some margin. Furthermore, these people exactly at 50 are drawn very disproportionately from those who either say they do not know what the scale means or who give the most irrelevant guesses at meaning. Clearly the 50 point is a convenient default choice for those who want to avoid the embarrassment of admitting they have no personal sense of self-location, for lack of understanding what that commitment would mean. When this massive fact is taken into account, the seeming edge in ideological sensitivity held by French voters over American voters is entirely dissipated and the two populations seem very similar, just as the more qualitative data on perceived meaning would imply.

But a final question remains. If the French public does indeed suffer a great deal of ignorance and confusion about left-right locations, how can it possibly generate a string of mean locations for ten parties that are very nearly a dead match for those given by a large panel of experts, our Assembly candidates?

Again, the answer is twofold and much simpler than meets the eye. First, large numbers of the most ideologically confused of our French respondents do not in fact try to place the parties at all, or only attempt to do so for the two or three most prominent parties. As an average over the ten parties, 39 percent of respondents drop out of the assignment of left-right positions to parties. Hence, the most confused are not represented in these means at all. And the admixture, which exists in the French electorate just as it does in the American one, thereby contributes nearly double the weight to the formation of these means than any quick glance at the data would lead us to realize.

The second answer is simply the power of aggregation. Up to now we have summarized these assignments by aggregating them into means. What this conceals is the scatteration of estimates from one voter to another. It turns out that this scatteration is vast in the mass sample by comparison with the elite sample, where our informants tend to converge rather closely on the same locations for the same parties.

It is not easy to find vivid ways of conveying the dispersion that underlies these means in the mass sample, but let us try. First, it is important to understand that the right-hand end of the left-right dimension is not much used for either self-location or party assignment, so that the full range of 100 points is a misleading standard of comparison. In the mass sample, for example, the mean location ascribed to the left-most party is about 60 points from that assigned the right-most party. Against this backdrop, it may be of interest that on the average, the standard deviations of the party locations are almost 20 points. This signifies that it takes a band of more than 30 points to encompass even ± 1 standard deviation of respondent estimates for the locations of given parties on the average. Or to put the matter another way, the average deviation from the consensual mean, averaged over the ten parties, is more than ± 15 points, thus spreading over a band of more than 30 points centered on the group mean for each party. Or again, if such deviations are confusing, we can note that over ten parties, more than a quarter of all respondents on the average suggest party locations more than 20 points to the left or to the right of the ultimate means, and individual left-right orderings of the parties are quite chaotic despite the fact that we are dealing here with only the more informed and sophisticated 60 percent of the French electorate.

In short, then, the drawing of means hides a sea of noise in these placements, as aggregation always does. The signal extracted from this noise is very recognizable because it is undoubtedly shaped in large measure by the small minority of the electorate that is nearly as well informed about these matters as are our elite informants. Of course the mass means do not look quite as similar to the elite means as a statement of correlation seems to imply. That is, because they are saturated with guesswork and the use of the 50 point as a default to hide ignorance, the mass means are very visibly shrunken in toward a value of 50 relative to those offered by the elites. But the order and general spacing of the mean party assignments from the mass sample map neatly against those from the elite, and a statement of correlation, which automatically wipes out the differences in sheer range of the means, hides the last tell-tale trace of marked confusion. The *signals* from the two samples are very similar. What does it matter if the elite responses are primarily signal and the mass responses are primarily noise?

Thus it is quite possible, thanks to the hidden power of aggregation, to arrive at a highly rational system performance on the backs of voters, most of whom are remarkably ill-informed much of the time.[1]

Of course we do not intend to imply that the magic of aggregation is the only phenomenon whereby less than informed voters can undergird a system performance that seems quite informed. In our earlier work on the prevalence of ideology in the electorate, we pointed out that mechanisms of social cueing, or what we called "ideology by proxy," would have the effect of amplifying the apparent ideological quality of an electoral response. This would occur quite simply in the degree that persons with little ideological orientation themselves took as a model for vote decisions the behavior of close acquaintances who did follow politics closely and coded it in ideological ways.

Other essays in this volume explore the dynamics and power of such social cueing, and point out quite properly that it does broaden the "rationality" of the electoral response well beyond what might be deduced from talking to voters as individuals. But mere statistical aggregation works powerfully to produce effects running in the same direction and much more automatically. That is, the prevalence of social cueing in political behavior is a cultural variable, depending for example on such things as the degree of privatization of attitudes, the availability of relevant mass media cues, and whether multiple persons from the same household or only the male head vote routinely. The effects of aggregation are, by comparison, asocial and acultural. They can be counted on to happen in every polity.

THE PROBLEM OF REPRESENTATION

We have now accumulated two simple ingredients. One is the enormous maldistribution of information in the electorate. The other is the miracle of aggregation that helps transmute a sow's ear into a silk purse. Let us mix these with a third, the phenomenon of popular representation, to see what results.

Popular representation and aggregation are linked inextricably. It is hard to imagine how the one might represent the many with any fidelity, save through some intervening act, be it mental if not physical, of aggregation.

The case could not be better made than with an ancient and little-known vignette from the Miller-Stokes (1963) study of representation in the American Congress. The published analyses of the Miller-Stokes data come from a second-generation analysis, after a first-generation analysis had failed rather dismally. This first round of analyses was organized according to a conception that what had been sampled were dyadic bonds linking each constituent to his or her representative. There were as many such bonds to be included in the analysis as the N of constituents across all the voter samples, and what was to be looked at were the congruence correlations between the constituents' attitudes and those of their representatives in Congress, as reflected in either personal conviction or roll-call vote.

The results of this first analysis were highly disconcerting. The dozens of congruence correlations in the Miller-Stokes diamond paradigm were a bleak desert. The good news was that at least the squares of all of these correlations could be taken to three digits instantaneously and without mechanical aids whatever. The bad news was that the result was everywhere the same: r^2 equaled .000. There was no trace of popular representation.

Once back to the drawing board, it was decided that the data should be assembled in another form. Instead of 1,500 constituent-representative dyads, perhaps the focus should be shifted to the 120 or so representatives, each one responding to some single aggregated value representing district sentiment such as a mean. When the data were recast in this form, and another kind of enhancement was added to eliminate the further noise of attenuation due to the tiny samples of opinion from each district, the results fairly leaped into that living color that is familiar from the project's publications. The signal had once again been rescued from the sea of noise, and a popular representation function of substantial fidelity was plain to see.

This kind of aggregation experiment can be instructively carried in other directions as well. In connection with our early work on the ideological sophistication of the American electorate, mentioned earlier, we had also drawn contrasts between the apparent internal structuring of attitudes, or their constraint, for the voter sample in the Miller-Stokes study as opposed to the elite sample of congressional candidates (Converse, 1964). Within our French representation data we can look at the same general contrasts. As in the American case, the signs of internal structure in the elite attitudes are far clearer than for the mass sample. In addition, for France we can make mass-elite stability comparisons not available to us for the United States. The French elite issue attitudes are markedly more stable than those in the mass sample and are so for items identically worded in both samples, so that allegations of mere shoddiness in question wording can be discounted. But in addition to these individual-level contrasts, we set aside as an experiment the individual mass data in favor of means for each of the eighty-six legislative districts in our sample. These aggregate means, like the individual data, could be examined for their intercorrelations at a point in time as well as for their stability over two waves of our panel study.

In this district-aggregated form, the apparent constraint and stability of what I shall now call "district sentiment" moves upward from the customary low levels observed for individual voters to high levels that actually are much like those observed for our elite samples. Districts with local sentiment to the conservative side of one issue tend to be conservative on other issues as well with a predictability that may well be an order of magnitude greater than is the case for the same prediction where individuals are concerned. And districts that are distinctively conservative at one election tend to be distinctively conservative at the next election as well.

In short, this is the partisan political world as aggregate analysts have long observed it. And given the fact that aggregate voter data and political elite data seem very similar in their "strength of signal," it is not surprising that these analysts from the aggregate vineyards are often bemused at the least and at times quite incredulous at survey-based discussions of voter ignorance, lack of ideology, confusion as to issue positions, and the like.

If representation requires aggregation, then a representative who sees himself or herself as a delegate must also become something of an aggregate analyst. There may be no magic in an arithmetic mean as a way of summarizing a district position on a given issue. But it is likely to be some measure of central tendency.

The big question that normative theory leaves open is not whether aggregation takes place, but rather aggregation over what? Classical theory assumed the total district, although a very plausible alternative would redefine the constituency as a set of supporters of the winner, in the fashion that Clausen (1973) and others have suggested. Measures of central tendency are, of course, at their weakest when they integrate over rampant heterogeneity, and as both Fenno (1978) and Fiorina (1974) have argued from their quite different approaches, district heterogeneity is the most troubling practical problem confronting the deputy who seriously wishes to represent district sentiment. In a polarized district there is surely no quicker way to liquidate heterogeneity from the representative's task than to decide to represent only one's own supporters, rather than the full district. And to justify this view of representation, we perhaps can take solace in Weissberg's (1978) definition of "collective representation," which points out that typically losers in one district ultimately get represented by some more congenial deputy who wins in some other district.

Whatever unit of aggregation we decide is the more proper, it is clear that without the miracle of aggregation, the deputy eager to represent the district in an instructed delegate mode would have a difficult and perhaps impossible task. Indeed, within our own French study it is clear that deputy accuracy in reading even a central tendency does decline as district heterogeneity advances.

Our final question concerns the source of the district signal in the general case, given that when we dissect the constituency (in either the global or the supporter definition) by looking beneath any central tendency we find a great maldistribution of information. If some people are more responsible than others for the definition of these signals, then there is a real sense in which these people are being more fully represented than their comrades in the district. And of course it is very tempting to assume that constituency signals tend to get defined chiefly by the informed constituents, a conclusion that would go hand in glove with the observation that aggregated results seem to follow sharper patterns intelligible to us than we might expect from conversations with individual voters.

Such a conclusion needs to be handled in a gingerly fashion, although I believe there is a substantial grain of truth in the observation. If the metaphor of signal and noise could be taken literally as a perfect analog, and self-compensating noise were in fact limited to those less informed, then we could give the observation full confidence. But it is only a metaphor, and perhaps it is seriously wanting.

The observation requires two states in nature, both eminently testable and in fact reasonable in terms of other things we now know. One is that less informed people tend *on average* to take more middling positions on issues than is true of more informed ones. At least since McClosky, Hoffman, and O'Hara's (1960) findings on convention delegates, there has been a growing corpus of evidence that this is, more often than not, true. We have already explored above another dramatic special case of the same phenomenon: our French respondents least sure as to what "left" and "right" signify tend to flock to the center of the continuum in their self-descriptions. The second requirement, where territorial representation is concerned, is a much weaker one: it merely says that there cannot be some active phenomenon, such as a doctrine of countervailing forces, which ensures that in district after district the well informed tend to polarize in two blocs, with a district mean that is unerringly middling as well. This is, of course, a requirement which we could largely relax if we redefine the constituency to include only supporters.

At least one other caveat is worth mentioning. This is the lively possibility that, due to phenomena of issue publics, we should refrain from thinking of the electorate as rigidly stratified into fixed blocs of people who are generally informed or generally uninformed. In other words, some people are informed on some things and others on other matters. Such a possibility is a little less depressing because the signals flow from where the information lies in the voter system, but not always from the same individuals.

Empirical evidence seems to give some partial support to an issue-public model, but also supports in a loose way a more general hierarchical model in which those who tend to monopolize information in one area also are well informed in others. Thus the real world is probably a mix of the two models.

We cannot evaluate the issue public possibility within our own representation studies because we lack compelling data about information held by individual voters from one issue domain to another.

On the other hand, we can evaluate the more rigid model by asking whether representation fidelity seems higher when the constituency is limited to the more educated half of its electorate, relative to that for the constituency defined as the less educated half. Here the answer in our French data is quite clearly positive: representation fidelity, indexed by the size of congruence correlations, is unquestionably higher for the better educated constituents (Converse and Pierce, 1986).[2]

Congruence alone does not guarantee active influence any more than correlations guarantee causality. Representatives in France, as in most other places, are relatively well educated, and when issue positions are broadly correlated with education, their positions tend in a natural way to resemble those of their more educated constituents in any event. Thus phenomena of "descriptive representation" alone would produce the same signs of higher congruence of representative positions with the better educated constituents independent of any short-term influence from constituent to representative. However, there is no reason to define descriptive representation as irrelevant to the kind of responsiveness sought in a democratic process. And in the case of our French data, there are reasons to believe that there is at least some active influence beyond the functioning of descriptive representation alone.

Such patterns, as is so often the case, have both pleasing and troubling implications. The pleasing ones are that whatever influence constituent signals have upon representatives, and hence upon national decision making, the signals tend to be defined disproportionately by the more informed of the constituents. If better decisions require better information, then this is a welcome result.

The more troubling implication is that the representation system in spirit follows a "one-person, one-vote" formula rather less than the letter of the law would suggest, and those poorly informed tend to suffer at least partial disenfranchisement as a result. How much this troubling implication is palliated by the reflection that in an information-rich environment there is a substantial element of choice in whether or not one is informed, and hence more effectively enfranchised, is probably a matter best left to personal taste.

NOTES

This chapter was originally presented as the keynote address at the Conference on Information and Democratic Processes, University of Illinois at Urbana-Champaign, March 1986.

1. I proffer this generalization with some hesitance, because it appears to walk directly into a stiff intellectual gale from the opposing direction. I refer to the paradox of committee voting, in which the contributions of individual voters, rational by construction, can turn out in the process of aggregation to be subverted into nonsense. I assume it is obvious what differentiates between these two cases, but surely they must not be confused one for the other.

2. The actual data presented in Converse and Pierce (1986) are based on a partition into higher and lower status, as measured by an index that includes occupation and income as well as education. However, the finding holds for education taken alone.

CONCLUSION

17

Information and the Study of Politics

James H. Kuklinski

The idea of "information" has overtaken political scientists. Lest there be any doubt, consider these recent book and article titles: "The Value of Biased Information: A Rational Choice Model of Political Advice" (Calvert, 1985); *How People Tame the Information Tide* (Graber, 1984); "A Primer of Information-Processing for the Political Scientist" (Hastie, 1986); "A Partisan Schema for Political Information Processing" (Lodge and Hamill, 1986); and "Sequential Elections with Limited Information" (McKelvey and Ordeshook, 1985a). Not every author has taken the plunge, of course, and by no means do the preceding titles represent the discipline as a whole, but even research not explicitly so entitled increasingly is adopting some kind of "informational" perspective. So why the newly acquired focus?

One answer is that the focus is not new. As early as 1913, Walter Lippmann was pointing to citizens' lack of information about the prevailing issues of the day as the major impediment to effective political representation in the United States. More recently, but still more than twenty-five years ago, Philip Converse (1962) published "Information Flow and the Stability of Partisan Attitudes," an influential article that placed information at the center of the voting act and examined how its flow through the social fabric conditions political judgments. A thorough search would undoubtedly uncover other works with information as their integrating and primary theme (cf. Cox, 1974).

Although the business-as-usual position has merit—it certainly serves to remind that the new is rarely new—most political scientists, I suspect, would acknowledge a "true change," a discernible shift, in the transcendent way that investigators frame their research questions. And that is the point: "information" has become a disciplinary language, not a term that a few adventurous political scientists introduce into their work. Nearly everyone attending a political convention today will acknowledge familiarity with "information processing"; ten years ago, the term would have brought blank stares.

Of course, the changing nature of American society and politics has done much to reshape disciplinary perspectives. Sensationalism aside, we have truly experienced an information explosion. In many observers' eyes, the most expansive sector of the economy, as the United States enters the 21st Century, will be the provision of information in its various forms. Continuous television news broadcasts like those on CNN, computerized stock exchange programs, 800-number investment centers—all speak directly and convincingly to this prediction.

One can look backward as well, to a more dramatic case in point, covering a long period of time. I refer to the transformation of our system of political representation. Although the governmental structure has changed little in two hundred years, members of Congress and their constituents today stand in a fundamentally different relationship to each other than they did at the Founding and for many years thereafter. Well into the 20th Century, citizens and representatives knew little if anything about each others' wishes and actions. Facing the perils of an untamed wilderness, national legislators would unhappily and cautiously trek back and forth between capitol and home—by horse and buggy, no less (Young, 1966). When in the familiar confines of their districts, they communicated not with the proverbial common citizen, but rather with local and state leaders. Today's representatives, in contrast, know the distribution of "public opinion" on a proposal as soon as it is announced, even when they might wish otherwise. Whereas Gallup and Harris once dominated the poll scene, today the major television networks as well as many other corporations regularly and frequently conduct nationwide surveys on every conceivable issue. Indeed, some scholars equate the proliferation of polls with the fabrication of public opinion (Ginsberg, 1986). On the other side, the media routinely report (and report on) individual congressional members' activities, so that no one escapes public scrutiny. Many U.S. senators, especially, have become household names. In short, two hundred years of technological progress has transformed our system of representation from informationally void to informationally based.

Not only do political scientists react to the changing nature of the environment they study, but they also borrow heavily from other disciplines. Economics and psychology, in particular, serve as sources of ideas and inspiration for researchers wishing to get an "edge up" on their colleagues. In both fields, the dominant theoretical perspectives, which have strongly influenced disciplinary research, begin with information.

Among psychologists, *information processing,* a term to which I referred earlier, has spawned a new and thriving subfield, social cognition. This subfield examines how people perceive, process, store, and retrieve social information (Fiske and Taylor, 1984; Wyer and Srull, 1984). With political scientists' quick adoption of social cognition concepts has come the introduction of information-based terms such as *schema, memory,* and *cognitive processing* (cf. Lodge and Hamill, 1986).

The growing number of political scientists who look to economic theory begin with one of the most venerable assumptions in all of the social sciences, utility maximization. Political economy research has gone through two stages, first assuming that people possess complete information and then assuming limited information. As this theoretical perspective has gained respect within the discipline, it has brought information to the fore of the study of politics (McKelvey and Ordeshook, 1985a, 1985b; Shepsle, 1972).

It is easy to understand the genesis of the "new" informational perspective in political science, but what, if anything, does the discipline gain from it? Or, to use the language of two psychologists who at the time were speaking to the schema concept in social cognition, "what does it buy us" (Fiske and Linville, 1980)?

If the preceding chapters are any indication, a general informational framework can integrate what scholars have traditionally viewed as disparate and unrelated research enterprises. Those interested in the effects of social context on the vote rarely cite social choice theorists, who in turn pay little heed to students of context or political psychology, a not unexpected state of affairs given that the various efforts have traditionally represented competing research paradigms. Ask these same scholars to adopt an explicitly informational conception, however, and they quickly discover common ground, or, at least, realize that they are all providing pieces to the same puzzle: How, and how well, does American representative democracy function in light of limited and badly fragmented political information?

Of course, this general question consists of a variety of more specific queries. What are the most effective (and ineffective) sources of citizen information? How do citizens perceive and use the political information that is available to them? Can the political system as a whole function at an acceptable level even when its individual citizens fail most tests of informedness? If so, how? Note how this litany of inquiries moves naturally and easily from matters of the individual citizen to overall system performance. In facilitating the transition, an informational perspective encourages, indeed begs, across-level analysis, which has been sorely absent from research on politics. One of the remarkable conclusions of this volume is that "the system" works, despite an abysmally low level of information among citizens and between citizens and representatives.

Note the term *works*. Perhaps the greatest potential value of an informational perspective to political science is that it returns questions of democratic theory to the center of the empirical study of politics, and, consequently, builds a bridge with earlier research. I can recall vividly, as a graduate student in the early 1970s, the excitement that accompanied reading debates over the capabilities and capacities of individual citizens and thus the nature of governance in the United States. Berelson, Dahl, and McCloskey, to name some of that era's intellectual leaders, posed questions—and offered answers—about which few could remain neutral. Although it would be folly to suggest that these "life-and-death" issues have since fallen by the wayside, the intensity of discussion has indisputably diminished, largely, I think, due to the lack of an integrating framework that forces researchers to juxtapose individual- and system-level findings. "Information" may provide such a framework.

Thinking in terms of information also returns elites to a central place in governance. During the 1960s, largely in response to the civil rights and the anti-Vietnam War movements, notions of representative democracy took on a participatory cast, as exemplified in Miller and Stokes's study of congressional representation (1963) and the outpouring of research that followed it. That seminal work, now deservedly in the political science hall of fame, failed explicitly to recognize the great asymmetry in information between national legislators on the one hand and the citizens who elect them on the other. How can citizens effectively instruct their representatives on a policy when the latter, by virtue of their positions, know more about it? Or, to be more direct, can political representation truly operate as nearly twenty-five years of research has depicted? Probably not, and both principal-agent and signaling theory, each rooted in some realities about the distribution of information, offer seemingly more tenable conceptions of citizen-representative interactions.

So, is "information" a panacea, a conceptual approach that will integrate the discipline and lead political scientists to the "big" questions? To answer in the affirmative would fringe on fraudulent advertising, at least at this time. For one thing, many of the research enterprises presented in this volume and elsewhere could exist quite independently of any reference to information. For another, no one, to my knowledge, has explicitly and precisely defined the very term that motivates this book. Suggesting that information is an obvious concept will not do. These caveats notwithstanding, I anticipate an outpouring of new and exciting research—all oriented around information—during the next decade.

References

Abelson, Robert P., Donald R. Kinder, Mark D. Peters, and Susan T. Fiske. 1982. Affective and Semantic Components in Political Person Perception. *Journal of Personality and Social Psychology*, 42:619–630.

Abelson, Robert P., and Ariel Levi. 1985. Decision Making and Decision Theory. In Gardner Lindzey and Elliot Aronson, eds., *Handbook of Social Psychology*, Vol. 1. 3d ed. New York: Random House.

Aldrich, John H., Tse Min Lin, and Wendy M. Rahn. 1987. Learning during the 1984 Nomination Campaign. Unpublished manuscript.

Aldrich, John H., John L. Sullivan, and Eugene Borgida. 1986. "Waltzing before a Blind Audience?": The Anomaly of Foreign Affairs and Issue Voting in the 1984 Presidential Election. Unpublished manuscript.

Almond, Gabriel A., and Sidney Verba. 1963. *The Civic Culture: Political Attitudes and Democracy in Five Nations*. Princeton: Princeton University Press.

Alt, James E., and K. Alec Chrystal. 1983. *Political Economics*. Berkeley: University of California Press.

Anderson, John R., and Gordon H. Bower. 1973. *Human Associative Memory*. Washington, DC: Winston.

Anderson, Norman H. 1971. Integration Theory and Attitude Change. *Psychological Review*, 78:171–206.

Anderson, Norman H. 1981. *Foundations of Information Integration Theory*. New York: Academic Press.

Arrow, Kenneth J. 1951. *Social Choice and Individual Values*. New York: John Wiley.

Asch, Solomon E. 1951. Effects of Group Pressure upon the Modification and Distortion of Judgments. In Harold Guetzkow, ed., *Groups, Leadership, and Men*. Pittsburgh: Carnegie Press.

Axelrod, Robert. 1981. The Emergence of Cooperation among Egoists. *American Political Science Review*, 75:306–318.

Axelrod, Robert. 1984. *The Evolution of Cooperation.* New York: Basic Books.

Ball, Terence. 1976. From Paradigms to Research Programs: Toward a Post-Kuhnian Political Science. *American Journal of Political Science,* 20:151–177.

Bargh, John A. 1984. Automatic and Conscious Processing of Social Information. In Robert S. Wyer, Jr. and Thomas Srull, eds., *Handbook of Social Cognition,* Vol. 3. Hillsdale: Lawrence Erlbaum.

Barnes, Samuel H. 1971. Left, Right, and the Italian Voter. *Comparative Political Studies,* 4:157–175.

Baron, David P. 1987. A Legislative Theory of Political Parties. Unpublished manuscript.

Baron, David P. and John A. Ferejohn. 1987. Bargaining in Legislatures. Unpublished manuscript.

Barry, Brian. 1970. *Sociologists, Economists and Democracy.* New York: Macmillan.

Bartels, Larry M. 1988. *Presidential Primaries and the Dynamics of Public Choice.* Princeton: Princeton University Press.

Beck, Paul Allen, and M. Kent Jennings. 1979. Political Periods and Political Participation. *American Political Science Review,* 73:737–750.

Becker, Gary S. 1958. Competition and Democracy. *Journal of Law and Economics,* 1:105–109.

Behr, Roy L. 1986. The Effects of Media on Voters' Considerations in Presidential and Congressional Elections. Doctoral dissertation, Yale University.

Behr, Roy L., and Shanto Iyengar. 1985. Television News, Real-World Cues, and Changes in the Public Agenda. *Public Opinion Quarterly,* 49:38–57.

Bellezza, Francis S., and Gordon H. Bower. 1981. Person Stereotypes and Memory for People. *Journal of Personality and Social Psychology,* 41:856–865.

Berelson, Bernard R., Paul F. Lazarsfeld, and William N. McPhee. 1954. *Voting: A Study of Opinion Formation in a Presidential Campaign.* Chicago: University of Chicago Press.

Berscheid, Ellen. 1984. Vocabularies of Emotion circa 1984. Presidential Address, American Psychological Association.

Birnbaum, Michael H. 1973. The Devil Rides Again: Correlation as an Index of Fit. *Psychological Bulletin,* 79:239–242.

Black, Duncan. 1958. *The Theory of Committees and Elections.* Cambridge: Cambridge University Press.

Blau, Peter M. 1957. Formal Organizations: Dimensions of Analysis. *American Journal of Sociology,* 63:58–69.

Blinder, Alan S. 1979. *Economic Policy and the Great Stagflation.* New York: Academic Press.

Blinder, Alan S., and Douglas Holtz-Eakin. 1984. Public Opinion and the Balanced Budget. *American Economic Review,* 74(2):144–149.

Bloom, Howard S., and H. Douglas Price. 1975. Voter Response to Short-

Run Economic Conditions: The Asymmetric Effect of Prosperity and Recession. *American Political Science Review,* 69:1240–1254.

Bodenhausen, Galen V., and Meryl Lichtenstein. 1987. Social Stereotypes and Information-Processing Strategies: The Impact of Task Complexity. *Journal of Personality and Social Psychology,* 52:871–880.

Bodenhausen, Galen V., and Robert S. Wyer, Jr. 1985. Effects of Stereotypes on Decision Making and Information-Processing Strategies. *Journal of Personality and Social Psychology,* 48:267–282.

Bower, Gordon H., Stephen G. Gilligan, and Kenneth P. Monteiro. 1981. Selectivity of Learning Caused by Affective States. *Journal of Experimental Psychology: General,* 110:451–473.

Brady, Henry E., and Paul M. Sniderman. 1985. Attitude Attribution: A Group Basis for Political Reasoning. *American Political Science Review,* 79:1061–1078.

Brennan, Geoffrey, and James M. Buchanan. 1984. The Logic of the Levers: The Pine Theory of Electoral Preference. Unpublished manuscript.

Brody, Richard A., and Benjamin I. Page. 1973. Indifference, Alienation and Rational Decisions: The Effects of Candidate Evaluations on Turnout and the Vote. *Public Choice,* 15:1–17.

Brown, Courtney. 1981. Group Membership and the Social Environment: Multiple Influences on Political Attitudes and Behaviors. Doctoral dissertation, Washington University, St. Louis.

Bruner, Jerome S. 1951. Personality Dynamics and the Process of Perceiving. In Robert R. Blake and Glenn V. Ransey, eds., *Perception: An Approach to Personality.* New York: Ronald Press.

Buchanan, James M., and Richard E. Wagner. 1977. *Democracy in Deficit: The Political Legacy of Lord Keynes.* New York: Academic Press.

Burnham, Walter Dean. 1970. *Critical Elections and the Mainsprings of American Politics.* New York: W. W. Norton.

Calvert, Randall L. 1985. The Value of Biased Information: A Rational Choice Model of Political Advice. *Journal of Politics,* 47:530–555.

Calvert, Randall L. 1986. Reputation and Legislative Leadership. Unpublished manuscript.

Calvert, Randall L., Mathew D. McCubbins, and Barry R. Weingast. 1987. A Theory of Political Control and Agency Discretion. Unpublished manuscript.

Campbell, Angus, Philip E. Converse, Warren E. Miller, and Donald E. Stokes. 1960. *The American Voter.* New York: John Wiley.

Campbell, Angus, Gerald Gurin, and Warren E. Miller. 1954. *The Voter Decides.* Evanston: Row, Peterson.

Carlston, Donald E. 1980. The Recall and Use of Traits and Events in Social Inference Processes. *Journal of Experimental Social Psychology,* 16:303–328.

Carmines, Edward G., and Lawrence C. Dodd. 1985. Bicameralism in Congress: The Changing Partnership. In Lawrence C. Dodd and Bruce I.

Oppenheimer, eds., *Congress Reconsidered*, 3d ed. Washington, DC: Congressional Quarterly Press.

Carmines, Edward G., and James A. Stimson. 1980. The Two Faces of Issue Voting. *American Political Science Review*, 74:78–91.

Carmines, Edward G., and James A. Stimson. 1986. On the Structure and Sequence of Issue Evolution. *American Political Science Review*, 80:901–920.

Carmines, Edward G., and James A. Stimson. 1988. *Issue Evolution: Race and the Transformation of American Politics*. Princeton: Princeton University Press.

Carver, Charles S., Ronald J. Ganellen, William J. Froming, and William Chambers. 1983. Modelling: An Analysis in Terms of Category Accessibility. *Journal of Experimental Social Psychology*, 19:403–421.

Chappell, Henry W., Jr., and William R. Keech. 1983. Welfare Consequences of the Six-Year Presidential Term Evaluated in the Context of a Model of the U.S. Economy. *American Political Science Review*, 77:75–91.

Chappell, Henry W., Jr., and William R. Keech. 1985a. A New View of Political Accountability for Economic Performance. *American Political Science Review*, 79:10–27.

Chappell, Henry W., Jr., and William R. Keech. 1985b. The Political Viability of Rule-Based Monetary Policy. *Public Choice*, 46:125–140.

Chubb, John E., Michael G. Hagen, and Paul M. Sniderman. 1986. Ideological Reasoning. *Brookings Discussion Papers in Governmental Studies*, No. 4.

Clausen, Aage R. 1973. *How Congressmen Decide: A Policy Focus*. New York: St. Martin's.

Clore, Gerald L., and John B. Gormly. 1974. Knowing, Feeling and Liking: A Psychophysiological Study of Attraction. *Journal of Research in Personality*, 8:218–230.

Cohen, Richard E. 1987. New Visibility. *National Journal*, 19:343.

Collier, Kenneth E., Richard D. McKelvey, Peter C. Ordeshook, and Kenneth C. Williams. 1987. Retrospective Voting: An Experimental Study. *Public Choice*, 53:101–130.

Conover, Pamela Johnston, and Stanley Feldman. 1984. How People Organize the Political World: A Schematic Model. *American Journal of Political Science*, 28:95–126.

Conover, Pamela Johnston, and Stanley Feldman. 1986. Emotional Reactions to the Economy: I'm Mad as Hell and I'm Not Going to Take It Anymore. *American Journal of Political Science*, 30:50–78.

Converse, Philip E. 1962. Information Flow and the Stability of Partisan Attitudes. *Public Opinion Quarterly*, 26:578–599.

Converse, Philip E. 1964. The Nature of Belief Systems in Mass Publics. In David E. Apter, ed., *Ideology and Discontent*. New York: Free Press.

Converse, Philip E. 1975. Public Opinion and Voting Behavior. In Fred I. Greenstein and Nelson W. Polsby, eds., *Handbook of Political Science*, Vol. 4. Reading: Addison-Wesley.

Converse, Philip E., Aage R. Clausen, and Warren E. Miller. 1965. Electoral

Myth and Reality: The 1964 Election. *American Political Science Review,* 59:321–336.

Converse, Phillip E., and Gregory B. Markus. 1979. Plus ca change . . . : The New CPS Election Study Panel. *American Political Science Review,* 73:32–49.

Converse, Philip E., and Roy Pierce. 1986. *Political Representation in France.* Cambridge: Harvard University Press.

Cox, Kevin R. 1974. The Spatial Structuring of Information Flow and Partisan Attitudes. In Mattei Dogan and Stein Rokkan, eds., *Social Ecology.* Cambridge: MIT Press.

Dahl, Robert A. 1961. *Who Governs?: Democracy and Power in an American City.* New Haven: Yale University Press.

Davis, James A., Joe L. Spaeth, and Carolyn Huson. 1961. A Technique for Analyzing the Effects of Group Composition. *American Sociological Review,* 26:215–225.

Davis, Otto A., Melvin J. Hinich, and Peter C. Ordeshook. 1970. An Expository Development of a Mathematical Model of the Electoral Process. *American Political Science Review,* 64:426–448.

Demski, Joel S., David E. M. Sappington, and Pablo T. Spiller. 1987. Managing Supplier Switching. *Rand Journal of Economics,* 18:77–97.

Denzau, Arthur, William H. Riker, and Kenneth A. Shepsle. 1985. Farquharson and Fenno: Sophisticated Voting and Home Style. *American Political Science Review,* 79:1117–1134.

Dodd, David H., and Raymond M. White, Jr. 1980. *Cognition: Mental Structures and Processes.* Boston: Allyn and Bacon.

Dooling, D. James, and Robert E. Christiaansen. 1977. Episodic and Semantic Aspects of Memory for Prose. *Journal of Experimental Psychology: Human Learning and Memory,* 3:428–436.

Downs, Anthony. 1957. *An Economic Theory of Democracy.* New York: Harper and Row.

Dreben, Elizabeth K., Susan T. Fiske, and Reid Hastie. 1979. The Independence of Evaluative and Item Information: Impression and Recall Order Effects in Behavior-Based Impression Formation. *Journal of Personality and Social Psychology,* 37:1758–1768.

Eckstein, Otto. 1983. *The DRI Model of the U.S. Economy.* New York: McGraw-Hill.

Edelman, Murray. 1964. *The Symbolic Uses of Politics.* Urbana: University of Illinois Press.

Einhorn, Hillel J., and Robin M. Hogarth. 1981. Behavioral Decision Theory: Processes of Judgment and Choice. *Annual Review of Psychology,* 32:53–88.

Elliott, Donald A. 1985. *The St. Louis Fed's Monetary Model: Whence It Came—How It Thrived, 1970–1983.* New York: Garland.

Elster, Jon. 1979. *Ulysses and the Sirens: Studies in Rationality and Irrationality.* Cambridge: Cambridge University Press.

Enelow, James M., and Melvin J. Hinich. 1982. Ideology, Issues, and the

Spatial Theory of Elections. *American Political Science Review,* 76:493–501.

Enelow, James M., and Melvin J. Hinich. 1984. *The Spatial Theory of Voting: An Introduction.* Cambridge: Cambridge University Press.

Eulau, Heinz. 1980. Editor's Note. *Political Behavior,* 2:215–218.

Eulau, Heinz. 1986. *Politics, Self, and Society: A Theme and Variations.* Cambridge: Harvard University Press.

Fair, Ray C. 1978a. The Effect of Economic Events on Votes for President. *Review of Economics and Statistics,* 60:159–173.

Fair, Ray C. 1978b. The Use of Optimal Control Techniques to Measure Economic Performance. *International Economic Review,* 19:289–309.

Fair, Ray C. 1984. *Specification, Estimation, and Analysis of Macroeconometric Models.* Cambridge: Harvard University Press.

Feldman, Stanley. 1982. Economic Self-Interest and Political Behavior. *American Journal of Political Science,* 26:446–466.

Feldman, Stanley, and Pamela Johnston Conover. 1983. Candidates, Issues and Voters: The Role of Inference in Political Perception. *Journal of Politics,* 45:810–839.

Fenno, Richard F., Jr. 1978. *Home Style: House Members in Their Districts.* Boston: Little, Brown.

Ferejohn, John A. 1986. Incumbent Performance and Electoral Control. *Public Choice,* 50:5–25.

Ferejohn, John A., and Morris P. Fiorina. 1974. The Paradox of Not Voting: A Decision Theoretic Analysis. *American Political Science Review,* 68:525–536.

Ferejohn, John A., and Morris P. Fiorina. 1975. Closeness Counts Only in Horseshoes and Dancing. *American Political Science Review,* 69:920–925.

Ferguson, Thomas. 1983. Party Realignment and American Industrial Structure: The Investment Theory of Political Parties in Historical Perspective. In Paul Zarembka, ed., *Research in Political Economy,* Vol. 6. Greenwich: JAI Press.

Festinger, Leon. 1957. *A Theory of Cognitive Dissonance.* Evanston: Row, Peterson.

Festinger, Leon, and Nathan Maccoby. 1964. On Resistance to Persuasive Communications. *Journal of Abnormal and Social Psychology,* 68:359–366.

Fields, James M., and Howard Schuman. 1976. Public Beliefs about the Beliefs of the Public. *Public Opinion Quarterly,* 40:427–448.

Finifter, Ada W. 1974. The Friendship Group as a Protective Environment for Political Deviants. *American Political Science Review,* 68:607–625.

Fiorina, Morris P. 1974. *Representatives, Roll Calls and Constituencies.* Lexington: D. C. Heath.

Fiorina, Morris P. 1981. *Retrospective Voting in American National Elections.* New Haven: Yale University Press.

Fiorina, Morris P. 1982. Legislative Choice of Regulatory Forms: Legal Process or Administrative Process? *Public Choice,* 39:33–66.

Fiorina, Morris P. 1985. Group Concentration and the Delegation of Legislative Authority. In Roger G. Noll, ed., *Regulatory Policy and the Social Sciences*. Berkeley: University of California Press.

Fishbein, Martin, and Icek Ajzen. 1975. *Belief, Attitude, Intention and Behavior: An Introduction to Theory and Research*. Reading: Addison-Wesley.

Fishbein, Martin, and Icek Ajzen. 1981. Attitudes and Voting Behaviour: An Application of the Theory of Reasoned Action. In Geoffry M. Stephenson and James H. Davis, eds., *Progress in Applied Social Psychology*, Vol. 1. New York: John Wiley.

Fiske, Susan T., and Donald R. Kinder. 1981. Involvement, Expertise, and Schema Use: Evidence from Political Cognition. In Nancy Cantor and John F. Kihlstrom, eds., *Personality, Cognition, and Social Interaction*. Hillsdale: Lawrence Erlbaum.

Fiske, Susan T., Donald R. Kinder, and W. Michael Larter. 1983. The Novice and the Expert: Knowledge-Based Strategies in Political Cognition. *Journal of Experimental Social Psychology*, 19:381–400.

Fiske, Susan T., and Patricia W. Linville. 1980. What Does the Schema Concept Buy Us? *Personality and Social Psychology Bulletin*, 6:543–557.

Fiske, Susan T., and Mark A. Pavelchak. 1986. Category-Based versus Piecemeal-Based Affective Responses: Developments in Schema-Triggered Affect. In Richard M. Sorrentino and E. Tory Higgins, eds., *Handbook of Motivation and Cognition*. New York: Guilford Press.

Fiske, Susan T., and Shelley E. Taylor. 1984. *Social Cognition*. New York: Random House.

Freedman, Jonathan L., and David O. Sears. 1965. Warning, Distraction, and Resistance to Influence. *Journal of Personality and Social Psychology*, 1:262–266.

Frey, Bruno S. 1983. *Democratic Economic Policy: A Theoretical Introduction*. New York: St. Martin's.

Friedman, Benjamin M. 1979. Optimal Expectations and the Extreme Information Assumptions of "Rational Expectations" Macromodels. *Journal of Monetary Economics*, 5:23–41.

Friedman, Milton. 1968. The Role of Monetary Policy. *American Economic Review*, 58: 1–17.

Friedman, Milton. 1977. Nobel Lecture: Inflation and Unemployment. *Journal of Political Economy*, 85:451–472.

Friedrich, Carl J. 1941. *Constitutional Government and Democracy: Theory and Practice in Europe and America*. Boston: Little, Brown.

Gibbard, Alan, and William L. Harper. 1978. Counterfactuals and Two Kinds of Expected Utility. In C. A. Hooker, J. J. Leach, and E. F. McClennen, eds., *Foundations and Applications of Decision Theory*, Vol. 1. Dordrecht, Holland: D. Reidel.

Giles, Michael W., and Marilyn K. Dantico. 1982. Political Participation and Neighborhood Social Context Revisited. *American Journal of Political Science*, 26:144–150.

Ginsberg, Benjamin. 1986. *The Captive Public: How Mass Opinion Promotes State Power*. New York: Basic Books.

Glynn, Carroll J., and Jack M. McLeod. 1984. Public Opinion du Jour: An Examination of the Spiral of Silence. *Public Opinion Quarterly,* 48:731–740.

Goldberg, Arthur S. 1966. Discerning a Causal Pattern among Data on Voting Behavior. *American Political Science Review,* 60:913–922.

Goldberg, Samuel. 1958. *Introduction to Difference Equations.* New York: John Wiley.

Graber, Doris A. 1984. *Processing the News: How People Tame the Information Tide.* New York: Longman.

Gramlich, Edward M. 1983. Models of Inflation Expectations Formation: A Comparison of Household and Economist Forecasts. *Journal of Money, Credit, and Banking,* 15:155–173.

Granovetter, Mark S. 1973. The Strength of Weak Ties. *American Journal of Sociology,* 78:1360–1380.

Granovetter, Mark S. 1978. Threshold Models of Collective Behavior. *American Journal of Sociology,* 83:1420–1443.

Granovetter, Mark S., and Roland Soong. 1988. Threshold Models of Diversity: Chinese Restaurants, Residental Segregation, and the Spiral of Silence. In Clifford C. Clogg, ed., *Sociological Methodology,* Vol. 18. Washington, DC: American Sociological Association.

Gray, Peter, Richard D. McKelvey, and Peter C. Ordeshook. 1986. Some Experimental Results on Retrospective Voting in Multidimensional Elections. Unpublished manuscript.

Greenstein, Fred I. 1960. The Benevolent Leader: Children's Images of Political Authority. *American Political Science Review,* 54:934–943.

Greenwald, Anthony G. 1968. Cognitive Learning, Cognitive Response to Persuasion, and Attitude Change. In Anthony G. Greenwald, Timothy C. Brock, and Thomas M. Ostrom, eds., *Psychological Foundations of Attitudes.* New York: Academic Press.

Griffitt, William, and Russell Veitch. 1971. Hot and Crowded: Influences of Population Density and Temperature on Interpersonal Affective Behavior. *Journal of Personality and Social Psychology,* 17:92–98.

Hamill, Ruth, and Milton Lodge. 1986. Cognitive Consequences of Political Sophistication. In Richard R. Lau and David. O. Sears, eds., *Political Cognition.* Hillsdale: Lawrence Erlbaum.

Hamill, Ruth, Milton Lodge, and Fredrick Blake. 1985. The Breadth, Depth, and Utility of Class, Partisan, and Ideological Schemas. *American Journal of Political Science,* 29:850–870.

Hamilton, David L., ed. 1981. *Cognitive Processes in Stereotyping and Intergroup Behavior.* Hillsdale: Lawrence Erlbaum.

Hammond, Thomas H., Jeffrey S. Hill, and Gary J. Miller. 1985. Presidential Appointment of Bureau Chiefs and the "Congressional Control of Administration" Hypothesis. Unpublished manuscript.

Hanushek, Eric A., and John E. Jackson. 1977. *Statistical Methods for Social Scientists.* New York: Academic Press.

Harris, Richard. 1971. Annals of Politics: How the People Feel. *New Yorker,* 47(July 10): 34–54.

Hastie, Reid. 1986. A Primer of Information-Processing Theory for the Political Scientist. In Richard R. Lau and David O. Sears, eds., *Political Cognition.* Hillsdale: Lawrence Erlbaum.

Hastie, Reid, and Bernadette Park. 1986. The Relationship Between Memory and Judgment Depends on Whether the Judgment Task is Memory-Based or On-Line. *Psychological Review,* 93:258–268.

Hauser, Robert M. 1974. Contextual Analysis Revisited. *Sociological Methods and Research,* 2:365–375.

Heider, Fritz. 1958. *The Psychology of Interpersonal Relations.* New York: John Wiley.

Herstein, John A. 1981. Keeping the Voter's Limits in Mind: A Cognitive Process Analysis of Decision Making in Voting. *Journal of Personality and Social Psychology,* 40:843–861.

Hess, Stephen. 1986. *The Ultimate Insiders: U.S. Senators in the National Media.* Washington, DC: The Brookings Institution.

Hibbs, Douglas A., Jr. 1977. Political Parties and Macroeconomic Policy. *American Political Science Review,* 71:1467–1487.

Hibbs, Douglas A., Jr. 1979. The Mass Public and Macroeconomic Performance: The Dynamics of Public Opinion Toward Unemployment and Inflation. *American Journal of Political Science,* 23:705–731.

Hibbs, Douglas A., Jr. 1982a. The Dynamics of Political Support for American Presidents Among Occupational and Partisan Groups. *American Journal of Political Science,* 26:312–332.

Hibbs, Douglas A., Jr. 1982b. On the Demand for Economic Outcomes: Macroeconomic Performance and Mass Political Support in the United States, Great Britain, and Germany. *Journal of Politics,* 44:426–462.

Hibbs, Douglas A., Jr. 1987. *The American Political Economy.* Cambridge: Harvard University Press.

Higgins, E. Tory. 1981. The "Communication Game": Implications for Social Cognition and Persuasion. In E. Tory Higgins, C. Peter Herman, and Mark P. Zanna, eds., *Social Cognition: The Ontario Symposium,* Vol. 1. Hillsdale: Lawrence Erlbaum.

Higgins, E. Tory, John A. Bargh, and Wendy Lombardi. 1985. Nature of Priming Effects on Categorization. *Journal of Experimental Psychology: Learning, Memory, and Cognition,* 11:59–69.

Higgins, E. Tory, and William M. Chaires. 1980. Accessibility of Interrelational Constructs: Implications for Stimulus Encoding and Creativity. *Journal of Experimental Social Psychology,* 16:348–361.

Higgins, E. Tory, and Gillian King. 1981. Accessibility of Social Constructs: Information Processing Consequences of Individual and Contextual Variability. In Nancy Cantor and John F. Kihlstrom, eds., *Personality, Cognition and Social Interaction.* Hillsdale: Lawrence Erlbaum.

Higgins, E. Tory, Nicholas A. Kuiper, and James M. Olson. 1981. Social Cognition: A Need to Get Personal. In E. Tory Higgins, C. Peter Herman, and Mark P. Zanna, eds., *Social Cognition: The Ontario Symposium,* Vol. 1. Hillsdale: Lawrence Erlbaum.

Higgins, E. Tory, and C. Douglas McCann. 1984. Social Encoding and Subsequent Attitudes, Impressions and Memory: "Context-Driven" and Motivational Aspects of Processing. *Journal of Personality and Social Psychology,* 47:26–39.

Higgins, E. Tory, and William S. Rholes. 1978. "Saying is Believing": Effects of Message Modification on Memory and Liking for the Person Described. *Journal of Experimental Social Psychology,* 14:363–378.

Higgins, E. Tory, William S. Rholes, and Carl R. Jones. 1977. Category Accessibility and Impression Formation. *Journal of Experimental Social Psychology,* 13:141–154.

Hinich, Melvin J., and Walker Pollard. 1981. A New Approach to the Spatial Theory of Electoral Competition. *American Journal of Political Science,* 25:323–341.

Hoare, Quintin, and Geoffrey Nowell Smith, eds. 1971. *Selections from the Prison Notebooks of Antonio Gramsci.* New York: International.

Hollander, Sidney, Jr. 1979. Comments and Letters: On the Strength of a Newspaper Endorsement. *Public Opinion Quarterly,* 43:405–407.

Homans, George C. 1958. Social Behavior as Exchange. *American Journal of Sociology,* 63:597–606.

Huckfeldt, R. Robert. 1983. The Social Context of Political Change: Durability, Volatility, and Social Influence. *American Political Science Review,* 77:929–944.

Huckfeldt, R. Robert. 1986. *Politics in Context: Assimilation and Conflict in Urban Neighborhoods.* New York: Agathon.

Huckfeldt, R. Robert, and John Sprague. 1983. Social Contexts, Political Environments, and the Dynamics of Voter Preference. Presented at the annual meeting of the American Political Science Association, Chicago.

Huckfeldt, R. Robert, and John Sprague. 1986. Networks in Context: Problems and Method. Presented at the annual meeting of the American Political Science Association, Washington, DC.

Isen, Alice M., Thomas E. Shalker, Margaret Clark, and Lynn Karp. 1978. Affect, Accessibility of Material in Memory, and Behavior: A Cognitive Loop? *Journal of Personality and Social Psychology,* 36:1–12.

Iyengar, Shanto. 1985. Report on the 1985 Suffolk County Pre-pilot Survey of Political Information. Presented at the NES Pilot Study Planning Conference, Cambridge.

Iyengar, Shanto. 1986. Whither Political Information? Presented at the NES Pilot Study Conference, Ann Arbor.

Iyengar, Shanto, and Donald R. Kinder. 1986. More Than Meets the Eye: TV News, Priming, and Public Evaluations of the President. In George Comstock, ed., *Public Communication and Behavior,* Vol. 1. New York: Academic Press.

Iyengar, Shanto, and Donald R. Kinder. 1987. *News That Matters: Television and American Opinion.* Chicago: University of Chicago Press.

Iyengar, Shanto, Donald R. Kinder, Mark D. Peters, and Jon A. Krosnick. 1984. The Evening News and Presidential Evaluations. *Journal of Personality and Social Psychology*, 46:778–787.

Jensen, Michael C., and William H. Meckling. 1976. Theory of the Firm: Managerial Behavior, Agency Costs and Ownership Structure. *Journal of Financial Economics*, 3:305–360.

Kagay, Michael R., and Gregory A. Caldiera. 1975. I Like the Looks of His Face: Elements of Electoral Choice, 1952–1972. Presented at the annual meeting of the American Political Science Association, San Francisco.

Kahneman, Daniel. 1973. *Attention and Effort*. Englewood Cliffs: Prentice-Hall.

Kahneman, Daniel, Paul Slovic, and Amos Tversky, eds. 1982. *Judgment under Uncertainty: Heuristics and Biases*. New York: Cambridge University Press.

Kalt, Joseph P., and Mark A. Zupan. 1984. Capture and Ideology in the Economic Theory of Politics. *American Economic Review*, 74:279–300.

Kau, James B., and Paul H. Rubin. 1979. Self-Interest, Ideology, and Logrolling in Congressional Voting. *Journal of Law and Economics*, 22:365–384.

Keech, William R. 1962. Classical Democratic Theory and the Classical Democratic Citizen. Unpublished manuscript.

Keech, William R. 1980. Elections and Macroeconomic Policy Optimization. *American Journal of Political Science*, 24:345–367.

Keech, William R., and Carl P. Simon. 1985. Electoral and Welfare Consequences of Political Manipulation of the Economy. *Journal of Economic Behavior and Organization*, 6:177–202.

Kelley, Stanley, Jr., and Thad W. Mirer. 1974. The Simple Act of Voting. *American Political Science Review*, 68:572–591.

Kernell, Samuel. 1977. Presidential Popularity and Negative Voting: An Alternative Explanation of the Midterm Congressional Decline of the President's Party. *American Political Science Review*, 71:44–66.

Kessel, John H. 1972. Comment: The Issues in Issue Voting. *American Political Science Review*, 66:459–465.

Key, V. O., Jr. 1966. *The Responsible Electorate: Rationality in Presidential Voting, 1936–1960*. Cambridge: Harvard University Press.

Keynes, John Maynard. 1935. *The General Theory of Employment, Interest, and Money*. New York: Harcourt, Brace.

Kiewiet, D. Roderick. 1983. *Macroeconomics and Micropolitics: The Electoral Effects of Economic Issues*. Chicago: University of Chicago Press.

Kinder, Donald R. 1983. Diversity and Complexity in American Public Opinion. In Ada W. Finifter, ed., *Political Science: The State of the Discipline*. Washington, DC: American Political Science Association.

Kinder, Donald R. 1986. Presidential Character Revisited. In Richard R. Lau and David O. Sears, eds., *Political Cognition*. Hillsdale: Lawrence Erlbaum.

Kinder, Donald R., and Robert P. Abelson. 1981. Appraising Presidential Candidates: Personality and Affect in the 1980 Campaign. Presented at the annual meeting of the American Political Science Association, New York.

Kinder, Donald R., and Susan T. Fiske. 1986. Presidents in the Public Mind. In Margaret G. Hermann, ed., *Political Psychology*. San Francisco: Jossey-Bass.

Kinder, Donald R., and D. Roderick Kiewiet. 1979. Economic Discontent and Political Behavior: The Role of Personal Grievances and Collective Economic Judgments in Congressional Voting. *American Journal of Political Science*, 23:495–527.

Kinder, Donald R., and Walter R. Mebane, Jr. 1983. Politics and Economics in Everyday Life. In Kristen R. Monroe, ed., *The Political Process and Economic Change*. New York: Agathon.

Kinder, Donald R., and David O. Sears. 1985. Public Opinion and Political Action. In Gardner Lindzey and Elliot Aronson, eds., *Handbook of Social Psychology*, Vol. 2. 3d ed. New York: Random House.

Kingdon, John W. 1966. *Candidates for Office: Beliefs and Strategies*. New York: Random House.

Kingdon, John W. 1973. *Congressmen's Voting Decisions*. New York: Harper and Row.

Klapp, Orrin E. 1954. Heroes, Villains and Fools, as Agents of Social Control. *American Sociological Review*, 19:56–62.

Klapper, Joseph T. 1960. *The Effects of Mass Communication*. New York: Free Press.

Kleppner, Paul. 1970. *The Cross of Culture: A Social Analysis of Midwestern Politics, 1850–1900*. New York: Free Press.

Kleppner, Paul. 1979. *The Third Electoral System, 1853–1892: Parties, Voters and Political Cultures*. Chapel Hill: University of North Carolina Press.

Klingemann, Hans D. 1979a. Measuring Ideological Conceptualizations. In Samuel Barnes and Max Kaase, eds., *Political Action*. Beverly Hills: Sage Publications.

Klingemann, Hans D. 1979b. The Background of Ideological Conceptualization. In Samuel Barnes and Max Kaase, eds., *Political Action*. Beverly Hills: Sage Publications.

Klingemann, Hans D. 1979c. Ideological Conceptualization and Political Action. In Samuel Barnes and Max Kaase, eds., *Political Action*. Beverly Hills: Sage Publications.

Klingner, Eric. 1975. Consequences of Commitment to and Disengagement from Incentives. *Psychological Review*, 82:1–25.

Koppstein, Peter. 1983. Parameterized Dynamical Systems Perspectives on Collective Action with Special Reference to Political Protest and Civil Violence. Doctoral dissertation, Yale University.

Kramer, Gerald H. 1971. Short-Term Fluctuations in U.S. Voting Behavior, 1896–1964. *American Political Science Review*, 65:131–143.

Kramer, Gerald H. 1983. The Ecological Fallacy Revisited: Aggregate- versus Individual-level Findings on Economics and Elections, and Sociotropic Voting. *American Political Science Review*, 77:92–111.

Krassa, Michael A. 1988. Social Groups, Selective Perception, and Behavioral Contagion in Public Opinion. *Social Networks*, 10:109–136.

Krehbiel, Keith, Kenneth A. Shepsle, and Barry R. Weingast. 1987. Why Are Congressional Committees Powerful? *American Political Science Review*, 81:929–945.

Kuiper, Nicholas A., and Timothy B. Rogers. 1979. Encoding of Personal Information: Self-Other Differences. *Journal of Personality and Social Psychology*, 37:499–514.

Kuklinski, James H. 1978. Representativeness and Elections: A Policy Analysis. *American Political Science Review*, 72:165–177.

Kuklinski, James H. 1988. Toward a Theory of Political Competition in Congress. Unpublished manuscript.

Kuklinski, James H., Daniel S. Metlay, and W. D. Kay. 1982. Citizen Knowledge and Choices on the Complex Issue of Nuclear Energy. *American Journal of Political Science*, 26:616–642.

Kuklinski, James H., and John E. Stanga. 1979. Political Participation and Government Responsiveness: The Behavior of California Superior Courts. *American Political Science Review*, 73:1090–1099.

Langton, Kenneth P., and Ronald Rapoport. 1975. Social Structure, Social Context, and Partisan Mobilization: Urban Workers in Chile. *Comparative Political Studies*, 8:318–344.

Lau, Richard R. 1982. Negativity in Political Perception. *Political Behavior*, 4:353–377.

Lau, Richard R. 1985. Two Explanations for Negativity Effects in Political Behavior. *American Journal of Political Science*, 29:119–138.

Lau, Richard R. 1986. Political Schemata, Candidate Evaluations, and Voting Behavior. In Richard R. Lau and David O. Sears, eds., *Political Cognition*. Hillsdale: Lawrence Erlbaum.

Lau, Richard R., and David O. Sears, eds. 1986. *Political Cognition*. Hillsdale: Lawrence Erlbaum.

Laumann, Edward O. 1973. *Bonds of Pluralism: The Form and Substance of Urban Social Networks*. New York: John Wiley.

Lazarsfeld, Paul F. 1957. Public Opinion and the Classical Tradition. *Public Opinion Quarterly*, 21:39–53.

Lazarsfeld, Paul F., Bernard R. Berelson, and Hazel Gaudet. 1944. *The People's Choice: How the Voter Makes up His Mind in a Presidential Campaign*. New York: Duell, Sloan and Pearce.

Ledyard, John O. 1984. The Pure Theory of Large Two-Candidate Elections. *Public Choice*, 44:7–41.

Levine, Steven R., Robert S. Wyer, Jr., and Norbert Schwarz. 1987. Are You What You Feel? The Affective and Cognitive Determinants of Self Esteem. Unpublished manuscript.

Levinthal, Daniel. 1984. A Survey of Agency Models of Organizations. Unpublished manuscript.

Lichtenstein, Meryl, and Thomas K. Srull. 1987. Processing Objectives as a

Determinant of the Relationship Between Recall and Judgment. *Journal of Experimental Social Psychology*, 23:93–118.

Lindbeck, Assar. 1976. Stabilization Policy in Open Economies with Endogenous Politicians. *American Economic Review*, 66(2):1–19.

Lingle, John H., and Thomas M. Ostrom. 1979. Retrieval Selectivity in Memory-Based Impression Judgments. *Journal of Personality and Social Psychology*, 37:180–194.

Lippman, Walter N. 1913. *A Preface to Politics*. New York: Mitchell Kennerley.

Lippman, Walter N. 1922. *Public Opinion*. New York: Harcourt, Brace.

Lippman, Walter N. 1925. *The Phantom Public*. New York: Harcourt, Brace.

Lipset, Seymour Martin. 1981. *Political Man: The Social Bases of Politics*, expanded ed. Baltimore: Johns Hopkins University Press.

Lodge, Milton, and Ruth Hamill. 1986. A Partisan Schema for Political Information Processing. *American Political Science Review*, 80:505–519.

Lord, Charles G., Lee Ross, and Mark R. Lepper. 1979. Biased Assimilation and Attitude Polarization: The Effects of Prior Theories on Subsequently Considered Evidence. *Journal of Personality and Social Psychology*, 37:2098–2109.

Lucas, Robert E., Jr. 1981. *Studies in Business-Cycle Theory*. Cambridge: MIT Press.

MacKuen, Michael B. 1981. Social Communication and the Mass Policy Agenda. In Michael B. MacKuen and Steven Lane Coombs, eds., *More Than News: Media Power in Public Affairs*. Beverly Hills: Sage Publications.

MacKuen, Michael B., and Courtney Brown. 1987. Political Context and Attitude Change. *American Political Science Review*, 81:471–490.

Mansbridge, Jane J. 1980. *Beyond Adversary Democracy*. New York: Basic Books.

Marcus, George. 1986. A Theory and Methodology for Measuring Emotions in Politics. Unpublished manuscript.

Markus, Gregory B. 1982. Political Attitudes during an Election Year: A Report on the 1980 NES Panel Study. *American Political Science Review*, 76:538–560.

Markus, Gregory B., and Philip E. Converse. 1979. A Dynamic Simultaneous Equation Model of Electoral Choice. *American Political Science Review*, 73:1055–1070.

Markus, Hazel, and Robert B. Zajnoc. 1985. The Cognitive Perspective in Social Psychology. In Gardner Lindzey and Elliot Aronson, eds., *Handbook of Social Psychology*, Vol. 1. 3d ed. New York: Random House.

Martin, Leonard L. 1986. Set/Reset: Use and Disuse of Concepts in Impression Formation. *Journal of Personality and Social Psychology*, 51:493–504.

Massad, Christopher M., Michael Hubbard, and Darren Newtson. 1979. Selective Perception of Events. *Journal of Experimental Social Psychology*, 15:513–532.

Matthews, Donald R., and James A. Stimson. 1975. *Yeas and Nays: Normal Decision Making in the U.S. House of Representatives*. New York: John Wiley.

May, Kenneth O. 1952. A Set of Independent Necessary and Sufficient Conditions for Simple Majority Decision. *Econometrica,* 20:680–684.

Mayhew, David R. 1974. *Congress: The Electoral Connection.* New Haven: Yale University Press.

Maynard Smith, John. 1982. *Evolution and the Theory of Games.* Cambridge: Cambridge University Press.

McClosky, Herbert, Paul J. Hoffman, and Rosemary O'Hara. 1960. Issue Conflict and Consensus Among Party Leaders and Followers. *American Political Science Review,* 54:406–427.

McCubbins, Mathew D., Roger G. Noll, and Barry R. Weingast. 1987. Administrative Procedures as Instruments of Political Control. Unpublished manuscript.

McCubbins, Mathew D., and Thomas Schwartz. 1984. Congressional Oversight Overlooked: Police Patrols versus Fire Alarms. *American Journal of Political Science,* 28:165–179.

McCubbins, Mathew D., and Thomas Schwartz. 1985. The Politics of Flatland. *Public Choice,* 46:45–60.

McGuire, William J. 1968a. Personality and Susceptibility to Social Influence. In Edgar F. Borgatta and William W. Lambert, eds., *Handbook of Personality Theory and Research.* Chicago: Rand McNally.

McGuire, William J. 1968b. The Nature of Attitudes and Attitude Change. In Gardner Lindzey and Elliot Aronson, eds., *Handbook of Social Psychology,* Vol. 3. 2d ed. Reading: Addison-Wesley.

McGuire, William J. 1985. Attitudes and Attitude Change. In Gardner Lindzey and Elliot Aronson, eds., *Handbook of Social Psychology,* Vol. 2. 3d ed. New York: Random House.

McKelvey, Richard D. 1979. General Conditions for Global Intransitivities in Formal Voting Models. *Econometrica,* 47:1085–1112.

McKelvey, Richard D., and Peter C. Ordeshook. 1984. Rational Expectations in Elections: Some Experimental Results Based on a Multidimensional Model. *Public Choice,* 44:61–102.

McKelvey, Richard D., and Peter C. Ordeshook. 1985a. Elections with Limited Information: A Fulfilled Expectations Model Using Contemporaneous Poll and Endorsement Data as Information Sources. *Journal of Economic Theory,* 36:55–85.

McKelvey, Richard D, and Peter C. Ordeshook. 1985b. Sequential Elections with Limited Information. *American Journal of Political Science,* 29:480–512.

McKelvey, Richard D., and Peter C. Ordeshook. 1986a. Information, Electoral Equilibria, and the Democratic Ideal. *Journal of Politics,* 48:909–937.

McKelvey, Richard D., and Peter C. Ordeshook. 1986b. Sequential Elections with Limited Information: A Formal Analysis. *Social Choice and Welfare,* 3:199–211.

McKelvey, Richard D., and Peter C. Ordershook. 1987. Elections with Limited Information: A Multidimensional Model. *Mathematical Social Science,* 14:77–99.

McPhee, William N. 1963. *Formal Theories of Mass Behavior*. New York: Free Press.

McPhee, William N., Bo Andersen, and Harry Milholland. 1962. Attitude Consistency. In William N. McPhee and William A. Glaser, eds., *Public Opinion and Congressional Elections*. New York: Free Press.

McPhee, William N., and Robert B. Smith. 1962. A Model for Analyzing Voting Systems. In William N. McPhee and William A. Glaser, eds., *Public Opinion and Congressional Elections*. New York: Free Press.

Meehl, Paul E. 1977. The Selfish Voter Paradox and the Thrown-Away Vote Argument. *American Political Science Review*, 71:11–30.

Miller, Arthur H., Martin P. Wattenberg, and Oksana Malanchuk. 1986. Schematic Assessments of Presidential Candidates. *American Political Science Review*, 80:521–540.

Miller, Warren E. 1956. One-Party Politics and the Voter. *American Political Science Review*, 50:707–725.

Miller, Warren E., and Donald E. Stokes. 1963. Constituency Influence in Congress. *American Political Science Review*, 57:45–56.

Moe, Terry M. 1984. The New Economics of Organization. *American Journal of Political Science*, 28:739–777.

Monroe, Kristen R. 1984. *Presidential Popularity and the Economy*. New York: Praeger.

Moon, J. Donald. 1975. The Logic of Political Inquiry: A Synthesis of Opposed Perspectives. In Fred I. Greenstein and Nelson W. Polsby, eds., *Handbook of Political Science*, Vol. 1. Reading: Addison-Wesley.

Mosley, Paul. 1984. *The Making of Economic Policy: Theory and Evidence from Britain and the United States since 1945*. New York: St. Martin's.

Muth, John F. 1961. Rational Expectations and the Theory of Price Movements. *Econometrica*, 29:315–335.

Nexon, David. 1971. Asymmetry in the Political System: Occasional Activists in the Republican and Democratic Parties, 1956–1964. *American Political Science Review*, 65:716–730.

Nisbett, Richard, and Lee Ross. 1980. *Human Inference: Strategies and Shortcomings of Social Judgment*. Englewood Cliffs: Prentice-Hall.

Noelle-Neumann, Elisabeth. 1974. The Spiral of Silence: A Theory of Public Opinion. *Journal of Communication*, 24:43–51.

Noelle-Neumann, Elisabeth. 1977. Turbulences in the Climate of Opinion: Methodological Applications of the Spiral of Silence Theory. *Public Opinion Quarterly*, 41:143–158.

Noelle-Neumann, Elisabeth. 1984. *The Spiral of Silence: Public Opinion—Our Social Skin*. Chicago: University of Chicago Press.

Nordhaus, William D. 1975. The Political Business Cycle. *Review of Economic Studies*, 42:169–190.

O'Gorman, Hubert J., and Stephen L. Garry. 1976. Pluralistic Ignorance— A Replication and Extension. *Public Opinion Quarterly*, 40:449–458.

Olson, Mancur. 1965. *The Logic of Collective Action: Public Goods and the Theory of Groups*. Cambridge: Harvard University Press.

Orbell, John M. 1970. An Information-Flow Theory of Community Influence. *Journal of Politics*, 32:322–338.

Osgood, Charles E., George J. Suci, and Percy H. Tannenbaum. 1957. *The Measurement of Meaning*. Urbana: University of Illinois Press.

Osterhouse, Robert A., and Timothy C. Brock. 1970. Distraction Increases Yielding to Propaganda by Inhibiting Counterarguing. *Journal of Personality and Social Psychology*, 15:344–358.

Ostrom, Thomas M. 1984. The Sovereignty of Social Cognition. In Robert S. Wyer, Jr. and Thomas K. Srull, eds., *Handbook of Social Cognition*, Vol. 1. Hillsdale: Lawrence Erlbaum.

Ostrom, Thomas M., John B. Pryor, and David D. Simpson. 1981. The Organization of Social Information. In E. Tory Higgins, C. Peter Herman, and Mark P. Zanna, eds., *Social Cognition: The Ontario Symposium*, Vol. 1. Hillsdale: Lawrence Erlbaum.

Ostrom, Thomas M., and Harry S. Upshaw. 1968. Psychological Perspective and Attitude Change. In Anthony G. Greenwald, Timothy C. Brock, and Thomas M. Ostrom, eds., *Psychological Foundations of Attitudes*. New York: Academic Press.

Page, Benjamin I. 1976. The Theory of Political Ambiguity. *American Political Science Review*, 70:742–752.

Page, Benjamin I. 1978. *Choices and Echoes in Presidential Elections: Rational Man and Electoral Democracy*. Chicago: University of Chicago Press.

Page, Benjamin I., and Richard A. Brody. 1972. Policy Voting and the Electoral Process: The Vietnam War Issue. *American Political Science Review*, 66:979–995.

Page, Benjamin I., and Calvin C. Jones. 1979. Reciprocal Effects of Policy Preferences, Party Loyalties and the Vote. *American Political Science Review*, 73:1071–1089.

Page, Benjamin I., and Robert Y. Shapiro. 1983. Effects of Public Opinion on Policy. *American Political Science Review*, 77:175–190.

Page, Benjamin I., Robert Y. Shapiro, and Glenn R. Dempsey. 1987. What Moves Public Opinion? *American Political Science Review*, 81:23–43.

Patemen, Carole. 1970. *Participation and Democratic Theory*. Cambridge: Cambridge University Press.

Peabody, Robert L., Norman J. Ornstein, and David W. Rhode. 1976. The United States Senate as a Presidential Incubator: Many Are Called but Few Are Chosen. *Political Science Quarterly*, 91:237–258.

Peltzman, Sam. 1984. Constituent Interest and Congressional Voting. *Journal of Law and Economics*, 27:181–210.

Pennington, Nancy, and Reid Hastie. 1986. Evidence Evaluation in Complex Decision Making. *Journal of Personality and Social Psychology*, 51:242–258.

Peterson, Merrill D. 1975. *The Portable Thomas Jefferson*. New York: Viking Press.

Petty, Richard E., and John T. Cacioppo. 1981. *Attitudes and Persuasion: Classic and Contemporary Approaches*. Dubuque: W. C. Brown.

Petty, Richard E., Thomas M. Ostrom, and Timothy C. Brock, eds. 1981. *Cognitive Responses in Persuasion.* Hillsdale: Lawrence Erlbaum. ·

Pitkin, Hannah Fenichel. 1967. *The Concept of Representation.* Berkeley: University of California Press.

Polsby, Nelson W. 1971. Strengthening Congress in National Policymaking. In Nelson W. Polsby, ed., *Congressional Behavior.* New York: Random House.

Popkin, Samuel, John W. Gorman, Charles Phillips, and Jeffrey A. Smith. 1976. Comment: What Have You Done for Me Lately? Toward an Investment Theory of Voting. *American Political Science Review,* 70:779–805.

Putnam, Robert D. 1966. Political Attitudes and the Local Community. *American Political Science Review,* 60:640–654.

Rahn, Wendy M. 1987. Candidate Image during Nomination Campaigns. Unpublished manuscript.

Repass, David E. 1971. Issue Salience and Party Choice. *American Political Science Review,* 65:389–400.

Riker, William H. 1982. *Liberalism Against Populism: A Confrontation Between the Theory of Democracy and the Theory of Social Choice.* San Francisco: W. H. Freeman.

Riker, William H. 1984. The Heresthetics of Constitution-Making: The Presidency in 1787, with Comments on Determinism and Rational Choice. *American Political Science Review,* 78:1–16.

Riker, William H., and Peter C. Ordeshook. 1968. A Theory of the Calculus of Voting. *American Political Science Review,* 62:25–42.

Rosenberg, Shawn W., Liza Bohan, Patrick McCafferty, and Kevin Harris. 1986. The Image and the Vote: The Effect of Candidate Presentation on Voter Preference. *American Journal of Political Science,* 30:108–127.

Rosenstone, Steven J. 1985. Explaining the 1984 Presidential Election. *The Brookings Review,* 3:25–32.

Ross, Lee, and Craig A. Anderson. 1982. Shortcomings in the Attribution Process: On the Origins and Maintenance of Erroneous Social Assessments. In Daniel Kahneman, Paul Slovic, and Amos Tversky, eds., *Judgment under Uncertainty: Heuristics and Biases.* New York: Cambridge University Press.

Samuelson, Paul A., and Robert M. Solow. 1960. Analytical Aspects of Anti-Inflation Policy. *American Economic Review,* 50:177–194.

Sani, Giacomo. 1974. A Test of the Least-Distance Model of Voting Choice: Italy, 1972. *Comparative Political Studies,* 7:193–208.

Schachter, Stanley, and Jerome E. Singer. 1962. Cognitive, Social, and Physiological Determinants of Emotional State. *Psychological Review,* 69:379–399.

Schattschneider, Elmer E. 1960. *The Semisovereign People: A Realist's View of Democracy in America.* New York: Holt, Rinehart and Winston.

Schelling, Thomas C. 1971. Dynamic Models of Segregation. *Journal of Mathematical Sociology,* 1:143–186.

Schelling, Thomas C. 1978. *Micromotives and Macrobehavior*. New York: W. W. Norton.

Schlozman, Kay Lehman, and Sidney Verba. 1979. *Injury to Insult: Unemployment, Class, and Political Response*. Cambridge: Harvard University Press.

Schotter, Andrew. 1985. *Free Market Economics: A Critical Appraisal*. New York: St. Martin's.

Schwarz, Norbert, and Gerald L. Clore. 1983. Mood, Misattribution, and Judgments of Well-Being: Information and Directive Functions of Affective States. *Journal of Personality and Social Psychology*, 45:513–523.

Schwarz, Norbert, Hans-Jurgen Hippler, Brigitte Deutsch, and Fritz Strack. 1985. Response Scales: Effects of Category Range on Reported Behavior and Comparative Judgments. *Public Opinion Quarterly*, 49:388–395.

Sears, David O., and Jack Citrin. 1982. *Tax Revolt: Something for Nothing in California*. Cambridge: Harvard University Press.

Sears, David O., Richard R. Lau, Tom R. Tyler, and Harris M. Allen, Jr. 1980. Self-Interest vs. Symbolic Politics in Policy Attitudes and Presidential Voting. *American Political Science Review*, 74:670–684.

Segal, David R., and Marshall W. Meyer. 1974. The Social Context of Political Partisanship. In Mattei Dogan and Stein Rokkan, eds., *Social Ecology*. Cambridge: MIT Press.

Shanks, J. Merrill, and Warren E. Miller. 1985. Policy Direction and Performance Evaluation: Complementary Explanations of the Reagan Elections. Presented at the annual meeting of the American Political Science Association, New Orleans.

Shepsle, Kenneth A. 1972. The Strategy of Ambiguity: Uncertainty and Electoral Competition. *American Political Science Review*, 66:555–568.

Shepsle, Kenneth A., and Barry R. Weingast. 1984a. Political Solutions to Market Problems. *American Political Science Review*, 78:417–434.

Shepsle, Kenneth A., and Barry R. Weingast. 1984b. Uncovered Sets and Sophisticated Voting Outcomes with Implications for Agenda Institutions. *American Journal of Political Science*, 28:49–74.

Shepsle, Kenneth A., and Barry R. Weingast. 1987. The Institutional Foundations of Committee Power. *American Political Science Review*, 81:85–104.

Sherman, Steven J., Karin Ahlm, Leonard Berman, and Steven Lynn. 1978. Contrast Effects and Their Relationship to Subsequent Behavior. *Journal of Experimental Social Psychology*, 14:340–350.

Sherman, Steven J., and Eric Corty. 1984. Cognitive Heuristics. In Robert S. Wyer, Jr. and Thomas K. Srull, eds., *Handbook of Social Cognition*, Vol. 1. Hillsdale: Lawrence Erlbaum.

Simon, Herbert A. 1945. *Administrative Behavior: A Study of Decision-Making Processes in Administrative Organizations*. New York: Free Press.

Simon, Herbert A. 1981. *The Sciences of the Artificial*, 2d ed. Cambridge: MIT Press.

Simon, Herbert A. 1982. *Models of Bounded Rationality*. 2 Vols. Cambridge: MIT Press.

Sinclair, Barbara. 1986. The Role of Committees in Agenda Setting in the U.S. Congress. *Legislative Studies Quarterly*, 11:35–45.

Sniderman, Paul M., and Richard A. Brody. 1977. Coping: The Ethic of Self-Reliance. *American Journal of Political Science*, 21:501–521.

Sniderman, Paul M., Richard A. Brody, and James H. Kuklinski. 1984. Policy Reasoning on Political Values: The Problem of Racial Equality. *American Journal of Political Science*, 28:75–94.

Sniderman, Paul M., Michael G. Hagen, Philip E. Tetlock, and Henry E. Brady. 1986. Reasoning Chains: Causal Models of Policy Reasoning in Mass Publics. *British Journal of Political Science*, 16:405–430.

Sniderman, Paul M., Barbara Kaye Wolfinger, Diana Muntz, and James A. Wiley. 1986. Values Under Pressure: AIDS and Civil Liberties. Presented at the annual meeting of the American Political Science Association, Washington, DC.

Snyder, Mark, and William B. Swann, Jr. 1978. Hypothesis-Testing Processes in Social Interaction. *Journal of Personality and Social Psychology*, 36:1202–1212.

Snyder, Mark, and Seymour W. Uranowitz. 1978. Reconstructing the Past: Some Cognitive Consequences of Person Perception. *Journal of Personality and Social Psychology*, 36:941–950.

Sorrentino, Richard M., and E. Tory Higgins, eds. 1986. *Handbook of Motivation and Cognition*. New York: Guilford Press.

Speier, Hans. 1950. Historical Development of Public Opinion. *American Journal of Sociology*, 55:376–388.

Spence, A. Michael. 1974. *Market Signaling: Informational Transfer in Hiring and Related Screening Processes*. Cambridge: Harvard University Press.

Spiller, Pablo T. 1988. Politicians, Interest Groups and Regulators: A Multiple Principals Agency Theory of Regulation (or Let Them Be Bribed). Unpublished manuscript.

Sprague, John. 1982. Is There a Micro Theory Consistent with Contextual Analysis? In Elinor Ostrom, ed., *Strategies of Political Inquiry*. Beverly Hills: Sage Publications.

Srull, Thomas K., Meryl Lichtenstein, and Myron Rothbart. 1985. Associative Storage and Retrieval Processes in Person Memory. *Journal of Experimental Psychology: Learning, Memory, and Cognition*, 11:316–345.

Srull, Thomas K., and Robert S. Wyer, Jr. 1979. The Role of Category Accessibility in the Interpretation of Information About Persons: Some Determinants and Implications. *Journal of Personality and Social Psychology*, 37:1660–1672.

Srull, Thomas K., and Robert S. Wyer, Jr. 1980. Category Accessibility and Social Perception: Some Implications for the Study of Person Memory and Interpersonal Judgment. *Journal of Personality and Social Psychology*, 38:841–856.

Srull, Thomas K., and Robert S. Wyer, Jr. 1986. The Role of Chronic and Temporary Goals in Social Information Processing. In Richard M. Sorrentino and E. Tory Higgins, eds., *Handbook of Motivation and Cognition*. New York: Guilford Press.

Srull, Thomas K., and Robert S. Wyer, Jr. 1987. Person Memory and Judgment. Unpublished manuscript.

Stokes, Donald E. 1966. Some Dynamic Elements of Contests for the Presidency. *American Political Science Review*, 60:19–28.

Stokes, Donald E., Angus Campbell, and Warren E. Miller. 1958. Components of Electoral Decision. *American Political Science Review*, 52:367–387.

Strack, Fritz, and Leonard L. Martin. 1987. Thinking, Judging and Communicating: A Process Account of Context Effects in Attitude Surveys. In Hans-Jurgen Hippler, Norbert Schwarz, and Seymour Sudman, eds., *Social Information Processing and Survey Methodology*. New York: Springer-Verlag.

Strack, Fritz, Norbert Schwarz, and Elisabeth Gschneidinger. 1985. Happiness and Reminiscing: The Role of Time Perspective, Affect, and Mode of Thinking. *Journal of Personality and Social Psychology*, 49:1460–1469.

Sullivan, Denis G., and Roger D. Masters. 1988. "Happy Warriors": Leaders' Facial Displays, Viewers' Emotions and Political Support. *American Journal of Political Science*, 32:345–368.

Sullivan, John L., John H. Aldrich, Eugene Borgida, and Wendy M. Rahn. (n.d.). Candidate Appraisal and Human Nature: Man and Superman in the 1984 Election. *Political Psychology*. Forthcoming.

Taylor, D. Garth. 1982. Pluralistic Ignorance and the Spiral of Silence: A Formal Analysis. *Public Opinion Quarterly*, 46:311–335.

Taylor, Shelley E. 1982. The Availability Bias in Social Perception and Interaction. In Daniel Kahneman, Paul Slovic, and Amos Tversky, eds., *Judgment under Uncertainty: Heuristics and Biases*. New York: Cambridge University Press.

Taylor, Shelley E., and Jennifer Crocker. 1981. Schematic Bases of Social Information Processing. In E. Tory Higgins, C. Peter Herman, and Mark P. Zanna, eds., *Social Cognition: The Ontario Symposium*, Vol. 1. Hillsdale: Lawrence Erlbaum.

Taylor, Shelley, and Susan T. Fiske. 1978. Salience, Attention, and Attribution: Top of the Head Phenomena. In Leonard Berkowitz, ed., *Advances in Experimental Social Psychology*, Vol. 11. New York: Academic Press.

Tingsten, Herbert. [1937] 1963. *Political Behavior: Studies in Election Statistics*. Trans. Vilgot Hammarling. Totowa, NJ: Bedminster.

Tufte, Edward R. 1975. Determinants of the Outcomes of Midterm Congressional Elections. *American Political Science Review*, 69:812–826.

Tversky, Amos, and Daniel Kahneman. 1973. Availability: A Heuristic for Judging Frequency and Probability. *Cognitive Psychology*, 5:207–232.

Tversky, Amos and Daniel Kahneman. 1974. Judgment under Uncertainty: Heuristics and Biases. *Science*, 185:1124–1131.

Upshaw, Harry S. 1965. The Effect of Variable Perspectives on Judgments of Opinion Statements for Thurstone Scales: Equal-Appearing Intervals. *Journal of Personality and Social Psychology*, 2:60–69.

Upshaw, Harry S. 1978. Social Influence on Attitudes and on Anchoring of Congeneric Attitude Scales. *Journal of Experimental Social Psychology,* 14:327–339.

Upshaw, Harry S. 1984. Output Processes in Judgment. In Robert S. Wyer, Jr. and Thomas K. Srull, eds., *Handbook of Social Cognition,* Vol. 3. Hillsdale: Lawrence Erlbaum.

Verba, Sidney, and Norman H. Nie. 1972. *Participation in America: Political Democracy and Social Equality.* New York: Harper and Row.

Watts, Meredith W. 1974. Semantic Convergence in the Measurement of Political Attitudes. *Political Methodology,* 1: 133–148.

Weingast, Barry R., and W. Marshall. 1987. The Industrial Organization of Congress: (or Why Legislatures, Like Firms, Are Not Organized as Markets). Unpublished manuscript.

Weissberg, Robert. 1978. Collective vs. Dyadic Representation in Congress. *American Political Science Review,* 72:535–547.

Wiebe, G. D. 1973. Mass Media and Man's Relationship to His Environment. *Journalism Quarterly,* 50:426–432, 446.

Williams, John. 1986. Managing Presidential Support Through the Use of Macroeconomic Policy. Presented at the annual meeting of the Midwest Political Science Association, Chicago.

Wright, Gerald C., Jr. 1978. Issue Strategy in Congressional Elections: The Impact of the Primary Electorate. Presented at the annual meeting of the Midwest Political Science Association, Chicago.

Wright, Gerald C., Jr., and Michael B. Berkman. 1986. Candidates and Policy in United States Senate Elections. *American Political Science Review,* 80:567–588.

Wyer, Robert S., Jr. 1974. *Cognititve Organization and Change: An Information-Processing Approach.* Hillsdale: Lawrence Erlbaum.

Wyer, Robert S., Jr. 1981. An Information-Processing Perspective on Social Attribution. In John H. Harvey, William Ickes, and Robert F. Kidd, eds., *New Directions in Attribution Research,* Vol. 3. Hillsdale: Lawrence Erlbaum.

Wyer, Robert S., Jr. and Donal E. Carlston. 1979. *Social Cognition, Inference, and Attribution.* Hillsdale: Lawrence Erlbaum.

Wyer, Robert S., Jr. and Sallie E. Gordon. 1984. The Cognitive Representation of Social Information. In Robert S. Wyer, Jr. and Thomas K. Srull, eds., *Handbook of Social Cognition,* Vol. 2. Hillsdale: Lawrence Erlbaum.

Wyer, Robert S., Jr., and Jon Hartwick. 1980. The Role of Information Retrieval and Conditional Inference Processes in Belief Formation and Change. In Leonard Berkowitz, ed., *Advances in Experimental Social Psychology,* Vol. 13. New York: Academic Press.

Wyer, Robert S., Jr., and Thomas K. Srull. 1981. Category Accessibility: Some Theoretical and Empirical Issues Concerning the Processing of Social Stimulus Information. In E. Tory Higgins, C. Peter Herman, and Mark P. Zanna, eds., *Social Cognition: The Ontario Symposium,* Vol. 1. Hillsdale: Lawrence Erlbaum.

Wyer, Robert S., Jr., and Thomas K. Srull, eds. 1984. *Handbook of Social Cognition.* 3 Vols. Hillsdale: Lawrence Erlbaum.

Wyer, Robert S., Jr., and Thomas K. Srull. 1986. Human Cognition in Its Social Context. *Psychological Review,* 93:322–359.

Wyer, Robert S., Jr., Thomas K. Srull, Sallie E. Gordon, and Jon Hartwick. 1982. Effects of Processing Objectives on the Recall of Prose Material. *Journal of Personality and Social Psychology,* 43:674–688.

Wyer, Robert S., Jr., Fritz Strack, and Robert Fuhrman. 1984. The Acquisition of Information about Persons: Effects of Task Objectives and Personal Expectancies. Unpublished manuscript.

Young, James Sterling. 1966. *The Washington Community 1800–1828.* New York: Columbia University Press.

Zaller, John. 1986a. Analysis of Information Items in the NES 1985 Pilot Study. Presented at the NES Pilot Study Conference, Ann Arbor.

Zaller, John. 1986b. The Effects of Political Involvement on Public Attitudes and Voting Behavior. Presented at the annual meeting of the American Political Science Association, Washington, DC.

Contributors

John H. Aldrich is professor of political science at Duke University. He has published numerous books and articles on such topics as voting behavior, campaigns and elections, and political parties, including *Before the Convention*. He has taught at Michigan State University and the University of Minnesota. With John Sullivan, he has served as co-editor of the *American Journal of Political Science*. He is working on a book about American political parties.

Eugene Borgida is professor of psychology and adjunct professor of law and political science at the University of Minnesota. His primary research areas are social cognition and psychology and law.

Edward G. Carmines is professor of political science at Indiana University, Bloomington. He has coauthored *Measurement in the Social Sciences*, *Statistical Analysis of Social Data*, and *Issue Evolution: Race and the Transformation of American Politics*.

Henry W. Chappell, Jr. is associate professor of economics at the University of South Carolina. His publications have appeared in a variety of journals in economics and political science. His current research interests include topics in the politics of macroeconomic policymaking and models of political advertising.

Philip E. Converse was formerly the Robert Cooley Angell Distinguished Professor of Sociology and Political Science at the University of Michigan and director of the Institute for Social Research at the university. In September 1989, he became the director of the Center for Advanced Study in the Behavioral Sciences at Stanford. He has coauthored a number of books, including *The American Voter*, *The Human Meaning of Social Change*, *The Quality of American Life*, and *Political Representation in France*, and published many articles on public opinion and political behavior.

John A. Ferejohn is the William Bennett Munro Professor of Political Science and Senior Fellow of the Hoover Institution at Stanford University.

He has written extensively on Congress, elections, public policy, and issues of democratic theory.

Morris P. Fiorina is professor of government at Harvard University. He has written widely on American national politics, with special emphasis on electoral and legislative processes. His books include *Representatives, Roll Calls, and Constituencies, Congress—Keystone of the Washington Establishment,* and *Retrospective Voting in American National Elections.* His book *The Personal Vote: Constituency Service and Electoral Independence* (coauthored with Bruce Cain and John Ferejohn) received the Legislative Studies Association's 1987 Richard F. Fenno Prize for the best book published in the field of legislative studies.

James M. Glaser is a graduate student in political science at the University of California at Berkeley.

Robert Griffin is a graduate student in political science at Stanford University.

Robert Huckfeldt is professor of political science at Indiana University in Bloomington. He is the author or coauthor of *Dynamic Modeling, Politics in Context,* and *Race and the Decline of Class in American Politics.* Along with John Sprague, he is engaged in a study of social structure and social influence in an election campaign.

Shanto Iyengar is associate professor of political science and communications studies at the University of California, Los Angeles. He is completing a book dealing with media framing of political issues. His interests include political communication, political psychology, and American politics.

William R. Keech is professor of political science at the University of North Carolina at Chapel Hill. He is author of *The Impact of Negro Voting: The Role of the Vote in the Quest for Equality* and co-author of *The Party's Choice,* a study of American presidential nominations. His research interests include the politics of macroeconomic policymaking and the theory of representative government.

Michael Krassa is assistant professor of political science at the University of Illinois. His research examines the interactions of social and structural influences on political information, attitudes, and behaviors.

James H. Kuklinski is professor of political science and research professor, Survey Research Laboratory, at the University of Illinois. He has written on political representation and is conducting research on the affective and cognitive bases of public opinion and democratic values.

Michael MacKuen is associate professor of political science at the University of Missouri, St. Louis. He has written numerous articles on the effects of economic conditions, the mass media, and interpersonal communications on political behavior.

Richard D. McKelvey is professor of political science at the California Institute of Technology. He is the author of numerous articles in the area of social choice theory, mathematical models of voting, and game theory.

Peter C. Ordeshook is professor of political science at the California Institute of Technology. He is the author or co-author of *Game Theory and Political Theory, An Introduction to Positive Political Theory* (with William H.

Riker), and *Balance of Power: Stability in International Systems* (with E. M. S. Niou and G. F. Rose).

Victor C. Ottati is assistant professor of political science at the State University of New York, Stony Brook. His research examines the affective and cognitive mediators of political judgment.

Wendy M. Rahn, a Ph.D. candidate at the University of Minnesota, is a member of the faculty of the political science department at The Ohio State University. Her research interests involve aspects of political cognition, including candidate evaluation and voter decision making.

Kenneth A. Shepsle is professor of government at Harvard University. He is the author or coauthor of *Politics in Plural Societies: A Theory of Democratic Instability* and *The Giant Jigsaw Puzzle: Democratic Committee Assignments in the Modern House.* He has edited *The Congressional Budget Process: Some Views from the Inside* and *Political Equilibrium,* and has written numerous articles on formal political theory, congressional politics, public policy, and political economy. His research focuses on formal models of political institutions, congressional politics, and congressional and English parliamentary history.

Paul M. Sniderman is professor of political science at Stanford University. He has written extensively on democratic values. His books include *Personality and Democratic Politics, A Question of Loyalty,* and *Race and Inequality.*

Pablo T. Spiller is the William B. McKinley Professor of Economics and Public Utilities at the department of economics and Ameritech Research Fellow at the Institute of Government and Public Affairs at the University of Illinois. He has written in political economics, regulation, and industrial organization issues. He is working on a rational choice theory of the Supreme Court.

John Sprague is professor of political science at Washington University in St. Louis. He is author or coauthor of *Lawyers in Politics, Voting Patterns of the U.S. Supreme Court, Systems Analysis for Social Scientists, The Dynamics of Riots,* and *Paper Stones.* Along with Robert Huckfeldt, he is engaged in a study of social structure and social influence in an election campaign.

James A. Stimson is professor of political science at the University of Iowa. Well-known for his work in voting and public opinion, congressional decision making, and methodology, he has coauthored *Yeas and Nays* and *Issue Evolution.*

John L. Sullivan is professor of political science at the University of Minnesota. His fields include political psychology and research methods. He has completed a number of studies on political tolerance and is engaged in a major project on patriotism.

Robert S. Wyer, Jr. is professor of psychology at the University of Illinois. His research interests lie in the area of social information processing, with particular emphasis on the cognitive representation of information about people and events.